International Relations, Political Theory and the Problem of Order

At the turn of the millennium, and now after the fall of the Berlin wall, the best way to map the trajectories of contemporary international relations is hotly contested. Is the world more or less ordered than during the Cold War? Are we on the way to a neo-liberal era of free markets and global governance, or in danger of collapsing into a new Middle Ages? Are we on the verge of a new world order or are we slipping back into an old one?

These issues are amongst those that have dominated International Relations theory in the late 1980s and 1990s, but they have their roots in older questions both about the appropriate ways to study international relations and about the general frameworks and normative assumptions generated by various different methodological approaches. This book seeks to offer a general interpretation and critique of both methodological and substantive aspects of International Relations theory, and in particular to argue that International Relations theory has separated itself from the concerns of political theory more generally at considerable cost to each.

Focusing initially on the 'problem of order' in international politics, the book suggests that International Relations theory in the twentieth century has adopted two broad families of approaches, the first of which seeks to find ways of 'managing' order in international relations and the second of which seeks to 'end' the problem of order. It traces three specific sets of responses to the problem of order within the first approach, which emphasize 'balance', 'society' and 'institutions', and outlines two responses within the second grouping, an emphasis on emancipation and an emphasis on limits. Finally, the book assesses the state of International Relations theory today and suggests an alternative way of reading the problem of order which generates a different trajectory for a truly global political theory in the twenty-first century.

N. J. Rengger is Reader in Political Theory and International Relations at the University of St Andrews. He is the author of *Political Theory, Modernity and Postmodernity; Dilemmas of World Politics;* and *Retreat from the Modern.*

The New International Relations
Edited by
Barry Buzan
University of Warwick
and Richard Little
University of Bristol

The field of international relations has changed dramatically in recent years. This new series will cover the major issues that have emerged and reflect the latest academic thinking in this particular dynamic area.

International Relations, Political Theory and the Problem of Order

Beyond International Relations theory?

N. J. Rengger

London and New York

First published 2000
by Routledge
11 New Fetter Lane, London EC4P 4EE

Simultaneously published in the USA and Canada
by Routledge
29 West 35th Street, New York, NY 10001

Routledge is an imprint of the Taylor & Francis Group

© 2000 N. J. Rengger

Typeset in Baskerville by Routledge
Printed and bound in Great Britain by Biddles Ltd,
Guildford and King's Lynn

British Library Cataloguing in Publication Data
A catalogue record for this book is available from the British Library.

Library of Congress Cataloging-in-Publication Data
Rengger, N.J. (Nicholas J.)
    International relations, political theory and the problem of order:
    beyond international relations theory? / N.J. Rengger.
    (The New International Relations Series)
    Includes bibliographical references and index.
    Romanized record.
    1. International relations–Political aspects.   2. International
    relations–Philosophy.   3. Political science–Philosophy.
    4. International relations–Methodology.   I. Title.   II. Series:
    New International Relations.
    JZ1251.R46   1999   99–32333
    327.1'01–dc21

ISBN 0–415–09583–2 (hbk)
ISBN 0–415–09584–0 (pbk)

For VMH, MWJ, EH

who remind me that Aristotle was, as usual, right:

Nobody would choose to live without friends, even if he had all other Good things.

Nichomachean Ethics, 115a4

And

for HDR 1926–1997

Father, teacher, teller of tales and friend,

'with whom I shared all the counsels of my heart'. Farewell.

Contents

Series editor's preface

Political theory and International Relations theory have drifted into a rather odd and unsatisfactory relationship. This has happened despite the role that some classical political theory plays in most introductory courses to IR, where Thucydides, Hobbes, Kant, Rousseau, Bentham, Mill and others are paraded as foundational formulations of the problems of peace, war and international political economy. These roots are mostly noted as part of the intellectual history of IR, and occasionally argued over in the context of debates about the validation of more contemporary versions of realist, liberal and Marxian doctrine. But these obeisances do not constitute any kind of coherent contact between the discourses of political theory and IR. While political theorists have focused more and more on the logical and normative dimensions of what goes on inside the state, IR theorists have turned more and more to the interactions between states and the structures of the international system as a whole. A few brave souls have tried to sustain contact: think of Stanley Hoffmann, Michael Walzer, Michael Joseph Smith and Michael Doyle in the United States; Brian Barry, Chris Brown, Andrew Linklater and Hidemi Suganami in the United Kingdom. But it is probably true to say that most of the core debate in political theory largely ignores the international dimension, and most of the core debate in IR is largely ignorant about the concerns of mainstream political theory.

In part the blame for this can be laid at the feet of the usual demons: narrow academic specialization, and the bizarre intellectual barriers erected by both the creation of jargon-based discourses and the institutionalization of disciplines. But there is a deeper problem of style as well. As Hidemi Suganami (*On the Causes of War*, 1996) nicely observes, there exists a more general division between those people who find the minutiae of philosophical argument cosmically important to understanding the real meaning of things, and those who see it mostly as irritating nit-picking that distracts from the really important things by posing questions that cannot be answered, and treating them as necessarily prior to dealing with more practical matters. The philosophical mind revels in always finding another logical difficulty, no matter how arcane, that undoes everything that comes before it. This continuous drive towards highly abstract forms of demolition quite quickly bores and frustrates audiences whose concerns are more pragmatic, and who think that there are urgent problems that we need at least to get to grips with, if not solve.

In this audacious and thought-provoking book, Nick Rengger tackles this difficult and lamentable state of affairs head on. In the context of a breathtaking survey of the main bodies of thought in the two areas, he argues that the growing alienation of political theory and IR has weakened both, and proceeds to show how they can and must be remarried if either is to have any hope of successfully addressing its agenda. His linking theme is the problem of order, what it is, and how to achieve or avoid it, and how to rediscover the central normative question of politics: how to live well? This is a work that achieves real depth and authority while covering a huge swathe of thinking in a remarkably compact manner. It commends itself for making a sustained argument that should affect how both political theory and IR conduct their business and understand their subject. On a more mundane level it will also attract because of its wide-ranging literature survey; its short, pithy and incisive summaries of many schools of thought; and its grand tour of the disciplines. For those in IR, it contains both a masterful overview of the discipline (realism, the English school and constructivism, liberalism, critical theory, postmodernism) and a useful crib for all whose training has left them ill-equipped to deal with the currently fashionable impact of philosophy of knowledge questions on debates about IR theory.

Preface

By temperament and training, I am a political theorist, and as a member of this rather endangered company in the modern academy, I have long agreed with Judith Shklar, surely among the most influential political theorists of the last fifty years, that political theory is the place where history and ethics meet. In our own day, therefore – and whatever may have been true of earlier periods[1] – this must mean that one of the central sites for that meeting is the increasingly blurred and contested boundary between the ethics and politics of (allegedly) 'settled' communities – usually, though not always, states – and the ethics and politics of the *relations* between such communities. That distinction, in other words, that usually issues in separate spheres called 'domestic politics' and 'international relations', respectively.

Given this allegiance, I have for a long time been primarily concerned to probe both political theory *and* international relations in terms of their relations with one another, though over the years the balance of my interests has shifted from questions of intellectual history and context to more straightforwardly normative questions. For example, when writing a book about the 'modernity debate' in contemporary political theory, as I did a few years ago,[2] I made a point of emphasizing the extent to which that debate had ramifications for the way we talk of 'domestic' politics – that is to say, *as opposed to* – 'international' politics.

This trajectory has also, rather naturally, formed the basic staple of my teaching, whether that teaching has been courses that I have specifically offered on political theory *and* international relations or the more 'usual' courses political theorists teach; those courses, that is, on the history of political thought usually known as the 'canon'. In the latter case, I have usually made a modest attempt to broaden said canon, or at least to suggest that students should bear in mind that the 'canon' as currently constructed was developed at a time when the state was seen as (at least) the inevitable political form of the modern age and (more infrequently) necessarily the best one. Thus, theorists who did not happily fit into the straitjacket of modern reflections about the centrality, even the inevitability, of the state tended not to make it onto the 'canonical' list. This is even true for theorists recognized in other contexts as central, even seminal, thinkers, for example Grotius or Leibniz.[3]

Given these general interests, however, it is also not surprising that amongst the courses I was asked to teach fairly early on was a course in 'International Relations Theory', usually referred to in the inevitable shorthand of the modern academy as 'IR theory', and, as always, the best way to learn a subject is to teach it and doing so was a wonderful introduction to the way 'IR theory' has/had traditionally been taught.

Initially, I was – I have to admit it – surprised at what was traditionally taught in such courses and even more at what was not. Normative questions tradition-ally did not appear. Nor really did historical ones. The international system, it would seem, had operated more or less as a repeating decimal from time immemorial – or at least since Thucydides. Before long, however, these features themselves began to intrigue me. *Why,* I wondered, did scholars of international relations make *these* assumptions, develop these kinds of theories and not others? Inevitably, my courses in 'IR theory' *did* have normative and historical elements to them, however much I also tried to do justice to the more usual questions that were the staples of such courses elsewhere, and I also tried to offer various answers to those questions that had intrigued me.

I have now taught such a course, in slightly different forms, and to both grad-uate and undergraduate audiences, at the Universities of Leicester, Aberystwyth, Bristol and St Andrews, most years since 1986, and have participated in similar courses, or seminars connected with such courses, while on leave at both the LSE in 1992 and the University of Southern California in 1995. I have also found it difficult to stop my interest in this area from spilling over into print and have thus contributed, in a small way, to the academic debate over 'International Relations Theory' and specifically to developing what is now often (and I think mislead-ingly) called a 'post-positivist' approach to 'International Relations Theory', in a number of articles in various learned journals and books.[4]

Over the last few years I have often thought I would like to offer some more organized reflections on the current state of 'International Relations Theory'. I wanted to push it into ever closer relations with those aspects of social and polit-ical theory that seem to me to be most interesting and which, in any case, I think are approaching it from the other direction. However, I put off actually doing so since I was already heavily committed – characteristically, indeed, *over*committed – on a number of other fronts.

One such front was a book on the question of order in world politics. I have long been fascinated by what I call the 'problem of order'. It seems to me that the search for a practically efficacious and normatively justifiable conception of political order has been a central question for political theory for much of its history and yet it has also been one which has exercised declining influence on political theorists, at least since the late seventeenth or early eighteenth century. This is especially true of the problem of 'world order'. Indeed, on my reading the last political philosopher unimpeachably of the first rank seriously to raise the question of 'world order' explicitly is Leibniz (though I would accept that good cases might be mounted for Kant, Hegel and Marx!).

However, the 'order book', as I kept referring to it, resolutely refused to display any order of its own. At one stage I had a draft of over 140,000 words and yet it was, frankly, a mess: a combination of intellectual history, political theory and international ethics that simply would not cohere. Leaving aside the intellectual irritation this created, this situation also created other problems. The deadline for the book came – and went. I faithfully – and repeatedly – committed myself to produce the manuscript for my bewildered and increasingly acerbic editors and – equally repeatedly – failed to do so with uncharacteristic consistency.

I cannot say what finally jogged me into realizing that I could combine my desire to write something in general about 'International Relations Theory' and 'political theory' with my concern to address – in outline at least – 'the problem of order'. All I can say is that once this became my aim, the book fell into place remarkably easily (and fairly quickly). A good deal of the material that existed in the original drafts I happily hacked out leaving a focus on the 'problem of order' as a vehicle to examine 'International Relations Theory' as it has commonly been understood over the last century, and I then added a good deal of material, heavily revised, from the various articles I had published on IR theory, and rounded the whole lot off with some more general discussions, about political and international theory and their possible trajectories.

Given my remarks above, few will be surprised that the overall purpose of the book is to engage in a *critique* of the literature of IR theory, though I hope a sympathetic one. However, it is probably as well to say at this point that I am equally critical of a good deal of 'political theory'. If IR theorists have – and in large part I think they have – forgotten the significance of the traditions of political theory for what they study,[5] it is IR theorists, in large part, who have kept the question of order at the forefront of their minds, where political theorists and philosophers – with a few honourable exceptions – have been pretty much content to forget it. For this, however much we would wish to abandon or moderate their characteristic modes of expression, we are very considerably in their debt.

There are, of course, many 'theories' of international relations and it is usual in books of this kind to discuss international relations in terms of those theories.[6] Whilst I certainly will be discussing those theories in this book – indeed it is a central task of the book to do so – I have chosen what many will doubtless see as an entirely characteristic off-centre way of doing it. Rather than simply focus on 'realism' or 'liberalism' (or whatever), I shall argue that, as far as the 'problem of order' is concerned at least, IR theory has contained five broad 'responses' or 'approaches' to what I shall call the 'problem of order',[7] divided into two broad families. Each of these responses concentrates on one aspect of international relations as the key to unlocking the solution to the 'problem of order'. These 'keys', then, are, in the order in which I shall discuss them here, balance, society, institutions, emancipation and limits. Most well-known 'theories' of international relations, I argue, have tended to focus on one of these 'keys' at the expense of the others. Thus, realists tend to focus on 'balance' and liberals on 'institutions'. However, there are plenty of exceptions or ambiguous cases: Raymond Aron, for example, or Arnold Wolfers or John Herz. The point of this is to bring into sharper relief the overall position that I shall explore in more detail in the final chapter, to wit that the focus on order allows us to see three broad trajectories for IR theory, two of which I shall wish to question, the third of which I shall broadly endorse.

Thus, the chief function of this book is to offer what I hope is both an interesting and provocative survey of contemporary 'International Relations Theory' through a concentration on the 'problem of order' and an argument for supposing that political theory as traditionally understood is much more significant for it than has usually been thought to be the case by either side. I do not suppose, of course, that I have covered everything of relevance in contemporary IR theory. Any book of this sort is bound to be impressionistic to some degree and so I do not feel inclined to apologize for emphasizing those bits of IR theory I think most interesting – whether I agree with them or not – and saying less about those bits I find least interesting. What I hope it achieves is to send IR theorists back to the study of the international with a sense that political theory (at least in some forms) is both necessary and helpful and to strengthen the sense that today at least, a political theory that is not also an international theory is hardly worthy of the name.

Notes

1   In fact, I believe that this is largely true for most earlier periods also, though certainly in differing ways. See Chris Brown, Terry Nardin and N. J. Rengger, *Texts in International Relations* (Cambridge: Cambridge University Press, forthcoming).

2   *Political Theory, Modernity and Post-modernity: Beyond Enlightenment and Critique* (Oxford: Blackwell, 1995). I shall take up one of the arguments pursued in that book in the last two chapters of this one.

3   For an attempt to broaden the canon quite explicitly with a focus on the 'international' aspects of political thought see Brown *et al.*, *Texts in International Relations*.

4   They will be referred to where relevant in the main text. However, for those of a bibliographic turn of mind, the essays are: 'Going Critical? A Response to Hoffman', *Millennium: Journal of International Studies*, 1988, 17(1): 81–9; 'Serpents and Doves in Classical International Theory', *Millennium: Journal of International Studies*, 1988, 17(3); 'Incommensurability, International Theory and the Fragmentation of Western Political Culture', in John Gibbins (ed.), *Contemporary Political Culture* (London: Sage, 1989); 'The Fearful Sphere of International Relations', *Review of International Studies*, 1990, 16(3); 'Culture, Society and Order in World Politics', in J. Baylis and N. J. Rengger (eds), *Dilemmas of World Politics* (Oxford: Clarendon Press, 1992); 'Modernity, Postmodernism and International Relations' (with Mark Hoffman), in J. Doherty *et al.* (eds), *Postmodernism and the Social Sciences* (London: Macmillan, 1992); 'A City which Sustains all Things? Communitarianism and International Society', *Millennium: Journal of International Studies*, 1992, 21(3) (reprinted in a revised form in Rick Fawn and Jeremy Larkins (eds), *International Society after the Cold War: Anarchy and Order Reconsidered* (London; Macmillan, 1996)); ' World Order and the Dilemmas of Liberal Politics', Center for International Studies at the University of Southern California (Working paper No. 4, June 1995); 'On Cosmopolitanism, Constructivism and International Society', *Deutsche Zeitschrift für Internationale Beziehungen*, 1/1996; 'Clio's Cave: Historical Materialism and the Claims of Substantive Social Theory in World Politics', *Review of International Studies*, 1996, 22: 213–31; 'Negative Dialectic? Two

Modes of Critical Theory in World Politics', in Roger Tooze and Richard Wyn Jones (eds), *Critical Theory and International Relations* (Boulder, CO: Lynne Rienner, forthcoming).

5 I should emphasize, by the way, that this is certainly not true of all of them, even those who on their contemporary reputations would be assumed to be furthest away from the sort of political theory I favour. Kenneth Waltz, for example, is an extremely able political theorist (as his first book, *Man, the State and War* demonstrates) and has written illuminatingly and interestingly on political theorists and international relations, as in his 1962 article 'Kant, Liberalism and War', *American Political Science Review*, 1962, 50: 331–40.

6 I should say here that I am not, for the moment, entering into the question of what, exactly, constitutes 'theory'. This will, indeed, be something that crops up from time to time in what follows, but for now I simply use the term in a very loose, imprecise and all-embracing sense, implying generalised reflection on world politics.

7 I do not suppose these four responses are exhaustive. There are unquestionably others. However, these have been the major twentieth-century responses, for both international relations and International Relations, as I seek to show in the Introduction.

Amongst those approaches I might be said to have neglected, probably the best known and most wide ranging would be the approach to the problem of order offered by various advocates of natural law theory over the last century or so. A whole chapter could have been devoted to this and I should, I think, at least suggest why I have chosen not to devote a chapter to it. In the first place, my own view is that natural law theory as a whole is split, with some advocates offering a version of what I call here (in Chapter 2) the 'societal' response – though a much stronger version than that which is offered by (say) the English school – whilst others amount to a version of the emancipatory strategy outlined in Chapter 4, and in each chapter I do try and say something about natural law. However, natural law theory has hardly been a major theory of international relations this century, for all its longevity and power – and for all that it has certainly been a prominent contributor to debates in international ethics. It might well be the case – as we shall see in the final chapter, I think in some respects it is the case – that versions of natural law are likely to be much more influential in the twenty-first century than they have been in the twentieth. However, if this is so, it will come about precisely because the major strategies for 'managing' world order in the twentieth in certain respects seem to have failed.

Another possible candidate for inclusion would be what we might call 'extreme responses' to the problem of order, such as those found in a good deal of fascist or Nazi literature, both official and unofficial. There is a good deal that could be said also, in this context, about the philosophical underpinnings of such responses, especially those of Heidegger and Carl Schmitt. However, such views have certainly not been part of 'International Relations Theory' – though inasmuch as they have influenced aspects of realist thought I do touch on them in the first chapter, and inasmuch as they influence a prominent recent train of thought I discuss them in Chapter 5. Nor have they, except perhaps briefly in the mid century, been responses around which political action has been oriented, whereas the four major responses discussed above have both representation in 'IR theory' and have been responses that have been implicated in policy.

Another interesting and not unrelated phenomenon, which I do touch on briefly in Chapter 1, is the thought of those political theorists – or activists – who follow the late Leo Strauss, many of whom certainly do have 'policy' positions stemming from a deliberately obscure – even 'hidden' – conception of political order. Perhaps the best known writer influenced by Strauss, for example, who is discussed in these pages is Francis Fukuyama. However, a full discussion of the Straussian conception of order would take me too far away from my main purpose in this book and so I pass over much of interest and relevance, to take it up again, I hope, another day. Equally, there is clearly a good deal to be said about Marxist conceptions of political order. I touch on these briefly in Chapter 4 and give full reasons there as to why I do not address them in the detail that it might be thought they deserved.

All of this is just to say that there are clearly other conceptions I might have discussed. However, I have chosen here to focus on those which have received the most prominent attention in both international relations – the world – and International Relations – the field of study. All accounts must draw limits somewhere!

Acknowledgements

I owe so much to so many people in connection with this book that I do not really know where to begin in thanking them. However, Gerry Segal, my erstwhile colleague at Bristol, now firmly esconced at the International Institute of Strategic Studies, and especially Barry Buzan, for whom the name peripatetic might have been invented, must have pride of place. As editors of the series in which this book appears, they commissioned me to write it, accepted the radical change(s) in the nature of the project with (relatively) good grace and put up with the continual non-appearance of the manuscript with far more tolerance than I deserved. I am pleased that they do not seem to be too displeased with the final result, though, in truth, I suspect that they are so surprised that there actually *is* a final result that pleasure or displeasure does not really come into it.

I obviously owe many debts of gratitude to a very wide range of scholars in political science, international relations and cognate disciplines whose territory I have trampled on and whose collegiality and good humour I have sorely tried over a number of years. Audiences at various conferences and universities heard various parts of this book in various stages of development, and I am, it goes without saying, very grateful for all the comments and criticism I received on these occasions.

I gave papers related to the book, or that have become – however tenuously or unrecognizably – part of the book, at the British International Studies Association annual conferences in 1991 and 1992, at the LSE (in 1992), the University of Essex (1993), the European Consortium for Political Research joint sessions in Leiden (1993), the University of Exeter (1995), the University of Manchester (1995), the Carlyle Club (1995), the University of Southern California (1995), the University of Dundee (1996), the University of Edinburgh (1997), the University of Leeds (1997), the University of Munich (1998) and the University of Westminster (1998).

Particular and personal thanks are due to a number of scholars of both international relations and political theory who have discussed the book – or ideas that it contains – with me and/or read and commented on portions of the manuscript. Special thanks then to Hayward Alker, Brian Barry, Samuel Brittan, Ken Booth, Chris Brown, David Campbell, Terrell Carver, John Charvet, Bill Connolly, James Der Derian, Michael Donelan, Hugh Dyer, Peter Euben, Ian

Forbes, Murray Forsyth, Mervyn Frost, John Groom, Richard Higgott, Mark Hoffman, Bonnie Honig, Andrew Hurrell, Robert Jackson, Maurice Keens-Soper, Caroline Kennedy-Pipe, Fritz Kratochwil, Andrew Linklater, Richard Little, James Mayall, Al Murray, Onora O'Neill, Gwyn Prins, Charles Reynolds, Martin Rhodes, Justin Rosenberg, Michael Shapiro, Steve Smith, Stephen Smith, Judith Squires, Hidemi Suganami, Ann Tickner, Henry Tudor, John Vincent, Ole Wæver, Rob Walker, Nick Wheeler, Howard Williams, and Pete Wright.

I have no idea where to start in thanking the Department of Politics at the University of Bristol, my institutional and intellectual home for eight memorable years. I was able to begin thinking about this book during a sabbatical term that the department's enlightened study leave policy allowed me and I was able to start the rethink that led to its current shape during a second period of leave in 1995–6. In addition to giving me this time free from teaching and administration, during the whole period of gestation the department supported the writing of the book in ways too numerous to mention properly. My colleagues in the department, most particularly Eric Herring, Vernon Hewitt, Mark Wickham-Jones, Terrell Carver, Judith Squires and, latterly, Richard Little, provided an especially stimulating environment for the kind of academic border crossing in which I seem to specialize, as did – outside the department – Chris Bertram, Gavin D'Costa, Catharine Edwards, Keith Graham, Michael Liversidge and Paul Smith.

I was also the beneficiary of an exponential increase in the numbers of research students in international relations and political theory at Bristol. Many thanks are due to these students for invigorating discussions, sharp criticism and many a pint – or large glass of the house claret – at *Col Jaspers* (now, alas, deceased). Thanks, then, to Richard Shapcott, Dave Fisher, Simon Francis, Keith Spence, Charlotte Hooper, Cecile Dubernet and Julian Ellis. One of those research students, now I am happy to say launched on his own scholarly way, will recognize just how much my views on realism owe to our conversations, discussions – and disagreements – during the three and a half years he was working on his own thesis on that subject, which I had the privilege of supervising. Al Murray's own book, *Rearticulating Realism*, based on the thesis, has now appeared. We disagree about realism still, but any non-realist – as well as most realists – will have to come to terms with the way Al has reconstructed this most flexible of twentieth-century traditions. Last, but never least, my undergraduate and masters students in various classes and at various universities have always showed consistently amazing levels of tolerance as I tried out on them various ideas contained herein. Their comments and insight – though not, I have to say, their essays – were always welcome.

During the time when some of the ideas for this book were first taking shape, I was on study leave at the Centre for International Studies at the LSE. Members of both Government and International Relations Departments, as well as (so to speak) my fellow fellows, were very generous with their time and discussed at length many issues that eventually became a part of this book – as well as many things that did not! For making my stay at the LSE such a pleasurable and profitable one, therefore, particular thanks are due (in no particular order) to James Mayall, Michael Donelan, Justin Rosenberg, Brendan O'Leary, Brian Barry, John Charvet, Janet Coleman, Michael Banks, Carsten Holbrad, Tom Miller, Spyros Economedes, Peter Wilson, Hayo Krombach, Hilary Hewitt, Elaine Childs and, last but not least, the *Beavers Retreat*! Very distant ancestors of parts of the book were, in fact, first given as papers at the LSE. One paper was given to the International Relations Department general seminar and a second to the 'Rational Choice Group' convened by Brian Barry. Thanks to the IR seminar participants for characteristically acute comments. Thanks too, as well as apologies, to those bewildered rational choice theorists (I must mention especially Patrick Dunleavy, Keith Dowding, Des King and Michael Nicholson) who arrived at Brian and Anni's flat expecting (not unreasonably) to hear a paper on rational choice and who put up with a rather rambling paper on realism and justice (distant echoes of which they might hear in Chapters 1 and 2 of the present book) with great tolerance.

A second vote of thanks should go to the Centre for International Studies at the University of Southern California. At the behest of Hayward Alker and Ann Tickner, this institution took its reputation in its hands and invited me out in the April of 1995 to give a presentation on some theme from this book. I chose to give a version of what is now Chapter 3. Not only was it a splendid and extremely pleasant stay for me, but the level of discussion and comment on the paper and indeed on the wider project was quite overwhelming. To Hayward and Ann (of course), and also to Jeff Knopf, my overkind and helpfully critical discussant during the actual seminar, I am, therefore, deeply indebted. However, not content with this, USC invited me back during the Autumn Semester of 1995 as a visiting fellow. I was able, therefore, to continue the dialogue with Hayward and Ann. I also discovered that, in addition to his talents as a discussant, Jeff Knopf makes the best coffee on the west coast. That was lucky for me, but unlucky for him since the centre gave me the office opposite him. (Glad to see you managed to finish that book in the end, Jeff!) I was also able to get to know the people at USC much better and am grateful to be able to pay tribute to their hospitality and friendliness. To all those who enriched my stay 'over there', especially Johnathan Aronson, Judith Grant, Steve Lamy, John Odell and the staff at the (now also, alas, defunct) *Crowne Plaza* at (or around) USC, Richard Rosecrance at UCLA and Peter Euben at UCSC, my grateful thanks.

Another acknowledgement is called for here. While I was in California, and through Hayward's good offices, I met Stephen Toulmin, whose work in many areas of philosophy and ethics I had long admired. We found that we had so many interests in common that we decided it would be entirely unfair to keep our views on them to ourselves and so, in due course, we intend to inflict them on an unsuspecting humanity. Although the impact on this book was more indirect, Stephen and Donna's hospitality, conversation (and single malt) all deserve a fitting tribute as does Dandy's forbearance!

Discussing forbearance, of course, I have to add that the biggest vote of thanks of all goes to Vanessa and, latterly, to Corinna, who have valiantly coped with my absences (mental as well as physical), my tendency to stay up till all hours of the night reading 'just one more chapter' and my concern with a subject – order – about which, I suspect, they felt that my knowledge was only academic. I am not sure whether the book is any the better for them being around, but I certainly know that I am.

I have one final acknowledgement I wish to make. My parents, as always, supported me in ways far too numerous to mention throughout the writing of this book. It is, therefore, very difficult still for me to realize that my father, who died in January 1997, will not now be there to read the final version and respond to it in his own inimitable way, as he did with everything I have written from my undergraduate dissertation onwards. There are no words that can express what I owe to him, or how much I miss him. As I came to finish the book there was no doubt that this book must be his. However, among the many things he taught me, one of the most cherished for us both was the value of friendship. Since he always welcomed my friends into his own life, and since he had the chance of getting to know them, I know that the three friends to whom I had intended to dedicate this book will not mind sharing the dedication of this book with him. As always, he would have enjoyed the company.

Several parts of this book have been published (usually in barely recognizable forms) elsewhere. It would be pointless to attempt to detail the borrowings and adaptions so let me simply list the published articles of mine from which I have drawn material for the book:

'Modernity, Postmodernism and International Relations' (with Mark Hoffman), in Joe Doherty *et al.* (ed.), *Postmodernism and the Social Sciences* (London: Macmillan, 1992).

'No Longer a Tournament of Distinctive Knights? Systemic Transition and the Priority of International Order', in Mike Bowker and Robin Brown (eds), *From Cold War to Collapse: Theory and International Politics in the 1980s* (Cambridge: Cambridge University Press, 1993).

'A City which Sustains all Things? Communitarianism and International Society', *Millennium: Journal of International Studies*, 1992, 21(3): 353–69. Reprinted in a revised form in Rick Fawn and Jeremy Larkins (eds), *International Society after the Cold War: Anarchy and Order Reconsidered* (London; Macmillan, 1996).

'World Order and the Dilemmas of Liberal Politics', Center for International Studies at the University of Southern California (Working paper No. 4, June 1995).

'On Cosmopolitanism, Constructivism and International Society', *Deutsche Zeitschrift für Internationale Beziehungen*, 1/1996.

'Clio's Cave: Historical Materialism and the Claims of Substantive Social Theory in World Politics', *Review of International Studies*, 1996, 22: 213–31.

'Negative Dialectic? Two Modes of Critical Theory in World Politics', in Roger Tooze and Richard Wyn Jones (eds), *Critical Theory and International Relations* (Boulder, CO: Lynne Rienner, forthcoming).

I am, of course, grateful to all publishers and editors for permission to reprint.

I should add finally that while all of the good ideas in this book are mine, any mistakes I make are, naturally, the fault of somebody else!

Introduction

International Relations theory and the problem of order

'Conceptions of order ... are always accompanied by the self interpretation of that order as meaningful ... that is about the particular meaning that order has. In this sense, self interpretation is always part ... of the reality of order, of political order, or, as we might say, of history.

Eric Voeglin

'Theory', in any area of academic enquiry, is almost always a contested term. In the social sciences today, it is perhaps more contested than almost anywhere else. Until relatively recently, however, this was not really true of International Relations.[1] Save for an (alleged) debate between Hedley Bull and Morton Kaplan in the pages of *World Politics* in the mid 1960s, and occasional polemical broadsides like Morgenthau's *Scientific Man versus Power Politics*, the 'great debates' that have supposedly shaped the study of international relations – realism versus idealism, for example, – have been debates *between* 'theories' – in the sense of general world views – rather than debates *about* 'theory' – what kind of theory is most appropriate for the study of international relations.

This is, however, no longer true. Today, debates about what *constitutes* theory as well as debates between different theories dominate the general discussion of international relations[2] and the two sets of debates are becoming increasingly intertwined. This book will, amongst other things, be concerned to develop an account of how this intertwining is taking place and what its implications are. However, in order to give us something substantive to focus on, I want first to explore what I shall call throughout this book, 'the problem of order'.

Order in the history of political thought

Order is one of the oldest and most discussed topics in political enquiry. From Greek tragedy and philosophy, to Roman conceptions of *Imperium* and *auctoritas*, medieval notions of trusteeship and the complex interrelations of law, power and order, to the natural lawyers of the Renaissance and early modern period and beyond, it was a constant and highly contested theme in political, philosophical and theological reflection. In more recent times, though as we shall see its unity was sundered and it was parcelled out between different disciplines (order in the natural world for the natural sciences, order in the social world for the moral and political sciences), it retained an important role in political enquiry at least until the mid nineteenth century.[3]

While 'order' has thus been much studied, it has not, I think, been much studied of late, at least in the moral and political sciences. Partly this is because the topic has tended to fall between the stools that are the disciplines of the modern academy. Understanding topics such as 'order' illustrates why the fragmentation of knowledge in the modern age, inevitable though it undoubtedly is, carries with it problems that we must be sensitive to: political order is a topic that, treated with the depth it should be, cannot be corralled by increasingly narrow specialisms.

However, it is also fair to say that treating 'order' – even political order only – as a whole would require a very substantial work indeed, and would take us a long way into many of those aforementioned disciplines. Such a task is not what I shall attempt here, though my treatment of order will be informed by that wider set of questions. Rather, what I want to do in this book is to view the evolution of the problem of 'political order' in the twentieth century specifically through that area where the question has been chiefly and most interestingly put, to wit, the question of international (or world) 'order' in the 'theory' of international relations.

It is significant, I want to emphasize, that while the most pertinent discussions of the 'problem of order' in the twentieth century have indeed been located in that amorphous, fuzzy and rather ill-defined 'field', usually called International Relations,[4] the discussions of this topic in the field also show very considerable ambivalence and tension. Part of the overall argument of this book is to suggest why this is the case. However, at this early stage we might just say that, whereas the 'problem' of political order 'within communities' – at least in theory – could be said to have been resolved through the institution of the nation-state (a mistaken belief, in my view, but a plausible and widely held one if one is using the conceptual language of modern Western politics), the very fact of the existence of multiple and often widely diverse 'communities' coupled with the fact of their interactions and interrelations makes the 'problem of order' at the 'international' level inescapable. Accounts of 'international' or 'world' order are the inevitable result as is the fact that accounts of international relations cannot but try and deal with the problem of order.

This is perhaps even truer today when it is at least arguable that the world of international relations is being radicalized beyond recognition by myriad forces: social, political, economic and technological. The catch-all term that is most often used in this context, of course, is 'globalization', and although I shall have little to say about this as a discrete set of phenomena in this book, at least until the last two chapters, the debate it has engendered is never far away from my concerns.

As I remarked in the Preface, my own background is in political theory, and so I think it is important at this point to emphasize that I take political theory to task as well for its neglect of this self-same topic. In a book first published in

1989, on the eve of the revolutionary events that were to shake the world of international relations – and also International Relations – to its foundations, the philosopher Stephen Clark remarked that, in his view, 'the overwhelming practical issue for political philosophers in this present day is to look out for an image of international order that can plausibly claim the loyalties of any sufficient number'.[5] He went on to say, rightly as I think, that

> it is astonishing that political philosophers have had so little to say in this, preferring to debate the nature of welfare rights within the state, redistributive justice within the state, civil disobedience within the state and so on, as though all human kind even lived, of their own will and spirit, in such states and as though the international scene were of no moment and the world itself – by which I do not mean the socio-political world – were not at stake.[6]

Clark went on to cite, in agreement, Kant's famous remark that the problems of 'domestic' political theory – the problems of perfecting a civil constitution – are subordinate to those of 'international' political theory – the problem of law governed relations between communities[7] – and to emphasize again how central a workable, defensible conception of world order is to this task.

I think Clark (and Kant) were, and are, right. Political theorists and philosophers, at least for the last 150 years, have largely left these questions alone, preferring, as Clark remarks, to debate questions that can (in the academy at least) be safely corralled within the 'boundaries' of the so-called nation-state. I do not think this attempt was ever very well founded; be that as it may, it is certainly coming apart at the seams now. Thus, it is high time that political theory started to think hard about the question of world order.[8] To do so, however, among its first responsibilities – both intellectually and as a matter of simple courtesy – is to come to terms with the manner in which those thinkers and scholars who have, in varying ways, thought about such questions have addressed it: in other words, it must engage International Relations theory and thus that dialogue forms the heart of this book.

The 'evolution of the problem of order'

Let me start here, however, with a general background sketch of how the problem of order itself might be said to have evolved in political thought. As I said above, 'the problem of order' has an old and distinguished history. However, it would not be true to say that it has remained unchanged throughout that history. Specifically, and for the purposes of the present discussion, I want to suggest that the problem of order has taken a distinctive form in the last 150 years or so, which we might call the problem of order within 'modernity'. This latter term is, of course, a highly contested one, and so I should emphasize that I understand it in a very particular way. Since I have defended this understanding in some detail elsewhere[9] I will not do so again, but its essence turns on the distinction between what I term 'modernity as mood' and 'modernity as socio-cultural form'. Simply put, this distinction separates out two ways of conceptualizing 'modernity'. The first consists in a focus on *the way we 'understand' and react to* what is held to be the implications of the modern; it is, in other words, largely a philosophical, theological, ethical and, perhaps, ontological question. The second, by contrast, focuses on particular changes in the material, techno-logical and/or socio-economic realms said to be *constitutive of the modern*.[10]

My argument in the earlier book was, amongst other things, that any account of modernity is, in fact, a compendium of both modernity as mood and moder-nity as socio-cultural form. The central question about discussions of modernity, therefore, is the relation between these two conceptions: which one, so to speak, dominates and how does each relate to the other in any given conception? The ramifications of this view in general do not concern me here, rather it is a way of framing what I take to be the central 'problem of order' for the modern world. The problem of order displays a particular character in the modern world in large part because of the way that a range of particularly influential readings of 'modernity as mood' have been related to certain claims about the development of modernity as socio-cultural form. Its 'modern' character is not, of course, entirely *distinct* from earlier versions of the problem, but it is *distinctive*.[11] In this book, it is largely with the 'problem of order in modernity' with which I shall be concerned and specifically with the way this problem has been manifested in the major traditions of political thought concerned with international relations. There are obviously other aspects of the problem of order, equally or even more important in the context of the historical story that might be told about it, that I do not concern myself with here. However, before I can come on to my main theme, I must offer at least a sketch of how I see the 'problem of order' in general evolving in the history of Western thought and practice and what makes it distinctive in modernity. Of course, what follows is – and given my main concern in this volume can only be – a sketch, the barest outline of an otherwise enormously complex and multi-faceted tale,[12] but as with all stories, one must start somewhere.

As with most aspects of the 'Western' tradition of political thought, we start with Classical Greece. As I remarked above, in the classical world 'order' was a much discussed, indeed disputed, term. However, one central theme in classical reflection was the unity of the world and the cosmos. 'Order', in this context, was often seen as the reflection of the unity of the natural world. Natural and 'human' order were in that sense perfectly at one.[13] In early Christian thought this strand of classical thought was often strongly emphasized with creation and divine providence being substituted for the eternal natural order.[14] Later on, however, the tension between classical and Christian thought became much more prominent. On this reading, 'order' in the sense implied above is impos-sible because of the fall. Human beings are sinful creatures and cannot attain even temporary virtue without strict control. Both versions are available in the thought of St Augustine, but it is the later, more pessimistic Augustine who becomes most influential on the developing Christian world.[15] For this

Augustine, it is not the promotion of 'order' as the realization of harmony with the natural world that is the business of the secular and spiritual authorities, rather it is the minimizing of instability, disorder and conflict. This is simply because the nature of the fall, as Augustine understood it, made it impossible for human beings to attain such harmony. Human order, such as can be attained, is no longer an integral part of the rational ordering of nature but is, so to speak, a separate part of God's providence located in the human realm of governmental institutions and law.

Such a division has fateful consequences for the conception of political order bequeathed to the Latin West. However, before we move on to see precisely how, it is worth pointing out here that, although similar influences were at work in the other repository of Christian thought, Byzantium, the results were rather different. In part because the political and generally socio-economic circumstances of the Greek East compared very favourably with those of the Latin West of Augustine's time, Byzantine reflections on the problem of order tended to offer a 'Greek' face to the world for much longer than in the West. The echo of Greek thinking about order as natural harmony of the human and divine can be found in early Byzantine thought, especially in the work of Eusebius, the Christian theologian and apologist for Constantinian conceptions of kingship. Eusebius's synthesis of Greek and Roman monarchical theory with Christian theology was hugely influential in the early Church, both East and West.[16] For this reason Byzantine political thought contains little overt reflection of the 'problem of order' after Eusebius's time. For the thousand or so years until the Byzantine tradition was finally scattered after the capture of the city by the Ottomans in 1453, the Eusebian tradition, albeit somewhat modified and reinterpreted, remained central. The emperor was seen as an 'incarnate law' (*lex animata, Nomos Empsuchos*) sent by God and thus beyond question or reproach. Of course, alternative currents did exist, particularly after the crisis of the eleventh century, but they were largely insignificant. In fact, perhaps the most revealing treatise in Byzantine political thought for the purpose of its working conception of political order is the *De Administrando Imperio* of Constantine Porphyrogenitus.[17] This private manual of statecraft, written by the emperor (Constantine VII) for his son and heir (the later Romanus II) is quite unlike the usual, public advice books for monarchs. It is written in plain language, rather than the rhetorical style favoured by imperial apologists, and it is particularly revealing about how the empire should conduct foreign policy, and on how the empire should view both itself and others. What it reveals is a conception of political order based on a greatly exaggerated Eusebian tradition, not dissimilar in tone to the way much ancient Chinese writing tends to view 'barbarians'. Influential though it became (in particular on Russian ideas of statecraft) it remained a largely distaff conception of political order for the West.[18]

There, rather than a reflection of an essentially unitary whole, order became seen as an 'ordering' of groups in society and between societies. As Pope Zacharias had accepted, when acknowledging Pippin III as King of the Franks, such acceptance was necessary that 'order may not be confounded'.[19] Order thus became both the overall patterning of a society and indeed of all societies (Christian ones anyway) and the precise relations between different parts of such societies, clerical and lay, high and low. This had the added significance, of course, that in a system such as feudal Europe with multiple and overlapping forms of authority and institutional structures, order in both senses applied across institutional and authority frontiers. It also meant that 'order' was related to an eschatological pattern, God's divine plan, which allocated a place to everyone and everything, and the administration of which was in the hands of the ruler or rulers (whether spiritual or temporal or – as in the most famous theological–political doctrine of the age, the Gelasian doctrine of 'the two swords' – both).[20]

Order, sovereignty and modernity

However, central as these themes were and are for the student of political order, it is with the emergence of the modern state, between the thirteenth and seventeenth centuries and with the consolidation of the same in the eighteenth and nineteenth centuries, that the problem of order took on the form it has had ever since and the form with which I shall principally be concerned in this book. While there were strong elements of continuity (as is well known the Treaty of Utrecht in 1713 still contained references to the *Respublica Christiana* that Europe was supposed to be in medieval thought, and the idea of the orders of social classes persisted still longer) there was also a good deal that was markedly different.

The central difference came about, I suggest, through the evolution of that most protean of modern political concepts, 'sovereignty'. In this volume I cannot possibly treat this notion with the attention it deserves and so I shall simply offer a sketch of a view of the relation between sovereignty and order which I freely accept would require a book in itself to describe and justify fully. Simply put, this view suggests that the establishment of sovereignty in early modern Europe instantiated, for better or worse, *a particular way of being political* and thus recast the basic assumptions of the problem of order.[21] The crucial aspect of this way of being political as far as the problem of order was concerned was the division of politics into an 'inside' and an 'outside', the inside of legitimately constituted territory and the outside of an 'anarchic' war of all against all.

Thus, 'inside', 'order' increasingly became a province of legal regulation within such states while 'outside' the whole problem became what could achieve 'order' in the absence of the legitimacy conferred by sovereignty.[22] In fact, this is a logical corollary of placing order within the realm of human institutions and is therefore perfectly consistent with Augustinian notions, even though the general Augustinian world view had long since been superseded in the minds of the political elites of modern Europe. However, in an almost Blumenbergian fashion,[23] the possibility of an Augustinian frame for understanding this situation remained, a point which we will see resurface in Chapter 1 when we look at realist accounts of order and the notion of balance.

If one wishes to see, writ small as it were, a microcosm of the differences between the 'old' and the 'new' conceptions of order as I have sketched them here, one could not do better than to study the differences between Leibniz and Hobbes. As has long been recognized, there was in Hobbes' political thought, and indeed in his general cast of mind, something remarkably 'modern' as the 'modern European West' defines that elusive term.[24] Without delving into the minefield of contemporary Hobbes scholarship let me suggest that among the aspects of his thought that were rightly perceived as 'modern', if by that term is meant qualitatively different from and newer than the 'medieval and renaissance' conceptions, was his thoroughgoing and very radical nominalism which, in the political realm, issued in his commitment to a very radical notion of sovereignty indeed. The 'sovereign' creates order not just in fact but in name also. By definition, therefore, there can be no 'order' where there is no sovereign and since there is no sovereign in the 'international realm' there is no order. Hence the 'problem' of international relations and Hobbes' understanding of it as a 'warre of all against all'.[25]

There could be few thinkers as opposed to this view as Hobbes' near contemporary Leibniz. Leibniz spent a hugely varied career, and one which also spanned a multitude of fields, arguing for the essential unity of theology, metaphysics, mathematics, ethics and politics. Perhaps no thinker since classical antiquity had such an ambition in developing an all-encompassing system. In his attitude to international relations, Leibniz was perfectly consistent with this ambition. He was the last thinker of the very first rank to reason quite seriously about the politics of the *Respublica Christiana* and locate his conception of order within that frame. In his most self-consciously 'medieval' work of political theory, the *Caeserinus Furstenerius*, he argues that the two heads of Christendom are the Pope and the Holy Roman Emperor and goes on to describe what Patrick Riley has called the 'supranational authority' which he thought that these two should have:

> the emperor is the defender or rather the chief or if one prefers the secular arm of the Universal Church: that all Christendom forms a species of republic, in which the Emperor has some authority … that it is mainly for him to destroy schisms, to bring about the meeting of [ecumenical] councils, to maintain good order … so that the Church and the Republic of Christendom suffer no damage.

Of course, it is true that Leibniz as he grew older also grew more resigned to the emergence of a different 'way of being political', but he never abandoned the hope – or the conviction that it was a realistic hope – that the framework of the *Respublica Christiana* could remain as a guide and constant beacon. Even in late works like the *Codex Iuris Gentium* of 1693 and in almost his last work of note, his commentary on the Abbé de St Pierre's *Project for Perpetual Peace* (1715), we find Leibniz returning yet again to various ways of institutionalizing in the new situation the old frameworks of the *Respublica Christiana*.[26]

As we shall see in the conclusion of this book we might do well to remember Leibniz – as well as several other 'pre-modern' thinkers in the current context. However, the immediate future lay with Hobbes.[27] It is in the mid eighteenth century that we get the first fully formed 'theories of international relations' in the modern sense, as well as, by the end of the century, the first embryonic senses that the system itself might one day be transformed – Kant's own idea for perpetual peace, of course.

However, it is also worth pointing out that in the late eighteenth and early nineteenth century two other factors became increasingly important. In the first place, the growing role and conceptual power of natural science began to challenge much of those aspects inherited from the medieval period in so far as those aspects were also predicated on the notion of a 'divine plan'. Second, and still more significantly for our purposes, the rise of 'History' (with, that is to say, a capital 'H') raises the question of order anew. As Karl Lowith has pointed out, nineteenth-century conceptions of history, so strongly influential on the whole of nineteenth-century scholarship in many different fields, consider the human world only and largely ignore the rest of the world. In so far as it was possible to say that history had a 'meaning', its meaning was locatable in purely human terms.[28] This divide reinforces, of course, the division of order as 'natural' on the one hand and 'human' (institutional, political) on the other with the two gods of the nineteenth century, science and history, neatly aligned with a separate type of order. Yet the great debates in the nineteenth century (and indeed beyond) have thrown into question the status of both science and 'History' and have thereby fragmented still further the possibility of a coherent understanding of 'order'.

Most influential, in the context of this latter development, has been the deep questioning of notions of 'progress' in both thought and, so to speak, experience in the twentieth century. The nineteenth-century argument was highly diverse and complex in its manifestations but in essence, in both fields, fairly simple. If order implies pattern, and the pattern can no longer be found in the assumption of a divine plan, it must be found either in nature or in history. Given that political order was, as we have seen, perceived as a function of laws and institutions, it perforce fell into the province of history. The great twentieth-century political doctrines, liberalism and socialism, in all their rich variety were, *par excellence*, doctrines of progress. Their great opponent, conservatism (as a doctrine, rather than a disposition) was, as it were, an 'anti doctrine' that challenged the notion of what progress was and what it might bring but, except on its more lunatic fringes, did not challenge its essence. As one of the twentieth century's greatest spokesmen for conservatism has put it, in a different though related context, 'a plan to resist all planning, might be preferable to its opposite but it is still part of the same style of politics'.[29]

Many have suggested that much of the ideological crisis of the twentieth century, from the rise of fascism to the emergence of post-structuralism and the challenge to (in Lyotard's words) 'meta-narratives', lies in the perceived crisis of faith in progress that was the legacy of the great nineteenth-century debates on science and faith, religion and history, coupled with the near universal trauma in European high culture created by the First World War. Some time before then, however, the crisis was memorably sketched by Nietzsche in the 1890s.[30] For Nietzsche, the logic of the last *fin de siècle* was a logic of 'decadence', but this was necessary for the new beginning he sought to create in the minds, and more importantly the wills, of his readers. Such a new beginning was indeed a 'new order', because it relied on the utter destruction of the decaying remnants of the old, which believed in 'progress' and therefore 'meaning' in history. For Nietzsche wished to return to a world where the natural truth of the cosmos is understood again, as it was by his beloved Greeks, and yet could only do this by calling into being a new world through an act of will that negates in principle the belief in harmony and natural order that was the hallmark of the classical vision. Many of Nietzsche's followers, whether acknowledged or not – and most especially Max Weber – doubted that this was possible but still saw the power of Nietzsche's critique of modernity and were thus caught in an acute dilemma: on the one hand a desirable, but increasingly unobtainable, world which in principle at least could be 'ordered'; on the other an increasingly all-encompassing 'iron cage', all too powerful and all too real but not really ordered by human agency at all.

It is my contention that the debate about order in general has not really moved from this spot. The fundamental 'problem of order' is still how order can be attained in the human community, after what should it seek to pattern itself, and who or what should impose the pattern. In terms of world order, however, the questions become much starker. Should there be some form of world authority to impose some pattern? If so, what pattern and what authority? If not, is order simply, as Augustine taught, the minimizing of disorder, conflict and instability? How should this be done? What weapons are appropriate for the task? What unusable or impermissible? And is there a goal to be aimed at, progress to be made along a path towards that goal? Do our existing mechanisms enhance or inhibit our chances of reaching such goals? Or is such talk doomed to futility, as Nietzsche so eloquently, and terrifyingly, predicted and as a number of his modern followers have, with more irony than terror, echoed?

What is distinctive about this version of the 'problem of order', of course, is the extent to which it is posed as a series of exclusive dichotomies. Either/or, to quote a Kierkegaardian phrase, is the hallmark of modernity. In terms of the 'problem of order', the question is simple. Can order be meaningful at all, in the absence of something – God's plan, History, Nature – which guarantees it? How could we find this out? How can we instantiate our answer, whatever it turns out to be? And especially in the context of 'international order', what vehicles can we use that are consonant with the legitimacy of the inside/outside distinction, or are there none that are so consonant?

Today, of course, such questions are deeply intertwined with the second aspect of the 'modernity debate', modernity as socio-cultural form. It is the *material* features of the late modern world that have often led many contemporary observers to talk of potentially radical new world orders in which the state is disappearing, markets are global and politics virtual.[31] If history has been challenged, so to speak from within, so too has science. The models and methods of nineteenth- and early twentieth-century natural science – experimentation, falsifiability, predictability – are being augmented, some would say overwhelmed, but in any event changed by new worlds of chaos and catastrophe, of virtual reality and artificial intelligence, of bio- and nanotechnology and so on. Of course, the implications of these developments are hotly disputed; the potential they have for the radical change of our world, whether for better or worse, is not.[32] Yet what real significance might they have for the way of being political that the problem of order within modernity makes manifest?

It is with the attempts to answer the 'outside' aspect of this question that I will largely be concerned here. Of necessity, however, this will involve claims about the 'inside' as well, claims to which I shall return at the end of the book. However, before I can survey what alternative answers have been proffered, I must say something about those who have done the proffering; in other words, about that sometimes strange and often hybrid entity, 'International Relations Theory'.

International relations theory and world order

As the above story suggests, political thinking about the character of community and the interrelations between communities is a permanent feature of political reflection in the West – and indeed not only the West[33] – though both the questions and the answers change through time.[34] However, with the rise of the distinction between 'domestic' and 'international' politics, the activity of theorizing about each began, gradually at first, to be separated as well. With the rise of the national state in the late eighteenth and early nineteenth centuries, this tendency became still more marked.

The recognition of the growing changes in political, social and economic life were, of course, partly responsible for the gradual establishment of the new 'social' sciences – also in the late eighteenth and early nineteenth centuries. By the end of the nineteenth century, Political Science, Sociology, Anthropology, Geography and Economics were gaining footholds in the major universities of the major states as History had a century before.[35] However, International Relations as a subject tended to be seen as part and parcel of one of the other 'disciplines' (History or Politics or Law), when it was seen at all. 'International Relations', as a self-conscious scholarly enterprise, was born later, as a direct result of a shattering political event and its aftermath, the First World War.

As is well known, the first chairs and departments devoted to questions of international politics were established just before or just after the Great War[36] and mainly, though not wholly, by people who had played a part in the events of that war. The significance of this is threefold, I think. In the first place, academic 'International Relations' from the beginning started from the prevailing assumption (both academically and practically) that the 'international' and the 'domestic' were distinct areas and that the source of the 'problem of order' –

and probably, therefore, the solution too – lay at the 'international level'. Thus 'domestic' political questions could be safely left to the students of politics (and perhaps sociology), a compliment that was often returned by the political scientists and, especially, by the political theorists. Thus, and despite the fact that even today many courses in 'international relations' contain some discussion of – to take just one example close to my own heart – the history of political thought, the tendency has always been to get students to read those brief selections of (say) Hobbes, Rousseau, Kant, etc., that address 'international relations' as academic International Relations (in the twentieth century) *already* understood it: as separated into 'domestic' and 'international' realms. Very rarely were students of 'international relations' expected to read Hobbes' *Leviathan* (for example) in its entirety,[37] to treat his account of politics *tout court* as a necessary whole; necessary, that is, in order to understand how Hobbes saw – if indeed he did – the distinction between 'domestic' and 'international' politics, amongst many other things. Still less are students of international relations expected to look at the context and intellectual milieu of a particular work, as a now very influential version of intellectual history and political theory would counsel.[38]

In the second place, and following on from the circumstances of its birth, 'International Relations' has always had something of a disputed identity, both intellectually and practically. In the latter context, as a self-conscious 'subject' – I hesitate to use the term 'discipline' – it was born with a very clear practical remit. The Wilson chair at Aberystwyth, for example, was endowed to investigate the origins of conflagrations like the Great War with a view to preventing a future occurrence.[39] The very fact that a new academic approach was felt by some to be needed indicates that, at least implicitly, existing academic subjects were not doing that job. More to the point, the erection of such a discipline was a standing rebuke to existing political and institutional forms in the international arena (which had, after all, at best failed to prevent the catastrophe).

The fact that International Relations was perceived to have a very clear practical task meant, and continues to mean, that it is one of the branches of the social sciences closest to the political world, both for good and ill. The rise of what I will refer to in this book as 'mainstream' academic International Relations in the United States after the Second World War displays a similar trajectory and similar tensions, driven in part at least by the Cold War, directly or indirectly.[40]

There is nothing intrinsically wrong, of course, with academic enquiry having a practical importance. But this fact adds to the intellectual ambiguity of what kind of an academic enquiry International Relations is. If it is 'separate' from, say, political science (the subject to which it is most usually yoked), then what is the character of its separateness? In most cases – and certainly by most self-conscious 'political scientists' – International Relations is treated as a 'sub-field' of political science; however, for many International Relations scholars, perhaps most notably Quincy Wright, but more recently many others as well, political science is but one amongst a number of fields that, together, make up International Relations properly understood.[41]

I do not intend to argue that toss here – though I shall return to it in the

Epilogue – rather I want to suggest that this volatility in the study of international relations has resulted in two things: first, an understandable desire to get on with 'doing' International Relations without too much concern about what is being done *elsewhere*; and, second, the complete impossibility of this actually being realized, except by simple fiat. The result is that International Relations as a *discipline* has often tried to keep itself aloof from the wider debates in the human sciences, in order to 'get on with its subject matter'. It has sometimes succeeded, but only at the cost of increasing its internal tensions, sailing ever more closely to the wind of prevailing political and/or intellectual fashion and developing internal 'theoretical' debates that are usually ill-defined echoes of debates elsewhere.[42]

The third point that needs to be made here concerns the *location* of the birth of International Relations as a separate subject of study. The creation of specific chairs (and thus departments, associations, journals, etc.) was, to begin with at least, concentrated in the 'liberal' countries that were victorious in the war, namely Britain and the United States. It is not the case of course that the only work *relevant to* 'international relations' (however understood) was done there; much was done in Europe and, especially as the century progressed, elsewhere as well. Most cultures and civilizations have, after all, long and important traditions of reflection about the subject matter of International Relations, however understood: relations between political communities, war, trade, cultural diversity and its implications.[43] However, the major chairs, journals, institutes and so on had been established in Britain and even more importantly – especially after the Second World War – in the United States and these set much of the 'tone' with which 'international relations' was discussed in the academy. Along with the methodological developments I will discuss a little later on, it is this which lends plausibility to Stanley Hoffmann's famous remark about International Relations being an 'American Social Science'.

This has also largely led to what I shall call the 'shape' of the debates that currently dominate international studies. International Relations bears the marks of its birth in the sense that the debates that initially framed it – 'Realism versus Idealism', for example – were Anglo-Saxon debates, or where they were not, were debates over which a clear Anglo-Saxon gloss was laid. As time went on and those who came from different traditions began to make their mark on the discipline – for example, a Morgenthau, a Wolfers or a Herz – they did so on a discipline already framed by a certain Anglo-American framework, a situation which continues to this day.

Thus, before reflecting on the vicissitudes of the problem of order in contemporary IR theory – and in order to frame my own discussion of IR theory itself – I want briefly to refer to a much discussed article which seeks to 'shape' the current debate on IR theory in general.

Contemporary International Relations theory in contest

This article is Robert Keohane's 1988 Presidential Address to the International Studies Association (ISA), 'International Institutions: Two Approaches'.[44] This essay has in many ways provided the launching pad for the evolution of a good deal of theoretical debates in the late 1980s to the mid 1990s. In the halcyon days of yore, before the Research Assessment Exercise and Teaching Quality Assessment emerged to blight the life of the humble British scholar, scholars at certain ancient British universities used to mark an essay that was in other respects unquantifiable as α/γ (alpha/gamma). Keohane's essay, I suggest, is the alpha/gamma of contemporary international relations theory – both excellent and suggestive and deeply flawed and underhanded at one and the same time.

The essay is based around a distinction between, as the title suggests, two approaches to the study of international institutions, though it quickly becomes clear that it is approaches to the study of international relations more generally that are at issue. However, the focus on institutions is appropriate – as we shall see in Chapters 2 and 3 of this study especially – in that, as Keohane remarks, it is on the issue of the effectiveness of 'institutions' that the two approaches differ most fundamentally, notwithstanding any other differences there might be within them.

Keohane refers to these two approaches as 'rationalist' and 'reflectivist', but rather than seeing them as distinct in substantive terms (though of course they often are) he frames the division largely in methodological and epistemological terms – in other words, he sees the division as primarily one driven by different conceptions of what theory is, rather than simply clashes between two rival theories. The 'rationalist' approach, which includes the currently dominant modes of IR theory in the United States, neo-realism and neo-liberalism, accepts what Keohane, following Herbert Simon, calls a 'substantive' conception of rationality, which characterizes rational behaviour as 'that [which] can be adjudged objectively to be optimally adapted to the situation'.[45] For Keohane (and for Simon) such a conception of rationality must be put together with assumptions about the structure of utility functions and the formation of expectations, though, of course, context is important as well. Thus 'rationalistic' accounts of international relations or international institutions are capable of considerable variation: hence, for example, the differences between neo-realists and neo-liberals on the role of institutions in promoting co-operation – though as Ole Wæver has pointed out, and as we shall discuss in more detail below, such differences as these are remarkably narrow.

In contrast to this rationalist approach, 'reflectivist' approaches, for Keohane, concentrate on the role of 'impersonal social forces as well as the impact of cultural practices, norms and values that are not derived from calculations of interests'.[46] The thinkers he has in mind are many and varied but the best known, he suggests, would include Hayward Alker, Richard Ashley, Friedrich Kratochwil and John Ruggie, all of whom emphasize the importance of inter-subjective meanings for (and of) international institutional activity. For Keohane, these writers emphasize that individuals, local organizations, and even states develop within the context of more encompassing institutions. Institutions do not merely reflect the preferences and power of the units constituting them; the institutions themselves shape those preferences and that power. Institutions are therefore constitutive of actors as well as vice versa.[47]

Keohane admits that all of the above writers are different from one another and that there are many differences between them. He admits also that the fairest label would probably be 'interpretive', 'since they all emphasize the importance of historical and textual interpretation and the limitations of "scientific"[48] models in studying world politics'.[49] However, Keohane also thinks such a label would be appropriate for what he terms 'strongly materialist historical sociological approaches indebted to Marxism' and 'political theoretical arguments emphasizing classical political philosophy or international law'. Thus, he decides upon the label 'reflectivist' since all of his intended thinkers 'emphasize the importance of human reflection for the nature of institutions and ultimately for the character of world politics'.[50]

Keohane's argument then moves on to suggest that students of international institutions (in particular) and – at least by implication – students of world politics more generally should direct their attention to the relative merits of these two approaches. 'Until we understand the strengths and weaknesses of each,' he says, 'we will be unable to design research strategies that are sufficiently multifaceted to encompass our subject matter and our empirical work will suffer accordingly'.[51] After a brief discussion of how we should understand institutions,[52] Keohane offers his own view (should I say reflection?) on the relative merits of the two approaches. Rationalistic theory, he thinks, is 'good at posing questions and suggesting lines of inquiry but it does not furnish us with answers'.[53] It has well-developed research programmes but also obvious blackspots (history or, anyway, historicity) that have been seized on by its reflective critics, Keohane suggests correctly. However, for all their critical edge, reflectivist scholars, he thinks,

> lack ... a clear reflective research program which could be employed by students of world politics ... until the reflective scholars or others sympathetic to their arguments have delineated such a research program and shown in particular studies that it can illuminate important issues in world politics, they will remain on the margins of the field, largely invisible to the preponderance of empirical researchers, most of whom explicitly or implicitly accept one or another version of rationalistic premises.

'Such invisibility would be a shame,' Keohane adds, 'since the reflective perspective has much to contribute'.[54] He concludes his comparison with a clear indicator that, for him – for all the critical success of reflectivist approaches – it is the rationalists who are still in the driving seat. 'Reflective approaches are less well specified as theories,' he says, '...supporters of this research program need to develop testable theories and to be explicit about their scope ... above all (they) need to carry out systematic empirical investigations, guided by their ideas'.[55]

Keohane's essay ends with a claim that one blindspot shared by both approaches is a lack of concern with domestic politics. Although both could develop interesting accounts of this, Keohane thinks – he mentions specifically Robert Putnam's work on 'two-level games' in the rationalist camp[56] and the reflectivist discussions and critiques of state sovereignty – neither has yet done so; the clear suggestion is that they should.[57]

This essay is interesting and paradoxical for a number of reasons. Keohane clearly points to the fact that dominant modes of IR theorizing, at least in the United States – in other words, the 'rationalists' – are governed by assumptions taken initially from Economics and more or less admits that, notwithstanding the popularity of such methods in political science as a whole – indeed in a good deal of social science as a whole – and, indeed, not withstanding his own commitment to them, they are clearly deficient in certain respects. This admission should be welcomed. Admitting that such methods are incomplete does not mean that they have no place in the human sciences; they clearly do. On the other hand, Keohane equally clearly stacks the deck in 'rationalism's' favour. What 'reflectivist' scholars have to do to prove their worth is, effectively, to become methodological rationalists. They have to develop 'testable theories'; 'research programs' and the like. Almost all of the 'reflectivists' discussed by Keohane – with the possible exception of Ruggie – would, I think, demur at the claim that this is what they 'have' to do to be taken seriously and would suspect that inasmuch as they did this, they would already have lost the game.

Another significant point is the extent of the contortions Keohane goes through in order to 'name' his reflectivists, especially given their enormous diversity which he himself admits. Ashley (at least by 1988) was clearly a post-structuralist, Ruggie and Kratochwil had already outlined the essentials of what has now become 'constructivist' IR theory, and Alker, then as now, is virtually unpigeonholeable.[58] To suggest that these thinkers have something in common that they do not share with (say) Robert Cox (whom I imagine Keohane might have in mind when discussing his 'strongly materialist historical sociological approaches indebted to Marxism') seems perverse, especially given that Keohane subsequently seems to use Cox as a 'reflectivist'.[59] Moreover, the 'political-theoretical arguments emphasizing classical political philosophy and international law' – which is where I suppose I would place myself – require substantial filling out. I suspect they refer to what I will discuss (in Chapter 2) as the English school, in which case I would not wish to locate myself there at all. In any case, and supposing that they do, then – as we will see – they would largely share the so-called 'reflectivist' emphasis as well.

So why 'reflectivism' as Keohane defines it? The short answer, of course, is that I do not know. However, let me offer a suggestion. The advantages of limiting his concerns to the four named thinkers are twofold. First, all of them work – or at least did then[60] – in the United States. Including Cox and/or the

English school would, perforce, dilute the 'purity' of the sense that 'mainstream' International Relations is essentially 'rationalist' in orientation, if by this term is meant subscription to a certain style of neo-positivist methodologies, broadly economistic in tone. That claim would probably be true in the United States; indeed it would be true of most political science *tout court* in the United States. However, it would most certainly not be true in Britain or elsewhere in the Anglophone world and would be even less true in certain European countries. Of course, it *is* true that 'rationalist' IR theory is well represented in Europe (especially in Scandinavia and Germany) and also in some places outside Europe, for example Japan and Korea. However, it becomes much less easy to 'group' thinkers together into a 'school of thought' if you confuse things by crossing either the 49th parallel or, still more significantly, the Atlantic Ocean.

This has the second advantage that the 'debate' that Keohane is seeking to invite can be managed in relatively straightforward ways and, so to speak, on the home ground of the largely US-based International Relations (or at any rate Political Science) journals. Since the mid 1980s there has been a growing worry on the part of many in International Relations that somehow it is all becoming far too eclectic; what was methodologically relatively united is dividing like (choose your preferred metaphor) bacteria or factions of the old left. For those already convinced of the advantages of 'disciplinary' unity at least over broad questions of method such developments naturally seemed problematic.[61]

I want to suggest, however, that this methodological diversity is not only welcome, but inevitable. It is largely the result of International Relations being gradually reintegrated with the wider questions of social and political science and theory that it had chosen – not always explicitly – largely to ignore from 1945 onwards – and indeed, as I shall suggest below, to some extent from its inception as an academic discipline. In this context the rise of 'rationalist' IR theory is, in fact, *itself* a sign of this development in that the assumptions of 'rationalism' are essentially those of rational and public choice theory and game theory which have become omnipresent in the social sciences of the mid to late 1990s,[62] spreading out from their initial home in economics.[63] However, I do not think you can really pick and choose. If one form of theoretical discourse from outside the 'discipline' could become influential in International Relations, it is hardly surprising if others do as well. 'Interpretive' or 'reflective' scholarship simply represents *other* aspects of the human sciences being brought to bear on questions of world politics. As the social sciences become more interpenetrated such 'spillover' will become increasingly common – and will affect all social sciences to a greater or lesser extent.

I agree with Keohane that dialogue between these various differing approaches is important. However, I would add that, contrary to what he seems to suppose, dialogue does not necessarily presume agreement and is, in any case, a two-way process. It should happen not just, so to speak, in the citadels of ratio-nalism, but in those of reflectivism also. And if it does, then it seems to me we cannot decide in advance what would come out of the dialogue. We cannot, for example, assert *in advance* that we 'have' to develop testable theories, for we might come to agree – certainly with many post-structuralists but also many radical philosophers of science who are not post-structural at all[64] – that 'testing a theory' in the sense meant is neither possible nor desirable. In other words, I would see Keohane's invitation to dialogue as structured in too narrow and one sided a way. If he genuinely wishes dialogue, then surely a lot more must be placed on the table than he has so far seemed prepared to place there.

All of this is relevant in the current context in that a good deal of contemporary theory has more than half an eye on this set of questions, in addition to any specific substantive question they might be dealing with. We might call this the question of the order of the 'discipline' of International Relations, and for many theorists it certainly has a higher priority than any explicit reflection on the problem of order as I shall define it in a moment. In particular, a number of theorists seem intent either on trying to knock their methodological opponents out – neo-realists and neo-liberals ganging up, as it were, on reflectivists – or on portraying their own favoured theory as the root to theoretical reintegration – ignoring the point I made above, that dialogue presupposes the notion of an *ongoing* conversation, an agreement to disagree, if you like.

This has added a rather strident and unpleasant tone to a good deal of both methodological and substantive debate in international studies. Recently, the philosopher James Sterba has criticized a 'war-making' style of discussion, in which arguments are 'attacked, shot down (like a plane) or sunk (like a ship) [or] Theses are defended, defeated or demolished'.[65] Arguments of this kind are only right or wrong, black or white. Grey does not figure in this colour scheme. In our context, the assumption is obvious. Realists and liberals – or rationalists and reflectivists – cannot both be right. Yet I shall try and suggest in what follows that this form of debate has actually obscured a good deal of commonality in positions that are usually seen as diametrically opposed and, as a result, has led to considerable confusion over what sorts of trajectories might be available for IR theory as we approach a new century.

Contemporary international theory and the problem of order

As we will see, the attempt to keep 'International Relations' unsullied by the wider human sciences has, in any event, failed. However, in terms of the problem of order, the multiple ambivalences of IR theory have chiefly meant that it has had difficulties articulating a clear understanding of world order even while – more or less explicitly – recognizing the centrality of doing so. The reason for this can be best illustrated if we examine one of the most interesting contemporary conceptualizations of the problem of order as such.

It is doubly significant in that it is by Raymond Aron, one of the few scholars or commentators based outside Britain and the United States to have had a major impact on International Relations. He was also, of course, a scholar with a foot in a number of intellectual camps (sociology, political science and philosophy, as well as International Relations) as well as a committed observer, public intellectual and political commentator.[66] In a paper first published in 1960, he argued[67] that there are five possible meanings of order for world politics. Two of these meanings, he suggests, are purely descriptive (order as any arrangement of reality, order as relations between the parts of said reality). One is purely normative (order as the conditions of the good life). The remaining two are hybrid and, in Aron's terms, analytical – that is, partly normative, partly descriptive (order as the minimum conditions for existence, order as the minimum conditions for co-existence). Aron's view is that it is the latter two – and especially the conditions for co-existence – that are the most fruitful for contemporary world politics.

In the light of the analysis of the problem of order offered above we can see that Aron's argument is particularly acute. 'Order' *must be both* 'normative' and 'explanatory'. In IR theory, as we shall see, it has, in fact, always been both, though not always explicitly. That is part of the problem. With the exception of mavericks like Aron, however, *explicit* discussions of Order are not as common in twentieth-century IR theory[68] as it might be thought they would have to be, though of course there are exceptions. Thus, before moving on to discuss the shape this book will take, I want to run briefly through some general discussions of order in the International Relations literature as a precursor to defending my own particular way of dividing them up.

To begin with, then, let me start with one of the few good studies to take the notion of world order seriously to have appeared recently:[69] R. D. McKinlay and Richard Little suggest that order be seen as a combination of what they call 'pattern' and 'goal satisfaction'. If order is pattern then disorder is deviation from a pattern, of course. However, they argue,

> the conceptualisation of order purely as pattern is inadequate once we focus on systems involving human intervention. The reason is that humans endow their behaviour with purpose and meaning. Human behaviour is goal oriented and it is necessary to incorporate goal orientation into a conceptualisation of order.[70]

This version of order is certainly an improvement on the usual neglect of what we might call the 'agent-centred' aspect of order,[71] common to broadly positivistic theories. Seeing order as 'goal satisfaction' certainly opens up a space for normative and ethical considerations that is absent in much other work and, as we shall see, it is central to much liberal writing about world politics in that liberal assumptions are generally reformist and, as a result, need to place some weight – though how much and in what way is, precisely, a matter of great dispute – on the possibilities of intentional, directed change in world politics. However, there is little sense in this formulation of what I called above the 'dialectic' of order, of Aron's sense of the tensions, ambiguities and contradictory character of order.

An alternative conceptualization, worth pondering both for its own sake and because of the influence of its author on the development of both constructivist and critical theory over the last few years, is that provided by Friedrich Kratochwil in his 1978 book *International Order and Foreign Policy*.[72] Kratochwil announces at the beginning of his study that his objective in the book is to 'develop an approach to the problem of international order and to demonstrate the heuristic fruitfulness of this approach ... [throwing] some light on the general problem of the establishment, the maintenance and the transformation of international order'.[73] He also emphasizes that his approach differs from those of more radically inclined scholars (he specifically mentions Richard Falk, amongst others, to whom we will turn in a moment) in that

> the analysis of international order requires a study of the processes by which particular conventions – or 'rules of the game' ... arise, persist, change and decay ... crucial to this approach is the belief that human action is 'rule governed' and that *in the process of interaction*, the meaning of the various moves on each side becomes intelligible to the participants, when they start to acquire a common background knowledge [emphasis added].[74]

It is in his first chapter that the operative conceptions of world order and international order are discussed and developed. After a brief discussion of the problems of defining order and of the classical and medieval background to conceptions of order, Kratochwil develops his account of order as such, as dependent upon norms working via socialization and absent centralized authority, following in this regard Hume's famous account of conventions. With this in mind, Kratochwil then broadly endorses Hedly Bull's separation of international and world order (which we will discuss in more detail in Chapter 2), the former being patterns of behaviour supportive of the society of states and the latter being patterns of behaviour supportive of human social life as such, and then goes on to emphasize that the focus of his study is international order thus understood and that its central concerns are the iterative bargaining relationships that consequently characterize international politics and out of which international order will emerge, if it emerges at all.

This conception of order, we might observe, is closer still to Aron's: both normative and explanatory and concerned with interaction, and thus at least open to what I termed the 'dialectical' aspect of Aron's treatment. It is also worth noting the anticipation of Kratochwil's later 'constructivist' position (indeed the constructivist position *tout court*), which emphasizes interaction, rules and norms[75] and which also marks at least a partial distance from the Utopianism inherent in much critical theory and which is also present in the work of the author who writes a foreword to Kratochwil's book and who for many years was one of the only dissenting voices in international studies broadly conceived and who is still among the most prolific, namely Richard Falk.

His work,[76] too, has had a pronounced concern with order, up to and including the title of the research project with which he is most associated, the World Order Models Project (WOMP).[77] When, for example, considering the notion of order in 'the international system', Falk suggests that there are three categories of theory, which he calls system maintaining, system reforming and system transforming.[78] In general 'realists' are usually held to be system-maintaining theorists, liberals (and also many globalists, pluralists, institutionalists, idealists) system reforming. In the system-transforming camp are a motley collection of Marxists and critical theorists, some post-structuralists and, of course, Professor Falk. It is worth pointing out the similarity of Falk's typology with perhaps the most famous categorization of international relations theory in Britain, Martin Wight's 'Machiavellians, Grotians and Kantians' (or Realists, Rationalists and Revolutionists).[79] However, it is also worth pointing out that, as with the McKinlay and Little view discussed above, it is the 'dialectical' sense of order that is missing.[80]

However, in all of the above treatments one thing at least remains constant: order in any of the senses discussed above is a quite different sort of problem from its corollary at the domestic level. The link between them has been well articulated by Stanley Hoffmann, another writer who has been concerned with the 'problem of order', and who effectively echoes Aron, who had a profound influence upon him. 'The problem of world order', he writes,

> is quite different from that of domestic political order or from that of order within the social groups that exist within the political unit. What charac-terises international order is anarchy (i.e the absence of central power above the units); it is also the absence or weakness of common norms. Thus one immediately sees where the problem lies. It is both analytical and normative: can there be both anarchy and order?[81]

This recognition of the two ways in which order can be seen is common to a good deal of the literature of world politics.[82]

Indeed, as was pointed out above, in the history of political thought more generally, the concept of political order as a problem, both generally and norma-tively, is far more central than it is, or has been, to most contemporary scholars of international relations (or, for that matter, political science more generally). For Hoffmann, there are two models of order visible in the history of political thought, which he calls, respectively, 'precarious peace/troubled order' and the 'state of war'.[83] The former model, he suggests, arises out of the decay of the old medieval order and the rise of territorial states. It is much the same as that set of beliefs that others have referred to as the 'morality of states' doctrine or the 'international society' approach (of which more later) and can be presumed to include (though he does not mention any names) the secular natural lawyers like Grotius and Pufendorf together with some of those nostalgic about the old medieval order (Leibniz, as we have seen)[84]. The latter model is that which we find by contrast, Hoffmann argues, in the work of Thucydides, Machiavelli, Hobbes, Rousseau, Kant, Hegel and Marx, though how they understand and interpret this model, of course, differs enormously.

Recently summing up his own understanding of the literature of world order, James Rosenau has suggested that however we understand the specifics of world order, we should understand it in general terms as 'the routinized arrangements through which world affairs are conducted'.[85] While, as we shall see, I dissent strongly from the basic thrust of Rosenau's argument, his understanding, like Kratochwil's, has the advantage that it forces us to concentrate on how such arrangements operate and change. Moreover, it forces us to ask the question 'what *are* the "routinized arrangements" through which world affairs are conducted?' Clearly, these would include obviously formal institutions (international organizations, the United Nations and so on) as well as 'regimes' (formal, like the non-proliferation treaty or the UN agreements on the law of the sea, and, perhaps, informal) and the practices of state-to-state co-operation (both bilateral and multilateral). According to some (e.g. Wight and Bull) they would also include the manner of conflict in world politics (war, intervention). Of course, as Hoffman rightly notes, the sense of 'world', here, is at least as important as the sense of order.[86] He is also surely correct to stress that 'world order' is far more than simply the logic of 'inter-state relations' (however that logic is seen); the question is, how much more? Does it include the growing network of transnational groupings etc. that some have seen fit to call a nascent global civil society,[87] for example? Should it, if it does not? Once we start to look at the implications of these questions, as we will see, the relative clarity and attractiveness of the Aronian understanding of world order becomes rather more problematic and, as we shall see, it becomes much less easy to see who is 'system maintaining' or 'system reforming' or even what these terms might actually mean. As Aron himself admitted in his memoirs, he did not make as much as he might have done of what we might call the 'non-state centric' aspects of world politics.[88]

Another feature of all of the above treatments of order is a tendency to suggest that contemporary 'responses' to the problem of order tend to be three-fold: maintain the system, reform the system, overthrow the system. Yet, as I shall want to argue in a moment, this is both too simplistic and not really focused on responses to the problem of order as such: rather, responses to the problem of order frame how we might be, and to what extent we can be, system maintaining, reforming or transcending.

However, all this is by way of a preliminary. Let me now move on to how I intend to address these issues in this book.

The argument of the book

I want to suggest that for most of the twentieth century – which for self-conscious IR theory can effectively be understood, as Eric Hobsbawm has recently understood it, as a 'short' century[89] – there have been two very broad families of responses to 'the problem of (international and world) order'. These fairly neatly divide into two general sets of responses, which can be subdivided respectively into three and then two specific responses.

Often, but by no means always, these responses are associated with a particular tradition of thought about international politics, although there is a good deal of overlap and interpenetration. The bulk of the book will thus examine these particular responses, in what I take to be their most impressive and influential versions, rather than simply looking at 'realism' or 'liberalism' or whatever. As I say, it is largely the case that each response is, so to speak, the favoured one of a particular tradition (or traditions) of thought, but it is worth emphasizing that discussing the issue this way necessarily cuts across the 'methodological and epistemological' divisions so important to the modern discussions of International Relations; the responses are thus one of the central sites for the interpenetration of the two sets of debates I spoke of earlier.

The first broad family of responses all broadly accept the 'problem of order', as it was discussed above, and see the task of IR theory, *inter alia*, as dealing with, solving and/or managing international relations in the light of this fact. They are all, thus, responses that seek to *manage* the problem of order. In this context, I suggest that there are three basic sets of responses, each of which concentrates on one aspect of the 'routineized arrangements' of contemporary world politics and locates in it the effective answer to the 'problem of order'. I shall therefore call them after these aspects: balance, society, institutions; and I shall examine each in turn. However, a few words about each might be helpful by way of introduction.

In the first case, 'balance' was the solution to the problem of order that the European states system believed itself to have evolved, once the practices of sovereignty became embedded in European life and it became the central pivot of discussion about international affairs well into the twentieth century. It is, as is well known, the central concern still of that tradition of political thought most associated with international relations (as well as International Relations), polit-ical realism. Realism, of course, is widely considered the central tradition of thought in international relations. In terms of the orientation of most explicit 'IR theorists' this century, that judgement is probably true. In terms of the char-acter of world politics during that century, I think we have witnessed a growing divergence between the way international relations has been studied and what has actually been going on in international relations. The twentieth century will be seen from the perspective of history, I suspect, to be that century where both the obvious – and widely recognized – failings and shortcomings of the 'tradi-tional' way of organizing the relations between and within political communities led to catastrophe and thus to the attempt to construct such relations anew. One of the central sites of this attempt – even where it has been denied (as by realists) – has been the creation, and also the debate over the possibility, of institutions at the international, and now global, level.

However, this was an accepted fact by at least one body of thought closely asso-ciated with 'realism', the so-called 'English school' of international relations. Its focus on the society of states – and not just a 'system' – required them to be sensi-tive to the role of institutions in international society and especially to the norms instantiated in such institutions. Here, it met with the concerns of reformers of international politics of various stripes whose favoured 'response' to the problem of order throughout the twentieth century has been to seek to 'institutionalize' and thus 'liberalize' world politics. Thus the second two chapters of the book consider variants of this 'institutionalization' thesis in international relations.

The second response, the broadest here, which I call simply 'society', focuses on the social aspect of order, on the fact that it is *created*. On this view, the international system is also a society, with norms and rules which can be understood and reshaped. It is on these rules and norms that order relies. Again, this is a way of thinking with deep roots in European thought, from the sixteenth century onwards, and often shares much with versions of realism. In contemporary IR theory, such a view is most closely associated with the 'English school'.[90] As I remarked above, it emphasizes 'institutions' but it sees the relevant institutions as being, for example, war or the balance of power at least as much as 'formal' institutions (such as the United Nations). As we saw above, however, a different variant of this approach has recently emerged that also emphasizes the 'construction' of such norms. This 'constructivist' international theory is an especially popular response as the twentieth century comes to an end, for reasons I shall discuss later, and it is allowing a developing mix of societal theories about world politics in general and the problem of order in particular to emerge. Especially interesting also in this context is the division made much of by Hedley Bull between 'International Order' and 'World Order' and what he thinks follows from it, and the ways in which younger scholars from both English school and constructivist approaches are working around each other, finding many areas of common ground.

The third response, which I have termed 'institutions' properly so called, has been the response favoured throughout the nineteenth and twentieth centuries by those who, seeing themselves often as heirs to the Enlightenment, believed a better way of 'ordering' the affairs of states must be found and who saw their worst fear come true between 1914 and 1918. In other words, it has tended to be the touchstone of liberal and reformist thinking in world politics.[91] It has remained a constant concern of liberals – though certainly not only of liberals – from that day to this. In brief this view holds that world order is best achieved through certain kinds of institutions – both international and/or domestic and both formal and/or informal – that can mitigate the struggle for power that tends to dominate in the international realm and can perhaps also shape and shove the preferences and behaviour patterns of states themselves and thus encourage co-operative rather than conflictual behaviour. This commitment is shared by liberals of remarkably different stripes, and vastly different methodological commitments, and has been largely responsible for much of the most interesting reformist thinking and practice in international relations this century, as well as a range of the most powerful IR theories of the century as well. It has also pioneered the thinking through the implications of the political economy of international relations, a central concern for contemporary theory, as is now widely accepted.

All three of the above responses, however, take the basic practices of politics – the problem of order created by and through practices of sovereignty – as a given. Though there are many differences between them there is little sense at the close of the twentieth century that IR theory is problematizing that way of being political itself.[92] The second family of responses, however, does precisely this. It emphasizes that in varying ways and to varying degrees we have reached the 'end of order'; that is to say, in the form in which it currently exists, they suggest that the problem of order is irresolvable. These responses are thus concerned with the 'ending' of the problem of order.

However, there is a marked division between these responses. For one group, the implications of this argument are that we need to emancipate ourselves from both the structures of politics as they are presently constructed and as we presently conceptualize them. For another, it is what we might call the '*question of* the problem of order' that is chiefly at issue, best signalled by the recognition of our limits, however conceived.

Thus, in the second part of the book, I offer discussions of each of these responses. In Chapter 4 I will focus largely on that body of theory associated with themes from, *inter alia*, Frankfurt school critical theory, feminist thought and so-called 'Gramscian' thinking in IR and IPE, as well as some more conventional 'Western Marxist' thinking on questions of international relations. In many respects much of this work builds on some 'institutionalist' insights and there are, indeed, possible areas of overlap between aspects of the 'revolutionalist' agenda and the more conservative 'English school' or constructivist approaches; though how plausible such amalgamations are we shall investigate later. I suggest, in any event, that the hallmark of this response is its commitment to 'emancipation'.

In Chapter 5, I shall focus on those bodies of work which are more pessimistic, at least about emancipation from the structures that have given rise to the problem of order. Specifically, I look at two versions of the 'end of order' thesis that emphasize, in different ways, 'limits': the work of some of the most influential 'post-structural' theorists working in IR; and finally the work of one of the most generally influential writers on contemporary 'post-positivist' theory, Jean Bethke Elshtain.

Finally, in my concluding chapter – which I call an epilogue since one cannot really 'conclude' an argument of this sort – I offer a general discussion of where we are now, given the discussions that have gone on before, and, finally, seek to outline a third orientation which I suggest forms a more appropriate trajectory for what I will (by this time) be calling international *political* theory, than either managerial or end of order options, though it has a fair amount in common with the latter: one built around the constant discussion and negotiation of the ends, purposes, processes and institutions of ethico-political life, a process I call 'ordering ends'.

Notes

1   International Relations, that is the 'discipline'.
2   Of course, it is also true that a good deal of work relevant to international relations goes on without any explicit theoretical discussions. Think of the important studies of Cold War history produced over the last twenty years or so, for example. I am very far from saying all good work should be explicitly theoretical. Nonetheless, 'theory' – however understood – is widely considered to hold the 'commanding heights' of the discipline. In one sense, as we shall see, I think it does. However, in another sense I am strongly opposed to 'theory'. International Relations, in my view, is part of prac-

tical not theoretical philosophy, to use Aristotelian terms. It is the elevation of 'theory' (narrow sense) to a position it does not warrant in this kind of endeavour that is part of the problem of contemporary International Relations; or so I shall argue.

3   Accounts of political order as such are not very plentiful. Most important scholarly works on the history of political thought in the relevant periods will, however, usually contain discussions of the key components of the appropriate notion or notions of order. An impressionistic selection worth consulting would include Andrew Lintott, *Violence, Civil Strife and Revolution in the Classical City* (London: Croom Helm, 1982), Clifford Orwin, *The Humanity of Thucydides* (Princeton, NJ: Princeton University Press, 1994), Paul Rahe, *Republics, Ancient and Modern* (Chapel Hill, NC: University of North Carolina Press, 1992), R. W. and A. J. Carlyle, *A History of Medieval Political Theory in the West* (London: William Blackwood 1903–36), Antony Black, *Political Thought in Europe 1250–1450* (Cambridge: Cambridge University Press, 1992), J. H. Burns (ed.), *The Cambridge History of Medieval Political Thought* (Cambridge: Cambridge University Press, 1988), Quentin Skinner, *The Foundations of Modern Political Thought*, 2 vols (Cambridge: Cambridge University Press, 1978), Anthony Pagden (ed.), *The Languages of Political Theory in Early-Modern Europe* (Cambridge: Cambridge University Press, 1987 (see especially Maurizio Viroli's essay on Rousseau's concept of *ordre*), Anthony Pagden, *Lords of All the World: Ideologies of Empire in Spain, Britain and France 1500–1800* (New Haven, CT: Yale University Press, 1995), Richard Tuck, *Sorry Comforters: Political Theory and International Order from Grotius to Kant* (Carlyle Lectures in Oxford, 1992, forthcoming), Murray Forsyth, *Unions of States: The Theory and Practice of Confederation* (New York: Holmes and Maier, 1981). A detailed treatment of order in the history of international political thought will also be found in Chris Brown, Terry Nardin and N. J. Rengger, *Texts in International Relations* (Cambridge: Cambridge University Press, forthcoming). Additional relevant material will be cited where appropriate later.

4   In keeping with by now accustomed usage, I refer to the academic field of study by capitalizing, hence 'International Relations', and the object of its study without such capitals, hence 'international relations'.

5   Stephen Clark, *Civil Peace and Sacred Order: Vol. 1 Limits and Renewals* (Oxford: Clarendon Press, 1989), pp. 96–7.

6   Clark, *Civil Peace and Sacred Order*, p. 97.

7   I shall return to Clark in the Epilogue.

8   I should emphasize here that I am not ignoring those political theorists who have made 'order' a central concern, most obviously Eric Voeglin. Voeglin's five-volume study, *Order and History* (all volumes published by Louisiana State University Press, 1956–87), is clearly a major attempt to 'situate' the 'problem of order' generally. However, not only would Voeglin not see the problem of order quite in the way I do here, but his way of addressing it would take me too far away from the central concerns of this book. Without defending this in any detail, let me suggest that Voeglin's treatment of order has to be seen as one way of rewriting the 'historical' side of the nineteenth-century treatment of order that I shall discuss in a moment. While not denying its power or its interest, it does not seem to me that this treatment would actually resolve the problem any more than the accounts I shall be discussing in more detail in this book. However, I accept that this is a case I should make in more detail, and I issue a promissory note that I shall do so in the near future. In addition to the five volumes of *Order and History*, Voeglin's major works worth looking at in this context are *The New Science of Politics* (Chicago: University of Chicago Press, 1951), *Anamnesis: Zur Theorie der Geschichte und Politik* (Munich: Piper Verlag, 1966) and several of his essays, increasingly gathered together in his *Nachlass*; see especially his remarkable essay 'World Empire and the Unity of Mankind', *International Affairs*, 1962. For other treatments of Voeglin's arguments that repay study, see Fred Dallmayr, 'Eric Voeglin's Search for Order' in *Margins of Political Discourse* (Notre

Dame, IN: University of Notre Dame Press, 1984); some (although not all) of the essays in Ellis Sandoz (ed.), *Eric Voeglin's Significance for the Modern Mind* (Baton Rouge, LA: Louisiana State University Press, 1991); David Levy's thoughtful and sensitive treatment in *Political Order: Philosophical Anthropology, Modernity and the Challenge of Ideology* (Baton Rouge, LA: Louisiana State University Press, 1987), and see also the excellent and exemplary collection of the Voeglin–Strauss correspondence, together with essays by each and critical commentaries by various other thinkers, in Peter Emberly and Barry Cooper (trans. and ed.), *Faith and Political Philosophy* (Pittsburgh, PA: Pennsylvania University Press, 1993).

9   In my *Political Theory, Modernity and Postmodernity: Beyond Enlightenment and Critique* (Oxford: Blackwell, 1995).

10 I should add, of course, that I do not claim that such distinctions can be made analytically useful. Rather it is a point about the *kind* of claims that tend to be made about modernity. Part of my argument was that all such claims are, of course, in fact, claims about both.

11 Again there are points of contact with Voeglin's conception of the relations of political (and more generally philosophical) symbols – race, state, class, justice or, in our case, order – and experience. However, I will not develop this point here.

12 I hope to tell this story in rather more detail and in the context of some of the major thinkers who have helped create it, on a later occasion.

13 This is obviously an enormous simplification of a vast and complex topic. For one thing there were a large variety of Greek views on order, whether understood in general, or specifically in ethical and political contexts. For the purposes of this book, however, I am focusing on that conception of order, and especially 'good order' (*Eunomia*) which was perceived in antiquity at least, to be the main contribution of Plato and, to a lesser extent, Aristotle. It was this view that became central for the modern West, which is my chief concern here. Of course, it is worth pointing out that the extent to which Plato and Aristotle actually held to the views ascribed to them, even by their own schools, is a matter of considerable scholarly debate. For good discussions of the varieties of Greek thinking on this and related topics see Richard Sorabji, *Time Creation and the Continuum* (London: Duckworth, 1983), and T. A Sinclair, *A History of Greek Political Thought* (London: Routledge & Kegan Paul, 1967). I have offered my own reading of classical thought on these questions in the relevant chapters of Brown *et al.*, *Texts in International Relations*, and 'Waiting for the Barbarians? Classical Thought, Community and Culture', Paper presented to the International Ethics section of the International Studies Association, April 1997.

14 For illuminating discussions of early Christian ideas on order and its Platonic and neo-Platonic overtones, see Henry Chadwick, *The Sentences of Sixtus: A Contribution to Early Christian Ethics*, (London: Texts and Studies, 1959), Arnaldo Momigliano, 'Pagan and Christian Historiography in the Fourth Century', in A. Momigliano (ed.), *The Conflict between Christianity and Paganism in the Fourth Century* (London: 1963). A brilliant discussion of the most influential Christian theorist of 'political order' before Augustine – Ambrose of Milan – can be found in J. Beranger, *Principatus. Etudes de notion et d'histoire politiques dans l'antique greco-romaine* (Droz: Galle, 1973).

15 For Augustine a superb general treatment is Peter Brown, *Augustine of Hippo* (London: Faber, 1967). A brilliant, if idiosyncratic, treatment of Augustine's political thought which foregrounds the question of order tellingly, if controversially, is R. A. Markus, *Saeculum: History and Society in the Theology of St Augustine* (Cambridge: Cambridge University Press, 1970). A more mainstream approach is offered in H. A. Deane, *The Political and Social Ideas of St Augustine* (New York: Columbia University Press, 1963). The significance of Augustinian ideas for the tradition of political realism in international affairs is superbly discussed in Alastair Murray, *Reconstructing Realism* (Keele: Keele University Press, 1997), and 'The Moral Politics of Hans Morgenthau', *Review of Politics*, January 1996.

An idiosyncratic, but nonetheless very pertinent and powerful, reading of Augustine's thought that specifically foregrounds his role as a necessary dialogical partner for contemporary politics is William E. Connolly, *The Augustinian Imperative: A Reflection on the Politics of Morality* (London: Sage, 1993).

16 The most celebrated and important of Eusebius's work on these themes is the *Triakontaeterikos*, or tricennial orations. They can be found in F. Winkleman (ed.), *In Praise of Constantine: A Historical Study and new Translation of Eusebius' Tricennial Orations* (Berkeley, CA: University of California Press, 1975).

17 The most easily available edition is *De Administrando Imperio* (Vol. 1), ed. J. Moravscik and H. Jenkins (Corpus Fontium Historiae Byzantinae), Dumbarton Oaks, Centre for Byzantine Studies, 1967. A good new English translation is badly needed.

18 On the evolution of Byzantine thought in general, see George Ostrogorsky, *History of the Byzantine State* ([1940] Oxford: Blackwell, 1989), Ernest Barker, *Social and Political Thought in Byzantium: From Justinian I to the last Palaeologus* (Oxford: Clarendon Press, 1956), F. Dolger, *Byzanz und die europaische Staatenwelt. Ausgewahlte Vortrage und Aufsätze* (Buch-Kunstverlag Ettal, 1956), and Arnold Toynbee, *Constantine Porphyrogenitus and his World* (Oxford: Oxford University Press, 1973).

19 See the discussion in *The Cambridge History of Medieval Political Thought*, pp. 262–6. Zacharias's Latin phrase is *ut non conturbaretur ordo*.

20 A good general treatment of the notion of international order in the medieval period can be found in Tony Black's excellent *Political Thought in Europe 1250–1450*. See especially chapter 10, 'Empire and Nation', which has a sympathetic and well-argued reconstruction of medieval ideas about international society and the *Respublica Christiana*. A different but equally well-articulated view is found in Geoffrey Baraclough, *History in a Changing World* (Oxford: Basil Blackwell, 1955). See chapters 2, 3, 7 and 8.

21 Other works that touch on this theme and on which I draw for my argument here would include R. B. J. Walker, *Inside/Outside: International Relations as Political Theory* (Cambridge: Cambridge University Press, 1992), Jens Bartelson, *A Genealogy of Sovereignty* (Cambridge: Cambridge University Press, 1995), Anthony Pagden (ed.), *The Languages of Political Theory in Early Modern Europe* (Cambridge: Cambridge University Press, 1987), and Anthony Pagden, *Lords of All the World: Ideologies of Empire in Spain, Britain and France 1500–1800* (New Haven, CT: Yale University Press, 1995), Friedrich Kratochwil, 'Of Systems Boundaries and Territoriality: An Inquiry into the Formation of the States System', *World Politics*, 1986, Vol. 39, and most recently, Jean Bethke Elshtain, *New Wine and Old Bottles: International Politics and Ethical Discourse* (Notre Dame, IN: University of Notre Dame Press, 1998).

22 It is also during this period, of course, that the notion of sovereignty begins to take on the colouring that has shaped and determined contemporary international law and a good deal of domestic politics. In the medieval period, juristic notions of sovereignty oscillated between an understanding of sovereignty which placed all 'sovereignty' in the hands of the emperor (of the Holy Roman Empire) rather than in the hands of kings and one which accepted that kings had *de iure* sovereign power over their territories. The key change in medieval political thought was predicated on the assumption (first articulated in detail by Bartolus of Sassferrato) that the *de facto* sovereignty of kings was a genuine form of sovereignty but different from the emperor's. By the fourteenth century Bartolus and the civilian movement in the Italian city states and principalities had produced a rounded theory of territorial sovereignty which was to influence strongly the developing European states system. However, in the fifteenth to seventeenth centuries the notion of sovereignty was refined still further. This notion was a central plank in the evolution of a recognizably modern concept of the state – as well, of course, of the 'states system' – as Quentin Skinner has shown. As he also points out, however, this conception of the state is not, of course, 'our' conception; there is no discussion of the post-Enlightenment

conception of the relation between the nation and the state nor is there any understanding of the role that the world market might (putatively) have on the state. For
good discussions of these themes see Burns (ed.), *The Cambridge History of Medieval
Political Thought*, pp. 454–76, Skinner, *Foundations of Modern Political Thought, passim*,
and Martin Wight, *Systems of States* (London: Leicester University Press, 1977), chapters 1, 4 and 5.

23 In his *The Legitimacy of the Modern Age* (Cambridge, MA: MIT Press, 1983), Hans
Blumenberg famously argues that the modern age is the 'second overcoming' of
Gnosticism, the first one having been attempted by Augustine. But this attempt
retained aspects of Gnosticism within it which were later to compromise fatally the
medieval world view thus paving the way for modernity. For a more detailed discussion of Blumenberg and his significance see my *Political Theory, Modernity and
Postmodernity*, chapter 1.

24 I would emphasize that I do not mean to imply by this usage a simplistic analogy of
Hobbes' thought with modern thought, after the fashion of those who see Hobbes as
a rational choice theorist *avant la lettre*. Rather, I am suggesting as, perhaps most influentially, Quentin Skinner has suggested that Hobbes' political thought marks a key
point in the *evolution* of modern political thought teaching it not only certain key
concepts and practices – of which the central one is sovereignty, in my view – but also
a certain tone or style. For Skinner's argument see his *Reason and Rhetoric in the
Philosophy of Hobbes* (Cambridge: Cambridge University Press, 1996).

25 For those who have a mind to follow up the ins and outs of Hobbes' scholarship on
these points, I suggest a good beginning can be found in Iain Hampsher-Monk's *A
History of Modern Political Thought: Hobbes to Marx* (Oxford: Blackwell, 1994). The most
persuasive general account of Hobbes in contemporary political thought is, I believe,
Quentin Skinner's; see especially his *Reason and Rhetoric in the Philosophy of Hobbes*.
However, relevant also to my concerns is Carl Schmitt's protean – and deeply flawed
– presentation of Hobbes and also his close colleague Leo Strauss's version in his *The
Political Philosophy of Hobbes* (Chicago: University of Chicago Press, 1963).

26 See, for the most thoroughgoing account of Leibniz' writing on these topics in
English, Patrick Riley's *Leibniz' Universal Jurisprudence: Justice as the Charity of the Wise*
(Cambridge, MA: Harvard University Press, 1996). Riley has also edited the best
extant English compendium of Leibniz' political works, *Leibniz: Political Writings*
(Cambridge: Cambridge University Press, 1992). For discussions of both Hobbes and
Leibniz, especially on International Political Thought, see Brown *et al.*, *Texts in
International Relations*.

27 It is worth emphasizing here that, according to a very powerful recent tradition of
modern political thought, Hobbes' triumph was bought at the expense also of an
alternative conception of freedom and politics than the liberal one, specifically what
most would call 'republican' and what Skinner has recently called 'neo-Roman'. As
we shall see current attempts to reinvigorate that tradition have some parallels with
classical realist thought, a parallel that its current advocates would, I suspect, wish to
resist. For good accounts of this story see Paul Rahe, *Republics, Ancient and Modern*
(South Carolina: University of South Carolina Press, 1992), Philip Pettit, *Republicanism*
(Oxford: Clarendon Press, 1997), and Quentin Skinner, *Liberty Before Liberalism*
(Cambridge: Cambridge University Press, 1997).

28 See especially Karl Lowith, *Weltgeschichte und Heilsgeschehen* (Stuttgart: Kohlshammer,
1955). See also his essays, 'Nature, History and Existentialism', *Social Research*, 1952,
19(1).

29 This is, of course, Michael Oakeshott. See his essay 'The Political Economy of
Freedom', in *Rationalism in Politics* (London: Methuen, 1962).

30 Recent discussions of Nietzsche's political thought that repay careful reading in
this context begin with Tracy Strong's superb study *Nietzsche and the Politics of
Transfiguration* (Berkeley, CA: University of California Press, 1975; 2nd edition,

1988) and continue with the excellent studies by William Connolly, *Political Theory and Modernity* (Oxford: Blackwell, 1988), Mark Warren, *Nietzsche and Political Thought* (Cambridge, MA: MIT Press, 1988), Keith Ansell-Pearson, *Nietzsche contra Rousseau* (Cambridge: Cambridge University Press, 1991), David Owen, *Maturity and Modernity: Nietzsche, Weber and Foucault* (London: Routledge, 1994). A good general background to Nietzsche's thought can be found in Keith Ansell Pearson, *An Introduction to Nietzsche as Political Thinker: The Perfect Nihilist* (Cambridge: Cambridge University Press, 1994).

31 A number of the advocates of these views will be touched on in the following pages. I will merely mention some names here, to whet the appetite, or jade the palate, depending on your taste: Kenichi Ohmae, Jean Baudrillard, Paul Virilio, Jean Marie Guehenno, James Der Derian.

32 For some general debates and discussions touching on these matters, though they tend to be seen and discussed from perspectives that are not as aware of the social, political and ethical ramifications as they might be, see, amongst others, Jerry E. Bishop and Michael Waldholz, *Genome: The story of the most astonishing scientific adventure of our time – the attempts to map all the genes in the human body* (New York: Simon and Schuster, 1990), Dorothy Nelkin and Laurence Tancredi, *Dangerous Diagnostics: The Social Power of Biological Information* (New York: Basic Books, 1991), R. C. Lewontin, *The Doctrine of DNA: Biology as Ideology* (Harmondsworth: Penguin, 1993), Michael Heim, *The Metaphysics of Virtual Reality* (Oxford: Oxford University Press, 1993), John Searle, *Minds, Brains and Science* (Oxford: Oxford University Press, 1990).

33 Other, non-Western, traditions of political thought show related problems. See, for elaborations, the discussions in David E. Cooper, *World Philosophies* (Oxford: Blackwell, 1996) and some of the discussions in Brown *et al.*, *Texts in International Relations.*

34 See Brown *et al.*, *Texts in International Relations* for a more detailed elaboration of this.

35 For fascinating and useful discussions see, *inter alia*, John Kenyon, *The History Men* (London: Weidenfeld and Nicolson, 1983), Donald Winch *et al.*, *That Noble Science of Politics*, and David Ricci, *The Tragedy of Political Science.*

36 The first being the Woodrow Wilson Chair of International Politics at the University College of Wales, Aberystwyth, in 1919, shortly followed by the Montague Burton Chairs, principally at the LSE and Oxford, though Montague Burton bequests at other Universities exist (e.g. Edinburgh). Chairs in the same area sprang up in US universities at around the same time and research institutes devoted to the 'science of international politics' – most notably the Royal Institute for International Affairs, Chatham House, in London, and the Council on Foreign Relations, in New York – were all part of the same trend and established at the same time (around the mid 1920s). For fuller discussions see Hedley Bull, 'The Theory of International Politics, 1919–69', in B. Porter (ed.), *The Aberystwyth Papers* (Oxford: Clarendon Press, 1972).

37 In fairness, I should say that certainly when I was an undergraduate very few students of politics were expected to do that either. Typically, the last two books of *Leviathan*, 'Of a Christian Common Wealth' and 'Of the Kindom of Darknesse', were not read – though I should add that my teacher in the history of political thought did insist we read them – which, as most Hobbes scholars would testify, gives you a very impoverished view of Hobbes' ideas.

38 This approach is particularly associated with the University of Cambridge and, especially, with Quentin Skinner. For a discussion of the approach, which includes a number of Skinner's extremely influential methodological essays, see James Tully (ed.), *Meaning and Context: Quentin Skinner and His Critics* (Cambridge: Polity Press, 1988).

39 See the account in Brian Porter (ed.), *The Aberystwyth Papers.*

40 By indirectly, I mean to imply in part that many of the most influential methods in International Relations (and indeed Political Science) were developed and distributed

in a Cold War context (think of game theory at RAND, for example). For discussions see William Poundstone, *Prisoner's Dilemma* (Oxford: Oxford University Press, 1992).

41 See, for example, Wright, *The Study of International Relations* (New York: Appleton Century Crofts, 1955), p. 502, and Alker, *Rediscoveries and Reformulations: Humanistic Methodologies for International Studies* (Cambridge: Cambridge University Press, 1996), pp. 19–20.

42 A favourite example of mine in this regard is the so-called 'interparadigm debate' much discussed (largely) by scholars based in Britain in the 1970s and early to mid 1980s. This debate was held to be between three alleged 'paradigms', realism, pluralism and structuralism. Effectively, though there were variations, this was a version of the 'conservatism vs liberalism vs Socialism/Marxism' debates going on elsewhere at the time. However, International Relations seemed to feel the need to put a gloss on it that made it specific to the 'discipline' of International Relations. The result, in my view, was a highly tendentious debate that misused the anyway rather overused and loose notion of a 'paradigm', and which added little if anything to anybody's understanding of international relations. If one wished to use the term paradigm at all – and I would not – all three 'theories' discussed are parts of the 'paradigm' developed by the modern West. For a discussion of the interparadigm debate – and indeed other aspects of the 'disciplinary' obsessions that characterize a good deal of contemporary theoretical debate in International Relations – see Steve Smith, 'Self Images of a Discipline', in Ken Booth and Steve Smith (eds), *International Relations Theory Today* (Cambridge: Polity Press, 1994).

43 See, for example, the discussions of Islamic and Judaic thought on these questions in Brown *et al.*, *Texts in International Relations*. Good discussions of Indian, Chinese, Japanese and African thought, along with Western, Islamic and Judaic thought, which touch on political thinking generally and international relations specifically, can be found in David Cooper's excellent *World Philosophies: An Historical Introduction*.

44 Initially published in *International Studies Quarterly* in 1988, the version I discuss here is that found in Keohane's collection of essays, *International Institutions and State Power* (Boulder, CO: Westview Press, 1989).

45 Keohane, *International Institutions and State Power*, p.161. The reference to Simon is to 'Human Nature in Politics: The Dialogue of Psychology with Political Science', *American Political Science Review*, 1985, 79: 293–304.

46 Keohane, *International Institutions and State Power*, p. 160.

47 Keohane, *International Institutions and State Power*, p. 161.

48 It is worth adding here that Keohane, in keeping with mainstream Social Science as a whole, has a rather narrow and limited notion of what constitutes 'science'. I would probably not go as far as Hayward Alker in referring to them as holding a 'nineteenth-century' view of science – though few contemporary International Relations scholars would come close to Alker in terms of their mastery of general social scientific techniques and knowledge of the relevant literatures and methods in the natural as well as the social sciences – but I would certainly agree with the general thrust of this criticism. Ironically, in this respect, as I shall come back to in the Epilogue, they are curiously like many of their most detested opponents among the 'critical theorists'. However, let this stand for the moment.

49 Keohane, *International Institutions and State Power*, p. 161. 'Interpretive', in this context, is in fact a term I have used in a paper written with Mark Hoffman to describe both critical theoretic and post-structurally derived contemporary IR Theory. Our view is that, used properly, it would apply to a number of other approaches as well. Why Keohane chooses a different word is a point I will come to in a moment. For our usage of 'interpretive' see N. J. Rengger and Mark Hoffman, 'Modernity, Postmodernism and International Relations', in Joe Doherty *et al.* (eds), *Postmodernism*

and the Social Sciences (London: Macmillan, 1992), though the paper was originally written in 1988.

50 Keohane, *International Institutions and State Power*, p. 161.

51 Keohane, *International Institutions and State Power*, p. 161.

52 To which we will return in Chapter 3.

53 Keohane, *International Institutions and State Power*, p. 168.

54 Keohane, *International Institutions and State Power*, p. 173.

55 Keohane, *International Institutions and State Power*, p. 174.

56 See Putnam, 'Diplomacy and Domestic Politics: the Logic of Two-level Games', *International Organization*, 1988, 42: 427–60. It is worth pointing out that two books have taken the 'rationalist' research programmes further on this point. The first, edited by Putnam, together with H. Jacobsen and P. Evans, *Double Edged Diplomacy* (New York: Columbia University Press, 1993), and the second edited by Keohane and Helen Milner, *Internationalization and Domestic Politics* (Cambridge: Cambridge University Press, 1995).

57 This is no longer true. Helen Milner, a former student of Keohane's, has developed a powerful and very sophisticated theory of how domestic politics influences international relations particularly on the question of international co-operation. I shall discuss it briefly in Chapter 3 later on. See Milner, *Interests, Institutions and Information: Domestic Politics and International Relations* (Princeton, NJ: Princeton University Press, 1997).

58 For anyone who wants evidence of what I think is his genuine originality and very real power then his recent *Rediscoveries and Reformulations: Humanistic Methods for International Studies* (Cambridge: Cambridge University Press, 1996) is superb. It is, however, worth noting that Alker has been a powerful influence on a wide range of 'interpretive' theory in international studies – for example, Ashley, who was an Alker student, as were a number of other prominent 'interpretivists' such as Thomas Biersteker. However, Alker's influence is hardly confined to them; see for example the work of another of his students, Joshua Goldstein. See *inter alia*, Bierteker and Weber (eds), *State Sovereignty as Social Construct* (Cambridge: Cambridge University Press, 1995), and Goldstein, *Long Waves: Prosperity and War in the Modern Age* (New Haven, CT: Yale University Press, 1988).

59 See the reference in Keohane, *International Institutions and State Power*, p. 171.

60 Kratochwil has subsequently moved to a Chair at Munich, where he was a student. However, it is more than possible that he will return to the United States; certainly his graduate work was undertaken there and his reputation was built there.

61 The most detailed treatment of this phenomenon can be found in Kal Holsti's *The Dividing Discipline: Hegemony and Diversity in International Theory* (London: Allen and Unwin, 1985).

62 It is also worth pointing out that many of these techniques themselves either originated in, or developed initially in, a context created by international relations (the world), that is the Cold War. See for good discussions of how game theory developed in just this way, William Poundstone, *Prisoner's Dilemma*.

63 A more general point here is to note the general thrust of the book on methodological issues that Keohane was co-author of, with King and Verba, *Designing Social Inquiry*.

64 Most obviously Paul Feyerabend. See his *Against Method* (London: New Left Books, 1975). My own view of this is much closer, however, to Stephen Toulmin's. See, in particular, the argument in his superb book *Cosmopolis* (Chicago: University of Chicago Press, 1992).

65 See James Serba, *Justice for Here and Now* (Cambridge: Cambridge University Press, 1998), p. 1. Serba is referring specifically to philosophy, but the comment holds good for much of the social sciences also.

66 He wrote a political column in the Paris-based newspaper *Le Figaro* for many years.

67 At a conference in 1965, as reported by Stanley Hoffmann, rapporteur of the conference. See Stanley Hoffmann (ed.), *Conditions of World Order* (New York: Simon and Schuster, 1970), pp. 1–2.

68 The chief exception, of course, being bodies like the World Order Models Project, on which a bit more below, and the English school, which we will focus on in Chapter 2. However, there are honourable exceptions. See, for example, Fritz Kratochwil's excellent *International Order and Foreign Policy: A Theoretical Sketch of Post War International Politics* (Boulder, CO: Westview Press, 1978), though the view he takes is not dissimilar to some English school writing. He even makes effectively the same distinction between international and world order.

69 R. D. McKinlay and R. Little, *Global Problems and World Order* (London: Frances Pinter, 1986).

70 McKinlay and Little, *Global Problems and World Order*, p. 15.

71 The debate between 'agency' and 'structure' is a well-known, indeed almost old hat, debate in the philosophy of social science, which has, of late, broken cover within International Relations. See, for example, Martin Hollis and Steve Smith, *Explaining and Understanding International Relations* (Oxford: Clarendon Press, 1990), Alexander Wendt, 'The Agent-Structure Debate in International Relations', *International Organization*, 1987, 41: 335–70, and the exchange between Wendt and Hollis and Smith in the *Review of International Studies*, 1991, 17(4): 383–92; 1992, 18(1): 181–5 (Wendt); and 1991, 17(4): 393–410 (Hollis and Smith).

72 See Kratochwil, *International Order and Foreign Policy*.

73 Kratochwil, *International Order and Foreign Policy*, p. 1.

74 Kratochwil, *International Order and Foreign Policy*, p. 2.

75 Kratochwil has (so far) most fully developed his position in his *Rules, Norms and Decisions: On the conditions of legal reasoning in international relations and domestic affairs* (Cambridge: Cambridge University Press, 1989).

76 Falk, of course, has written on various aspects of world politics for well over thirty years. However, his formal training is in international law and both his general intellectual approach (broadly critical and interpretive) and his political position (essentially opposed to the current structure and configuration of world power) has put him in opposition to most conventional 'IR' theory.

77 The principal figures involved in this have been Richard Falk, Saul Mendlowitz and Samuel Kim, though many others have been connected over the years.

78 In *The End of World Order* (New York: Holmes and Maier, 1983).

79 See, for an elaboration of this categorization, Wight, *International Theory: the Three Traditions*, ed. Brian Porter and Gabrielle Wight (London: Leicester University Press, 1992).

80 It is present, though I think in a greatly reduced and inchoate form in Wight's conception of 'the three traditions', a point which has a good deal of significance for so-called 'English school' conceptions of order, as we will see in Chapter 2.

81 Stanley Hoffmann, 'Is There an International Order?', in *Janus and Minerva: Essays in the Theory and Practice of International Politics* (Boulder, CO: Westview Press, 1987), pp. 85–6.

82 See, for example, aside from Hoffmann, Ian Clark, *The Hierarchy of States* (Cambridge: Cambridge University Press, 1989), James N. Rosenau and Ernst-Otto Czempiel (eds), *Governance without Government: Order and Change in World Politics* (Cambridge: Cambridge University Press, 1992), pp. 9–11, R. D. McKinlay and R. Little, *Global Problems and World Order*, (London: Frances Pinter, 1986). Of course, each of these writers (to say nothing of many others) has slightly different ways of conceptualizing this difference. Thus, for example, Rosenau refers to analytic and normative conceptions of order, while McKinley and Little refer to order as 'pattern' (descriptive) and order as 'goal satisfaction' (normative). Nonetheless, the basic meaning is the same.

83 For a full discussion see Hoffmann, *Janus and Minerva*, pp. 92–5. Hoffmann has also, of course, published a famous book with the title the state of war. See Hoffmann, *The State of War: Essays in the Theory and Practice of International Politics* (New York: Praeger, 1965).

84 For a good discussion of the background to Leibniz' thought, to which I shall return in Chapter 6, see Patrick Riley, *Leibniz' Political Writings* (Cambridge: Cambridge University Press, 1988), introduction. The writings most relevant here are the *Ceaserinus Fursterinus (De Suprematu Principum Germaniae)* and the *praefatio* to the *Codex Iuris Gentium*.

85 Rosenau, in Rosenau and Czempiel, *Governance without Government*, p. 22.

86 Hoffmann, *Conditions of World Order*, p. 2.

87 See, for example, Ronnie Lipschutz, 'Towards a Global Civil Society', *Millennium: Journal of International Studies*, 1992, 21(3): Summer, and David Held, *Democracy and the Global Order*, (Cambridge: Polity Press, 1995).

88 Aron, *Memoirs: Fifty Years of Political Reflection* (New York: Holmes and Meier, 1990), p. 303.

89 That is to say, as a 'short' century, roughly speaking running from 1914 to 1991. See Hobsbawm, *Age of Extremes: The short twentieth century* (London: Heinemann, 1994).

90 Also called the 'classical tradition', the 'Grotian tradition', etc. More of this later.

91 Which is not, of course, to say that it is the only concern of liberals or even – always – the major one.

92 This is not entirely fair. Some liberals, especially economic liberals like Kenichi Ohmae, see a radical change coming about through economic globalization, but in the event their preferred response turns out once more to be a version of the 'institutionalization' thesis. See the discussion in Chapter 3.

Part I

Managing order?

1 Balance

From at least the mid seventeenth century, and arguably at least from the Renaissance onwards, one principle has been widely seen as the dominant way of securing 'order' in the chaotic and anarchic world of interstate politics, in Europe to begin with and later the world. This principle became known as the 'balance of power'. As Hume famously remarked, however, 'it is a question whether the idea of the balance of power be owing entirely to modern policy or whether the phrase only has been invented in these later ages'.[1] Many have seen the operation of something like what we would today call the balance of power working in all ages, or at least in all ages and places where something resembling a 'states system' has existed.[2] Whether that is true or not, however, it was certainly during the eighteenth, nineteenth and twentieth centuries that the principle reached its apogee as a response to the 'problem of order' in the context of the European states system and in the twentieth century in particular it became the centrepiece of the most protean and widely discussed approach to international relations of all, to wit, political realism.

Of course, the balance of power has not solely been the province of self-confessed 'realists'. As we shall see, many others recognize its force, however much they might also think that it was incomplete or were critical of the way it was deployed. Moreover, the 'balance of power' is not a concept that is limited to the 'international'. Many aspects of 'domestic' politics can be seen in roughly these terms and a good deal of contemporary political science analyses them as such.[3] Equally, it is by no means only 'realism' – at least narrowly conceived – that has seen the concept of balance as central to the maintenance of world order. Both those who seek to preserve order in the context of a system of states and those (few though they may have been) who dreamt of *replacing* such an order with an imperial or hegemonic order – perhaps Napoleon in the immediately heady days after the first consulship or his elevation to the imperial title in 1804 is the most obvious candidate here – emphasized the significance of 'the balance' as the central feature of existing international order; whether, in other words, their aim was to maintain it, or overthrow it.

The centrality of 'balance' as a way of thinking about international order is thus made manifest in many aspects of the thinking and practice

of international relations over the last 200 years. One of the most important traditions of thinking in this context, for example geopolitics,
emphasized the importance of the notion of 'balance' from the start and
sought to give advice on how to balance effectively given the 'geopolitical'
realities.[4] Despite various periods of eclipse, this tradition is still alive and
vigorous at the dawn of the twenty-first century and, indeed, in some
respects is enjoying something of a renaissance amongst Anglo-American
scholars of international relations.[5]

Moreover, as I have already mentioned, and as I will discuss in more detail in
the next chapter, perhaps the most influential British (or anyway British-based)
theory of international relations, the so-called 'English school', also saw the
balance of power as a central feature of the last 200 years of world politics. Two
of its central figures, Herbert Butterfield and Martin Wight, both published
independent essays on it,[6] and in Wight's more general work the concept also
figured prominently, as a central 'institution' of international society.[7] The very
mention of that term, however, illustrates a subtle difference between English
school usage and more traditional 'realist', geopolitical and *machtpolitik* uses; or
so, at least, I shall argue.

Despite this widespread use, however, it is chiefly political realism that has
argued, and continues to argue, that the balance of power is the primary, indeed
perhaps the only, guarantor of order in a world of states; and it is realism – in
some form or other – that has tended to dominate international relations (the
external practice of states) as well as International Relations (the academic study
of the external practice of states), throughout the twentieth century. Therefore, it
is the realist framing of the notion of balance with which I shall primarily be
concerned in this chapter.

To examine properly the appropriateness of the notion of balance as a
response to the problem of order we will therefore need to look in some detail at
the ways in which realists have deployed it. Thus, this chapter will have three
main sections together with a short conclusion. To begin with, I shall look at a
number of realist attempts to deploy the notion of balance as the central mechanism for sustaining international order. In the first section, I shall look at the
so-called 'classical realist' account of the balance of power – the ideas usually
associated with the likes of Hans Morgenthau, George Kennan and Rheinhold
Niebuhr amongst others – and examine how they related the idea to the problem
of order. In the second section, I shall then look at the currently most influential
version of realism within academic International Relations – neo-realism – and
examine how it deploys the concept in this context. In the third section, I shall
then examine three attempts at rewriting and reconstructing realism and its view
of the relations between balance and order; the 'structural' (and grand historical)
realism of Barry Buzan, Richard Little and Charles Jones, the 'evaluative political realism' of Roger Spegele and the 'Augustinian–pragmatic' realism of
Alastair Murray. The fourth and final section then offers a critique of these
attempts and tries to point up some of the obvious problems the notion of
balance has in dealing with order as I discussed it in the Introduction, closing

with a view about the likely prospectus for realism which suggests two very different trajectories for realism in the twenty-first century.

Classical realism: 'moral realpolitik' and the balance of power

It is realism, then, that has sought to make this understanding of balance the 'holy grail', as it were, of IR theory, however much other thinkers accept its relevance. Of course, realists have long sought to argue that they stand in a long line of thinkers and practitioners to do so, running from Thucydides onwards. Such a list usually includes – as a minimum – Machiavelli and Hobbes as major intellectual figures, and the likes of Richelieu, Metternich and Bismarck as practical ones.[8] It would quite often be expanded to include Augustine, say, and Rousseau.[9] Whatever the validity of such claims – and I should say that I am pretty unconvinced by them – I am not going to discuss any of these worthies in what follows.[10] The reason is very simple. At least as a self-conscious outlook, 'realism' is a creature of the nineteenth and – especially – the twentieth centuries and it is on the writers who have developed it in this context that I will concentrate here.[11]

Origins

As many have pointed out, it is Max Weber who is perhaps the first to state an identifiably 'realist view'[12] and it is largely Weber who sets the scene for the more usual – in International Relations anyway – figures who dominate the tradition. It is worth noting, in this context, that in terms of German domestic politics Weber was a liberal, a national liberal, to be sure, but a liberal nonetheless. It is not perhaps impossible, therefore, to combine some sense of liberalism with political realism, a link I shall come back to a bit later on in both this chapter and Chapter 3.

Of course, it is also true that the sources of twentieth-century realism are many and varied. A reaction against so-called 'Idealist' writing in the interwar period is perhaps the most widely cited 'trigger' for the self-conscious realist thinking and clearly there was a powerful negative reaction against some of the assumptions widely assumed (at any rate) to have been propagated by writers like Alfred Zimmern, Gilbert Murray, Robert Cecil, G. Lowes Dickinson, Leonard Woolf, Arnold Toynbee and, in the United States, James Shotwell.[13] One of the allegedly canonical statements of realism – E. H. Carr's *The Twenty Years Crisis*[14] – was explicitly written with many of these writers as targets.

However, many of the leading realists – most obviously Morgenthau, Kennan and Niebuhr – came to realism from very different routes. In Morgenthau's case, the most direct influence was, unquestionably, Weber, though other more subterranean influences may also have been at work. In Niebuhr's, the most powerful influence would seem to have been the Augustinianism that developed in the course of his work for his Gifford Lectures, *The Nature and Destiny of Man*.

Unquestionably, too, the political events and experiences of the interwar period in particular also left their mark, as they did on many of the actors who were to become noted realist policymakers, particularly in the United States, most obviously on Kennan and on that 'practitioner' who, along with Henry Kissinger, is perhaps the best known advocate of realism in US politics, Dean Acheson.[15]

It is perhaps also not entirely irrelevant that the full flowering of twentieth-century realist theory took place not in Europe (where perhaps it was regarded as too obvious to need 'theorizing') but in the United States, and specifically in the contexts both of the emergence of the United States as an unambiguous world power between 1940 and 1950 and of the requirements and needs of a number of US-based European exiles. A number of the most celebrated 'realists' were of European origin, émigrés who made their names and reputation in the United States but whose formative experiences and education had been European. This is true, for example, of Morgenthau and of Arnold Wolfers,[16] and also of Kissinger, of course, though he was younger.

It is perhaps an interesting irony that realism became dominant in the academic study of international relations partly through the numerical dominance of US-based scholarship – Stanley Hoffmann's celebrated 'American Social Science' of International Relations[17] – but partly due also to the influence of European-trained or domiciled thinkers who fled Europe in the run-up to the Second World War or just after.[18]

Obviously any attempt to summarize the views of all of these thinkers, writers and practitioners would be as impossible as it would be impolite and I shall not even attempt to do so here. Rather I shall look at the manner in which the balance of power is treated by realists in general, and in particular by the most influential 'older' realist theorists – usually termed the 'classical' realists – and especially by Morgenthau, unquestionably the most influential realist 'theorist' for the study of international relations.[19] In the next section, I shall then contrast this with the currently most influential version of realism in academic circles – usually called neo-realism – where I will focus in particular on the arguments of Kenneth Waltz, who largely created this version of realism, though I shall also look at some recent reworkings of Waltzian themes in the hands of some of the more influential younger 'neo-realists', especially Stephen Walt and John Mearsheimer. Finally, I shall look at some contemporary re-evaluations of realist thinking that I call 'revisionist realisms'.

Before I do any of this, however, I want to make one final point. 'Realism', in general discussions of international relations, even in some academic discussions, is perhaps most commonly seen as a version of what, in nineteenth-century German thought, was called *Machtpolitik* and which the Renaissance and early modern period called *raison d'état*, or reason of state.[20] There is a lot that could and should be said about this. I will simply say that, as I understand them, and powerful though the influence of aspects of this tradition were on the realists, they must be seen as distinct from this tradition. As indicated above, a view of politics as simply about power – and thus wholly 'explanatory' – could offer no real account of the problem of order and certainly not attempt a solution to it. Realism most certainly tried to do both. Ergo it must, at least superficially, develop a view of politics that goes beyond the simple *machtpolitik* made famous by Treitschke and so ably chronicled by Meinecke.

Framework

Classical realism is hardly all of a piece. Any body of thought which contains Acheson, Kennan, Morgenthau, Niebuhr, Kissinger – to say nothing of (allegedly) Metternich, Talleyrand, Castlereagh and Bismarck as well – could scarcely be seen as being so. However, to all intents and purposes there are a set of shared views which the twentieth-century realists at least tended, in broad terms, to share and which provide the general background for the way that they think about international order and the role of the balance of power in maintaining that order. As Michael Smith has said,

> realism contains three main aspects, which various theorists emphasise differently. First, and most broadly, realism purports to be a general theory explaining the essence of international politics. Second some writers draw on the precepts of realism – without necessarily regarding it as a general theory – to advocate, criticise or justify specific policies for a given state. Finally the notion of realism is often advanced as a particular solution to the vexed problem of the place of moral considerations in foreign policy.[21]

As he also points out, it is fruitless to look for 'true' realism (as fruitless as it would be to look for 'true' liberalism), though, as we shall see, neo-realism has elicited the claim that it is not, perhaps fully, 'realistic' in the sense meant by classical realist thought.

In Smith's view, and it is one shared with some minor qualifications by most recent scholars of realism,[22] there are four key components of the 'general set' of realist beliefs. First, the assumption that human nature is universal, however varied its manifestations may be, and that among the most important aspects of this universal human nature is a universal *animus dominandi*, a lust to dominate, whether such a view be put in theological terms (as it was by Niebuhr) or in more secular terms (as it has been more generally put). Second, 'realists assume that the important unit of social life is the collectivity and that in international politics the only important collectivity is the state, which recognises no authority above it'.[23] Third, they believe that power and its pursuit by individuals and states is both 'ubiquitous and inescapable. From Weber to Kissinger [and one might add from Kissinger to Waltz] conflicts of power constitute the essence of international politics'.[24] Fourth, it follows that the real issues of international politics can be understood in terms of the rational analysis of competing interests defined as power.

A number of things need to be said about these four assumptions. In the first place, as Smith notes, the first two assumptions in particular imply certain things about the character of change in world politics. Since a common charge against realism is its inability to conceive of radical change it might be sensible to pause on this point a moment. A change in the *character* of world politics – as opposed to relatively epiphenomenal features such as the particular players (Imperial Rome, Angevin England, Renaissance Florence, absolutist France, the modern United States) or some of the temporally and spatially specific rules – is possible but only, for realists, by the 'workmanlike manipulation of the perennial forces that have shaped the past as they will shape the future'.[25]

Many realists, especially Morgenthau towards the end of his life, and Kennan still, were convinced that such a change was necessary.[26] However, they also knew how dangerous and difficult it might be, even how impossible it might be. This is perhaps a reason for the melancholic tone of a good deal of what we might call 'late' classical realist thought. Nonetheless, they did not give up hope. Kennan tellingly prefaced the conclusion to a recent book[27] with a remark of Gandalf's taken from Tolkien's *The Lord of the Rings*: 'Do not despair ... despair is only for those who see the end beyond all hope'.

A second point is that classical realist thought never supposes that the exigencies of power eliminate ethical demands, which are also part of universal human nature. All of the classical realists thought long and hard about the dilemmas of ethics and international politics. One quotation from Morgenthau will have to stand for them all, but it is one with which, I suggest, they would almost all agree.

> To act successfully, that is according to the rules of the political art, is political wisdom. To know with despair that the political act is inevitably evil, and to act nevertheless, is moral courage. To choose among several expedient actions the least evil one is moral judgement. In the combination of political wisdom, moral courage and moral judgement man reconciles his political nature with his moral destiny. That this conciliation is nothing more than a modus vivendi, uneasy, precarious, and even paradoxical, can disappoint only those who prefer to gloss over and distort the tragic contradictions of human existence with the soothing logic of a specious accord.[28]

The third point, of course, is that in this context, 'order' can *only* be the way in which the structures of the world and the structures of our 'moral destiny' can best co-exist and, as Morgenthau puts it:

> In the absence of an integrated international society, the attainment of a modicum of order and the realisation of a minimum of moral values are predicated upon the existence of national communities capable of preserving order and realising moral values within the limits of their power.[29]

The question thus arises, how best, given all of the above, can this order be achieved and, once achieved, maintained?

The answer, of course, is that it is achieved and maintained through the balance of power. On the classical realist understanding, the balance of power is not simply a convenient tool for *machtpolitik*; rather it is a *moral* policy precisely because it is the only tool that can promote 'order' – which as Niebuhr says must 'implicate justice' rather than ignore it[30] – while at the same time allowing for the inevitable multiplicity of a states system.

Al Murray has recently argued convincingly[31] that the classical realist's treatment of the balance of power is foreshadowed, and in certain respects framed by Niebuhr's arguments in his Gifford Lectures, *Human Nature and the Destiny of Man*. In these lectures, Niebuhr starts from the view that all institutions and human practices are necessarily incomplete and imperfect and that the corruption and imperfection of human nature requires temporal power.[32] Such power, however, must also be checked otherwise it will turn into tyranny. As Murray puts it,

> the achievement of even a measure of justice … presupposes some social equilibrium of power, for in its absence, moral and social restraints are ineffective. … In any international order 'an implied hegemony of the stronger powers is both essential and inevitable [but] with this comes the threat of a new imperialism. Against this danger of tyranny, [there must be] an institutional balance of power to protect states.[33]

In essence the other classical realists all agreed with this formulation.[34] In *Politics among Nations*, for example, Morgenthau referred to the balance of power as the 'necessary outgrowth' of power politics and even called it a 'universal concept', and argues that 'the balance of power and policies aimed at its preservation are not only inevitable, but an essential stabilising factor in a society of sovereign nations'. Or, as Michael Smith has paraphrased the position, 'only power can restrain power'.[35] However, it is also worth emphasizing that Morgenthau stresses the different ways in which the balance of power can be deployed and the different methods that can be used to promote it and stresses still further the centrality of what he refers to as the 'moral and political unity of Europe' which allowed it to operate successfully. In the absence of such unity, which Morgenthau believed was largely absent in the Cold War period, the balance of power becomes more difficult to operate effectively but, if anything, even more important.

A number of things are worth emphasizing about this argument. The first is the dependence on a view of human beings as essentially appetitive, power seeking and possessing, as Niebuhr put it, an *animus dominandi*. It is this that critics usually refer to when they talk about realists having a simplistic view of 'human nature'. However, I think we should remember that none of the realists denied the possibility of human excellence, though they certainly did not think it was always very conspicuous. Rather their view was that statesmen could not afford to assume that virtuous behaviour would occur. The 'ethics of responsibility' developed by Weber and taken over by most of the realists, though especially by

Morgenthau, require what we might today call 'risk-averse' behaviour from the statesman. As Morgenthau puts it,

> The political actor has, beyond the general moral duties, a special moral responsibility to act wisely … what is done in the political sphere by its very nature concerns others who must suffer from unwise action. What is here done with good [or even neutral] intentions but unwisely and hence with disastrous results is morally defective; for it violates the ethics of responsibility to which all action affecting others, and hence political action par excellence, is subject.[36]

This is thus the source of the realists' constant emphasis on 'prudence'; and inevitably it reinforces the sense that 'balance' is the best we might hope for.

A second point is the extent to which for most of the classical realists, the balance of power is very *difficult* to create properly; it requires constant maintenance and very considerable diplomatic and political skill. This is easier when there is a degree of shared normative assumptions – a point emphasized especially by Niebuhr and Morgenthau[37] – but it is difficult even then. This is particularly interesting in the light of the developments of realist thought I shall discuss below, where the tendency is to speak of the balance of power as necessarily emerging as a result of the logic of the system. This, the classical realists would most vehemently have contested.

It is perhaps Morgenthau who makes most of this aspect of realist thought, but not, interestingly, in *Politics among Nations* but rather in the first book he published after arriving in the United States, *Scientific Man versus Power Politics*.[38] In this book Morgenthau launches a powerful criticism of the development of social and political philosophy in the modern West culminating in the belief that science could solve all problems, especially political ones. This was, amongst other things, a broadside against the recently inaugurated attempt to put political science on a 'scientific' footing represented by the likes of Charles Merriam's *New Aspects of Politics*. For Morgenthau, politics was, *par excellence*, the *human* science, it depended on will, action and belief and could not be reduced to structures/processes, however important they were.[39] It is therefore especially ironic that the realism which his *Politics among Nations* helped to make dominant in the US study of international relations should very quickly have been taken over by precisely the scientism and formalism he most detested. However, this capture was perhaps not complete until the next generation of realist thinkers became dominant, most especially one: Kenneth Waltz.

Neo-realism: the inevitability of the balance of power

In the 1970s, as is well known, realism took a new turn. The author of a well-known, influential and relatively straightforward realist text, *Man, the State and War*,[40] published in 1979 a text that sought to revolutionize realist thinking. In this he has largely succeeded, though whether for good or ill is a different question. The author was Kenneth Waltz, of course, and the text, *Theory of International Politics*.[41]

In *Man, the State and War* Waltz had famously argued that of the three usual 'images' of the origins of war – human nature, the internal constitutions of states and regimes and the character of the international system – it was the 'third image', the international system, which was actually the one in which a serious theory about the origins of war could be found. The book was influential in many areas. As is well known, and as has been recently emphasized by Barry Buzan,[42] it helped shape the so-called 'levels of analysis' debate, which has remained an important topic in mainstream IR theory ever since.[43] Waltz' 'third image' or 'systemic' view being contested, as it was at the time, by those – often but not exclusively liberals – who argued that it was the 'second image' – that is to say, the internal constitution of states – at least in some form, is where the real source of the problem is to be found. (We will see a recent version of this thesis in Chapter 3 in the liberal peace argument.) As we have just seen, classical realist thought often saw the failures of peace in a first-image way, though some – especially Morgenthau – sought to combine differing explanations.

In any event, it is this argument that in many respects forms the basis for Waltz' hugely influential recasting of realist thought in *Theory of International Politics*. However, the manner of the two essays is at least as important as their matter. *Man, the State and War* displays an impressive familiarity with traditional questions of the human sciences as well as considerable knowledge of and skill in political thought more generally.[44] *Theory of International Politics*, however, is couched in a much more strongly 'scientific', economistic, style. In part of course this simply reflects the changes of academic fashion between 1959 and 1979 in the US academy, or at least the social scientific branches of it. However, it also represents a substantial shift, I would say, in Waltz' conception of his task, one with substantial implications for the problem of order.

Waltz' theory

Before I turn to this, however, let me summarize, as far as I can, the basis of Waltz' case and its implications for our current concern with the balance of power. Fortunately, Waltz' theory is sufficiently well known for me to be able to offer a brief summary, without doing too much violence to his argument. Waltz starts by dividing theories of international relations up into two types, those which see causes operating primarily at the 'state' (second-image) level, which he terms 'reductionist' theories and those which see causes operating primarily at the systemic (third-image) level, which he terms 'systemic'.[45] The former group, which Waltz thinks have been dominant in IR theory, explain international politics, therefore, in terms of the interactions and characteristics of the major units which make it up, that is states. He further argues that reductionist theories do not just, as a matter of fact, mistake or ignore certain aspects of international politics – the systemic aspects – they *must* do so. For reductionist theories to be true, Waltz famously says, 'we would have to believe that no important causes intervene between the aims and actions of states and the results their actions produce. In the history of international relations, however, results achieved seldom correspond to the intentions of actors'.[46]

The result of this argument, of course, is that there must be a set of factors which are properties of the *system*, not of the units, and which represent the 'structural', 'constraining' factors that make international politics what it is. It is these factors, Waltz thinks, that a systemic theory should address. A theory of international politics, Waltz says, should be systemic; theories of foreign policy, in contrast, must be reductionist. It follows, then, that a theory of international politics as such is different from a theory of foreign policy. The problem is that virtually all previous theories of international politics (he specifically discusses Aron, Morgenthau, Morton Kaplan and Richard Rosecrance) have been reductionist in that they have failed to appreciate this distinction and its implications.

Waltz then goes on to argue that a systemic theory of international politics must comprise a structure and a set of interacting units. Structure, of course, is a hugely contested concept in social science as Waltz acknowledges; however, he goes on to argue that the crucial trick is to avoid describing the structure in terms of the units, which we might call the 'reductionist fallacy'. Seeking to avoid this, Waltz suggests that a systemic structure is shaped by three defining characteristics: the principles by which the parts are arranged, the characteristics of the units and the distribution of capabilities across the units.

It is the first of these that is perhaps the most significant in the context of the problem of order for it is the one part of his analysis where the notion of order enters at all. Waltz suggests that, at least as far as political systems are concerned, there are only two ordering principles: hierarchy and anarchy. A hierarchical system is one where the units stand in a relationship to one another that is constitutionally and legally organized in terms of a hierarchy of power. An anarchical system is one where no such formal relations are present; it is therefore, to use one of Waltz' best known terms, a 'self-help' system. For Waltz, the key distinction between domestic and international politics can be conceived of in these terms: domestic politics is hierarchical, international politics anarchical.

From this it follows that the 'characteristics of the units' in anarchical systems are not differentiated. This gives rise to one of Waltz' ugliest, but most quoted, phrases: that in international systems the units are 'functionally undifferentiated'. It is worth emphasizing, in this context, that Waltz explicitly accepts that states are not the only actors in international politics, but clearly he says the most important are the cluster around the sense of functional similarity. The result of this view is simple: the 'character of the units' has no effect on their likely behaviour in the context of the system. Something which does, however, is the distribution of capabilities across the units. This is the only way in which international systems change, and it is a function of the system rather than the units because it is the position of the units in the system relative to one another, not their capabilities as such, that Waltz is referring to.

The inevitability of the balance of power

The way he structures this theory means that for Waltz, as for the classical real-ists discussed above, the balance of power becomes the central tool of statecraft. However, there is a profound difference between Waltz' deployment of it and his predecessors.

For Waltz, states are 'functionally undifferentiated' and this means that the 'ordering principle', anarchy, forces all states to become 'like units'. However, the point about the relative position of the units in the system implies that we can roughly see the characteristics of a system in terms of its major players and that their relationship will frame the system's structure at any given time. Thus in post-war world politics, the fact that there were two major powers, the Soviet Union and the United States, led to a 'bi-polar' system, which replaced the multi-polar system of the eighteenth and nineteenth centuries. For Waltz, bi-polarity is preferable to multi-polarity since it reduced the possible number of conflicts and is easier to control (this is flatly contrary to the view of other realists like Morgenthau and Kissinger who, though for slightly different reasons, thought multi-polar systems were likely to be more stable than bi-polar ones).[47]

This argument has led to a number of Waltz' best known and most contro-versial theses, all of which revolve around his contention that 'balancing' is central to any anarchic system with functionally undifferentiated units. It is important to see that for Waltz, unlike the classical realists, states really have only two alternatives in terms of general systemic behaviour: balancing *against* another state or states, or 'bandwagoning' – going along *with* it – and in general terms, balancing is far the likelier option. The 'balance of power' in the Cold War, however, was affected by something other than bi-polarity. It was affected by the invention of nuclear weapons which had a pronounced impact upon the relative capabilities of the units, especially the great powers and which therefore further enhanced the stability already created by bi-polarity. This has led Waltz to argue in work subsequent to *Theory of International Politics* that the managed and controlled spread of nuclear weapons would, in fact, be a positive develop-ment, not a negative one as most conventional opinion has assumed.[48]

The developing neo-realist agenda

Waltz' recasting of realism has become hugely influential. It is probably true to say that it now dominates US IR theory, its only challenger a version of liber-alism with a similar 'rationalist' methodological orientation (more of which later) and it is widely influential elsewhere. It is also a theory which has developed a powerful penumbra of subsequent additions and modifications. Although Waltz had initially called it 'structural' realism, it was quickly christened 'neo-realism' and the name has stuck. The next generation down from Waltz have given neo-realism additional sophistication and power but have largely continued along the lines Waltz mapped out, though they have certainly moved in some different directions. A particularly influential 'second-generation' neo-realist, for example, is Stephen Krasner, whose work has developed, along with that of Robert Gilpin, a powerful neo-realist agenda in International Political Economy, an area which Waltz hardly touched at all.[49] This development has also been at the centre of the work of other prominent neo-realists such as Joseph Grieco, who has been at the heart of the 'neo-realist/neo-liberal debate' that dominated mainstream IR theorizing during the 1980s.[50]

The balance of power has remained a central concern, of course, and it has figured prominently in a number of the central charges neo-realists have made against their largely liberal opponents. Perhaps the best known recent example of this is the work of John Mearsheimer, a formidable controversialist,[51] who has taken the lead in criticizing the latest developments in neo-liberal and more radical theories of world politics.[52]

However, one of the most interesting departures in recent neo-realist theory has been made by a 'third-generation' theorist, significantly one trained by Waltz himself, Stephen Walt. It is doubly significant in the present context because Walt's reformulation of neo-realist theory centres on the balance of power. For Walt, neo-realism is indeed the best way of understanding the system, but it does require supplementing. His first book, *Origins of Alliances*,[53] was a sophisticated and powerful recasting of neo-realist theory which suggested that states balance not simply against *power* but against perceived *threat* – a function, he argued, of aggregate power, perceptions of intent and the offence–defence balance.

In his second book, *Revolution and War*,[54] Walt deepened the analysis by arguing that revolutions tend to produce situations where the perception of threat, both on the part of the revolutionary state and on the part of its neighbours, is heightened and thus, in the short term at least, this will often lead to war. Thus, he argues that gradually revolutionary states are, so to speak, 'socialized' into the rules of the game, and thus increasingly they behave like any other state in an anarchic self-help system, thus reinforcing a central element in Waltz' analysis. He also remains firmly wedded to the traditional 'levels of analysis' problematic where states are 'unit-level actors' as opposed to 'system-level' ones. For Walt, revolutions are unit-level events with 'systemic' (that is to say, international) consequences. However, he also believes that 'balance of threat theory' suggests the importance, even for neo-realism, of 'unit-level' factors, and in this respect at least seems to be arguing for a less rigid division between the various levels of analysis and a less clear distinction between systemic and reductionist theories, which would surely be resisted by Waltz.

Neo-realism, order and balance

The above makes very clear, I think, the centrality of 'balance' for neo-realism. However, there is one major difference between classical and neo-realists which we need to discuss. Neo-realists give very little attention, if any, to the problem of order in the sense I have discussed it in this book. It would pay us, therefore, to pause a moment and ask why this is so and what implications it might have for their understanding of the balance of power.

Part of the problem, of course, is the methodological assumptions which neo-realism makes and the epistemological and ontological positions on which those assumptions depend. Waltz was very critical of Aron precisely because Aron claimed that the field of International Relations was resistant to theory (of Waltz' type) owing to its necessarily diverse and, as we saw in the Introduction, dialectical subject matter, both explanatory *and* normative, precisely where he located the problem of order – a point that, as we saw, would have been echoed, though in a different way, by Morgenthau. Yet Waltz effectively reduces 'theory' to the explanatory – indeed to a certain kind of explanation[55] – and, as Aron observed, this cannot therefore offer an account of 'order'; it can only offer a description of the 'pattern'. Effectively, I suggest this is what Waltz' discussion of the 'ordering principle' of the system amounts to. There is no sense that this principle has any normative component whatever for Waltz.

As a result, however, the 'balance of power', in Waltz' terms at least, is not couched in terms of a response to the problem of order, because neo-realism no longer sees 'order' as a problem, in the sense discussed in the Introduction. It is reduced simply to the status of an 'organizing principle' of a system with no normative warrant at all. In this context, neo-realism, so to speak, 'refuses' the problem of order: it is concerned with a different set of questions. Yet, in refusing it, neo-realist accounts run into a classic problem, I suggest. If the balance of power will necessarily occur, as a result of the logic of the system, there is no sense that it requires the diplomatic skill and subtlety Morgenthau and others insisted it did. Yet, if it does not, there is no way one can claim it was done well or badly. If one does wish to claim, as for example I think Walt would, that it can be done more or less well, then we are back I suggest to the very mixture that so irritated Waltz in Aron, and thus, we are back to asking what is it that the balance exists *for*: the defence of the national interest, of course; but what does that exist for and so on. We end up, I suggest, back with the sense brilliantly developed by the classical realists that it is only in balance that a system of states can find order at all and that this is a normative, not simply a descriptive, statement. However, let me come back to this in the final section in a moment.

The revisionists

It should not be thought, however, that neo-realism has the field to itself in the late 1990s. Partly as a result, I think, of a growing sense of unease about neo-realism's failure seriously to address normative questions in the way the predecessors did, there are an ever widening range of revisionist readings of realism appearing, some of which take neo-realism as their starting point but a number of others of which are much closer in spirit, and sometimes in fact, to classical realism.[56]

In this chapter I do not, of course, have time to do anything other than gesture at what I think are among the most significant of these revisionist approaches and so, in the former category, I want to discuss in particular the recent work of Barry Buzan and Richard Little (and at least in their first venture into this terrain, Charles Jones);[57] and in the latter category the recent work of Roger Spegele and Alastair Murray.[58] In each case, I shall focus on whether their revisionism leads in general terms to a 'new' or different way of viewing the problem of order or the notion of balance.

Buzan and Little: theory meets history

Both Barry Buzan and Richard Little have impressive bodies of work behind them and both have been seen, and see themselves as, in varying ways, contributing to realist thinking. Buzan has become one of the most influential contemporary writers on security questions; his *People, States and Fear*[59] is probably the most widely read non-American text in the field, and over the last few years, together with a number of colleagues at the Centre for Peace and Conflict Research at the University of Copenhagen,[60] where he is a research director, he has established an approach to broad questions of security that has become suffi-ciently widely known to merit a canonical description as 'the Copenhagen school'.[61] He has also written on a wide variety of other topics, including, most recently, military technology and security and a bravura attempt to define the character of the contemporary and its likely trajectories.[62] Richard Little, by contrast, has tended to work in more general areas of international relations. Intervention,[63] the balance of power and general IR theory are the areas where he has chiefly worked, co-editing one of the most widely used texts in British International relations[64] as well as, as I discussed in the Introduction, co-authoring one of the few book-length studies to foreground the question of order.

Their major joint work so far is *The Logic of Anarchy*, co-authored with Charles Jones. This book, as they make clear in their introductory overview, takes as its starting point Waltz's neo-realism, but also seeks a greater degree of continuity with the older realist tradition (Carr is especially prominent, especially for Jones). They call their own view 'structural realism' and suggest that three elements mark it as an extension of realism. The first is a continued insistence on the primacy of the political, though they add that they deny Waltz' assumption that all power is reducible to political power. The second is a focus on the state and the third the acceptance of 'Waltz' basic definitional framework for an interna-tional structure, albeit with very specific changes to his specific formulation'.[65] There are, they then go on to say, three basic differences between their structural realism and Waltzian neo-realism. First, a much more comprehensive and more open definition of structure is deployed. The second is the claim that structure is not seen as the only systemic-level factor in play. What they term 'interaction' also plays a central role. The third difference is that the analogy with microeco-nomics so important to Waltz is dropped and replaced with a more sociological, linguistic approach.

'The combined effects of these differences', they argue,

> open four possibilities not available to neo-realism. First is that structure becomes a way of addressing history and not something to be detached

from it ... the second possibility ... allows the explicit linkage of units and structure through the logic of structuration ... the third possibility ... [breaks] out of the narrow logic of political interaction that dominates neorealism ... to look at the whole range of interactions (economic, societal, environmental as well as military and political) that have shaped both the units and the structures of the system ... the fourth possibility, arising out of our revision of the philosophical posture of realism ... [develops] a philo-sophically realist methodological position which mitigates the binds of relativism and reflexivity that have restricted so much self proclaimed post-modernist and poststructural work.[66]

In this context it would not be appropriate, of course, to attempt an overall interpretation of this ambitious work. Rather, I shall merely focus on those aspects of it most relevant to the way the notion of balance can be understood according to this version of realism. The relevant sections of the book for this task are the first two and it is on them that I shall, therefore, concentrate.

The key move made in the book is the development of what they call 'interac-tion capacity' as a key level of analysis *between* the 'system level' and the 'unit level'. By interaction capacity, Buzan, Jones and Little understand

a set of variables that clearly belong within a system theory of international politics, but which are neither structural nor unit level in character. They are aspects of absolute capacity that transcend the unit level, but are not struc-tural in the sense of having to go with the positional arrangements of the units. They are systemic not only because they represent capabilities that are deployed throughout the system, but also and mainly because they profoundly condition the significance of structure and the meaning of the term system itself. This is a different quality from selective unit capabilities that have system wide affects, such as Nuclear weapons, which Waltz rightly places within the unit level.

Thus 'interaction capacity', 'captures the importance of the absolute quality of capabilities as both a defining characteristic of the system, and a distinct source of shoving and shaping forces playing on the units alongside those from the structural level'. They also suggest that it might make sense to suggest that one could have both 'aggregative' and 'disaggregative' conceptions of interaction capacity (a move they earlier made in the 'structural' level as well). Thus their conception of structural realism looks like that shown in Figure 1.1.

The key implication of this reformulation of realism for our concerns here is that it changes in quite profound terms realism's approach to the notion of balance, without suggesting that 'balance' is not, indeed, in some sense, central to the effective operation of the system. This point becomes clearest in the second section of the book largely concerned with historical illustrations of the above schema. In chapter 8, for example, on 'the structure and logic of anarchy' itself, there is a rich discussion of a number of historical cases that throw

International political sector	
Structural level of analysis	**deep structure = organizational principle plus differentiation of units**
	distributional structure = systemic patterns in the distribution of unit attributes
Interaction level of analysis	**interaction capacity = absolute quality of technological and societal capabilities across the system**
Unit level of analysis	**process formations = action–reaction relations between units, particularly recurrent patterns of action–reaction**
	attribute analysis = unit behaviour explained in terms of unit attributes

Figure 1.1   The vocabulary of structural realism

Source: Buzan, Jones & Little 1993

considerable doubt on the simple way in which neo-realism predicts the emergence of a competitive balance of power.

For Buzan, Jones and Little, their approach allows for *differentiated* anarchic systems – that is, systems in which (for example) power remains highly decentralized in *both* units *and* system (they illustrate this with discussions of the Kula and Carthage) contrasted with systems where power is decentralized in the system but concentrated in some or all of the units (Rome, for example, *vis-à-vis* the Hellenistic kingdoms).

The balance of power inevitably differs on this view. The former type of system for example does not develop it whereas the latter does. However, this does not mean balance is irrelevant; rather, according to Buzan, Jones and Little, it allows you to see clearly where balance – and what kind of balance – is important in any given system. Their differentiated logic of anarchy can produce a variety of possibilities, which they represent graphically as shown in Figure 1.2.

The key distinction, of course, is between international systems and international society. In these contexts balance will, of course, exist, but only in the former will it necessarily take the shape predicted by neo-realism. In the latter, it is likely to be deeply intertwined with norms and rules and therefore be a very

State A

	Compete	Co-operate
Compete	international system	hegemony by B
Co-operate	hegemony by A	international society

State B (label for the left rows)

Figure 1.2 Differentiating the logic of anarchy
Source: Buzan, Jones & Little 1993

different kind of 'balance' – not simply a balance of 'power'. However, since 'anarchy remains the great constant',[67] balance of some sort there will inevitably be.

This project is clearly enormously impressive. As the authors claim, it offers new ways of thinking about systemic aspects of international politics without abandoning the central insight they think neo-realism brought, the role of structure. In future work, Buzan and Little are seeking to offer 'an explanatory theory of the whole history of the international system and some aspects of its future'.[68] However, it is remarkable how central balance remains even in this reconfigured structural realism. It will be a different kind of balance than that supposed by older realisms, whether classical or neo, and it may move this version of realism closer to aspects of the English school or constructivist thinking that we will examine in the next chapter (the 'societal' element in their analysis would certainly suggest this).[69] In that context it may be reasonable to see it as a bridge between seeing 'balance' and seeing 'society' as the central element in supporting and sustaining order. However, more of that later.

Spegele: evaluative political realism

Roger Spegele's work has taken realism – and the notion of balance – in a very different direction. Like all the 'revisionist' realists discussed here – much more so than Buzan and Little, if less so than Murray – he is critical of 'neo-realism', which he refers to as 'concessional realism'.[70] However, he is also critical of what he calls 'commonsense realism', meaning the view of realism as a centuries-old distillation of hard-nosed political wisdom. He suggests in contrast that he will develop a version of realism – evaluative political realism – which, while it builds on aspects of the usual (commonsensical) realist tradition, also departs from it in important ways.

Spegele's argument begins by disagreeing with what he takes to be the two most powerful opposed views to his own, which he terms 'positivist-empiricism' – effectively the methodological armoury of neo-realism (and also the neo-liberalism that we will encounter in Chapter 3) and 'emancipatory' International Theory (which is effectively what we will examine in Chapter 4). He then develops his own, evaluative, political realism by arguing,[71] first, that the 'scientific claims of international relations will be … modest and mainly grounded in what can be delivered by historical methodology', but that, also, and second,

> human beings are in certain ineliminable senses animals, and, as such, are part of the living environment in which international relations takes place … [this] involves accepting the consequences of an understanding of natural selection according to which … competition … is probably an inevitable genetic cum cultural property of human beings.

This also, he thinks,

> hinders socially engineered projects for world government which take no account of what it is for human beings to have a complex and full subjectivity, and, second, it depends on our commonsense explanations of international activity by charting the evolutionary history that underlies the proximate mechanisms which constitute the core of any realist conception of international relations.

Third, the evaluative political realist understands history in terms of individual actions and, fourth, he or she understands it in terms of the fact of the conflict of moral/political choices.

The key to Spegele's reformulation of realism, it seems to me, lies in what he refers to as his 'second thesis', to wit his replacement of the 'first-image' model of classical realism (broadly theological in origin and character, as we have seen) with one taken from evolutionary biology. Traditional realists, though for rather different reasons, would be happy to reject 'positivist empiricism' and 'emancipation'; equally, they would also have seen history as largely about individuals and as being chock full of 'tragic' moral choices and dilemmas, though again for rather different reasons. It is the second thesis they would reject.

The thesis is essentially very simple. 'For the evaluative political realist', Spegele writes,

> [we must avoid] two extremes: constructivism and naturalism. Constructivism … refuses to recognise that the human being is a natural kind and, like other natural kinds, has real properties discoverable by natural science. On the other hand, naturalism … refuses, quite wrongly, to countenance facts about … what it is to be a person, in contrast to an animal,

endowed with certain psychological needs and capacities that have to be satisfied in certain ways if human beings are to flourish.[72]

For Spegele, this thesis serves two purposes, First and foremost, for Spegele, it grounds realism's traditional claim to be based on 'human nature', without any even implicit theological overtones, and thus allows him to defend realism as both naturalistic and 'objective', though naturally partial and incomplete. It also allows him, he thinks, to reject 'post-modernist' claims about the infinite malleability of humans (as we shall see in the Epilogue not a claim his targets would, in any case, make, but more of that later). The second important point for Spegele is that it undercuts, as the whole approach does, the 'systemic' claims of neo-realism. As he says, it resuscitates the idea of the primacy of foreign policy 'understood in terms of how the heritage of different nation-states shapes the views of statespersons'.[73]

In terms of the problem of order, although it is significant, I think, that it does not even have an entry in his index, his second thesis provides us with a clear indication of his general view. 'Order', normatively speaking, will make sense only in terms of an evolutionary approach. Given that this approach is sceptical of radical policies for change, and given that it also emphasizes group life and solidarity, we are effectively where the traditional realists left us, only with a naturalistic, evolutionary grounding instead of a theological one. In this context, again balance is likely to be the major, if not the sole, technique of statecraft for promoting order in the international system.

Murray: pragmatic Augustinianism[74]

Murray is perhaps the revisionist with the strongest distaste for neo-realism. In his opening chapter – indeed his opening sentence – he refers to it as a 'heretical hegemony', and a good deal of his opening chapter is concerned with a powerful – and at times almost bitter – critique of neo-realism. He even seeks to deny it the name. Neo-realism, he says, 'has departed in fundamental ways from the concerns of realism, generating a partial and skewed realism which … barely deserves the name'.[75] His critique of neo-realism concentrates, understandably enough, on Waltz, and centres on Waltz' misreading of the classical realists and the damaging effects of his desire for 'theoretical parsimony'. For example, he takes issue with the claim that Waltz makes – discussed above – that classical realists have to assume that 'no important causes intervene between the aims and actions of states and the results their actions produce'. This claim, Murray says, ' is simply bizarre. The dissonance between intentions and outcomes was central to [classical realism's] approach'.[76] However, his fundamental charge cuts much deeper.

> The most fundamental result [of neo-realism] is that it cuts theory off from any concern with the normative. Informed by a vitally practical orientation, realism revolved around the problem of enhancing the mutual understandings by which actors relate to one another, and, in particular, around the

problem of reconciling the divergent value systems which inform the different actors in the international system ... this problem culminates in the attempt to inform the international order with a degree of legitimacy, a moral consensus, which will reduce its reliance on the *simple* balance of power [and] which will achieve some modus vivendi between the competing value systems of the different actors ... neo-realism abandons this concern ... consequently neo-realism represents a reformulation, not of realism but of realpolitik.[77]

Having disposed of neo-realism, however, Murray then confronts a second obstacle. If neo-realism is not realism, what is? He opts, I believe rightly, to deny that realism can be located in a transhistorical 'tradition' of figures that include Thucydides, Machiavelli, Hobbes, etc., but does suggest that one figure not usually discussed provides a framework which does exert a powerful influence: Augustine. His influence is largely second hand and second order (though very direct on some realists like Niebuhr) but powerful for all that. Murray thus describes the main current of realism, represented in the twentieth century by the likes of Niebuhr, Kennan, Morgenthau and, more controversially, Butterfield as 'Augustinian realism'.

The bulk of the rest of Murray's book consists of a reinterpretation of traditional realist themes, thinkers and concerns in this context, but his final section then moves on to discuss the contemporary applicability of this reformulated realism. He first of all wrestles with the awkward fact that his (in my view powerful and suggestive) identification of classical realism with an Augustinian framework points up the one chief problem from his point of view: realism's unambiguous relation to Judaeo-Christian – and especially Christian – theology. He looks at one prominent attempt to side-step that problem – Henry Kissinger's reformulation – which he believes fails, before moving on to his own solution which is effectively to cannibalize aspects of American pragmatism and use them to suggest that realism can coalesce around the defence of Western (or potentially other) material interests and values, and that if we do so, we replicate the dilemmas so presciently analysed by the classical realists, substituting the belief in 'Western values' for belief in God. Though he does not quote it, his position here is not dissimilar to that identified by Isaiah Berlin in his famous aphorism 'to recognise the relative validity of one's beliefs and to stand for them unflinchingly is what distinguished the civilised man from the barbarian'.

However, he is quite clear about what this requires. His final chapter emphasises uncompromisingly what he terms, 'The Essential Relevance of the Balance of Power'. On the values-centred realism he develops, he remarks that

realism ... is ... centrally about the values we hold, and about building a framework for international order which reflects and supports such values ... in practical terms this implies, first and foremost, an emphasis on maintaining a balance of power [which, in a footnote, he significantly suggests already is, for traditional realism, a balance of threat à la Walt].[78]

For Murray, then, there is little doubt about the centrality of the balance of power, even if it is fact in the service of values, not just power. Moreover, he is the clearest of the revisionists about the central link between balance and order. We seek balance to preserve an international order that we value *normatively*, not just because it produces stability. It is perhaps a nice irony that the youngest of the revisionists ends up by sounding like no one as much as that realist whom Kennan called 'the Father of us all'.

Realism, balance and order: an interrogation

So how does 'balance' stand as an approach to order in world politics at the end of the twentieth century? At one level, I think, it remains at the centre of the realist conception of international politics; just realism remains the central home of the notion of balance, however much revisionists like Buzan, Jones and Little might be pushing it in the direction of the sorts of societal constructivist theses we will be examining in a moment. Of those realists we have discussed here, the traditional realist approach, and that of Murray which in so many ways builds upon it, are the only ones which draw a clear link between order and balance and make the former dependent on the latter. I want to argue that this at least is consistent and coherent, though also that there are formidable problems with it. I shall come back to them in a moment. What, however, of the other versions of balance, and of realism, touched on above?

Neo-realism need not detain us long, in this context. In all its many variants, it emphasizes balance, but is silent (indeed, as I argued above, must be silent) on the question of 'order', as understood above. It is, therefore, a 'theory' that tell us little about the relationship between the two, since on its own methodological presumptions there cannot be one! For all its sophistication and technical virtuosity, neo-realism is and can only be silent on all of the most important questions facing contemporary world politics, since only a *normative* defence of 'order' (even understood as they do) could justify the actions and policies they usually claim to recommend. Otherwise there is no reason, save a simply prudential one, why neo-realists should not 'recommend' hegemony – several effectively seem to do just this! But, surely, even hegemony needs some justification?

The key villain of the piece here is, of course, Waltz' substitution of a mechanistic concept of 'structure' for the agent-centred – and therefore normatively sensitive – concerns of the traditional realists. In part, therefore, the assessment of whether neo-realism will continue to flourish will depend on whether one thinks this substitution an advance or a retreat. Since I think that a coherent approach to the 'problem of order' is a *sine qua non* of any intelligible account of world politics and since neo-realism cannot provide one, I cannot but think of it as a retreat. My guess is that neo-realism will, at least in the short term, continue to flourish in the United States academy, where there is powerful institutional and methodological sustenance for it, though even here I think, the growing recognition within neo-realist ranks (think for example of the work of a Snyder or a Walt) that perceptions, ideas (and, therefore, I would argue also norms) matter suggests a weakening of the foundations even here. Elsewhere, I suspect, it will quickly wither. A 'balance' erected on so slender a foundation will not last long.

The 'structural realism' of Buzan, Jones and Little is much to be preferred. However, their way of developing realism seems (to me at least) to be leaving not only 'balance' but also realism on a rather different trajectory. Not, of course, that there is not much of great interest in such a trajectory. There clearly is. However, I think that there is also a problem, at least as far as the relationship between balance and order today is concerned, whatever might have been the case in the past. On my reading, at least, their model suggests we are currently occupying the 'international society' quadrant. In which case, it is likely that 'balance', important though it is, will become part of a complex 'societal' matrix of norms, regimes, etc. This may well be a better description of contemporary world politics than anything in conventional realism, but, in that case, it surely moves us on to the second way of addressing the problem of order. In other words, one of the revisionist strategies of realism seems to suggest that the best way of integrating balance and order is to see both as dependent on some notion of world (or international) society. Effectively this is to push realism into the path of international society, the response to the problem of order I examine in the next chapter, and, as we shall see, this has problems of its own. I shall, in any event, take it up again there.

Spegele's 'evaluative' political realism is clearly more concerned with the problem of order as I have presented it here. However, his version of realism also suffers, I think, from a failure to address adequately the implications of his 'evolutionary' approach. Spegele takes care to try and distinguish his evolutionary approach from what he calls 'naturalism' – the refusal to recognize that humans are, so to speak, *unique* animals, unique, that is, in having human personalities. For Spegele, 'human nature', that composite so beloved of the classical realists, is a compound of 'animal' and 'person' components. He wants to argue that 'something more than a biological concept of human nature is required'[79] and that this something is what he calls the 'person' component of human nature. The problem is that once you take this view to lead to a certain normatively preferable approach, as Spegele clearly does, you are left with the familiar question: why should I adhere to it? Everything Spegele says might be true – as I do not think – but the argument has no *specific* normative force, beyond, so to speak, a personal appeal for us to see things this way and think that they hang together as Spegele says they do. It ends up effectively with a position that I suggest is more reminiscent of the Sophists of antiquity than it is of those ancients that Spegele most wishes to claim for his own, Thucydides and Aristotle.

A thoroughgoing naturalism – like, say, Thucydides or Santayana's[80] – offers us something subtly different, or so it seems to me, from the conventional 'realism' that, in some respects at least, Spegele subscribes to (though there are clearly points of contact): different and a lot more difficult. It seems to me, in fact, that Spegele either is likely to be forced into the arms of the more limited constructivists that we will examine in Chapter 2, if he wishes to maintain his 'middle way' between (radical) constructivism and naturalism, or he will have to become much more 'naturalistic', in which case I think he drifts away from realism. The greatest recent work of naturalistic political theory that I know of – Santayana's *Dominations and Powers*[81] – makes it clear just how different from realism such a view would be, for all the elements of contact. It is, after all, hardly a realist temper Santayana displays when he writes, at the opening of his treatise:

> Seen under the form of eternity all ages are equally past and equally present; and it is impossible to take quite seriously the tastes and ambitions of our contemporaries. ... I have my likes and dislikes, of which I am not ashamed. I neither renounce them nor impose them. I simply recognise them to be personal in me ... my endeavour is not to allow this inevitable bias of temperament or position distort my view of the facts, which include the perhaps contrary position or temperament of other people. Let them, I say, be themselves and fight their own battles and establish their own systems. In any case these systems will not be permanent.[82]

On my reading at least, naturalists of this sort have no real 'answer' to the 'problem of order' for the very simple reason they do not see it as a 'problem', merely as an inevitable feature of human existence and certainly not, in itself, a 'tragic' one.[83]

Which leaves us, therefore, with the traditional realists, and with the attempted reformulation of their thesis by the likes of Al Murray. Let me make it clear that, in many respects, it seems to me that their position is by far the most consistent – once you make one theoretical concession at least – which does not, of course, mean that it is necessarily correct.

The 'concession' required is in general terms to understand that human beings must be seen – somehow, in some way – as deeply divided beings, whose best efforts are always and permanently threatened by their appetites and fragility. It is this view, expressed in different ways by different realists, that is one of the reasons for the persistence of realist thinking in the twentieth century, I think, for at one level it is so obvious as to be virtually banal. Who could deny it? The point, for realists, however, is that on their view alternative conceptions, at least in international relations – societal, liberal and radical – argue that all alternative conceptions believe that this is, in fact, two hypotheses rather than one, and that while one aspect of the thesis would indeed meet general acceptance, one would not. That humans are frail, limited beings is generally accepted; that they *must* be, and that all their good efforts will, one day or another, and because of that fragility, fail, is not. It is the specific concern of all classical realists to assert the interdependence of both these theses.

Both are true and it is this that makes political life *in toto* a fraught and contested realm, even a tragedy. The very powerful sense of the tragic aspects of human life is an oft-noted feature of realist thought, but it is worth pointing out that it is most prominent in realists like Morgenthau and Kissinger on whom the influence of Weber was perhaps strongest.

This, however, is where, I suggest, we can see the merest crack opening up in realist thinking, a crack, however, which threatens to become a fissure wide enough to undermine the otherwise impressive coherence and consistency of their world view. The points they make about human nature, war and so on, and on which they base their claim that balance in a states system is the only way to secure order, usually derive their power from this central assumption of a *necessarily* divided human essence. The fault lies not in ourselves but in our stars. Yet Augustine did not believe that, nor does Niebuhr. Christians cannot, in one sense, *have* a strong sense of the tragic, for the possibility of redemption is ever present. Even if they accept (as I think Niebuhr does) both theses, the 'tragic' implications someone like Morgenthau draws from them are absent.

But in that case, it seems to me, you have what amounts to weaker and stronger versions of the classical realist case. In the stronger version, order is permanently precarious and always fragile because everything is. Thus a balance between forces, between powers and perhaps a hard-fought delaying action against the irrevocability of ultimate defeat is all that can be hoped for. On this view there is no 'solution' to the problem of order. It is simply an endless problem, with an infinite number of possible manifestations and an endless set of possible ways in which the various aspects of any context can be 'balanced'. This is the realism, I would say, of Weber, of Morgenthau and, at bottom at least, of Kissinger.

The weaker version, by contrast, suggests that although politics is indeed finite and limited, there are ways forward that might not be merely bound one day to fail, but that such ways depend upon international order and *that in the contemporary context*, this is best secured by the balance of power. This is the realism of Niebuhr, and of Christian realism in general, and it shares a good deal, as we will see in a moment, with the 'conservative' English school.

Note, however, the difference in the view of balance in each case. For the stronger view, balance is, whatever its specific context (balance of power, balance of forces), almost an existential condition of politics as such. It is perhaps not fanciful to see in this view something of an echo of the infamous claim of Carl Schmitt that politics is about friend/enemy relations and that liberalism will fail because it never recognizes the fact of the inevitability of conflict. Schmitt was, of course, but a powerful influence on Morgenthau, though someone about whom Morgenthau was bitter even fifty years later. In the shadow of Schmitt and Weber, Morgenthau's realism seeks to find one way that politics can be rescued from the inevitability of constant strife; and the one way he finds is through the notion of balance, ambiguous and tenuous though that is.

For the explicitly Christian realist, however, or perhaps simply for more optimistic or liberal ones (perhaps like the 'realist liberals' Herz and Aron), balance is a tool, a necessary mechanism to a greater good, but in no sense a good in itself. For these realists, perhaps like Buzan, Jones and Little above, circumstances will dictate the centrality of balance as a tool of statecraft and the extent to which it can be combined with other things. There is nothing inevitable about it and it is certainly not a condition of politics as such.

Seeing realism in International Relations in this way, I think, suggests that both realism and the ideas of balance particularly associated with it are highly unstable at the close of the twentieth century. And this is where revisionists like Murray come in. What I called Murray's 'Augustinian pragmatism' seeks effectively to split the difference between the weaker and stronger versions. 'Balance' is indeed an existential condition, in that 'our values' are always being negotiated and renegotiated and in that sense the 'balancing' we do to support them is a constant and permanent feature of our political lives. However, advances can be made and there is no sense in Murray's reformulation of realism of the 'tragic' element that he (rightly) detects in earlier versions. By replacing the 'transcendental' assumptions of a Morgenthau with the resolutely pragmatist ones of a Rorty, Murray destroys the sense of tragedy whilst retaining the sense of limits and fragility.

Yet it is not clear to me, at least, that this graft will take. Like many hybrids, this one is inherently unstable, likely to collapse into versions of cultural relativism, simple *machtpolitik* or a combination of the two. What held Morgenthau's realism together was a sense of *ineliminable* tension, as Murray rightly notes, but this tension was a creature of the belief in a core of values that were true necessarily and transcendentally. Without that, the tension dissolves, and what is one left with? Thus, even the classical realist synthesis, so brilliantly deployed by the Morgenthaus and the Kennans, is now on the verge of being an impossibility.

This, however, opens up the possibility that twenty-first-century 'realism' will revert to a version of a much more cynical *machtpolitik*, without traditional realism's moral depth, neo-realism's technical virtuosity and quite possibly no longer tied to the state – cyberpunk versions of the so-called new Middle Ages thesis. A variant of this can, I think, be found in some fashionable millennial worries such as the essay (later book) penned by Robert Kaplan entitled 'The Coming Anarchy'.[84] A still more insidious version is that which lies at the heart, on my reading at least, of Straussian political theory and practice,[85] and which is also growing in influence, especially in the United States. However, these developments have yet to take a definitive form. They are simply shadows of what 'realism' might become, without the normative frameworks that sustained traditional realism and assuming the waning of the higher sterility that neo-realism now threatens to become.

On this view, the failure of IR theory (and practice, indeed) to solve 'the problem of order' is actually the key to the *real* problem. For the likes of Kaplan, *all* attempts to 'create order' have actually been trying to deal with a problem that was always going to overwhelm them eventually, a view to which the more pessimistic traditional realists – like Kissinger – also inclined.

There are a wide range of variants of this view, of course, and it has a pronounced pedigree.[86] Historically, perhaps its strongest versions have been outlined by historians like Jacob Burckhardt, philosophers like Schopenhauer and Heidegger, pessimists like Oswald Spengler[87] and perhaps most presciently and powerfully of all by the thinker who became, I think, the ghost who haunted that most protean of modern realists, Hans Morgenthau, most: Carl Schmitt.[88]

The leitmotif of this view is a – more or less permanent – sense of crisis, conflict, decline and/or overambition. In a recent study of the idea of decline in Western history Arthur Herman[89] has suggested that this tradition itself has two faces, which he terms 'historical' and 'cultural' pessimism. The central division is visible in the differences between a historical pessimist such as Burckhardt, convinced that 'society' – in this case Western civilization itself – is too weak to save itself, but thinking that this is a tragedy and still worshipping at what Herman calls the 'shrine of the old society', and a cultural pessimist like Nietzsche, convinced that society is doomed and that it is a good thing that it is, that only when society has truly collapsed will some form of transformation be possible.

Historical pessimism has much in common with various forms of conservatism in twentieth-century thought, including at least aspects of realism, and also with the general sense of cultural malaise that obsessed many thinkers at the end of the last century, not least the great Max Weber himself. In its more benign forms it has issued in an emphasis on the importance of limits for the human project – a particular theme in some of the most pertinent conservative writing of the twentieth century.[90] Its emphasis on not overreaching ourselves – whoever the 'we' might be – on the necessary limits to human powers and aims and on the impossibility of securing 'order' at perhaps any level is less visible in explicit writing on international relations than might be expected; nonetheless its echoes abound (echoes of it can also be found in the writings of some of the English school, especially Butterfield, who will be my concern in the next chapter).

The alternative, of course, is the attempt to yoke realism – and balance – to something else, social constructivism, naturalism, liberalism, even post-structuralism,[91] with which in important and interesting ways traditional realisms, at least, turn out to have quite a bit in common.[92] In either of these versions, however, 'balance' seems likely to be at best a part, and certainly not the whole, of any approach to order in and for the twenty-first century. In that sense, the close of the twentieth century will also see, I suspect, the dwindling of the balance of power in terms of the grip it exerts and so, to borrow a phrase of A.J.P. Taylor, what he called the 'perpetual quadrille' of the balance of power does perhaps appear, finally, to be slowing down.

Notes

1   David Hume, *Essays* [*The balance of power*] (London: Routledge, 1907), p. 240.
2   The view that the characteristics of the European states system, and perhaps of other states systems in history that resemble it (such as the Greek system, the Italian city states of the Renaissance and the Chinese system during the so-called 'Warring states'

period), is, as we shall see in Chapter 2, especially associated with the so-called 'English school' in IR theory, and especially with the work of Martin Wight. There are many reasons for doubting that things are, in fact, this simple but I shall not go into this in detail here. We can say that, at the very least, in states systems that resemble one another something like the balance of power is held to appear, at least at intervals. Few have doubted that whatever might be the case more generally, it certainly did operate in the European states system at its zenith and was perceived to be operating for much of the twentieth century, and indeed, still is, according to some. For a defence of the view that states systems are different from other kinds of systems and that there have been a number of recognizably similar examples, see Martin Wight, *Systems of States* (Leicester: Leicester University Press, 1977).

3   And, indeed, a long tradition of writers have used the notion of balance as part and parcel of political understanding *tout court*. See for example Thucydides, *History*. It is also worth saying that a good deal of very modern IR theory is beginning to explore these themes once more. Kenneth Waltz, for example, in a recently published interview remarks that the theory says 'whenever conditions are such … this will apply' (Fred Halliday and Justin Rosenberg, 'An Interview with Ken Waltz', *Review of International Studies*, 1998, 24(3): 371–86). See also, for a different reading of the issue, Helen Milner, *Interests, Institutions and Cooperation: Domestic Politics and International Relations* (Princeton, NJ: Princeton University Press, 1998).

4   The classic statement of geopolitics, widely cited these days, but alas little read, is Halford Mackinder's 'The Geographical Pivot of History', *Royal Geographical Society Journal*, 1904, later amended and developed in his *Democratic Ideals and Reality* (New York: Henry Holt, 1919). His most important nineteenth-century precursor was Alfred Thayer Mahan, whose *The Influence of Sea Power upon History, 1660–1783* (Boston: Little Brown, 1890) was in part the target of Mackinder's arguments. Other central texts in geopolitics include John Seeley's celebrated *The Expansion of England* (Chicago: University of Chicago Press, 1971[1888]), Vidal de la Blanche, *Principles of Human Geography* (London: Constable, 1936), Nicholas Spykman, *America's Strategy in World Politics* (New York: Harcourt Brace, 1942), L. Struasz-Hupe, *Geopolitics* (New York: Putnams, 1942).

5   It has remained very much a living tradition in Europe more generally, particularly in France and Russia. A number of Anglo-American scholars and practitioners have also retained an affection for it as a term and, to varying degrees, as a tool, the most celebrated being, of course, Henry Kissinger, but his great rival, Zbigniew Brezinski, is equally convinced of the significance of geopolitical realities. Among scholars, Colin Gray has perhaps been the most consistent advocate of geopolitics in mainstream scholarship on international relations, though others, like Gerry Segal, have also continued to use the term. Amongst more radical international theorists, Daniel Deudney has provided perhaps the best recent statement. See, *inter alia*, Henry Kissinger, *Diplomacy* (New York: Simon and Schuster, 1994), Zbigniew Brezinski, *The Grand Chessboard: American Primacy and its Geostrategic Imperatives* (New York: Basic Books, 1997), Colin Gray, *The Geopolitics of Superpower* (Lexington, KY: University of Kentucky Press, 1988), and *War, Peace and Victory: Strategy and Statecraft for the Next Century* (Oxford, 1991), Gerry Segal and Daniel Deudney, 'Geopolitics and Change', in Michael Doyle and G. John Ikenberry (eds), *New Thinking in International Relations Theory* (Boulder, CO: Westview Press, 1997). In France geopolitics has remained central.

6   In their jointly edited book *Diplomatic Investigations* (London: George Allen and Unwin, 1966).

7   See especially his most famous work *Power Politics*, and especially the second edition edited by Hedley Bull and Carsten Holbrad after Wight's death: Wight, *Power Politics* (London: Macmillan, 1992).

8   For a classic typology of realist thinkers and practitioners, developed by the one figure who was most distinguished in both fields, see Henry Kissinger, *Diplomacy.*

9   Curiously enough, considering its provenance, there is no standard history of 'realist' thought which seeks to identify these thinkers truly as 'realists'. Realists are usually content with a cursory reference or two. The exception includes scholars like Smith, Rosenthal and Murray who are very clear that 'realism' in any identifiable sense is a twentieth-century idea whatever past thinkers or ideas shaped it.

10   Some discussions of the appropriateness of the historical lineage can be found in Chris Brown, Terry Nardin and N. J. Rengger (eds), *Texts in International Relations* (Cambridge: Cambridge University Press, forthcoming).

11   For good discussions of twentieth-century realism – and some sceptical comments about it – see Michael Joseph Smith, *Realist Thought from Weber to Kissinger* (Baton Rouge, LA: Louisiana State University Press, 1986), Joel Rosenthal, *Righteous Realists: Responsible Power and American Culture in the Nuclear Age* (Baton Rouge, LA: Louisiana State University Press, 1991), Alastair Murray, 'Reconstructing Realism', PhD Thesis (University of Bristol, 1996) – a revised version of the thesis has now been published as *Reconstructing Realism* (Keele: Keele University Press, 1997), and references to Murray's argument here are taken from this version – and Justin Rosenberg, *The Empire of Civil Society: A Critique of the Realist Theory of International Relations* (London: Verso, 1994).

12   The usual source of this is Weber's very well-known essay 'Politics as a Vocation'. The German version is much the best version to consult given that the most common English translations are not, in my view, always very accurate. This can be found in Weber's *Gesammelte Politische Schriften* (Munich, 1921), pp. 396–450. The recent Cambridge University Press version of Weber's *Political Writings* (1992) is the best English version, in my opinion. For commentaries on Weber which discuss his thinking about international relations, the most interesting of a large batch, in my view, are David Beetham, *Max Weber and the Theory of Modern Politics* (London; Allen and Unwin, 1974), Wolfgang Mommsen, *Max Weber und die Deutsche Politik, 1890–1920* (Tubingen: Mohr, 1959), Michael Smith, *Realist Thought from Weber to Kissinger*, Raymond Aron, 'Max Weber and Power Politics', in Otto Stammer (ed.), *Max Weber and Sociology Today* (New York: Harper Torchbooks, 1971), Lawrence Scaff, *Fleeing the Iron Cage* (Berkeley, CA: University of California Press, 1989), Karl Löwith, *Marx and Weber* (London: Routledge, 1992).

13   For good discussions of these writers, usually and pejoratively (and in my view also wrongly) referred to as the 'idealists', see Peter Wilson and David Long (eds), *Thinkers of the Twenty Years Crisis* (Oxford: Clarendon Press, 1996).

14   It is worth pointing out here that Carr is becoming something of a bone of contention in contemporary international theory. That he was critical of the 'idealists' is undoubtedly true. That he was not a 'realist', in the manner of Morgenthau, Kennan or Niebuhr – or even Wight and Butterfield – is equally true. Some – for example, Ken Booth and Andrew Linklater – have recently argued with some plausibility that Carr's work has a good deal in common with what would now be called 'emancipatory' IR theory, which we will look at in Chapter 4. In any event, I shall not discuss Carr in this chapter. For all his influence on realism, his assumptions seem to me to be rather distant from the concerns that have chiefly characterized realist writing for most of this century. For discussions of the 'revisionist case', see Andrew Linklater, 'The Transformation of Political Community: E. H. Carr, Critical Theory and International Relations', *Review of International Studies*, 1997, and Ken Booth, 'Security in Anarchy: Utopian Realism in Theory and Practice', *International Affairs*, 1991, 67: 527–45.

15   On Acheson's realism see his memoirs, *Morning and Noon* (Boston: Houghton Mifflin, 1965) and *Present at the Creation* (New York: Norton, 1969). An unusual but engrossing

account of Acheson can be found in Walter Isaacson and Evan Thomas, *The Wise Men: Six Friends and the World They Made* (New York: Simon and Schuster, 1986).

16 Arnold Wolfers' major book was *Discord and Collaboration: Essays on International Politics* (Baltimore, MD: Johns Hopkins University Press, 1962).

17 See his argument in 'An American Social Science: International Relations', *Daedalus*, 1977, CVI: Summer.

18 This is true for example of Morgenthau, of Kissinger, and of a number of other prominent realists – or quasi-realists – such as Arnold Wolfers and John Herz. It is also true, of course, of Hoffmann himself, though no realist he!

19 Though it is also worth noting that Morgenthau was both seen and saw himself as something of an 'outsider' in US academic circles. Most of his close friendships were with exiles like himself (most notably Hannah Arendt, to whom he eventually proposed and to whom he was both personally and intellectually very close), and his most influential book in international relations, *Politics among Nations: The Struggle for Power and Peace* (Chicago: University of Chicago Press, 1948 [1st edition]), was not amongst his favourites. I shall say more about this aspect of Morgenthau's thought in a moment. An excellent discussion of the relationship between Morgenthau and Arendt can be found in Elizabeth Young-Breuhl's excellent biography of Arendt, *For Love of the World* (New Haven, CT: Yale University Press, 1988).

20 For a masterful survey of the evolution of this latter term in the language of early modern political thought see Quentin Skinner, *The Foundations of Modern Political Thought*, 2 vols (Cambridge: Cambridge University Press, 1978). See also Friedrich Meinecke's classic *Die Idee der Staatsrason*, well translated by D. Scott as *Machiavelism: The Doctrine of Raison D'état and its Place in History* (London: Westview Press, 1984).

21 Michael Smith, *Realist Thought from Weber to Kissinger*, pp. 1–2.

22 Especially Murray and Rosenthal.

23 Smith, *Realist Thought*, p. 219.

24 Smith, *Realist Thought*, p. 220.

25 The phrase is Morgenthau's from *Politics among Nations*, quoted by Smith, *Realist Thought*, p. 220.

26 There will be many, doubtless, who will be surprised at this claim, so deep has the caricature of realism eaten into the soul of much modern political thought. The best recent commentators on realism, Smith, Rosenthal and Murray, all emphasize the point that the realists were far from being immune to the desirability, even the necessity, of radical change in world politics.

27 *Around the Cragged Hill: A Personal and Political Philosophy* (New York: Norton, 1993).

28 Morgenthau, *Scientific Man versus Power Politics*, p. 203. See also the discussion of this passage in Murray, *Reconstructing Realism*, p. 179.

29 Morgenthau, *American Foreign Policy* (London; Methuen, 1952), p. 98. This book is usually better known under its US title, *In Defence of the National Interest* (New York: Knopf, 1951). Again see Murray's discussion in *Reconstructing Realism*, p. 131.

30 A point he makes in *The Children of Light and the Children of Darkness* (London: Nisbett, 1945), p. 123.

31 In *Reconstructing Realism*.

32 As Murray argues, the dependence of this argument on an Augustinian framework is obvious and acknowledged by Niebuhr.

33 Murray, *Reconstructing Realism*, p. 181.

34 Detailed, and excellent, discussions can be found in Smith, *Realist Thought*, Rosenthal, *Righteous Realists*, and Murray, *Reconstructing Realism*.

35 Smith, *Realist Thought*, p. 144.

36 Morgenthau, 'The Evil of Politics and the Ethics of Evil', *Ethics*, 1945, Vol. 56. See also Murray, *Reconstructing Realism*.

37 This is one of the points which obviously links the realists with the English school that I will look at in the next chapter. Murray, in *Reconstructing Realism*, goes so far as to link

Butterfield, the first chair of the British Committee on the Theory of International Politics, with the realists. I would not go this far; there remained strong differences between, say, Niebuhr and Morgenthau on the one hand and Butterfield and Wight on the other. However, that there were many points of contact is also true. See also Morgenthau's appreciation of Wight in *Truth and Power: Essays of a Decade* (New York: Praeger, 1970).

38 (Chicago: University of Chicago Press, 1946).
39 It is worth pointing out here that this placed Morgenthau in a pronounced minority to most of his colleagues at the University of Chicago, in Political Science at least. There the rise of scientific styles of politics was championed amongst the professors of public administration and international law who dominated the department – one thinks immediately of Quincy Wright, whose mammoth *A Study of War* (Chicago: University of Chicago Press) also first appeared in 1942.
40 New York: Columbia University Press, 1959.
41 Reading, MA: Addison-Wesley, 1979.
42 Barry Buzan, 'The Levels of Analysis Problem Reconsidered', in Ken Booth and Steve Smith (eds), *International Relations Theory Today* (Cambridge: Polity Press, 1994).
43 Though it is worth pointing out that other writers, for example David Singer, who could certainly not be called a disciple of Waltz' were equally influential. See especially his two key essays, 'International Conflict: Three Levels of Analysis', *World Politics*, 1960, 12(3): 453–61, and 'The Levels of Analysis Problem in International Relations', in K. Knorr and S. Verba (eds), *The International System: Theoretical Essays* (Princeton, NJ: Princeton University Press, 1961).
44 Waltz was originally trained as, and expected to become, a 'traditional' political theorist. As fishermen say, the ones that get away are always the biggest!
45 The key chapter here is Waltz, *Theory of International Politics*, chapter 2.
46 Waltz, *Theory of International Politics*, p. 65. See also the discussion of this passage in M. Hollis and S. Smith, *Explaining and Understanding International Relations* (Oxford: Clarendon Press, 1990), p. 106.
47 It is worth pointing out that this view of Waltz' long predates *Theory of International Politics*. See his 'The Stability of a Bi-polar World', *Daedalus*, 1964, 93: 881–909.
48 Waltz' case for controlled proliferation was first put in an *Adelphi* paper for the International Institute for Strategic Studies, 'The Spread of Nuclear Weapons: More may be Better', *Adelphi*, 1981, No. 171. He has amended and modified this position over the years, in various articles, but still holds to it. His fullest exposition of the view has come in a debate with Scott Sagan, see Sagan and Waltz, *The Spread of Nuclear Weapons: A Debate*. It is worth emphasizing, as Waltz himself has recently done (in his interview with Halliday and Rosenberg cited above), that the point is that the *rapid* proliferation would be destabilizing, which is why, Waltz says, he talked of the 'spread' of nuclear weapons rather than the proliferation of nuclear weapons in his original *Adelphi* paper.
49 Krasner's particular strengths are well on display, for example, in his *Structural Conflict: The Third World against Global Liberalism* (Berkeley, CA: University of California Press, 1985). I should emphasize, of course, that Krasner is no mere clone of Waltz. His own work prior to the appearance of *Theory of International Politics* – for example, his *Defending the National Interest* (Princeton, NJ: Princeton University Press, 1978) – was a sophisticated and powerful elaboration of some traditional realist themes. However, he certainly has far more in common with Waltz than with the earlier generation of realists.
50 Representative samples of Grieco's work would include, 'Anarchy and the Limits of Cooperation: A realist critique of the newest liberal institutionalism', *International Organization*, 1988, Vol. 42, and *Cooperation among Nations* (Ithaca, NY: Cornell University Press, 1990).

51 I merely point out that he has also been involved in another controversy on an entirely different front: to wit, his biography of the British soldier and military thinker and writer, Basil Liddell-Hart, which has been widely attacked as being unfair to Liddell-Hart. Needless to say, Mearsheimer gives as good as he gets!

52 Without doubt the best known piece of Mearsheimer's is his 1990 article, 'Back to the Future: Instability in Europe after the cold war', *International Security*, 1990, 15: 4–57. This was debated for some time thereafter, with Mearsheimer taking on some of the major paladins of (various forms of) liberalism in international relations; see S. Hoffmann, R. Keohane and J. Mearsheimer, 'Back to the Future part 2: International relations theory and post cold war Europe', *International Security*, 1990, Vol. 15, and B. Russett, Thomas Risse-Kappen and John Mearsheimer, 'Back to the Future part 3: Realism and the realities of European Security', *International Security*, 1990/91, Vol. 15. Not content with this, however, Mearsheimer returned to the attack four years later with another article, 'The False Promise of International Institutions', *International Security*, 1994–5, 19: 5–49, which sparked an equally vitriolic debate which dragged in some of the newer constructivist theorists, including Alex Wendt, that we will examine in the next chapter.

53 Ithaca, NY: Cornell University Press, 1986.

54 Ithaca, NY: Cornell University Press, 1996.

55 Waltz has repeated many times, most recently in the interview with Halliday and Rosenberg cited above, that for him 'theory' has a very specific sense, one derived from certain debates in the philosophy of science. For instance, 'theory' is not the same as 'interpretation', and theories are about explaining some *particular* thing (not, in other words, everything). Thus his theory explains the international system (i.e. what it is about) but certainly does not explain the whole of international relations.

56 For a wide variety of 'realist' approaches that I shall not discuss here in detail see Benjamin Frankel's two edited books, *Realism: Restatements and Renewal* and *Roots of Realism* (both Ilford: Frank Cass, 1996).

57 See their *The Logic of Anarchy* (New York: Columbia University Press, 1993). See also the forthcoming jointly authored book by Buzan and Little, *The International System: Theory Meets History* (Oxford: Clarendon Press, forthcoming).

58 In addition to these writers I cannot forbear to mention that amongst the more influential – at least in the United States – versions of what is, ultimately, a form of realism at least is that developed by the friends, allies and students of the late Leo Strauss. This account is all the more remarkable for having almost no presence in the contemporary academic study of International Relations – one or two individuals excepted – though it has had really rather a profound impact on some US policy-makers. The character of this 'realism' is extremely heterodox and is generally expressed, as is usual with 'Straussian' political theory, in terms of commentaries upon the great texts of political (and international) thought, another one of the reasons why its presence in self-conscious IR theory is virtually nil. Since this book is largely concerned with 'self-conscious IR theory', I will spend no longer on this version of realism here. However, I should emphasize that it is, in my view, extremely powerful, extremely influential (outside 'IR theory', that is), extremely interesting and about as profoundly mistaken as it is possible to be. I shall return to this view briefly in a moment.

59 Brighton: Harvester, 1983; 2nd edition, 1991.

60 Especially, but not limited to, Ole Wæver.

61 The major statements of the school are O. Wæver, B. Buzan, Morton Kelstrup and Pierre Lemaitre with David Carlton, *Identity, Migration and the new Security Agenda in Europe* (London: Pinter, 1993), and Buzan, Wæver and Jaap de Wilde, *Security: A New Framework for Analysis* (Boulder, CO: Lynne Rienner, 1997). For debates over the school see Bill McSweeny, 'Identity and Security: Buzan and the Copenhagen School', *Review of International Studies*, 1996, 22: 81–93; Barry Buzan and Ole Wæver,

'Slippery? Contradictory? Sociologically Untenable? The Copenhagen school replies', *Review of International Studies*, 1997, 23: 241–50; Bill Mcsweeny, 'Durkheim and the Copenhagen School: A response to Buzan and Wæver', *Review of International Studies*, 1998, 24: 137–40.

62 It is worth pointing out that both these books are co-authored, the former with Eric Herring and the latter with Gerry Segal, so obviously the co-authors have at least as much right to be considered. In this context though it is interesting that while Segal is clearly a realist of sorts (perhaps, like Herz and Aron, a liberal realist), Herring would most certainly not claim to be one. However, Herring's own previous work in the security field shows the powerful impact of US styles of – largely realist inclined – security studies, however much his conclusions dissent from theirs. See Eric Herring and Barry Buzan, *The Arms Dynamics in World Politics* (Boulder: Lynne Reinner, 1998) and Barry Buzan and Gerald Segal, *Anticipating the Future: Twenty Millennia of Human Progress* (New York: Simon and Schuster, 1998).

63 *Intervention: External Involvement in Civil Wars* (London: Martin Robertson, 1976).

64 See R. Little and M. Smith (eds), *Perspectives on World Politics* (London: Croom Helm, 1976; 2nd edition, Routledge, 1990).

65 *Logic of Anarchy*, p. 11.

66 *Logic of Anarchy*, p. 12.

67 *Logic of Anarchy*, p. 245.

68 *Logic of Anarchy*, p. 245. This refers to their forthcoming book, *The International System: Theory Meets History* (Oxford: Clarendon Press, forthcoming). They have already outlined some aspects of this thesis in a series of articles: see, for example, Buzan and Little, 'The Idea of International System: Theory Meets History', *The International Political Science Review*, 1994, 15(3): 231–55.

69 It is also worth noting that both Little and Buzan have displayed a considerable warmth towards the English school in some of their more recent work.

70 See Roger Spegele, *Political Realism in International Theory* (Cambridge: Cambridge University Press, 1996), p. 14. Spegele's book is his summation to date of a number of previous articles through which he developed his heterodox realism. I shall only refer to the book here.

71 The following is all taken from the conclusion to his book, pp. 230–44.

72 Spegele, *Political Realism in International Theory*, p. 132.

73 Spegele, *Political Realism in International Theory*, p. 159.

74 As I indicated in the acknowledgements to this book, I was the supervisor of Al Murray's thesis. It might seem, therefore, an especially brazen piece of special pleading for me to discuss his work in this context. However, his work does seem to me to be a particularly interesting reformulation of realism and thus it seems appropriate to discuss its implications here.

75 Murray, *Reconstructing Realism*, p. 8.

76 Murray, *Reconstructing Realism*, p. 12.

77 Murray, *Reconstructing Realism*, pp. 18–19.

78 Murray, *Reconstructing Realism*, p. 246.

79 Spegele, *Political Realism in International Theory*, p. 150.

80 I should add, of course, that I am well aware that this description, certainly of Thucydides, would be contestable, but I hope to make good on it in later work.

81 George Santayana, *Dominations and Powers: Reflections on Liberty, Society and Government* ([1950] New Jersey: Transaction Books, 1995). Again, I hope to offer an extended reflection on Santayana on another occasion.

82 Santayana, *Dominations and Powers*, p. xxii.

83 As with natural law, Heidegger etc., this view is not one I discuss in detail here. As I say, another occasion.

84 Kaplan, 'The Coming Anarchy', *Atlantic Monthly*. The book is entitled *The Ends of the Earth: A Journey at the Dawn of the Twenty First Century*.

85 Picking up an earlier point, on my reading – I accept this reading would be contro-
    versial – the political theorist Leo Strauss – also, significantly, a pupil and then
    collaborator of Carl Schmitt – developed a view of life which is/was radically
    nihilistic, in that his view was that life has no meaning, that such radical absence can
    only be understood and accommodated by the few true 'philosophers'. Such knowl-
    edge is inevitably dangerous to any or all societies for it robs people of the comforting
    belief in God/gods, value, patriotism, etc. At the same time, such a recognition would
    destroy the possibility of the fortunate few to enjoy the one thing that might make life
    bearable: intellectual adventure and excitement for which society has to create and
    sustain the institutional and epistemic setting. Thus, for Strauss, philosophy must
    become 'political' – the real meaning of the classical term 'political philosophy' – in
    that it must 'hide' the truth and habituate others – especially the political elite – to the
    job of ordinary politics through the fostering of 'noble lies' about the importance of
    the gods, the value of patriotism, etc., whilst at the same time recruiting the truly
    talented genuine philosophers and revealing the truth to them, much as Socrates
    inspired and 'habituated' the – traditional and political – young Adeimantus and
    converted and 'recruited' the – brilliant, radical and potentially tyrannical – young
    Glaucon in Plato's *Republic* (on a Straussian reading, of course).
       These views would be largely irrelevant to a book like this one except for the
    growing influence 'Straussians' are having on (especially) US public and academic
    life. A number of prominent and active conservative political figures in the United
    States – William Kristol Jr, and William Bennet, to name but two of the best known –
    are Straussians and a number of other influential conservative commentators or
    essayists are fellow travellers, as it were. Perhaps the best known of these is Francis
    Fukuyama, who was trained by Strauss's best known – and probably most charismatic
    – student Allan Bloom, in whose John M. Olin Center for the Theory and Practice of
    Democracy at the University of Chicago, a good deal of the *End of History and the Last
    Man* was written. Most of the public figures who have acknowledged their indebted-
    ness to Strauss are, I would argue, Adeimantus not Glaucons. It is the academics,
    Bloom himself, Harvey Mansfield, Thomas Pangle and others who are the 'philoso-
    phers'; the others are the 'gentlemen' (these are Strauss' terms) who require
    habituating. The point, however, is a strongly conservative politics, autocratic in
    content, if not usually in form, and strongly 'realist' in foreign policy terms in the
    usual assumption of that phrase; amoral, concerned with force, fraud and power. For
    whatever might be the case internally in a state (good things in some sense if run by
    properly habituated statesmen) international politics is indeed a war of all against all
    in which anything is permitted. It is also a convenient way of 'siphoning off', as it
    were, the destructive impulses that otherwise might create havoc within polities.
       I should emphasize that this is a very schematic reading of a very complex and at
    times deliberately obscure set of views and that much more room than I have at my
    disposal here would be required to establish my case convincingly. I should also add
    that nothing I have said here detracts from the power that Strauss himself, as well as
    some of his better students, display in their interpretations of particular texts in the
    history of ideas – their usual mode of expression. These are often excellent, indeed
    inspiring, studies.
       The most sustained and powerful treatment of Strauss, his influence and the
    growing power of his ideas in the United States, which I am happy to acknowledge
    has influenced my own reading, though it is overly polemical for my taste, is offered
    by Shadia Drury in three books: *The Political Ideas of Leo Strauss* (London: Macmillan,
    1988), *Alexandre Kojeve: The Roots of Postmodern Politics* (London: Macmillan, 1995) and
    Leo Strauss and the American Right (London: Macmillan, 1998). I have discussed Strauss
    in some detail, though not as critically as I now would, in *Political Theory, Modernity and
    Postmodernity: Beyond Enlightenment and Critique* (Oxford: Blackwell, 1995).

86 Again, I cite the work of Leo Strauss and his friends and colleagues. However, a full discussion of this must await another occasion.

87 Representative works would include Burckhardt, *Force and Freedom*, ed. J. H. Nicholls (New York: Meridian Books, 1955), and *On History and Historians*, trans. H. Zohn (New York: Harper and Row, 1965); Schopenhauer, *Essays and Aphorisms*, trans. R. J. Hollingdale (Harmondsworth: Penguin, 1976).

88 For the best general discussion of Schmitt in English see John P. McCormick, *Carl Schmitt's Critique of Liberalism: Against Politics as Technology* (Cambridge: Cambridge University Press, 1997). Even this excellent book, however, sees Morgenthau as, effectively, a disciple of Schmitt. In fact, Morgenthau saw himself as Schmitt's arch opponent. Whether he was successful is, of course, a matter of opinion, but realism in Morgenthau's hands becomes not so much the carry-over of Schmitt's thought but its nemesis, by recognizing its force and subordinating it yet to constitutionalism. Those who want a full account of the relationship between Schmitt and Morgenthau and the extent to which Morgenthau's version of realism is a critique of Schmitt, however, will have to await the publication of my research student Mitchell Rologas's doctoral thesis.

89 Herman, *The Idea of Decline in Western History* (New York: Free Press, 1997).

90 For an extended discussion of the interrelationship between conservatism and the notion of a politics of 'limits' see Noel O'Sullivan, *Conservatism* (London: Dent, 1976). Perhaps the most influential, and certainly the most stylish, advocate of this position has been Michael Oakeshott. See especially his *magnum opus*, *On Human Conduct* (Oxford: Clarendon Press, 1975), though it is visible in many of his influential essays and lectures as well.

91 I have already mentioned the affiliation of some post-structuralists to traditional realism. For an interesting spin on this see Francis Beer and Robert Hariman (eds), *Post-Realism: The Rhetorical Turn in International Relations* (Minneapolis: University of Minnesota Press, 1996).

92 Not, perhaps, particularly surprising, given the influence of Nietzsche, post-structuralism's presiding deity, on Weber and Weber on realism.

2 Society

As I remarked in the Introduction, for most of the modern era the European experience of international relations has been profoundly ambivalent. As Stanley Hoffmann has put it, European thinking about international relations has tended to oscillate between seeing it as, in Rousseau's famous phrase, 'a state of war' and seeing it as a 'troubled peace'. If those who see balance as the key to order express, in however moderated a way, the view that international relations is a state of war, then the alternative view, that it is a troubled peace, has tended to be the view, first, of those who are often, in IR theory, referred to as 'Grotians' and, second, and more radically, of liberals. Both 'Grotians' and liberals have always placed greater weight than realists on the role international institutions do (as well as might) play in international affairs. However, as I also remarked in the Introduction, they have also differed between themselves as to the precise form and role of such institutions and just how, and to what degree, they might be able to secure order.

This difference has been recently exacerbated by the increasing dominance within some forms of liberal thinking – especially that dominant in Political Science and International Relations – of methodological and epistemological assumptions derived from economics, essentially the 'rationalist' mode of argument we met in the Introduction. An older tradition of thinking about international relations, however, has always been hostile to such moves, as have in more moderated ways influential newer forms of 'societal' thinking.

However, 'Grotians' do emphasize that order must be seen as parasitic on society, a sense of shared involvement and participation; a common, if attenuated, communal sense that seems perpetually present in international politics. Initially a ghostly echo of the old medieval idea of the *Respublica Christiana*, the idea is passed on to the idea of 'Europe',[1] then to the idea of the family of 'civilized' nations[2] and perhaps finally to what is today referred to as the 'international' (or global) community. In contemporary IR theory, this idea is perhaps most often referred to as a belief in the existence of an 'international society' – a 'society' that is more than *simply* an interacting system – and it is this notion above all others that the so-called 'English school' of international relations theory[3] – the chief champions of the 'Grotian' approach in the modern academy – have sought to delineate, define and develop. This approach has traditionally seen the *fact* of international society as central to the existence and maintenance of international order. It thus offers what we might term a 'societal' reading of the problem (and answer to the problem) of order.

However, of late a growing number of other scholars have increasingly come around to the view that international relations is a 'society of sorts' or at least that 'social construction' is very important to it; that its 'societal' character is central to our understanding of it. The most common term for this approach in IR theory is 'constructivist'. Although these scholars do not see things in quite the same way as the English school, the latter is an acknowledged influence on the former and there is increasingly some overlap as a number of younger members from each approach seek to draw the two closer together. This development also builds on some of the revisionist realist writing referred to above (e.g. that of Buzan, Jones and Little).

Thus, this chapter will look at both English school and constructivist thinking; for both suggest that it is in the 'social' character of international relations that any lasting solution to the problem of order will be found. Constructivist accounts of international relations in particular are now growing very rapidly and, according to some, they now represent a 'third way' between realist and liberal approaches.[4] Thus the chapter will close with an assessment of the plausibility of this view.

International society and international relations

We will start, then, with the English school itself, and with the notion of the 'society of states' and the conceptions of world order it develops. In its contemporary form the English school's approach to international society has been most powerfully shaped by Hedley Bull. Stanley Hoffmann has suggested that it is with the notion of international society that Bull, in fact, came into his own as a theorist of international relations:

> it is society rather than system which he, virtually alone among contemporary theorists of international affairs, stresses and studies. System means contact between states and the impact of one state on another; society means (in Bull's words) common interests and values, common rules and institutions.[5]

In this, however, Bull was following the lead established by Martin Wight.[6] For Wight, the idea of international society, found in past political thinkers as varied as Suarez, de Toqueville, de Visscher and Burke, is best defined as 'the habitual intercourse of independent communities, beginning in the Christendom of Western Europe and gradually extending throughout the world'.[7] The nature of this society, Wight goes on to argue, is

> manifest in the diplomatic system; in the conscious maintenance of the balance of power to preserve the independence of the member communi-

ties; in the regular operations of international law; in economic, social and technical interdependence and the functional international institutions established to regulate it. All these presuppose an international social consciousness, a world wide community sentiment.[8]

In Bull and Watson's edited collection, *The Expansion of International Society*, which can almost be read as an extended elaboration of Wight's argument, Bull identifies the First World War as the time by which 'international society', previously primarily self-consciously Eurocentric, had become a universal international society, and the period following the Second World War as that in which attempts were made 'to transform a universal society of states into one of peoples'.[9] Wight, however, implies that international society as he understood it accepted that states were not its exclusive members and suggests that it is only in the eighteenth century, with Wolff and Vattel, that there was seen to be a problem with the ascription of international rights to actors with, as it were, non-state personalities. Moreover, this transition was not, Wight believes, entirely eclipsed by the rise of the notion of state personality, expressed in more recent times by, amongst others, international lawyers such as James Brierly.[10]

In *The Anarchical Society*, Bull builds on Wight's argument, but departs from it in subtle but important ways. For Bull, the idea of international society is conceived by the natural law tradition of the sixteenth to the eighteenth century, most prominently, Vitoria, Suarez, Gentili, Grotius, and Pufendorf.[11] This period of international society, according to Bull, has five principal characteristics: Christian values; the aforementioned ambiguity as to the membership of international society; the primacy of natural, as opposed to positive, international law; the assumption of universal society (the *Respublica Christiana*); and finally, the lack of a set of institutions deriving from the co-operation of states. Bull's argument goes on to suggest, however, that the notion of the idea of international society develops through two further major stages: 'European international society' and 'world international society'. Bull's conclusion, echoing Wight's assertion of the tension implicit in his most famous essay, 'Western Values in International Relations',[12] is that the element of international society is only one element in world politics, but that '[t]he idea of international society has a basis in reality that is sometimes precarious but has at no stage disappeared'.[13] Bull concludes by attacking notions of 'international anarchy' that ignore the persistence of the idea of international society, as relying overly on an overstated domestic analogy that, in its turn, ignores the elements of uniqueness in the predicament of states and state systems. This uniqueness, according to Bull, was recognized by certain theorists of international society in the eighteenth century and is implicit in the gradual abandonment of the idea of the law of nature in favour of 'law of nations' and ultimately of the adoption of the term international law – initially by Jeremy Bentham.[14] Bull reinforces this claim by reiterating Wight's point that it was also in the eighteenth century that the key statement that states are the true and proper members of international society is made.[15]

Bull is, moreover, insistent that the notion of society in world politics is intimately connected with ideas of order in world politics. *The Anarchical Society* is, of course, subtitled 'A Study of Order in World Politics'. By order, Bull is clear that he means a pattern or regularity of social life such that it promotes certain goals and values – incidentally showing how close the English school is to Aron in this respect. This pattern will have three component parts: first, the fact that all societies seek to ensure that life will be in some measure secure against violence; second, that all societies will seek to ensure that all agreements, once made, will be kept; and third, that all societies will seek to ensure relative stability of possession. These Bull refers to as the elementary and primary goals of societies. As far as world politics is concerned, then, Bull suggests a crucial division: international order, which he describes as a pattern of activity conducive to the maintenance of the elementary and primary goals of the *society of states*, and world order, described as a pattern of activity conducive to the maintenance of the elementary and primary goals of *human social life as such*.

The latter notion, he thinks, is in important respects prior to the former. He puts it this way: 'World order is not only wider than international order or order among states, but also more fundamental and primordial than it, and morally prior to it'.[16] Thus, for Bull, not only is international society engaged in a transition from a society of states to one of peoples, but in addition it is also, and at the same time, engaged in an attempt at transition from international order to world order.

It is, therefore, the existence and character of international society that confers legitimacy on particular acts in international affairs and illegitimacy on others. The immunity of diplomats, the normative force of international law, and ultimately the coercive sanction of the internal community as a whole is manifested in and through, and only possible because of, the existence of international society.

Those who largely agree with Bull and Wight, at least about the centrality of international society, all express relatively similar assumptions.[17] Throughout the international society literature two basic assumptions are made. First, that international society is a fact, however tenuous and fleeting, of international relations; and second, that this fact creates obligations on the part of the members of the society concerned. It is these two assumptions that have made the alleged fragmentation of contemporary international society so dangerous for Bull. It threatened to undermine all the good that international society, through the promotion of international and world order, can do.

Inevitably, therefore, the notion of society deployed here is dependent on seeing society and culture as locked in a parasitic embrace. The values and shared understandings that mark out international society must be culturally generated and sustained, which, of course, implies that international and/or world order is equally dependent on such cultural generation and maintenance. Thus, the chief problem for theorists who wish to assert that international society is the crucial 'glue' that holds the international system together, is the alleged fragmentation of the 'Western' norms[18] that created the society in the first place and, in any case, their questioning or rejection by many in contemporary world politics. Bull himself believed that this fragmentation, although certainly threatened, had not yet fully occurred, and he was relatively optimistic about the prospects for international society.[19] However, as Hoffmann has remarked, this view gave rise to an unresolved tension in Bull's view:

> between Bull's awareness of the special importance of the great powers because of their evident stake in preserving international society and his awareness of their inadequacy in a global international system in which they cannot fulfill their traditional functions alone any more for two reasons: because of the greater capacity of smaller powers to resist and because of the greater potency of ideologies of resistance and of international inequality.[20]

I shall come back to these tensions in a moment but, for now, it is worth repeating that the theory of international society as put forward by Bull and other English school writers is *both* an empirical fact about how international relations works *and* a normative claim about what follows in international relations. This is unusual, for other writers who use the term tend to use it in one sense or the other. For Evan Luard,[21] for example, it is an explanatory concept in what amounts to an historical sociology of international relations,[22] whereas for Philip Allott international society is almost entirely a normative term because, for him, it does not yet exist but must be brought into being.[23] This dual sense that international society has in Bull's writings is, as I remarked above, close to the 'analytic sense' of Aron outlined above, and in this sense, I would argue that the English school rightly sees the parameters of the problem of order. However, it also the source of some of the problems with the English school notions of society and order, as we shall see.

International society: a critique

Before looking at the implications of this analysis for the problem of order *per se*, I want to pause for a moment to suggest a link between the way Bull and other English school writers set out their conception of society and order and that style of contemporary political theory usually called 'communitarian'.[24]

Communitarian political theory is part of a debate which largely dominated English-speaking political theory in the 1980s. The debate in question is usually referred to as the 'liberal–communitarian debate', though as we shall see there are good reasons for resisting the idea that it is a debate between 'liberals' and others – 'communitarians' – who are not liberals. In essence, the debate grew out of criticisms of the *locus classicus* of modern liberal thinking, John Rawls' justly celebrated 1971 book *A Theory of Justice*.[25] For many, the problem with Rawls' arguments was that they displayed too etiolated a notion of what human beings value and how they value them. Rawls posited, famously, an 'original position' wherein potential members of a putative just society would have to choose the organizing structures of that society in ignorance of the positions they would hold in the society once constituted; they would be choosing, Rawls said, behind a 'veil of ignorance'. The point, however, replied his critics, is that people hold values in ways that *cannot* be abstracted from, not even as a heuristic device. Communities are not made up of 'unencumbered selves'[26] but rather of people whose identities, frameworks of moral and political reference and sense of well-being are intimately and irrevocably bound up with the sense of community.

The set of authors usually considered under this rubric would generally be taken to include Michael Sandel, Michael Walzer, Charles Taylor and Alisdair MacIntyre. However, it is worth pointing out in this context that of these writers only MacIntyre could not plausibly be seen as a liberal of sorts (though certainly liberal in a different way to Rawls). Obviously the specifics of this as a debate within liberalism do not concern me in this book, though I shall return to them briefly in the next chapter; for now I simply want to assert some parallel between 'communitarian' ideas[27] and those of the English school.

There are two principal areas where the classical account of international society overlaps with contemporary communitarian thought. First, international society for the English school is contrived: 'artificial' in the Humean sense.[28] It is recognized by states and arises out of their situation in an anarchic world where there are elements of co-operation as much as conflict. As Bull writes:

> The element of international society has always been present in the modern international system because at no stage can it be said that the conception of the common interests of states, of common rules accepted and common rules worked by them, has ceased to exert an influence.[29]

As such, if international society is a genuine society, it is simply because its membership is composed of fictive persons – states, rather than biological ones. Bull effectively gives what Martin Wight termed the rationalist answer to the question 'what is international society?' 'It is a society but different from the state'.[30]

Many communitarians have stressed that their understanding of community is not simply co-terminus with the state. Charles Taylor, for example, elaborates a view of the 'modern' identity which implies a certain sense of community which is clearly communitarian but, equally clearly, non-statist.[31] Even Michael Walzer, perhaps the communitarian most obviously committed to what one of his critics has called 'the romance of the nation state',[32] has admitted that the rights people have 'follow from shared conceptions of social goods [that are] local and particular in character'.[33] Such conceptions need not be national or statist, therefore; they might grow out of shared conceptions of particular communities at particular times.[34]

Such, indeed, is how the Wight/Bull international society tradition portrays the idea of international society. The assumption that cultural homogeneity is necessary for a 'strong' international society' implies that there must be a link of the sort that Walzer and Taylor are talking about – even though Walzer certainly talks of communities as states most of the time. In other words, there is a similarity in the form of the international society and communitarian argument in that each assumes a degree of cultural homogeneity which generates certain shared concerns, interests and values which, in their turn, create, encourage and maintain a set of obligations. 'Within international society', Bull argued, 'order is the *consequence of a sense of common interests in the elementary goals of social* life'.[35] It is this 'sense of common interests' that creates international society which, in turn, creates the possibility of international order.

Thus, it seems clear that the forms that international society arguments take in the classical school are broadly communitarian. Neither Bull nor Wight nor any of their colleagues argue that there is a form of the good to which all societies – including the society of states – should bend their will; the *fact of the society* is the source of the obligations that spring from it. This creation is what allows us to talk of an international community or international society and which, therefore, allows us to explain and prescribe in its name.[36]

It would appear, then, that the foundations for a 'communitarian' international society are well laid. Yet there are problems. As already pointed out, international society has both an explanatory and a normative focus. These have an obvious connection in that, as far as its account of the nature of the international system is concerned, the tradition of international society is perfectly right to stress those aspects of the history of world politics that have often been dropped, ignored or marginalized by more mechanistic accounts. However, there are two points to be made here. The first, as implied earlier, is that the historical story told by theorists of international society is itself open to serious revision. To give just one example, understandings of the work of Grotius which emphasize that Grotius is following on from the 'tradition' of Vitoria[37] underrate the extent to which Grotius is *distancing* himself from the positions of Vitoria by echoing the work of writers opposed to the latter in important respects, such as Suarez, Sepulvada and Luis de Molina.[38] The significance of this is that it implies that (a) understandings of international society do not make sense outside wider ethical and political frameworks including self-conscious theories of the state, one of the sources of the differences between Grotius and Vitoria; and (b) that, as a result, the so-called 'tradition' of international society is in fact a scissors-and-paste construct taken from a wide variety of past traditions. As Roberts and Kingsbury have noted and as other thinkers (such as Alisdair MacIntyre)[39] also make patently clear, the notion of an intellectual tradition is deeply problematic and the use to which Wight and Bull, for example, put it is highly stipulative.

A second, and more profound problem, however, is the character of the 'rules' and 'norms' that are held to be the basis of the 'common values' which are manifested by international society. On this point, many of the theorists of international society are close to some realists (as we have seen these would include Reinhold Niebuhr, Walter Lippman, Hans Morgenthau and George Kennan) and some recent normative theorists (Terry Nardin)[40] in holding to a broadly conservative approach to international law and order. While not necessarily opposed to liberal conceptions, such views are certainly on the conservative end of liberal opinion.[41] Like these thinkers, the English school stresses that it is precisely human artifice and invention that has created international society, though it has often arisen, of course, from circumstances not of humans' own intentional making.

Two questions arise, however, over the character of the artifice and the forms of co-operation to which it gives rise. For 'international society' to be a 'fact', it must include norms, rules and procedures that are not simply rules of thumb but able to create illocutionary and normative force. This is where the empirical/explanatory and the normative arguments depend on one another. People must believe in these 'common values' for them to have any explanatory purchase and it is *because* they believe in them that they create obligations. Lastly, it is because they create obligation that international society can help to explain international order which is not just equilibrium or stability. This explanatory capacity is an important factor that separates the tradition of international society from various forms of realism.[42]

This emphasizes a significant point. International society is in important respects a quasi-contractarian type of argument despite its tacit Humean assumptions: because we have created certain institutions and we must rely on them for our continued peaceable existence we should accept the obligations that arise out of them.[43] However, in the form in which we have examined it so far, it is a 'communitarian' contractarianism and, therefore, it is in this context that the true significance of the 'communitarian' basis of international society becomes apparent. Unlike many other writers on world politics the theory of international society is voluntarist, not only in the obvious sense that if people do not accept an ethical view it is unlikely to receive much attention or act as a justifying reason for action, but also in the strong sense, in that it is our creation and acceptance of the norms of international society that *alone* creates the obligation to follow them. Thus, the appeals that Bull and others make on behalf of international society are a curious blend of the ethical and the self-interested; they are thus characterized by what we might call, following Humean language, 'weak' altruism, and there must be a question as to how powerfully such a view could support a world order, when what is required to create it are often likely to be so complex and difficult and when one of the things that most obviously stands in the way of it is the 'international order' necessary for the maintenance of the 'society of states'. In other words, how does the English school account of international society adjudicate between international order and world order when and if they conflict?

It is here that the link between 'communitarian' arguments and international society are most damaging for the latter. In his own attempt to solve the problem of how one adjudicates between different standpoints 'within', as it were, the community, Michael Walzer[44] suggests that dispute within a community is usually settled by whoever can give the most 'authentic' interpretation of the community. However, as Brian Barry has pointed out:

Surely the issue is not who can claim most of the tradition but who can claim the best of it but if once we allow a social critic to say that, although he is not offering the most authentic reconstruction of the whole cultural tradition, he is picking out the bits worth preserving, we cannot avoid asking: How does the critic decide which are the good bits?[45]

In the case of international society, the problem is all the more pressing. Bull, for example, expects us to ask questions of the sort 'what are the patterns of activity supportive of the society of states?' Can we answer this, however, unless there is, at least potentially, some standard outside the *existing* 'patterns of activity' which could allow us to say that A rather than B under circumstances X is more appropriate? As a form of ethical judgement this surely slides imperceptibly into a rather curious rule utilitarianism[46] with a sliding scale of values; in principle nothing is forbidden, it depends on whatever the 'consensus of shared values' happens to permit at any given time. Witness, for example, the ever increasing slippage in the laws of war from the early modern period to our own.[47]

Given the above, it seems that the nature of rule following within the international system neither can be explained by the existence of international society as understood by Bull or Wight nor can the notion prescribe ethical action in the required sense, as the consensus that forms international society and provides the framework for ethical decision is always a moving target. While it might be that states will co-operate for self-interested reasons, such actions do not need the Bullian notion of international society to explain them as writers such as Robert Axelrod, Robert Keohane, Kenneth Oye and Robert Jervis have shown.[48] The only way of asserting otherwise was if the existence of international society could provide a way of explaining international politics, and especially the normative component of international politics, that gives us *additional* reasons for supposing, for example, that a state's obligations should compel it to act even if it is not in its self-interest to do so. Yet one cannot provide, on the sort of communitarian logic that structures such accounts of international society, as they rely on ethical norms as the creation of a particular consensus on ethical values: if a state – or a community – does not share in them, while it might, of course, be *forced* to comply, it is under no ethical obligation to do so, merely a prudential one. Of course, it is precisely this problem that makes it easy to see why Bull, for example, oscillated so much between a semi-realist position (especially in his early work,[49] but also in some of his later writings as well) and the quasi-cosmopolitanism of the *Hagey Lectures*.[50] Yet this means that, while it provides more than just a useful corrective to many of the rationalistic interpretations of the international system currently on offer, the tradition of international society, as outlined and defended by the classical school, is surely running the risk of incoherence.[51]

'Constructivist' theory

If, however, English school theory is problematic, might there not be a better, though perhaps related, way of taking up the central English school concern? As I remarked above, a range of related approaches have evolved in IR theory of late which look as though they might well be good candidates. These approaches are now most usually referred to as 'constructivist' IR theory.[52]

Before saying anything in more detail about this development, let me just say that, as indicated above, I understand constructivist theory to be a group of *related* approaches, rather than one completely coherent approach, so references to constructivism will generally be avoided. The sources of constructivist theory are many and varied and the weight given to them will differ from theorist to theorist. Moreover, a number of self-confessed 'constructivists' have suggested that they see a number of different broad orientations in constructivist scholarship. For some, for example Cecilia Lynch, there are two such interpretations, which she calls 'modernist' and 'interpretive'.[53] Some others, perhaps most notably John Gerard Ruggie, suggest that one might see three broad orientations. Ruggie suggests that the first of these might be termed 'neo-classical' constructivism – as it is rooted in the sociological tradition of Durkheim and Weber, the 'classics' to which he refers – and it consists, with various amendments of content or temper in an

> epistemological affinity with pragmatism, a set of analytical tools necessary to make sense of intersubjective meanings … and a commitment to the idea of social science – albeit one more plural and more social than that espoused in the mainstream theories [he means by this term, of course, the 'rationalism' we discussed in the Introduction].[54]

Ruggie places himself in this category and adds that he thinks it is the basic orientation of scholars such as Friedrich Kratochwil, Nicholas Onuf, Emmanuel Adler, Martha Finnemore and Peter Katzenstein as well as the political theorist Jean Elshtain.[55] His second category he terms 'post-modernist constructivism'. This version traces its intellectual roots back to Nietzsche and in International Relations consists of scholars such as Richard Ashley, James Der Derian, David Campbell, R. B. J. Walker and feminists like Spike Peterson. It breaks with 'modernist' assumptions and holds out little hope for legitimate social science. Finally, he suggests that there is a third constructivist variant, 'located on the continuum between these two'. This he terms 'naturalistic' constructivism, and suggests it is exemplified in the work of Alexander Wendt and David Dessler.

I shall have something to say about all of these 'constructivisms' in the pages that follow. However, I suggest that Ruggie's second category is actually more of a category mistake. While I agree that some constructivists – I would put Kratochwil and Lynch at the head of this list – are rather more inclined to the interpretive end of the social scientific spectrum – and that they differ, in this context, from both Ruggie, on the one hand, and Wendt, on the other – I think that post-structuralists like Ashley, Der Derian, and others, are actually a very different kind of animal. What kind, exactly, I shall discuss in Chapter 5. For the moment, I shall simply, by fiat, rule them out of the constructivist camp. I would also point out at this point that Ruggie does not really discuss those theorists who will be the subject of my fourth chapter – though he does make a fleeting reference to an 'emancipatory constructivism'[56] – yet some of these are much closer, I would (and will) argue to constructivists like Lynch and Kratochwil than are the likes of Ashley or Der Derian.

In any event, and splitting the difference between Lynch and Ruggie, I suggest that broadly speaking there is a 'modernist' constructivist *core*, but that this is split between what Ruggie calls 'neo-classical constructivism' and 'naturalistic' constructivism. Then there are more interpretive constructivists like Lynch and Kratochwil, who sometimes incline quite closely to Ruggie, but sometimes are much further apart. It is obvious, of course, that it is the modernist variants that are the most influential in 'mainstream' academic International Relations, while it is the interpretive constructivists who are engaging in dialogue with the more general 'critical' voices in contemporary International Relations.

The way in which the mainstream constructivists (at least) position themselves can be taken from an argument offered by Alex Wendt, Ronald Jepperson and Peter Katzenstein in the second chapter of the last's recent book,[57] which is also cited favourably in Ruggie's general overview of the constructivist approach.[58] This suggests that the best way to see contemporary theories of International Relations (they are discussing, especially, security issues) is as shown in Figure 2.1.

The crucial corner, of course, is the top right-hand one, which though in the figure is referred to as 'sociological' perspectives, a note in the text makes it clear that 'constructivist' (and possibly institutionalist as well) is the authors' preferred

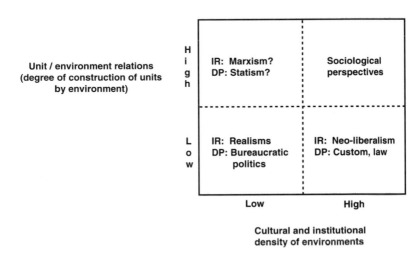

Figure 2.1

Key: IR, International Relations; DP, Domestic Politics[59]

nomenclature.[60] The first group of scholars they position in this quadrant is, significantly, the English school (they refer to it, as Bull sometimes did, as the 'Grotian Tradition' and say, still more significantly, that 'subsequent traditions are partly indebted to it') and they describe it as follows:

> From this perspective the international system is a society in which states, as a condition of their participation in the system, adhere to shared norms and rules in a variety of issue areas. Material power matters but within a frame-work of normative expectations embedded in public and customary international law. Scholars in this tradition ... have not focused explicitly on how norms construct states with specific identities and interests. But socio-logical imagery is strong in their work; it is not a great leap from arguing that adherence to norms is a condition of participation in a society to arguing that states are constructed, partly or substantially by these norms.[61]

The remaining bodies of work that they locate in this quadrant are also inter-esting for they include post-structural writing, feminist writing and the Gramscian variant of critical theory, all of which we will meet later on in the book and which together are usually what is referred to (misleadingly) as 'critical' theory in International Relations.[62] In other words, as Ruggie does – and as I do not – they link constructivist approaches (their own approach) with other accounts critical of the mainstream. This is relevant in that, as we will see, some see 'constructivist' approaches as holding the ring, as it were, between these 'post-positivist' accounts and mainstream ones. This is not, it would appear, how constructivists see things themselves. At the same time, however, they allow considerable scepticism of at least some of these other approaches to surface from time to time. In discussing identity, a key aspect of their analysis as it is for much post-structural theory, for example, they remark: 'the term identity here is intended as a useful label, not as a signal of some commitment to some exotic [presumably Parisian] social theory',[63] a clear repudiation of post-structuralism. This ambivalence is something to which I shall return.

Constructivist accounts of society and order

To outline the distinctive constructivist approaches to order and society, I want to start with perhaps the most influential general constructivist thinker in contem-porary International Relations, John Ruggie. Ruggie begins his recent survey of the emergence of what he calls 'social constructivism' by acknowledging the influence of the English school.[64] He suggests as well that earlier versions of liberalism (he specifically mentions neo-functionalism) also embodied many of the assumptions now characterized as 'constructivist'. Neither of these two accounts, however, develops the general approach now associated with construc-tivist theory. For Ruggie, the core assumptions take their starting point from the failures of the rationalist – he calls it neo-utilitarian – theory; that is, neo-realism (which we have just looked at) and neo-liberalism (which we will look at in the next chapter), but they have now evolved to a point at which distinctive features of their own are apparent. 'The most distinctive features of constructivism', he argues,

> are in the realm of ontology, the real world phenomena that are posited by any theory and are invoked by its explanations ... at the level of individual actors constructivism seeks ... to problematize the identities and interests of states ... at the level of the international polity, the concept of structure in social constructivism is suffused by ideational factors ... finally constructivism ... is non or post positivist in its epistemology.[65]

In many respects, I agree with Ruggie that most constructivists would accept at least two out of these three, especially the first two (I shall come back to the third a little later on). All constructivists – and they would share this view with many others, obviously the English school but also many of the 'critical' approaches I will examine in Chapters 4 and 5 – suggest that state identities cannot be seen simply as givens, rather they are constructed by mutual interactions in the 'society of states'. For example, as we saw Robert Jackson argue above, sovereignty as a *juridical* concept is conferred through processes of mutual recognition. Ruggie is emphatic that 'neo-utilitarianism provides no answer to the foundational question: how the constituent actors – that is territorial states – came to acquire their current identity and the interests that are assumed to go along with it'.[66] Constructivist arguments, however, do.

However, perhaps the central assumption Ruggie makes, as far as conceptions of society and order are concerned, lies in the second claim he thinks constructivists make. Here he draws on the work of the philosopher John Searle who develops the idea of 'collective intentionality'.[67] Constructivists, argues Ruggie, deny the neo-utilitarian assumption that ideational beliefs are necessarily 'beliefs held by individuals'; rather they make use of the notion of intersubjective beliefs which cannot be reduced to the form, 'I believe that you believe that I believe' and so on. Intersubjective beliefs can be 'social facts' which rest on 'collective intentionality' in the sense that 'I intend' only has meaning as part of '*our* intending'.

Constructivists, Ruggie argues, have explored the impact of collective intentionality at several levels in the international polity:

> At the deepest is the question of who counts as a constitutive unit of the international system. The mutual recognition of sovereignty ... is a precondition for the normal functioning of a system of sovereign states ... sovereignty, like private property or money, can only exist within a social framework that recognizes it to be valid – that is by virtue of collective intentionality.[68]

Collective intentionality for Ruggie also creates new rights and responsibilities (most interestingly, he thinks, examples like human rights) and at what he calls the 'most routine level', it creates meaning in the context of regimes.

Another central area for constructivists, according to Ruggie, is that they distinguish between different kinds of rules operative in international relations. *Regulative* rules regulate what he terms antecedently existing activity, for example the rule that says we should drive on the left (in Britain). *Constitutive* rules, by contrast, *define* an activity. Following Searle again he gives the example of chess, where the rules constitute in an important way the activity of playing chess. Neo-utilitarian IR theory, according to Ruggie, lacks any concept of constitutive rules, which is one of its most obvious weaknesses, a point which has been elaborated upon most powerfully by Kratochwil in a major book.[69]

These points taken together indicate clearly how, at least in general terms, constructivists would see the problem of order. Order is the term we give for the set of rules, constitutive and regulative, which together make up the practices of shared meaning and collective intentionality that frame a particular social practice. In the case of international relations, the frame is international society, as the English school was right to emphasize. Constructivists focus on the characteristics of that society and through that manage the problem of order by seeing how the framework is established, sustained and, most importantly at the present time, changed.

Most constructivists would agree, I think, with the general points Ruggie makes. Some, most influentially Kratochwil, would take a rather more radical stance on aspects of the constructivist agenda, as Ruggie himself admits. Others, however, are closer to the neo-utilitarian core than Ruggie.

Perhaps the best example here would be Alexander Wendt. His position has been outlined in a series of influential articles[70] and in a long trailed major book.[71] Wendt agrees, of course, in many ways with the agenda just outlined. Like Ruggie and Kratochwil, he suggests that we should focus on representations in international politics, not just on material forces. All realisms, but especially neo-realism, he thinks, offer a fundamentally materialist account which ignores representational issues. Representations, however, are fundamentally social things, indeed societal things, and this implies, of course, that they are constructed through processes of interaction. Anarchy, he states – in the title of his best known article – 'is what states make of it', *contra* Waltz, because it can only have the meanings attached to it by states in the processes of interaction.

In a still more recent article, Wendt characterizes the core claims of constructivism as follows:

1   states are the principal actors in the system;
2   the key structures in the states system are intersubjective rather than material;
3   state identities and interests are in large part constructed by those structures, rather than being determined exogenously to the system by human nature or domestic politics.

As he says – and as we saw above – the first view would be shared by realism (and neo-realism) as well as by at least some versions of neo-liberalism. The second, however, distinguishes 'constructivist' from neo-realist theory, which emphasizes material structures. The third, he says, 'brackets it from systemic theories that are rationalist in form [i.e. whether neo-realist or neo-liberal]'.[72] In the constructivist view, therefore, the

> structure of the states system contains both material and cultural elements … [and] in general constructivists give priority to cultural over material structures on the grounds that actors act on the basis of the meanings that objects have for them, and meanings are socially constructed.[73]

Wendt has given a number of examples of how this works in practice, among the most recent being his claim that what he calls 'collective identity' creates the possibility of 'common purposes and interests' and thus by investigating it we can trace 'the emergence of international authority out of anarchy'.[74] Indeed, he goes further and suggests that, unlike realism in general, and all forms of rationalism, constructivist accounts of the emergence of collective identity amongst states can point to the gradual (though by no means necessary or irrevocable) 'emergence of state powers at the international level that are not concentrated in a single actor but distributed across transnational structures of political authority … constituting a structural transformation of the Westphalian states system'.[75] Of course, he remarks that such a development has not gone very far 'any more than has the formation of collective identities that is one of its pre-requisites. It is a process, and even if it continues we are only in its early stages'.[76] However, he also makes the point that, assuming such a development, albeit embryonic, then

> the internationalization of political authority has at least two implications for IR theory. First it points towards a gradual, but structural, transformation of the Westphalian states system from anarchy to authority … a second implication is how this calls into question the premises of contemporary democratic governance. … As state actors pool their de facto authority over transnational space, they remove it from direct democratic control … [and this creates] a problem ultimately of transforming the boundaries of political community.[77]

This view leads Wendt to point to two final implications of his 'constructivist' method. As we saw above, realism – especially neo-realism – is often charged with being unable to account for 'structural change' and this is laid at the door of realism's 'state centricity'. Wendt suggests his argument implies that it is not with statism that the problem lies but rather with, in the case of neo-realism especially, 'materialism', since a 'materialist' focus cannot account for the sort of 'authority shift' Wendt thinks he detects. In the case of rationalist IR theory more generally, the problem is that inasmuch as it assumes that preferences and interests are 'exogenous' and constant, it cannot, by definition, take into account the shifting identities that are a key determinant of structural change.

Most constructivists, I think, would agree with most of this. If anything they would go further. Wendt is perhaps the most important of the so-called 'modernist' constructivists. Other – 'interpretive' – constructivists, for example Kratochwil and Nicholas Onuf, would have rather less clear allegiances to the 'state' and might take the sense of non-material forces rather further. They might also have less sympathy for at least aspects of the 'rationalist' mainstream than Wendt displays. Nonetheless, this example of constructivist reasoning shows a number of things extremely relevant in the present context.

In the first place, it is clear how close much of this is to the English school style of reasoning outlined above. The 'societal element' in constructivist thinking is clear and overlaps with a range of other positions that draw on English school work, including some of the revisionist realist readings we examined above (especially, for example, the work of Buzan and Little and also the 'new security thinking' of Buzan and some of his collaborators in the so-called 'Copenhagen school' principally, of course, Ole Wæver) and some critical theory (especially the work of Andrew Linklater which we will examine in more detail in Chapter 4).

Second, it is clear that inasmuch as constructivist thinking does indeed make the three basic assumptions outlined by Wendt, it is clear also that its treatment of the 'problem of order' will be analogous to the English school as well. On the basis of Wendt's argument discussed above, for example, 'order' would require a degree of 'collective identity' which could then support some international authority. Of course, the language is different and some of the methodological assumptions are alien to what we might call the 'voice' of the English school – Wight would probably have been as uncomprehending of a lot of the sociological literature cited by Wendt as he was of the early stages of what became 'rationalist' IR theory in the United States – but there is, as many have said, considerable commonality and overlap in their manner of treating these topics. The question, of course, is whether constructivist accounts are better able to deal with some of the objections cited above.

International order versus world order; towards a critical – or 'constructivist' – international society?

To confront this question, let me return, for a moment, to Bull's distinction between 'international order' and 'world order'. This is, I think, an important distinction and Bull seems right to suppose that there is, at the least, a tension between these two things. In his own work, however, and despite his claim in *The Anarchical Society* that world order is in some sense 'prior to' international order and various scattered remarks in the *Hagey Lectures* that suggest similar things, Bull almost always comes down on the side of international order as, at the very least, a necessary building block and is quite often more brutally dismissive of 'world order' types of arguments.[78] Some other English school writers – for example, Robert Jackson – have also articulated this. Indeed, Jackson explicitly repudiates the idea, which we will explore in more detail below, that there could be a 'critical' international society theory – at least inasmuch as this was based on what he calls 'post-modern theories of an anti-foundational kind' and suggests that the closest links of the English school lie with (traditional) forms of realism.[79]

However, in terms of the constructivist argument just discussed, we might suggest that what Wendt is suggesting is that the contemporary system is manifesting the gradual transition from a system where 'international order' is paramount to one where world order might, indeed, be prior and might indeed be available to undergird some more cosmopolitan idea of 'world order'. It is perhaps the sense that traditional understandings of international society have tended towards a very conservative view of the character and mechanisms of international society, as well as the recognition that alternatives might exist within the basic assumptions of the international society approach, that have prompted some of the younger scholars influenced by the English school to explore whether there might not be a way of reconceptualizing international society so as both to bolster its 'liberalism' and strengthen its ability to resist such criticisms.

One way of seeing the debate within the English school today is over the extent to which this English school approach to world order can be – so to speak – 'liberalized', even radicalized. If successful, it might be argued that this would be the best approach to take to the question of conceptualizing world order. This is being substantially aided, of course, by the emergence of the sorts of constructivist modes of thought we have just examined and which often are more radical than traditional English school arguments and yet which are happy – as we have seen they are – to acknowledge English school writing as an important influence.

From the English school perspective, the starting point in this attempt is often taken to be Bull's argument in the *Hagey Lectures*. In these lectures, Bull seems to move towards a more 'cosmopolitan' view, one stressing world order over international order. He adopts, in the words of two of his recent followers, a 'solidarist' rather than a 'pluralist' conception of international society.[80] However, as they also point out, he never fully reconciles this tension in the lectures, or, tragically, anywhere else. He was dead within a year of giving them.

In important ways this tension has remained perhaps the central dynamic of the English school.[81] It was, for example, central to the work of one of the most important 'second-generation' English school theorists, John Vincent. Vincent's first book, *Non-Intervention and the International Order*[82] was a fairly traditional (though very individual) presentation of the usual English school claims about 'the society of states', the importance of sovereignty, the centrality of non-intervention and so on. His second, however, *Human Rights and International Relations*[83] sought to grapple with the most important challenge to those assumptions, the growing claims for universal human rights. If the traditional English school view was that, as Robert Jackson has recently expressed it, 'World society was the client of the society of states, rather than the reverse',[84] Vincent's study of human rights led him in a rather different direction, though it is certainly true that he remained convinced that the 'society of states' view still had a lot of mileage left in it. Like Bull, he died tragically young, robbed of the opportunity to try and work towards the resolution of the dilemma he felt as keenly as anyone.[85]

Some younger English school theorists have gone further and made explicit common cause with the constructivists and have even suggested in this context that a 'critical international society' literature is beginning to evolve[86] that links international society literature to the constructivist arguments we looked at above and perhaps might even take it in the general direction of some of the critical theories that we will examine in Chapter 4 and in the Epilogue. Bull, Wight and their colleagues were themselves already 'constructivist' theorists of a sort, this argument runs, and in the later work of Bull and in Vincent in particular, there is the beginnings of a genuinely 'cosmopolitan' international society thesis that moves beyond traditional liberal theory and at least gestures in the direction of 'emancipatory' critical theory.[87]

The validity of these claims depends, however, on the inference that the English school is actually amenable to cosmopolitan claims and that, indeed, its strongest contemporary form would be a version of international society which emphasized cosmopolitan norms without surrendering the (communitarian and constructivist) shape of the theory. If this can, in fact, be made to stick, might it not be possible to overcome some of the problems just mentioned and to evolve an approach that could provide a way of adjudicating between international and world order when and if they conflicted?

It is worth emphasizing that this view has certainly received some powerful and heartfelt expressions. As we shall see, a number of critical theorists of international relations have a good deal of time for the English school and it is certainly true that many of the members of the school – especially Wight – lend themselves to readings that can be accommodated to the concerns of much critical or constructivist theory.[88] However, the problem is that even the new, radicalized English school still sees the existence and practices of an international society as having the central role in creating international and world order. These commitments are still, English school writers tend to suggest, at least primarily the commitments of states – thus it will be state elites who will largely 'create' the norms of the society – but nonetheless, they *are* creations, and thus can be altered, amended or recreated. As constructivists would say, the norms at least partially 'construct' the state identities involved and thus the responsibilities entailed by them.

But this is where the English school begins to be pulled in very different directions. Whilst many in the school, and arguably certainly the school's original leading thinkers like Bull, together with other prominent English school theorists such as Adam Watson[89] retain the clear focus on the state in a relatively unaltered form,[90] the liberalizers within the school, those within it sympathetic to 'critical' international society theory, want the school to be less concerned with 'states' (and thus 'international order') and more concerned with 'peoples' (and thus 'world order')[91] – the 'solidarist' rather than the 'pluralist' conception. For them, the great advantage of the English school's emphasis on 'the social construction of international society', as Tim Dunne has put it, offers at least the possibility of doing this, whilst retaining the English school's insights about the still central role of the state in contemporary world politics.[92]

The contemporary radicalizers of the English school have thus increasingly sought to relate its concerns to those shared by a number of 'critical' theorists. A special attempt has been made to link it with the (cosmopolitan) ethical concerns of critical theorists like Linklater and the (constructivist) methodological ones of someone like Wendt; some have even suggested important parallels between the work of some post-structuralists and the English school.[93] As well as taking seriously the 'constructive' elements in international relations – for example, the extent to which international society or 'world order' constructs (but does not determine) the identity (but not the behaviour) of states and vice versa – it is also argued that the English school is not necessarily opposed to one of the most important claims of 'critical' theory, to wit the claim that world politics and its practices and institutions should not be seen simply as 'constructed'; rather they should also be interpreted in ways that emphasize at least the possibility of human agency changing the structures and institutions of world politics for the better. In other words, on this view, 'society' should be linked to at least the possibility of 'emancipation'.

Of course, the view that world politics is largely a 'given' can be put in many ways. We might see it as a 'structure' that 'determines' the behaviour of its 'units' (as, for example, neo-realism would) or one in which individual preferences are king but that they are exogenous preferences and largely unaffected by the results of any actions (as the version of neo-liberalism currently being developed by some 'institutionalists', for example Andrew Moravscik, suggests).[94] However, for the radical English school and for some constructivists, as we have seen, such claims are false; rather world politics should be seen as a complex construction which can, at least in principle, be reconstructed.

This view receives a powerful articulation by Dunne in his recent argument putting the claims of the English school tradition to be taken seriously as a 'constructivist' theory of international politics. Dunne suggests that a central part of 'constructivism' lies in challenging arguments that give pre-eminence in social scientific explanation to 'systemic' or 'structural' or 'holistic' accounts.[95] Constructivist accounts need to emphasize the possibility of reconstituting the social world but to do so in the light of the realities of intersubjective constraints. Unlike the constructivism of a Wendt or an Onuf, however, 'the constructivism of Bull ... helps us to think about the constraining nature of the intersubjective structures which underpin international society.'[96] The centrepiece of such a constructivism, Dunne suggests, lies in the English school's conviction that international society is, '*through conscious deliberation* what *states* have made of it' (emphasis added). This conscious echo of Wendt's best known article[97] is designed, I assume deliberately, to focus attention on the obvious point that for at least the liberalizers among the English school, there is a good deal to be said for stressing the notion of at least *state* agency in international society.

Yet as we saw above, for Wendt constructivist theory is indeed about structures;

it merely sees those structures as being (primarily) intersubjectively constituted rather than being (primarily) materially constituted.

Yet alongside this disagreement there is also a central agreement. To both constructivist and English school scholars, the state remains, at least in certain key respects, uniquely the carrier of the possibilities of international society. Even for the critical theory friendly wing of the English school, states are 'qualitatively' different from other kinds of actors and agents in world politics and, in Dunne's phrase, 'the actions of *states* are given meaning by their conscious participation in common institutions'.[98] In this respect, he certainly resembles Wendt. For critical theorists like Linklater, however – as we shall see – the state has simply a derivative and secondary significance. While it is, of course, necessary to start with states (no sensible cosmopolitan denies their power), 'starting points' are just that, they exist to be transcended, overcome, bypassed, and, most fundamentally of all, transformed. Whereas, English school 'constructivism', though real enough, is a constructivism based on the state's capacities, a properly *cosmopolitan* constructivism would have to be based on both a much stricter notion of reason and a much more all-embracing conception of agency. 'International society' is not just what *states* make of it, it is what we all (individuals and institutions other than the state as well the state) make of it.

It is fair to say, of course, that the traffic on this point is not all one way. Linklater, in a recent article,[99] has suggested that he thinks that international society and his own cosmopolitan critical theory can indeed be combined, through the medium of a Habermassian discourse ethics and the institutional construction of a cosmopolitan democracy in which states begin to 'share' sovereign powers with other institutions both above and below them. Leaving aside the practicalities or likelihood of this even in Europe (which is Linklater's explicit concern), the way he puts this argument suggests merely that Bull (the English school writer he directly quotes) saw this as a possibility. It says nothing about whether the possibility, if actualized, would effectively have made Bull's general framework for the analysis of world politics defunct. Once 'the sovereign state' is no longer sovereign, you cannot surely have a 'society of states', that society that it is the glory and, indeed, the entire *raison d'être* of the English school to delineate and analyse.

There is a second point which brings us back to the question of how English school or constructivist theorists could adjudicate between 'international and world order' if necessary. As we will see in Chapter 4, cosmopolitan critical thinking like Linklater's is quite clear that it is norms that ought to be in the driving seat of our 'agency' when it comes to world politics and that these norms are, while certainly not fixed in advance, clearly not amenable to the sort of sliding scale logic that we have seen applies in the English school case. Whatever the faults of the cosmopolitan critical theory might be, it is clear that for them, we cannot simply base our norms on the stipulative agreements of state elites, which is the origin of the English school's fabled 'international society' and which also must be the source of the 'intersubjective meanings' that constitute, remember, *state* collective identities for Wendt.

For the English school, the basic problem lies in the root conception. If it is the mere *fact* of 'society' and the norms that the society constructs that in turn create identity, obligations or legitimacy or authority, and which in their turn interact and 'construct' the states and their elites in an ever returning circle, then *either* the norms of the society have to be worked out through the accepted institutions of representation – effectively still states and their agreements – which is, of course, what the traditional English school would have argued, and what some of its contemporary adherents like Jackson would still argue, *or* we have to have some other method for ascertaining what the shared norms and cultural consensus necessary for sustaining 'international society' are. Talking about a 'society of peoples' is all very well but how do 'peoples' express their agreement or dissent from particular 'norms of international behaviour' in the existing system?

It is important that this point is not misunderstood. My point is not to say that the 'critical' – or at any rate 'constructivist' – international society theorists are *wrong* to want to move the English school towards a more cosmopolitan conception of international society. Indeed, it seems to me that such a move is the absolute bare minimum required to make the notion of 'world order' as Bull defines it meaningful at all. The problem is that if this move is, indeed, made, I do not see any real use for the notion of 'international society' as outlined by the English school at all. You simply move onto the terrain already staked out by various critical theorists of world politics, so my question becomes, why bother with the English school conception of international society at all? It is – and must remain, if it is to be distinctive – a state-bound and state-centred conception, yet the move to cosmopolitanism would force it to abandon that.[100]

Conclusion: beyond international society?

This, it seems to me, is the real reason why the English school cannot – and not simply has not yet – come up with a way of resolving the problem of how to adjudicate between international and world order. To do this they would need either to plump for the traditional international society model – in which case it seems to me that international order would always have priority – or to shift to a much more strongly cosmopolitan view, in which case they would no longer be dealing in any meaningful sense with 'international society' at all: at which point the distinctive contribution of the English school simply evaporates. Much the same, I think, would be true about Wendt's constructivist reading. At the very least, if this path were to be taken by constructivist theory it would require that the first of Wendt's assumptions – that states are the principal actors in the system – be dropped. In this case a good deal of the way in which he, at least, has developed his arguments would require very considerable revision, at the very least.

In any event, the attempt to see constructivist theory as some kind of a 'half-way house' between positivistic and (allegedly) post-positivistic methodologies will not work, simply because the way 'rationalist' scholars like Keohane have posed the question does not allow any real choice; one either accepts certain assumptions about how one constructs appropriate research designs or one does not. More significantly, I think, the dominant constructivist approaches, most especially that of Wendt, with all its richness and sophistication, will have to recognize that their real theoretical heart lies with the project of critique. Otherwise, it will end up looking remarkably like 'classical realism' in many respects.[101] It is statist, it sees structures as a product of the relations between ideas and material forces – in Waltzian terms it is unambiguously reductionist. In this case, however, it will run into precisely the same problems that as I suggested classical realism does.

In this context, it seems to me that Jackson is in fact right about the English school; it is easily – and rightly at one level – seen as a subset of 'classical' realism: society linked with balance produces 'international order', rather than society linked with emancipation producing world order, as the liberalizers would prefer. Except, as we have already seen, the notion of balance in classical realist theory is itself incoherent. It does not – cannot – provide a solution to the problem of order, as I conceptualized it above.

Interpretive 'constructivists', however – most prominently, I suggest, Kratochwil – have already accepted the logic of this. Their real dialogue is, indeed, with critical (i.e. emancipatory) theory. Of course, there are still differences. Kratochwil has indeed argued persuasively for a responsible methodological pluralism[102] and much of his own work, as with much other constructivist writing, is happy to use many of the standard techniques and *discoursi* of the rationalists, without accepting one whit of their general position. Yet if this is so, then it would seem to me that the 'distinctiveness' of constructivist or English school thinking disappears; it simply becomes subsumed in a much more general critical project.

This, it seems to me, is the really crucial point in all of this. English school and constructivist thinking must simply decide which path open to them they are going to take. They could seek to retain their (rather different) distinctiveness; yet this would be, as I see it, a conservative move and would take both approaches back rather than forward and would effectively align them both with versions of realism, which accounts, of course, for the similarities between some of the newer revisionist realisms we looked at above and a good deal of contemporary English-school-derived, or constructivist, work. Or they could accept, as I think some have come close to doing, that they must throw their lot in with the critical project more generally,[103] in which case their distinctiveness is lost and the English school would, indeed, finally be 'closed', as Roy Jones proposed all those years ago, albeit for all the wrong reasons!

The problem, I suggest, with societal approaches like the English school and (at least modernist) constructivist views is that, as always, the middle of the road is just too dangerous a place to be. Sooner or later, you have to move to one side or the other.

Notes

1 For a good discussion of this subject see Iver Neuman's book in this same series, *Russia and the Idea of Europe* (London: Routledge, 1994).

2 For a good discussion of this see Gerritt Gong, *The Standard of Civilization in International Society* (Oxford: Clarendon Press, 1984).

3 I am very uncertain about terminology here as there are good reasons for rejecting all such labels. For convenience, references to the English school refer to the writings primarily of Martin Wight, Hedley Bull, Adam Watson and Herbert Butterfield and, to an extent, to the writings of some other members of the British Committee for International Theory, that they successively chaired. However, that there were many differences between these writers as well as similarities is quite apparent. There was especially, I think, a pronounced difference between Butterfield, Wight and Watson, on the one hand, and Bull on the other, specifically over the under-standing of the character of history and thus on the character of the appropriate 'units' that are the principal actors in history. Butterfield, Wight and Watson tend to a more 'Toynbeean', civilizational and cultural approach, Bull to a more statist one. I shall return to this briefly below. On the understanding of international society, however, they largely agreed, as discussed below. For discussions of the 'English school', see Roy E. Jones, 'The English School of International Relations: A Case for Closure', *Review of International Studies*, 1981, 7(1): 1–12; and N. J. Rengger, 'Serpents and Doves in Classical International Theory', *Millennium: Journal of International Studies*, 1988, 17(2): 215–25. More recent scholars associated with this view are discussed below.

4 See, for example, Stephen Walt's recent survey of the field in *Foreign Policy*, 1997/8, Winter.

5 Stanley Hoffmann, 'International Society', in J. D. B. Miller and R. J. Vincent (eds), *Order and Violence: Hedley Bull and International Relations* (Oxford: Clarendon Press, 1990), p. 22.

6 Aspects of this section are drawn from my analysis in 'Culture, Society and Order in World Politics', in John Baylis and N. J. Rengger (eds), *Dilemmas of World Politics* (Oxford: Clarendon Press, 1992), pp. 86–8.

7 Martin Wight, 'Western Values in International Relations', in Herbert Butterfield and Martin Wight (eds), *Diplomatic Investigations* (London: Allen and Unwin, 1966), pp. 86–98.

8 Ibid., pp. 96–7.

9 Hedley Bull and Adam Watson (eds), *The Expansion of International Society* (Oxford: Clarendon Press, 1986), pp. 125–6.

10 See, for example, James L. Brierly, *The Law of Nations*, 2nd edition (Oxford: Oxford University Press, 1936).

11 This development is covered brilliantly by Richard Tuck in his *Natural Rights Theories* (Cambridge: Cambridge University Press, 1979). Although he does not discuss Gentili, his account is very different and, in my opinion at least, much more satisfac-tory than Bull's. See, for a full appreciation of the development of modern natural law and the errors in Bull's version of it, Francisco de Vitoria, *Commentarios a la Secunda Secundae de Santo Tomas*, ed. V. B. de Heredia (Salamanca, 1934), *Domingo De Soto De Iustitia et Iure* (Salamanca, 1553), Francisco Suarez, *De Legibus ac Deo Legislatore* (Coimbra, 1612), *Alberico Gentili De Jure Belli Libri Tres* [1598] (London: James Brown Scott, 1964), Hugo Grotius, *De Iure Praedae* (The Hague, 1607), and *De Jure Belli ac Pacis* (Paris, 1625), and Samuel Pufendorf, *De Iure Naturae et Gentium* (1672). Part of the problem with the reading of these writers given by Wight, Bull and others is that they pay insufficient attention to the context of the evolution of these ideas. For example, in *The Anarchical Society* Bull references Kelsey's 1925 translation of Grotius' *De Jure Belli ac Pacis* (Oxford: Clarendon Press). As Tuck points out, however, (*Natural*

Rights Theories, p. 73, n. 31), many of the most easily available translations are based on the heavily revised printing of *De Jure* published in 1631. This can distort the perception of both Grotius' intentions and the internal structure of his thought. While this is only a minor point in the current context, it leads, I think, to some very significant distortions in Bull's view of the historical origin and provenance on the notion of international society. I have discussed these points more fully in 'Discovering Traditions? Grotius, International Society and International Relations', *The Oxford International Review*, 1991, 3(1): 47–50.

12 See Martin Wight, 'Western Values in International Relations', op. cit., in n. 12.

13 See Bull, *The Anarchical Society*, op. cit., in n. 9, p. 4.

14 See Jeremy Bentham, *The Principals of Morals and Legislation* (New York: Hafner, 1948), p. 326.

15 Bull's assertion of this point is backed up with a reference to Vattel's *Droit des gens* but, again, I think that the intellectual history of the eighteenth century is much murkier than Bull would have it. The notion of 'state personality' is already present in the writings of Pufendorf, but in both Pufendorf and Vattel it should not, I think, be taken to assume the existence of no other rights. As Tony Carty points out in *The Decay of International Law* (Manchester: Manchester University Press, 1986), p. 90, Vattel is asserting a legal category for the interpretation of state conduct when he asserts the principle of non-intervention and assumes states as entities; there is little else in his notion. Moreover, many other eighteenth-century theorists writing on international topics adopted very different perspectives, David Hume, for example. See Hume's *Essays*, especially his writings on the balance of power and the balance of trade.

16 Bull, *Anarchical Society*, op. cit., in n. 9, p. 315.

17 Among these would be, for example, Robbie Purnell in his *The Society of States* (London: Allen and Unwin, 1972), Murray Forsyth, H. M. A. Keens-Soper and Peter Savigear (eds), *The Theory of International Relations* (London: Allen and Unwin, 1970), and the group of writers involved in the project which has led (thus far) to three edited collections: Michael Donelan (ed.), *The Reason of States* (London: Allen and Unwin, 1978); James Mayall (ed.), *The Community of States* (London: Allen and Unwin, 1982); and Cornelia Navari (ed.), *The Condition of States* (Milton Keynes: Open University Press, 1991). Perhaps the two best recent statements are James Mayall, *Nationalism and International Society* (Cambridge: Cambridge University Press, 1990); and Robert Jackson, *Quasi-States: Sovereignty, International Relations and the Third World* (Cambridge: Cambridge University Press, 1990). I should stress that I do not suggest that these writers are at all slavish followers of Bull and Wight, only that they take the Bull/Wight notion of international society as their starting point.

18 For a discussion of this, though I have some doubts about this argument now, see N. J. Rengger, 'Incommensurability, International Theory and the Fragmentation of Western Political Culture', in John Gibbins (ed.), *Contemporary Political Culture* (London: Sage, 1989), pp. 237–50.

19 See the conclusion to Bull and Watson (eds), *Expansion of International Society*, op. cit., in n. 14.

20 Hoffmann, 'International Society', op. cit., in n. 10, p. 31.

21 See, for example, Evan Luard, *Types of International Society* (New York: Free Press, 1976).

22 A similar sense is observable in Marcel Merle, *Sociologie des relations internationales* 4th edition (Paris: Dalloz, 1988), although Merle does not use the term.

23 See Philip Allott, *Eunomia: New Order for a New World* (Oxford: Oxford University Press, 1990).

24 I stay within the usual terminology here, though as will be seen later, I take this orientation to be effectively a form of 'particularism'.

25 See Rawls, *A Theory of Justice* (Oxford: Oxford University Press, 1971).

26 A phrase made famous in this context by Michael Sandel, one of Rawls' chief 'communitarian' critics. See his 'The Procedural Republic and the Unencumbered Self', in *Political Theory* vol. 12 n.1 1984 pp. 81–96. The more general statement of Sandel's position can be found in his *Liberalism and the Limits of Justice* (Cambridge: Cambridge University Press, 1982).

27 Though I should add that a number of English school thinkers draw attention to the similarity between aspects of (especially) Bull's account and that of Michael Walzer, one of the most prominent so-called 'communitarians' who has also written a good deal about international relations – and very powerfully too. Robert Jackson, for example, in his 'Is There a Classical International Theory?', in S. Smith, K. Booth and M. Zalewski (eds), *International Theory: Positivism and Beyond* (Cambridge: Cambridge University Press, 1996), explicitly draws attention to this similarity on p. 216.

28 Hume famously refers to justice as an artificial virtue in both the *Treatise of Human Nature* and the second *Enquiry (Enquiry Concerning the Principles of Morals)*. In the *Treatise* he gives his best elaboration of the notion when he remarks that 'there are some virtues that produce pleasure and approbation by means of an artifice or contrivance which arise from the circumstances and necessities of mankind'. See *Treatise of Human Nature*, ed. L. A. Selby Bigge, rev. P. H. Nidditch (Oxford: Clarendon Press, 1978), p. 477. It is worth pointing out that Hume added that 'though the rules of justice be artificial they be not arbitrary' (Book 111, Part 2, Section 1, p. 484). This is effectively how Bull, especially, sees international society: arising from the circumstances and necessities of mankind and in that sense artificial, a human contrivance, but not an arbitrary one that can be changed at will.

29 Bull, *The Anarchical Society*, op. cit., in n. 9, p. 42.

30 See Martin Wight, *International Theory: The Three Traditions*, ed. Brian Porter and Gabrielle Wight (Leicester: Leicester University Press, for the Royal Institute for International Affairs, 1992), p. 48.

31 See Taylor, *Sources of the Self*, op. cit., in n. 4, especially parts 1 and 3.

32 See David Luban, 'The Romance of the Nation State', in Charles Beitz *et al.*, *International Ethics* (Princeton, NJ: Princeton University Press, 1981).

33 Walzer, *Spheres of Justice*, op. cit., in n. 4, p. xv.

34 It is worth pointing out here, however, that one so-called communitarian, to wit MacIntyre, has explicitly repudiated the term precisely because he thinks it carries, and is carried by, essentially statist assumptions. See his 'Response to my Critics', in John Horton and Sue Mendus (eds), *After MacIntyre* (Cambridge: Polity Press, 1992).

35 Bull, *The Anarchical Society*, op. cit., in n. 9, p. 65. Emphasis added.

36 This is also, incidentally, where the English school approach to international society would most obviously differ from that of natural law. For natural law, on any or all interpretations of it, international society is by definition more than simply the agreements humans make, however much it also incorporates that. For excellent discussions see the chapters by Robert George and Robert Friedman in David Mapel and Terry Nardin (eds), *International Society: Diverse Ethical Perspectives* (Princeton, NJ: Princeton University Press, 1998).

37 Bull's argument, of course, recently repeated and amplified by Adam Roberts and Ben Kingsbury in their excellent introduction to Hedley Bull, Adam Roberts and Ben Kingsbury (eds), *Hugo Grotius and International Relations* (Oxford: Clarendon Press, 1990).

38 For a detailed discussion, see Rengger, 'Discovering Traditions', in n. 16, pp. 48–9, and Tuck, *Natural Rights Theories*, in n. 16, chapters 4, 7 and 8.

39 See Roberts and Kingsbury, 'Introduction' to *Hugo Grotius and International Relations*, op. cit., in n. 37; Alisdair MacIntyre, *After Virtue* (London: Duckworth, 1981; 2nd edition 1987); MacIntyre, *Whose Justice? Which Rationality?* (London: Duckworth, 1988); and *Three Rival Versions of Moral Enquiry* (London: Duckworth 1990).

40 Terry Nardin, *Law, Morality and the Relations of States* (Princeton, NJ: Princeton University Press, 1983).
41 I will, in fact, return to these thinkers in Chapter 4.
42 Including those realist writers mentioned above, otherwise close to it.
43 For a very different, but related and explicitly contractarian, argument, see John Charvet, 'Contractarianism in International Political Theory' (unpublished paper, 1992).
44 See Michael Walzer, *Interpretation and Social Criticism* (Cambridge, MA: Harvard University Press, 1987) and *The Company of Critics: Social Criticism and Political Commitment in the Twentieth Century* (New York: Basic Books, 1988).
45 Brian Barry, 'Social Criticism and Political Philosophy', in *Liberty and Justice: Essays in Political Theory 2* (Oxford: Clarendon Press, 1991), pp. 18–19.
46 I draw here on the well-known distinction between act and rule utilitarianism whereby 'act utilitarianism' judges consequences on the basis of acts or classes of acts, and 'rule utilitarianism' judges them on the basis of rule following for certain classes of acts.
47 A good discussion is James Turner Johnson, *Ideology, Reason and the Limitation of War* (Princeton, NJ: Princeton University Press, 1975), and *Just War Tradition and the Restraint of War* (Princeton, NJ: Princeton University Press, 1981).
48 See, for example, Robert Axelrod, *The Evolution of Co-operation* (New York: Basic Books, 1984), and Kenneth A. Oye (ed.), *Co-operation under Anarchy* (Princeton, NJ: Princeton University Press, 1985). We shall return to aspects of this in the next chapter.
49 Such as Hedley Bull, *The Control of the Arms Race* (London: Weidenfeld and Nicolson, for the International Institute for Strategic Studies, 1961).
50 See Hedley Bull, *Justice in International Relations: The Hagey Lectures* (Waterloo, Ontario: University of Waterloo, October 1984).
51 There is, I should say, another alternative. One might argue, as Barry Buzan has done, and as – at least on some interpretations – Wight has done as well, that international and world order – and international and world society – are each requisite for the other. Since it is the work of the likes of Buzan and Little, and to some extent some constructivists, that have most recently developed this claim, I will consider it at the end of this essay, rather than here.
52 In the last few years, discussions of, and versions of, constructivist IR theory have grown from a trickle to a torrent. Early statements that, largely subsequently, have been labelled constructivist *avant la lettre*, as it were, would include Nicholas Onuf, *World of our Making: Rules and Rule in Social Theory and International Relations* (South Carolina: University of South Carolina Press, 1989), and Friedrich Kratochwil, *Rules, Norms and Decisions: On the Conditions of Legal and Practical Reasoning in International Relations and Domestic Affairs* (Cambridge: Cambridge University Press, 1989). Aside from Ruggie, the best known constructivist in IR theory is unquestionably Alex Wendt whose major book, *Social Theory of International Politics*, forthcoming from Cambridge University Press in autumn 1999, must be one of the most eagerly awaited books in IR theory for some years. Before it appears, his version of constructivist IR theory can best be seen in one now very well-known article, 'Anarchy is What States Make of it: The Social Construction of Power Politics', *International Organization*, 1992, 46: 391–425. The extent to which constructivist theory has now grown in reach and range, and its attraction to some of the best, younger, mainstream US scholars, are clearly on view in Peter Katzenstein (ed.), *The Culture of National Security* (New York: Columbia University Press, 1997).
53 I am borrowing this language from one of the best younger interpretive constructivists, Cecilia Lynch, whom I happily thank for a number of discussions of this point, particularly one very illuminating one at the ISA convention in Toronto in 1997. The best known 'interpretive' constructivist is, I think, Kratochwil, whose

position is certainly close in certain respects to critical theory. The best known 'modernist' constructivist is Wendt, who has picked up the 'Keohane challenge' referred to in the Introduction with a vengeance.

54 Ruggie, *Constructing the World Polity: Essays on International Institutionalization* (London: Routledge, 1998), p.35.
55 I have to say that I disagree with Ruggie here. Elshtain seems to me not really to be a constructivist at all, and Kratochwil, though certainly a constructivist, is rather more ambivalent about aspects of the sociological tradition than is Ruggie. However, more of this later.
56 Ruggie, *Constructing the World Polity*, p. 35.
57 *The Culture of National Security*, that is.
58 Ruggie, *Constructing the World Polity*, p. 39.
59 The map, as the authors say, stems, in fact, from Wendt, who has a version of it in his article (co-authored with Daniel Friedheim) 'Hierarchy under Anarchy: Informal Empire and the East German State', in Biersteker and Weber (eds), *State Sovereignty as Social Construct*.
60 See n. 33 on p. 44.
61 *The Culture of National Security*, p. 45.
62 The one approach they add, not well known in International Relations, as they say, is the sociologist John Meyer's work on the world polity, as well as the work of those associated with him. See, for an example, Meyer, 'The World Polity and the Authority of the Nation State', in Albert Bergsen (ed.), *Studies of the Modern World System* (New York: Academic Press, 1980).
63 *The Culture of National Security*, p. 34.
64 Ruggie, *Constructing the World Polity*, p. 11.
65 Ruggie, *Constructing the World Polity*, pp. 33–4.
66 Ruggie, *Constructing the World Polity*, p. 14.
67 See especially his *The Construction of Social Reality* (New York: Free Press, 1995).
68 Ruggie, *Constructing the World Polity*, p. 20.
69 See Friedrich Kratochwil, *Rules, Norms, Decisions, passim*.
70 Most particularly 'The Agent-Structure problem in International Relations Theory', *International Organization*, 1987: 41(3): 335–70; 'Anarchy is What States Make of it: The Social Construction of Power Politics', *International Organization*, 1992, 46(2): 391–425; 'Collective Identity Formation and the International State', *The American Political Science Review*, 1994, 88(2): 84–96; 'Constructing International Politics', *International Security*, 1995, 19: 71–81.
71 Still unpublished at the time of writing.
72 Wendt, 'Identities and Structural Change in International Politics', in Yosef Lapid and Friedrich Kratochwil (eds), *The Return of Culture and Identity to IR Theory* (Boulder, CO: Lynne Rienner, 1996), p. 48.
73 Wendt, 'Identities and Structural Change', p. 50.
74 Wendt, 'Identities and Structural Change', p. 52.
75 Wendt, 'Identities and Structural Change', p. 59.
76 Wendt, 'Identities and Structural Change', p. 61.
77 Wendt, 'Identities and Structural Change', pp. 60–1.
78 This is especially true of his early work. See, for example, his *The Control of the Arms Race* (London, 1962). However, even in later writings this comes through as well. I have explored Bull's thinking on arms control in 'Arms Control, International Society and the End of the Cold War', *Arms Control*, 1992, April.
79 See Jackson, 'Is There a Classical International Theory?', in Smith, Booth and Zalewski (eds), *International Theory: Positivism and Beyond*. He makes this claim on p. 213.
80 See Nick Wheeler, 'Pluralist or Solidarist Conceptions of International Society: Bull and Vincent on Humanitarian Intervention', *Millennium: Journal of International Studies*, 1992, 21(3): 463–87.

81 Murray Forsyth, 'The Classical Theory of International Relations', *Political Studies*, 1978, 13(1): 32–57.
82 R. J. Vincent, *Non-intervention and the International Order* (Princeton, NJ: Princeton University Press, 1978).
83 R. J. Vincent, *Human Rights and International Relations* (Cambridge: Cambridge University Press, 1986).
84 Robert Jackson, 'The Political Theory of International Society', in Ken Booth and Steve Smith (eds), *International Relations Theory Today* (Cambridge: Polity Press, 1994), p. 111.
85 It is unusual, I know, to introduce personal anecdote into a scholarly study but it is worth recording here that the last conversation I had with John Vincent, at a conference lunch at Madingley Hall in Cambridge, a few weeks before his shockingly abrupt death in 1990, concerned just this. He was bursting with enthusiasm, as always, and was glad that at last he saw the opportunity for some real work on this topic, which he believed was one of the central questions confronting both the study and practice of international relations.
86 Tim Dunne, for example, has suggested that Andrew Linklater, Philip Allott, Andrew Hurrell, Ole Wæver, myself and Martin Griffiths might qualify as 'critical international society theorists' (Dunne, 'International Society: Theoretical promises fulfilled?', *Co-operation and Conflict*, 1995, 30(2): 125–54). I can, of course, speak only for myself, but while this is a not implausible reading of some of my earlier work, my view on English school international society theory has always been sceptical and is now rather more than that. This is not to say that the international society tradition is either unimportant or uninteresting (I would hardly be discussing them in this book if I thought that) but it is to say that, as I see it, it is ethically profoundly confused at best and dangerous and harmful at worst.
87 A good example of this sort of claim can be found in the discussion of Vincent by Iver Neumann, a student of Vincent's, in Ole Wæver and Iver Neumann (eds), *The Future of International Relations: Masters in the Making* (London: Routledge, 1996). Neumann himself is very sympathetic to both constructivist and critical theory as can be seen in his *Russia and the Idea of Europe* (London: Routledge, 1994).
88 An example of the possible openings available in Wight's work can be found in Roger Epp's excellent chapter in Francis A. Beer and Robert Hariman (eds), *Post-realism: The Rhetorical Turn in International Relations* (Minneapolis: University of Minnesota Press, 1996). If, indeed, there is such a thing as a 'critical' international society theorist, then Epp probably comes closest to it.
89 See, especially, Adam Watson, *The Evolution of International Society* (London: Routledge, 1992).
90 Wight is again the principal exception, largely due to his theological cast of mind. As his exchange with Toynbee in the appendix to volume VII of *A Study of History* (Oxford: Oxford University Press, 1954) makes clear. His view is far less state centric than many of his colleagues. Again, Roger Epp has documented this very ably. See Epp *et al.*, in Beer and Hariman (eds), *Post-Realism: The Rhetorical Turn in International Relations*.
91 The paradigmatic statement of this view is Wheeler and Dunne, 'Hedley Bull's Pluralism of the Intellect and Solidarism of the Will', *International Affairs*, 1992, 72(1): 91–107. Though their edited book *Human Rights, Human Wrongs* (Cambridge: Cambridge University Press, 1998) makes similar points.
92 My argument here will focus on the 'liberalizing tendency' within the English school, as well as some critical theorists sympathetic to it (like Linklater). More conservative versions of the English school argument would doubtless have a different set of responses to cosmopolitan arguments but then they would probably reject these anyway and it is not part of my concern here to argue that particular toss.

93 This is a theme in James Der Derian's excellent edited collection *International Theory: Critical Investigations* (London: Macmillan, 1995).
94 See Moravscik's widely cited 'Liberalism and International Relations Theory', Harvard University CFIA Working Paper No. 92–6.
95 Dunne's article contains a detailed and concise discussion of the 'metatheoretical' debates in contemporary IR theory relevant to this, especially the levels of analysis problem and the agent–structure debate. See Dunne, 'The Social Construction of International Society', *European Journal of International Relations*, 1995, 1(3): 368–72.
96 Dunne, 'The Social Construction of International Society', p. 373.
97 Alexander Wendt, 'Anarchy is What States Make of it: The Social Construction of Power Politics', *International Organization*, 1992, 46(2): 395–425.
98 Dunne, 'The Social Construction of International Society', p. 384.
99 Linklater, 'Sovereignty and Citizenship in the Post-Westphalian State', *European Journal of International Relations*, 1996, 2(2). He is also writing a study linking English school theorizing to emancipatory and cosmopolitan theory with his Keele colleague Hidemi Suganami. See his discussion in *The Transformation of Political Community* (Cambridge: Polity Press, 1998), p. 10.
100 For a brief recent attempt which ends up, I think, simply asserting that statesmen should be liberals see Nick Wheeler, 'Guardian Angel or Global Gangster? A Review of the Ethical Claims of International Society', *Political Studies*, 1996, 44(2): 123–35.
101 This is a point that Wendt, Jepperson and Katzenstein effectively concede. See their lengthy note 14 overlapping pp. 13–14 in *The Culture of National Security*. Moreover, as I pointed out in the previous chapter, a number of revisionist attempts to reread realism can be read as being implicitly 'constructivist' in this sense.
102 See his concluding essay in *The Return of Culture and Identity to IR Theory*, and, in much greater detail, his argument in *Rules, Norms and Decisions*.
103 There is of course a different route altogether. But I shall come to this in the Epilogue.

3   Institutions

For all that realism has dominated IR theory in the twentieth century, it is in many ways liberal attempts to solve 'the problem of order' that have largely set the stage for alternative accounts. If, as Hobsbawm has suggested, we see the twentieth century as 'short', as essentially 'beginning' with the European suicide of 1914–18, then it is with the peace settlement of 1919 and its associated crises that the century 'begins' in terms of world order.[1] And, with all its flaws and problems, that settlement helped to create a framework of international institutions more formally committed to central liberal principles, activated and directed by liberal ideas and practices, than ever before. It was against that settlement and on the anvil of those aforementioned 'flaws and problems' that political realism in its twentieth-century form was initially hammered out, in explicit opposition to liberal ideas about world order, and against liberal ideas too that many members of the English school continued to rail, though in rather different ways.

Equally, at the other end of the 'short twentieth century' it is the alleged 'triumph' of liberal ideas and practices, heralded by the end of the Cold War and the collapse of the Soviet Union that has dominated much IR theory since 1989. If, as Michael Walzer has said, 'political theories are tested by events in the political world',[2] then the dominant theories of *international* politics, most prominently among them the latterly fashionable versions of realism, have not passed the test very well.[3] Liberalism, on the other hand, seems to do much better in this new world of global markets, increasing democracy, multilateral decision making and cultural difference.

Of course, liberal thought and practice in the twentieth century has been a central theme of political science for much of that century, hotly contested and endlessly debated, and many good accounts of it exist, from multifarious perspectives.[4] What I want to focus on here, however, is the central role *institutions* play in liberal thought and practice, especially in international relations and, especially, the *manner* in which they play that role. As we saw, of course, in many respects 'societal' thinking in international relations – both English school and 'constructivist' – also emphasizes the role that institutions can play. However, *liberal* institutions play a very specific set of roles and it is this feature of liberal theory on which I shall want to focus here.

This chapter thus has five main sections. In the first section, I offer a thumbnail sketch of liberal politics tracing how liberal politics sees institutions and how these are usually related to the goal of international order in general. The next three sections then each illustrates one concrete way that liberal international theorists have tried to make good on the claim that liberal institutions can support world order, and indeed, at least on some views, that it is the only thing that can. The final section then offers an argument that is sceptical of such claims and contends instead that liberal politics is in danger of being rent asunder by the evolution of world politics and that, as a result, its institutional emphasis needs, at the very least, to be greatly reconfigured.

Liberal politics, liberal institutions and liberal order

The 1990s opened with the triumph of liberal values being loudly heralded. Liberalism's two great opponents of the twentieth century, fascism and communism, had both been seen off and the result seemed to be that, as one of the most celebrated chroniclers of the triumph of liberalism put it – though someone whose view of liberal politics is, I think, more ambiguous than is usually assumed, of which more in Chapter 5 – 'at the end of history, there are no serious ideological competitors left to liberal democracy'.[5]

In the rather more chastened atmosphere of the late 1990s, surrounded as we are by the evidence of the persistence, indeed the rude health, of fundamentalisms, atavisms and nationalisms of every kind and by the unique and persistent ingenuity of human attempts at butchering other humans, a more modest liberalism is the order of the day, at least on the surface. Yet it is still rare, at least in the public discourse of liberal states, to find any serious doubts about the continuing viability of liberal politics or about the extent and worth of its ideological and material 'victory' over other forms of politics. In contrast, it is my contention in this chapter that an examination of liberal attempts to think through the 'problem of order' in world politics reveals just how problematic the continuing viability of liberal politics really is, and that it also forces advocates of liberal politics to face up to some of the most wrenching questions about itself. Whether it is possible also to resolve or at least begin to resolve some of these problems is a question I shall defer to the final section of this chapter.

I do not think, though, that any of this should come as a particular surprise – at least to liberals. As the wisest among them have always known – and I think here especially of Montesquieu, Kant, Tocqueville and Mill – liberal politics, no less than other political forms, is susceptible to particular dangers – dangers, that is to say, that are *particular to* liberal politics – as well as to those to which all political forms are heir. Or to put it slightly differently, and in the words of Judith Shklar whose thought we will examine in a moment, liberal politics is an *especially* difficult kind of politics.

Such liberals have consequently taken particular care to seek to avoid these dangers. Unfortunately, as we shall see, many of their contemporary followers have not been as careful and, in any case, the problems and aporias of contemporary 'international life' make such avoidance doubly difficult. Indeed, ironically, it is precisely the success of liberal politics in clearing the field of major perceived ideological rivals that has left its own problems ever more exposed. Therein lies both its danger and – possibly – its hope.

Among the most important of these problems is the centrality – and at the same time the ambiguity – for liberal politics of the assumed division of politics into 'domestic' and 'international' forms. Liberals have now to face the fact that the evolution of world politics is putting increasing pressure on that form of political association that they have historically chosen to be the principal carrier of the liberal project, to wit, the nation-state. Of course, it is far from clear that states cannot adapt to such pressures and much of the literature of 'globalization' – the most common catch-all term for this phenomenon – seriously underestimates, it seems to me, the extent to which 'the state' is a remarkably adaptive political form. Moreover, as we shall see, perhaps the most important central liberal assumption is suspicion of the state. Nonetheless, the very real changes in the global political economy, the very public rise of issues such as environmental pollution and degradation, the clear increase in such phenomena as multilateralism, and the exponential rise in the number, roles and capacities of various forms of international organizations and perhaps most of all the stunning and exponential increase in technological (and especially informational) change all point to a changing, possibly transforming, environment for world politics in the next century.[6] As I remarked in the Introduction, this raises the question of 'order' in a particularly acute form – what pattern? how applied? by whom? – but it also throws into question the way in which liberal and democratic politics choose, most often, to configure themselves; that is to say, within a relatively clearly defined territorial unit with identified and clear citizens who are the holders of rights and obligations.

These phenomena, and whether or not one holds them to be radically transformative, therefore put in question the dominant contemporary liberal approaches to politics in general and world order in particular. 'Liberal politics', of course, is a hugely contested term. In academic political theory over the last few years there has been a veritable explosion of interest in and discussion of liberal politics. If one wished to be unkind, one might say that such discussions have become a drug on the market following the so-called rebirth of liberal political theory[7] consequent upon the publication in 1971 of John Rawls' *A Theory of Justice*, the *locus classicus* of dominant forms of contemporary liberal theory. Added to that, of course, is the large amount of discussion of the processes of 'liberalization' and 'democratization' in the aftermath of the revolutions of 1989, the growing significance of economic liberalism globally and the increasing number of countries seen as 'liberal democratic' (what Samuel Huntington has referred to as the 'third wave of democratization')[8]. However, this amount of discussion (and indeed action) has not always increased the clarity of what, precisely, liberal politics consists of.

In this book, it is neither possible nor necessary to embark on an exhaustive discussion of the ins and outs of liberalism. Rather, what I want to suggest is that, at least in its modern form – roughly speaking the form which it has increasingly taken from the late seventeenth century onwards – liberalism has four basic aspects, combined together in different ways and to different degrees by various liberals.[9] The four also represent, in interesting ways, what we might call the 'layers' of the historical development of liberalism. I want to look briefly at each of these assumptions in turn.

The liberalism of fear

The first aspect claims that liberal politics is essentially constituted by the fear of the exercise of arbitrary power, whether exercised by states or their governments – the usual case – or by other types of collectivities or individuals. The most acute and powerful advocate of this form of liberal politics in recent years has been the political theorist Judith Shklar.[10] As she has put it this form of liberalism 'has only one overriding aim: to secure the political conditions that are necessary for the exercise of personal freedom'.[11] Its sources lie in the Europe of the fifteenth and sixteenth centuries but it includes among its advocates many of the most distinguished liberals of later times including, for example, Montesquieu and among writers of today, Tzvetan Todorov[12] and, most interestingly from the point of view of IR theory, Stanley Hoffmann. Shklar goes on to emphasize that this liberalism is 'entirely non-utopian. In that respect', she adds, 'it may well be what Emerson called a party of memory, rather than a party of hope'.[13] The memory most pressing for contemporary liberals in this context, Shklar suggests, is the history of the world since 1914, especially the huge increase in things like torture and the emergence of what she calls 'national warfare states'. Thus, contemporary liberal politics of this sort concentrates on actual or potential abuses of power in all regimes, including liberal ones; 'the assumption, amply justified by every page of political history, is that some agents of government will behave lawlessly and brutally in big or small ways most of the time unless they are prevented from doing so'.[14]

Constitutional liberalism

The second aspect of liberal politics is its emphasis on constitutionalism. Of course, 'constitutionalism' is older than liberalism[15] but in the eighteenth and nineteenth centuries the two formed a particularly powerful and felicitous fusion. It is this form of liberalism that is chiefly associated with the Enlightenment and with the American founding; when Richard Hofstader famously wrote that it was the fate of the United States not to have ideologies but to be one, it was of this that he was thinking. The great political thinkers of the Enlightenment – all liberals in one sense or another – Voltaire, Montesquieu, Hume, Bentham and Kant, for all their differences, were agreed on this; the best government was a government of laws and not of men.

Of course, constitutional liberalism is open to interpretation, but in essence it is summed up in that hoary phrase, the rule of law. Government by consent, by (probably) representative – though not necessarily democratic – institutions, a relatively plural and open society – these are the hallmarks of constitutional liberalism.

Individualism

Liberal politics is often seen, and rightly, as a politics that foregrounds the individual over and above the community. At its root it is simply the belief that it is the individual that counts and that it is the responsibility of society to rank individuals and their welfare highly. This has a wide range of possible implications, of course. Perhaps most important in the modern world, it is one of the main roots of economic liberalism. As Samuel Brittan has said in a recent influential account of economic liberalism '[the hallmarks of economic liberalism are first] individualist liberalism ... the market comes second as an instrument of human co-operation and capitalism third as the only known working embodiment of the market system'.[16] However, closely following this in importance and perhaps more important, at least in terms of its potential for liberal accounts of world order, is the way in which it has come to be used to legitimate 'rights talk' running on a parallel track, as it were, to the constitutional liberalism described above. Rights for liberals are above all – and whatever qualifications might be added[17] – the rights of individuals. In international relations it is this liberal emphasis on rights that has perhaps become the most important – and among the most controversial – aspects of 'liberal claims' about what a stable world order requires.

Cognitive liberalism

This, the final aspect of contemporary liberal politics, is also, probably, the most controversial. Few would doubt that, to some degree or other, the above three aspects are present in most, if not all, sincere liberal theory and actual liberal practice. This final aspect, however, is much less familiar. However, it has not gone unnoticed, even if others choose to call it by different names. Richard Bellamy, in one of the best recent general studies of liberalism, discusses the phenomenon I am referring to and calls it 'ethical liberalism'. He describes the characteristic assumption of this form of liberalism as combining 'a philosophical and a social thesis, the latter providing the former with a coherence it otherwise lacked'.[18] The philosophical thesis holds that it is possible to maximize an equal set of harmoniously existing liberties for all members of any given group (usually a national group). The social thesis assumes that societies would develop in such a way that would lead to the basic harmonization of life plans at least to the extent that root and branch clashes could be avoided.

This assumption is rooted in many of the same currents of thought that have strengthened constitutional and economic liberalism, specifically the thought and practice of the European Enlightenment and, especially, the belief in the methods and requirements of natural science. Science, on these assumptions, is

usually held to require a commitment to universalizable or harmonizable knowledge. It is thus no accident that many influential philosophers of science have
also been, implicitly or explicitly, liberals, perhaps the most famous – and most
explicit – example being Karl Popper.[19]

Institutionalism, cosmopolitanism and the forms of liberal 'order'

In the twentieth century, in North America, Western Europe and elsewhere
where liberal politics has been prominent, I want to suggest that one way of
combining these four aspects has proved especially popular, indeed dominant. I
will refer to this version of liberalism, as most of its adherents do, as
'cosmopolitan liberalism', though I emphasize that there are a number of
different variants of it, and I should emphasize also that in the Epilogue to the
book as a whole I shall want to reclaim the term 'cosmopolitan' for a rather
different approach. As Charles Beitz has said, 'cosmopolitanism' is defined in
general terms as inclusive and non-perspectival, that is to say it encompasses all
'local' points of view and it tries to see all things in relation to the whole.[20] Not
all cosmopolitans are liberals, of course – as we shall see in the next chapter
most critical theorists would also see themselves as cosmopolitans. In terms of
cosmopolitan *liberalism*, therefore, we might say that it emphasizes individualism
– and therefore rights – as being the most effective way of being 'inclusive',
suggests that constitutional structures are the only sure ways of securing such
rights and holds, in broad terms at least, that it is possible (though of course by
no means inevitable) that societies will develop in such a way as to permit the
effective harmonization of life plans. It is also important to note that *cosmopolitan
liberalism is, by definition, universalist.*[21]

The dominant modern forms of liberalism, as well as some forms of socialism
and conservatism, at least as they are practised in the West, are subsumable
under this general understanding. There are, of course, differences. Many
liberals – perhaps the best known is Isaiah Berlin – have denied the basic
assumption of what I have called 'cognitive liberalism' and suggested that politics, even liberal politics – or perhaps especially liberal politics – is marked by an
irreducible pluralism and that it is this fact that requires us to adopt constitutional politics as the best guarantor of the protection of the individual.[22] Still
others – most notably Will Kymlicka – have emphasized the significance of
seeing rights, sometimes at least, in terms of groups as well as individuals. The
currently most influential academic liberal, John Rawls, seems to have moved
from a position which emphasized individualism as the wellspring of liberal politics to one which emphasizes constitutionalism over rights.[23] Nonetheless, most
of these liberals are, to a greater or lesser extent, representatives of cosmopolitan
liberalism.

This view of liberalism also issues in a fairly clear conception of world order.
Again the emphasis is on rights and, subsequently, on the conditions for securing
such rights, in the first place an emphasis on constitutional forms and practices,

especially in the contemporary context, liberal democratic forms within states, and in the second place a concern for international institutional structures that consolidate and, if possible, enhance such rights and such practices. It sees world politics as largely composed of separate sovereign states whose behaviour patterns are largely determined by their domestic political regime. Thus, liberal states keep the peace with one another – the so-called 'liberal peace' thesis that I shall turn to in a moment – whilst being perfectly prepared to use force on other, non-liberal, states. War, in this context, is a regrettable but necessary aspect of international order. International order is also, however, a society with obligations and responsibilities accruing by virtue of membership and especially by virtue of the express consent given by states to international law, the chief mechanism for regulating and monitoring international order. However, most important of all, cosmopolitan liberals emphasize that growing institutionalization is the only way in which liberal forms can be 'globalized', especially in the context of globalization.

I want to emphasize two things here. First, both aspects of liberal order are versions of one central claim, to wit that *only* liberal institutions can improve the prospects for order in an Aronian sense, since only liberal institutions manifest liberal politics and liberal politics is the one form of politics that can, in fact, do justice to the complexity of the problem of order and hold open the prospect of a way of resolving it. The second is that in the twentieth century advocates of liberal politics in international relations have oscillated between the belief that the most appropriate institutions are state based – that is, fundamentally the view that liberal states themselves can solve the problem of order – and the view that what we need is to institutionalize – in a liberal way, naturally – world politics itself. In contemporary liberal theory, for example, variants of the first view can be found in Rawls' recent essay 'On the Law of Peoples',[24] variants of the second in the work of scholars like Thomas Pogge.[25]

In contemporary IR theory these views are both strongly represented. In the third and fourth sections of this chapter, I want to examine what I take to be particularly influential versions of each of these: in the first place what is usually called the liberal democratic peace thesis and in the second, perhaps the dominant form of liberal IR theory, so-called 'neo-liberal' institutionalism. Before I do this, however, I want to look at a rather different version of liberal politics in international relations, one that is perhaps best represented by Aron himself.

The liberalism of fear and the dialectic of order

In terms of the fourfold characterization of liberal thought I offered at the opening of this chapter, the cosmopolitan liberal position represents a version – or rather differing versions, depending on the particular advocate – of cognitive liberalism, suffused with admixtures of constitutionalism and individualism. The one tradition that is largely downplayed, when it is not ignored altogether, is the liberalism of fear. Yet this is perhaps the root of liberal thinking about order, and, as I remarked above, it has some powerful contemporary adherents.

I shall start by returning to Raymond Aron. As I suggested in the Introduction, Aron is among the most acute analysts of the problem of order this century. Of course, Aron's body of work is enormously diverse. It ranges from the philosophy of history, through political and social theory, to empirical sociology, narrative history, international relations and cultural and political criticism.[26] Part of the reason for his surprising neglect in the contemporary literature of political science and international relations, I suspect, has to do with the very range of his intellect. Proud hedgehogs, as modern social scientists tend to be, are always suspicious of elegant foxes, especially Gallic ones. Another reason, of course, is the hostility shown to Aron in his lifetime by the left in France (and elsewhere) of which he was such an acute – though often sympathetic – critic. 'Better wrong with Sartre than right with Aron', as the saying went, might now be amended to 'better wrong with (take your pick) Foucault/Derrida/Lyotard/Levinas/Baudrillard/etc. than right with Aron', but the sentiment is still real, even in a France where Aron's reputation stands higher than it has ever done.[27]

In this context, I want to offer a brief interpretation of Aron's assessment of the character and vicissitudes of liberal politics and I will then look at his general account of international relations. These discussions will then serve as a background and context for a reading of his interpretation of what I shall call the 'dialectic of liberal order' in world politics. However, I would also emphasize that Aron has been followed in this by a number of contemporary scholars, perhaps most importantly Stanley Hoffmann, but also more recently John Hall. Moreover the liberalism of fear, as I remarked above, is a view most particularly championed of late by the political theorist Judith Shklar, a close friend and colleague of Hoffmann's. I shall have occasion to refer to all their arguments in what follows. The sketch I give of this view is, therefore, to some extent a composite of their views, and should not be ascribed *in toto* to any of them. It will serve as a backdrop to the more usual institutional liberalism in international relations that I will discuss in the next two sections.

Aron's liberalism

As a number of writers have said, Aron was all his life a passionately committed supporter and defender of liberal democracy.[28] However, his version of liberalism is worth looking at in some detail as it is rather different from the most popular and common versions of liberal politics today, such as those we examined in the above two sections. A good place to begin is with his 1964 essay 'The Liberal Definition of Freedom'.[29] In this essay, Aron compares and contrasts the thoughts on freedom of two of the greatest nineteenth-century thinkers on these topics, Tocqueville and Marx. It comes as no surprise, of course, to realize that Aron is more sympathetic to Tocqueville. However, what is more surprising is the basic question that Aron thinks emerges from a comparison of the two thinkers. This is, quite simply, are contemporary Western societies (he calls them 'industrial' societies),

the heirs of liberalism, concerned primarily with subjective rights and representative institutions, or of the promethean ambition of the Marxists,
concerned with freedom in their own way but with a freedom that would
come about through the fundamental re-organization of society beginning
with its existing socio-economic infrastructure?[30]

More surprising than the question, even, is the answer that Aron wants to give it.
For, at least on one level, he thinks, the answer is both. As he points out,

> among the freedoms proclaimed by the Atlantic Charter there are two that
> would have been ignored by traditional liberals – freedom from want and
> freedom from fear – because want and fear, hunger and war, were inherent
> to human existence throughout the centuries. That poverty and violence
> have been as of now eliminated no one believes: that one day they might be
> why not hope? That the ambition to eliminate them is new and shows an
> arrogance that ... Tocqueville would not have shared or approved is beyond
> doubt. For this ambition emerges from equating the tyranny of things with
> the tyranny of men ... only men can deprive other men of the right to
> select a government and worship a god. But what men are responsible for
> and what men can conquer want and fear? No social condition must be
> accepted as independent of the rational will of men. This is nearly a textu-
> ally Marxist formula but it expresses the common faith or universal illusion
> of modern societies. From the moment this equivalence is raised or this
> ambition asserted, industrial (liberal) societies ... even if they in fact [are]
> liberal democracies, are permeated with a spirit fundamentally different
> from the one that inspired the framers of the American constitution.[31]

Aron's conclusion, however, is not quite what this difference might lead us to
think that it would be. Aron does not doubt that, in principle, these two principles can be combined and, indeed, he believes that, in practice, in modern
liberal democratic societies they are indeed combined. However, what Aron does
want to suggest is that the compound term – liberal democracy – is itself indica-
tive of a real tension in modern societies. As he puts it,

> [the] societies in which we live ... [are] democratic in essence if one means
> by that, as Tocqueville does, the elimination of hereditary aristocracies:
> [they are also] normally, if not necessarily, democratic if one means that no-
> one is excluded from citizenship and the spread of material well being. On
> the other hand [they are] liberal only by tradition or survival if by liberalism
> one means respect for individual rights, personal freedoms and constitu-
> tional procedures.[32]

In the terms which we used above then, we might say that Aron is suggesting
that cosmopolitan liberalism has become dominated by a particular fusion of
cognitive liberalism with individualism and that in the process the danger is that

the traditional constitutional procedures – that is to say, the institutions – and, especially, the liberalism of fear, that for Aron, as for Shklar, is at the root of classical liberalism, are being overwhelmed by it. I shall come back to this in a moment; however, let me now turn to Aron's international theory.

Aron and international relations

Aron's status as a 'theorist' of international relations is a curious one. He is well known as a contributor to both 'general' international theory (*Paix et la Guerre*) and to strategic studies[33] (*Le Grand Debat*) and yet contemporary 'theory' in either field makes almost no reference to him. In part this is simply a matter of academic fashion. None of the major trends within contemporary international theory – be they social scientific and positivistic, sociological or post-structural – have much in common with Aron and he was, in different ways, critical of them all. However, as I shall now argue, there is also a second reason.

Again, a good place to start is an essay, appropriately enough entitled 'What is a Theory of International Relations?'[34] In this essay, Aron makes clear what, for him, counts as the setting and agenda for international theory: 'I concluded (in Peace and War) that what constitutes the distinctive nature of international or interstate relations … rests in the legitimacy or legality of the use of military force'.[35] In part, the key here is Aron's use of the terms legitimacy and legality. For, as he emphasizes at the end of the essay,

> the whole approach, which proceeds from the determination of the international system as a specific social system to the prudence of the statesman through the analysis of sociological regularities and historical peculiarities, constitutes the critical or questioning equivalent of a philosophy.[36]

In other words, for Aron, a 'theory' of international relations includes both explanation and norms; neither, indeed, is really possible without the other.

In his general international theory, it is the way he deploys this conception that has caused most confusion. As he noted in the above essay, the term he uses to describe the fusion of theory and doctrine in *Peace and War* – Praxeology – brought a torrent of criticism. Yet he could not have been clearer as to its provenance. In the opening sentence of the fourth part of *Peace and War*, the section that he calls 'Praxeology: the antinomies of diplomatic Strategic conduct', he is as clear as it is possible to be: 'Normative implications are inherent in every theory', he says, before going on to say that, in his view, the essence of interstate relations raises two praxeological problems above all. He calls them the Machiavellian problem and the Kantian problem and identifies their essence as, respectively, the problem of legitimate means and the problem of universal peace.[37]

Again the emphasis is on 'legitimacy'. For Aron, 'legitimacy' was always a tension-filled, contradictory concept in the international realm. Just as international society is a unique kind of society, the only kind, Aron thinks, which accepts resort to force as potentially legitimate – a connection here to the English school – so the norms that govern such a society are unique, consisting of a compromise between – and not, please note, a synthesis of – what he calls the morality of struggle and the morality of law, each of which is the rationale of, respectively again, the Machiavellian and the Kantian problems.

Aron and order

The above two discussions serve as a necessary background for a consideration, finally, of the significance of order for Aron. Let me briefly recap on how he specifically conceptualizes it. In the paper first published in 1960 and that we have already had occasion to discuss, he argued[38] that there are five possible meanings of order for world politics. Two of these meanings, he suggests, are purely descriptive (order as any arrangement of reality, order as relations between the parts of said reality). One is purely normative (order as the conditions of the good life). The remaining two are hybrid and, in Aron's terms, analytical – that is, partly normative, partly descriptive (order as the minimum conditions for existence, order as the minimum conditions for co-existence). Aron's view is that it is the latter two – and especially the conditions for co-existence – that are the most fruitful for contemporary world politics.

In the first place, we can see, of course, how this conception of order flows naturally from his view of international theory. The 'conditions' for existence and co-existence are, given his praxeology, obviously both material and ethical and order is thus, almost by definition, constituted by the same tension and contradictory character which characterizes world politics more generally. As the subtitle to the fourth section of *Peace and War* makes clear, the poles of this contradiction are antinomies, and as Aron himself makes clear, they exist in permanent tension with one another, neither being collapsed into the other, each depending in part on its relation with the other.

Although Aron does not use this term, I will suggest that it is therefore convenient to refer to this way of viewing order as the 'dialectic' of order, dialectic here understood in the Elatic/Aristotelian/Hegelian sense of 'thinking in contradictions'. Aron stipulates that order is such a 'dialectical term, composed of contradictory and tension filled opposites: explanatory/normative; theory/practice; politics/ethics; struggle/law'.

What does this imply for *liberal* order, however? Here, I want to use as a foil for my own argument one of the best recent interpretations of Aron's thought on these questions, John Hall's recent book *International Orders*.[39] In this book, Hall suggests that the best way to conceive of international order is through what he calls a 'realism/liberalism mix'. His essential rationale for this is fairly straightforward. 'Realism cannot be abandoned', he says,

> as long as the world polity remains asocial ... still realism can be informed by liberalism in two ways. States are likely to be rational only when they have the capacity to think clearly *and liberal institutions, both inside and outside*

states, have helped and can help further towards this end ... secondly, whilst the homogeneity of the system which helps policy makers understand each other is not necessarily based on liberalism, the Kantian idea of liberal normative integration has some descriptive force and is still more powerful in prescriptive terms ... the first of these two points in effect argues that liberalism can provide the sociological base for realism, the second ... [helps to] imagine a world in which the necessary salience of realism would begin to diminish as other countries ceased to be objects of suspicion [emphasis added].[40]

Equally, of course, Hall thinks that liberalism is tempered and improved by realism. However, the major point for Hall is that the social conditions for realism are *provided*, at least in the modern world, by liberalism. This realism/liberalism mix is, he suggests, the essence of Aron's position, though Aron devoted, he says, 'curiously little attention' to the point just made.[41]

Now, I think that Hall is right to suggest that Aron's thought contains what we might call a realism/liberalism mix and I think, too, that he is right to suggest that under modern conditions it is liberalism that provides the grounding for realism, *if realism is seen as a focus on the character of the international system.* In other words, Hall is right to suppose that neo-realism is dependent on the social conditions of liberalism. The realism of a Kennan, a Niebuhr, even a Morgenthau, is, however, – as we have already seen – a rather different case.

Hall is also correct, I think, to emphasize what I earlier called the 'dialectical' character of the realism/liberalism mix, for Aron. His argument depends, as he suggests at the end of the first chapter, on neither collapsing into the other but the two being held together in a symbiotic – indeed contradictory – relationship.[42] However, I also think that Hall has a rather attenuated view of this dialectic, both in general and specifically as it relates to Aron's liberalism. If we recall the earlier discussion of Aron's notion of freedom, we will remember that Aron's concern was that the 'traditional' liberal concern with freedom from despotism was being conflated with what we might call the 'radical liberal' and Marxist claim to master nature in order to make a much larger freedom, freedom from want and fear, possible.

This suggests that, for Aron, the central core of liberal politics should be fear of arbitrary power: in other words, it is the liberalism of fear that should take precedence, and constitutional liberalism should be seen as a handmaiden of that. For Aron, then, strictly speaking the assumption of individualism is unnecessary – individuals in the required sense are already the central concern of the liberalism of fear – and those of cognitive liberalism positively dangerous, since they assume an historically and theoretically unlikely convergence of desire and possibility.

There is, of course, an obvious problem with this conception for an account of liberal world order. For Aron, international order is the normative/explanatory take on the conditions for existence and co-existence and this presumes that states are the entities which can provide for that. Yet, for the liberalism of fear, it is states who are usually the chief problem. It is the despotism of the state in any form that the classic liberals feared most, even if they also feared tyranny as the most likely way such despotism would be imposed. As Hall's discussion makes clear, and, indeed, as Aron's discussion of the same set of issues in *Peace and War* makes equally clear,[43] the possibility of liberal international order depends upon the possibility of correct – that is to say, normatively correct – action on the part of states, action that will enhance, rather than retard, liberal practice. This has two implications: first, we need to be sure that states actually can perform the tasks as set – without too much concern for the historical record as to whether they actually have done – and second, and perhaps more profoundly, we need to be sure that states, under contemporary conditions, are the *kinds* of actors which should perform the tasks the result of which will be 'order' in Aron's sense.

It is the recognition of this latter fact that has, I suggest, increasingly led liberals to look to international institutions as checks on sovereign power, just as liberal institutions act as such a check internally. However, as we shall see later on, this is a strategy that may not work under contemporary circumstances, at least without considerable reformulation. Before I can elaborate this point, however, let me move on to the two examples of contemporary liberal theory that focus on the specifically liberal sense of institutions.

The liberal democratic peace

First, I want to examine that thesis which has become the most talked of, and perhaps even the most widely accepted, claim made by liberal theory in world politics in recent years. This is the claim that liberal states do not fight one another; the claim, in other words, that there is emerging in world politics a 'liberal democratic peace'. I shall then supplement this argument, by focusing on a recent and very interesting claim that liberal states (and especially one liberal state) can justifiably act as an international hegemon. In both these cases, the basic argument is the same: liberal regimes are qualitatively different from other kinds of regimes; different and better and that, as a result, liberal regimes have a certain moral force in international affairs which should be parlayed into influence.

As I have just remarked this is now perhaps the most widely cited feature of the existing world order that has claims to be called a central plank of liberal politics. It is unambiguously universalist – all states configured in a certain way will share these characteristics, some unusual limiting conditions to one side – plausible – the kind of democracy assumed requires no great changes on those states already considered democratic – and offers a clear focus for a notion of liberal international order; it has both normative and explanatory power. In short it is almost the perfect cosmopolitan liberal strategy, which, of course, in part accounts for its popularity with liberals.

My strategy will be a very simple one. In a moment I shall start off by considering some of the better known formulations of the idea of the 'liberal democratic peace' with a view to providing a checklist, as it were, of the basic assumptions that seem to be going into the story. The most problematic assumption, I shall seek to suggest, lies in the claims that are being made about the character of liberal democratic regimes. Then, I shall seek to outline some of the more problematic aspects of the liberal democratic peace thesis before moving on to look at the argument for liberal hegemony.

The thesis stated

Let me start, then, with the theory of the 'liberal democratic peace' itself. I cannot forbear to remark at the outset how odd a theory it would have looked to almost any writer prior to the eighteenth century, whether or not they self-identified with liberalism or democracy. If Thucydides is to be believed, the most highly regarded democrat before that time, Pericles, not only did not accept the central contention of the 'democratic peace' – it would hardly in that context have been liberal, of course – (that democratic states do not fight each other) but regarded it as an absurd notion, unworthy of serious discussion.[44] After the time of Classical Greece, and due in no small part to the influence of Greek – and particularly Aristotelian – political science, especially to the rise of the theory of the mixed constitution,[45] and then to the dominance of models of government taken from Roman forms,[46] 'democracy' as such ceased to play a meaningful role in mainstream political thought and practice until the thirteenth and fourteenth centuries.[47] Even then, however, it hardly had a powerful or widespread role and liberalism, of course, did not really emerge in anything like its contemporary form until the eighteenth century.[48]

In the eighteenth and nineteenth centuries, of course, there were many who believed that liberalism – especially economic liberalism – would bring with it a decreasing salience of war. That optimism, however, is generally assumed to have been buried in the mud and agony of Flanders. In any case, the claims of our contemporary 'liberal democratic peace' theorists are rather more subtle – or at least better developed – than those of their nineteenth-century forbears. The key, of course, lies in the compound term. For all that many scholars and writers (carelessly, as it seems to me) use the term the ' liberal peace' (or indeed democratic peace) it is unambiguously clear that what is discussed today is the '*liberal democratic* peace', that is to say the 'peace' of (normatively) liberal states, with (procedurally) democratic systems.

The seminal force in the rearticulation of the theory in the last few years has unquestionably been Michael Doyle's work.[49] Doyle has been a powerful and articulate advocate of the dominant version of liberal world order and his presentation of the liberal democratic peace argument is, in many ways, the jewel in his crown.[50] Doyle's work has thus become the *locus classicus* of the theory of the liberal democratic peace, widely cited and discussed both inside and outside the academy.[51] There have, however, been a wide range of other writings which have drawn attention to this phenomenon[52] and my discussion here will be based on my understanding of the general arguments advanced across the whole of this literature, rather than by any one particular author.

Let me start with a basic outline of the theory as a whole. The essence of the approach is contained in one (empirical) observation – that democracies rarely (or, on some accounts, never) fight one another – and one (normative) assumption – that while democracies undoubtedly have as many conflicts of interests as other kinds of regimes, they do not see war as an appropriate method for resolving such disputes *between democracies*. This might be termed the first basic assumption of the thesis of the liberal democratic peace. The last point, however, leads on to the second basic assumption: that, although liberal democracies rarely (never) fight each other they *are* likely to fight non-democracies.

By far the largest discussion of the thesis of the liberal democratic peace has been around the empirical observation part of the first basic assumption, the *fact*, that is to say, of the democratic peace. Doyle's 1986 article made much of this, a point to which he has recently returned,[53] and it has been widely picked up elsewhere.[54] There is an obvious reason for this. If, after all, there were many examples of democracies fighting one another, the thesis would be far less plausible or interesting. A good deal of the critical literature too has picked up on this aspect and sought to suggest that, in fact, democracies have indeed, fought one another. I should emphasize that for my purposes here I am quite happy to concede that democracies (the definition of which I shall come to in a moment) have indeed fought each other very rarely, if ever – at least in the terms in which the thesis is usually expressed.

A second criticism widely picked up is also worth briefly addressing here. This is the claim that while empirically it might be true that democracies have rarely, if ever, fought each other, this is due to circumstances entirely separate from the fact of their being democracies. Notoriously, for example, this is the view of John Mearsheimer[55] who suggests that the European 'democratic peace' since the Second World War is perfectly consistent with neo-realist explanations emphasizing a 'third-image'[56] logic, to wit, that mutual fear (of the Soviet Union) forced the European states to band together on good old-fashioned balance of power principles and that the fact they were all (in some sense or other) democracies had nothing whatever to do with it. In this context, I would merely refer to the Aron/Hall point that I elaborated in Chapter 1. While this might be a telling argument against aspects of the liberal democratic peace argument, it is made possible by assumptions that are essentially liberal and so is hardly a knockdown argument against liberal world order as such. Moreover, it is both untestable and irrefutable. However, in this current context, I do not want to discuss the point in any detail. I am quite happy to concede both that there are occasions when the context is all and some occasions (at least) when the fact of democracy *is* the (relevant) context[57] which is, I think, all that the liberal democratic peace argument needs.

Let me now mention a distinction that is implicit in much of the literature but is made central (and most explicit) by Bruce Russett in one of the most comprehensive general books on the liberal democratic peace thesis. Russett suggests that within the general structure of the liberal democratic peace (he calls it just the 'democratic' peace) two broad families of assumptions can be found.

Characteristically (for Russett) they are described as 'models': the cultural/normative model and the structural/institutional model. Each of these 'models' explains what I termed above the two basic assumptions of the theory in slightly different ways. The cultural/normative model assumes that 'decisionmakers' will try and follow the norms of conflict resolution to which they are wedded 'domestically' and that they would expect other states' 'decisionmakers' to do the same. As a result, the major premiss of the *first basic assumption* – that violent conflicts between democracies will be rare (or non-existent) – is asserted because democratic decisionmakers expect to resolve conflicts by compromise and non-violence, and will expect other democratic decisionmakers to perceive the situation in the same way. The only possibility that this will not happen occurs if one or more of the democracies involved is politically unstable. The *second basic assumption* is held to be true because non-democratic decisionmakers use and would expect to have used against them violent and coercive forms of behaviour; thus democracies will be (rightly) suspicious of non-democracies and may in any case adopt 'undemocratic' measures in dealing with non-democracies.[58]

The structural/institutional model, by contrast, suggests the following different reasons.[59] Violent conflicts between democracies will be infrequent because democratic political systems and the associated checks and balances and the need for large-scale popular support for large-scale military action reduce the likelihood that such decisions will be made. Moreover, other states will see this and expect it and thus, in democracies, there will be expected to be time for processes of conflict resolution to work. However, violent conflicts between non-democracies or between democracies and non-democracies will be frequent because non-democracies are not so constrained, and as a result the calculations that structure relations between democracies do not apply. Democracies and non-democracies alike, in dealing with non-democracies, may make pre-emptive strikes, seek to force too many concessions and so on. Russett is far too old and cunning a fox, of course, to allow anyone to suppose that he thinks that these two accounts can be easily or simplistically kept apart. Each, clearly, runs into the other but, he wants to say, we should keep them separate because they may allow us greater richness in explanation through greater contextual sensitivity.

We now have a much clearer idea of the basic structure of the kinds of arguments that go to make up the thesis of the liberal democratic peace. It is time, therefore, to take stock and to look in a bit more detail at some of the terms and assumptions that mark this particular debate. Once we have done this, we can see, I suggest, the beginnings of a rather different critique than that which neo-realists like Mearsheimer have developed.

Some redefinitions

The first term that needs a rather more thorough look, I think, is war. As most theorists of the liberal democratic peace make perfectly clear they are concerned with interstate war. Russett is characteristically clear on this point. 'Here', he says, 'that term means war between sovereign "states" internationally recognised as such by other states'.[60] Russett accepts that this rules out all sorts of international conflict (some of it large scale, on his definition, i.e. a thousand or more battle deaths) such as colonial wars, wars of liberation, civil wars and so on. This is, admittedly, unfortunate, he says, but argues that such a strategy is necessary 'for the purposes of theoretical precision'.

On the face of it, this is a fair point, well made, but if we dig a little deeper some aspects of it begin to appear rather curious. To begin with, it assumes that the sorts of terms Russett here deploys possess an essential character and stability that they simply do not have. Terms like 'sovereign state', 'colonial war', 'war of liberation' and so on are surely themselves *political* terms, not simply juridical or definitional ones. The fact that certain states are so called because they are so understood by other states makes of the 'fact of statehood' a political fact, available for use as a political tool in the contest of interests and power. Major 'states' and their elites will, thus, clearly have far more influence on these political 'facts' than 'lesser' states and their elites. Terms such as 'colonial war' are not simply applicable in Russett's sense (his definition clearly effectively limits it to nineteenth-century European colonialism); they could be applied (and have been) to, for example, US-backed 'wars of liberation' in the modern world (against Nicaragua, in Afghanistan). Russett's definition is a stipulative one which can only have real plausibility if these terms have a stability and a non-contestable character that they cannot possibly possess.

A second, if often hidden, minefield of the debate over the liberal democratic peace, however, is the question of the proper understanding of democracy and what goes with it. By far the commonest way of understanding it is to see it as some version of what might be called 'procedural' democracy or what Mark Warren has called '*standard* liberal democracy' (SLD).[61] This is robustly described by Samuel Huntington as follows:

> a twentieth century political system is democratic to the extent that its most powerful collective decisionmakers are selected through fair, honest, and periodic elections in which candidates freely compete for votes and in which virtually all the adult population is eligible to vote.[62]

Doyle, Russett and most of the major theorists of the liberal democratic peace interpret democracy in this way, or something very like it.[63] Of course, in this they are hardly alone. It is by far the commonest understanding of democracy in political science more generally[64] and is also the one which is broadly that of most liberal democratic policymakers as well. There are, however, two other understandings of democracy that I will mention, as I shall want to return to them in the next two chapters.

The first is that understanding which we might call the 'Rousseauean' understanding of democracy or perhaps the radical understanding. I mean to include here what Warren calls the Self Transformation Thesis (STT), that is the claim that the practices of democracy themselves transform the character of political life and the assumptions, capacities, motives and ends of the involved agents. It is not simply Rousseauean, of course. Many modern writers have found this understanding of democracy elsewhere: in American thinkers such as Walt Whitman or Ralph Waldo Emerson, perhaps,[65] or even in avowedly anti-democratic thinkers such as Carl Schmitt, Nietzsche or Heidegger,[66] and there is a wide spread of views within the general understanding. However, for the purposes of the current argument I want just to highlight one aspect of this view: the claim that democratic culture is necessarily transformative and that among its most profound transformations is an attitude to the use of force in general and military force in particular.

The third view is perhaps a rather more idiosyncratic one. It is perhaps the rarest and the best recent statement of it is in John Mueller's *Quiet Cataclysm*. Mueller's view is simple. He agrees with the first view that the crucial aspect of democracy as a form of government is that it is responsive to the people. However, Mueller suggests that this is not necessarily related to competitive elections, (near) universal suffrage and so on. Rather he suggests that

> democracy – government that is necessarily and routinely responsive – takes effect when people agree not to use violence to overthrow the government and when the government leaves them free to criticize, to pressure and to try to replace it by any other means.[67]

Elections may, of course, make this process easier and smoother (though they may also make it rougher and more difficult); Mueller's point is simply that they are not necessary to it. Since Mueller refers to Sidney Smith in his presentation of this view[68] I shall call this view Smithian democracy, to contrast it with Rousseauean democracy.

Despite the significance of the various claims about 'democracy', however, unquestionably the most important set of assumptions in the liberal democratic peace thesis lies in the way it understands liberalism. Some theorists, indeed (and Doyle led the way in this as in much else), refer to it simply as the liberal peace. John Owen in his recent argument supporting the existence of a liberal democratic peace[69] has in fact made a specific point of arguing that it is liberalism, not democracy, that produces the liberal democratic peace. To use a social scientific term with which I am hardly enamoured but which seems appropriate in the context (and which Owen uses), for Owen liberalism is the independent variable in the thesis of the liberal democratic peace.

In his article (largely agreeing with Doyle here) Owen emphasizes social contract liberalism (i.e. the tradition that includes Hobbes, Locke and Kant) and makes it very clear that the version of liberal politics to which he thinks his argument applies is effectively a version of monistic cognitive liberalism or what we referred to in Chapter 2 as liberal cosmopolitanism. In fact, virtually all of the theorists of the liberal democratic peace assume a liberal cosmopolitan stance and it is this version of the dominant ethic of liberal order that is really on display in their arguments.

If we put together Owen's argument with the arguments of Russett and his colleagues, however, it would seem that Owen's argument that liberalism is the key independent variable creating the 'democratic peace' is only partially true in that it is liberal ideology *and* liberal institutions that create 'democratic peace' and either in the absence of the other would be much less likely to create democratic peace. Thus, we might say that on liberal cosmopolitan grounds the likelihood of the 'liberal democratic peace' is greatest when both cultural/normative and institutional/structural models are present; in other words, when both the regime (of states) and the regimes (in the international system) are liberal then, and most likely only then, is the democratic peace likely to be a reality.

The ideology of the status quo?

In this section, I want to offer some reasons for supposing that these arguments for the 'liberal democratic peace' are not only problematic in themselves but also serve to mask a rather more troubling feature of the literature of political science and international relations on these questions.

In the first place, let me just make one minor point. One does not need to accept John Mueller's provocative (and always entertainingly expressed) conviction that 'major war' is becoming obsolete[70] to recognize that the traditional 'war' (an interstate war, waged by sovereign adversaries with large numbers of casualties ('1,000 battle deaths or more')) is an increasingly rare bird in world politics. On one calculation over 90% of instances of war – or at least of 'armed conflict' – since 1945 would fall outside such definitions.[71] This merely emphasizes the point I made earlier about the stipulative – and normative – character of the definitions of 'war' that tend to be offered in discussion of the 'liberal democratic peace'. It is simply that peace here is seen as the absence of a certain kind of 'war'. Yet this kind of war is certainly less significant than previously and this has clear implications for the two basic assumptions of the liberal democratic peace thesis. As Mueller has sought to argue, it may be true that war aversion and liberal democracy are following a similar trajectory, but they may, in fact, have little directly to do with one another.[72] If war, defined as Russett does (and as he must do to include all the 'data' from the nineteenth and twentieth centuries they wish to include), is in decline anyway, it is perhaps not surprising that war between liberal democracies is rare, given that for most of the period there were very few of them and there was precious little, in any case, they had to fight about.

The most worrying aspect of the argument lies in a related point, however. I suggest that at the heart of the liberal democratic peace thesis – as it is understood by both advocates and critics – is a deeply misleading understanding of liberal democracy. This understanding is misleading because it ignores or misinterprets one of its own most important features. To develop this point let me return to the three understandings of democracy I outlined above.

The dominant understanding of democracy, which I earlier referred to as

SLD, very deliberately – and often explicitly – closes off certain avenues of discussion about what does and does not constitute democratic practice. In doing this it rules out the possibility that existing forms of democracy – liberal democracy – might, in fact, require radical alteration if they are to become meaningfully democratic. In other words these understandings of democracy are political in an additional sense from the obvious one; they work to defend a particular status quo, namely the present one.

Rousseauean understandings of democracy, however, insist that in their present form at least, liberal democracies are likely to be at best partial and inadequate democracies, or, if not that, then they require constant tending to ensure they work as genuine democracies are supposed to,[73] whereas the Smithian view suggests that both SLD and the Rousseaueans are asking too much of people or of systems.

The point is not simply to rehearse the obvious fact that democracy is a contested concept. Rather it is to highlight a curious silence on the part of most of the advocates of the liberal democratic peace. This silence, I suggest, is over the central role played by the state in the thesis. Of course, it is not that the state is ignored itself in the argument; quite the contrary. To use Keohane's terms, 'republican liberalism' is a fundamentally statist theory and 'sophisticated liberalism', inasmuch as it relies on multilateralism and so on, relies also on the category and norms of statehood. Moreover, SLD accounts, because of the way they have evolved and because of the emphases they have (on elections, universal suffrage, etc.) are also inevitably statist accounts.

However, Rousseauean and Smithian accounts are not so wedded to the state, or at least they do not have to be. Many critical poststructural theorists – I am thinking, for example, of writers as otherwise different as Andrew Linklater, David Held, William Connolly and Rob Walker[74] (all certainly among our Rousseaueans) – would hold that in order for it to be workable under contemporary conditions democracy must be de-territorialized, and/or globalized (I shall come on to discuss some of these ideas in a moment). Mueller's Smithian view is more pragmatic, suggesting that the key aspect of democracy is 'responsiveness' and implying that such 'responsiveness' could come in many forms, some certainly organized in states but many not. The point here is that theorists of the liberal democratic peace do not seem to see that by not taking alternative conceptions of democracy into account as part of the thesis, the liberal democratic peace is locked into an account that must focus on those instances of war that fit the statist premisses of SLD, which, as we have seen, represents a decreasing part of overall international conflict.

This has two particularly significant consequences, I think. The first is that it allows a largely inaccurate picture of liberal democratic states' hostility to 'war' to dominate the discussions of both those who agree with the thesis (largely liberals) and those who disagree (usually self-confessed 'realists'). That liberals have been hostile to war is unquestionably true,[75] that they have waged it with uncommon zeal is equally true. As we saw earlier, the theorists of the liberal democratic peace have suggested that this zeal occurs only against non-'liberal democratic regimes' and finds both normative and institutional reasons for this. However, I suggest an alternative reason. 'Wars' – in the sense implied by the liberal democratic peace thesis – are usually fought by 'states' to secure 'interests'. The marked absence of war between liberal democratic states certainly indicates that such interests as these states have *vis-à-vis* one another are unlikely to be achieved by war, but it also might indicate, I suggest, that the character of the state as such is the key 'variable'. There is, after all, no need to fight if you can achieve what you want without fighting. Broadly speaking, in the twentieth century, the major Western liberal democracies have been able to achieve what they wanted without fighting each other; though they have certainly had to fight others. The way the thesis of the liberal democratic peace is structured, however, ignores the fact that many of the 'others' they have chosen to fight have often not been fought by 'war' as defined above, rather they have been fought by covert war,[76] the support of proxies, economic sanctions (overt or covert)[77] and so on. Many of these 'others' were, however, 'democracies' – at least as Mueller understands the term – and some were – procedurally at least – liberal democracies. In other words, whether intentionally or not, the thesis of the liberal democratic peace has served to mask the clear fact that liberal democracies have behaved much as 'states' have always behaved – that is, badly – though of course the peculiarities of time, technology and culture should not be ignored.

They have masked this fact not so much by ignoring it (though many have certainly ignored it) but by suggesting implicitly or explicitly that it is unimportant or somehow gets in the way of 'theoretical precision'. Where such behaviour is noted, a usual excuse for it is to claim that all practice falls short of the ideal and, perhaps, to say as well that the concern of those who advocate the liberal democratic peace is to suggest trends, rather than to state irrevocable laws. Neither of these claims, however, refutes the basic point, which is that in terms of the practice of liberal democratic states – whatever liberal theory might say – they have been perfectly prepared to use highly unpleasant methods, up to and including lethal force, to achieve their ends.

This leads me to the second consequence which is starker still. By focusing on an aspect of international conflict that is, if my argument above was correct, of decreasing practical significance – but great rhetorical importance, for liberal democracies – the thesis of the liberal democratic peace actually helps to provide a normative justification for the role and power of the dominant states in contemporary world politics, a world politics that is still clearly and effectively structured around fundamental and increasing inequality and either active or passive coercive power. If we look at the reality of the 'embedded liberalism' Keohane refers to, we see a system that has allowed certain groups within the dominant states much greater freedom to pursue their own interests and which maintains a fairly clear control of the system, co-opting those members powerful enough to cause trouble and marginalizing or silencing those who would seek to change things.

There are, of course, many reasons for this and I suppose neither that it is always an intended effect of liberal statecraft nor that liberals or democrats are not, in many ways, attempting to overcome it. Indeed, one of the principal ways that liberals have sought to overcome it, human rights, will be my subject in a moment. Moreover, I do not suggest that many other states (or individuals, if it came to that) would act differently if they were the dominant powers. However, as long as the legitimacy of world politics is couched in terms of the discourse of the contemporary states system (sovereignty, self-determination and so on) such a situation will persist.

Of course, it is true that things can be seen as better or worse even within this system. It would be foolish to begrudge support to those liberals and others who genuinely seek to decrease the amount of suffering and hardship this situation creates. However, such a policy requires the sort of understanding of the character of liberal regimes and their strengths and weaknesses that no 'systemic' theory can provide (since, by definition, the character of the 'units' is largely irrelevant), and that most modern political science (or political theory if it comes to that) has failed to provide as well.

The liberal democratic state as hegemon: a justification?

To illustrate the sort of dangers that flow from not doing this, I now want to focus on an argument that is, I think, a reasonable extrapolation from the sort of 'liberal democratic peace' thesis we have been investigating, though in fact it is an argument of a rather different stamp. This is Lea Brilmayer's argument, on which I have already had occasion to comment briefly, to the effect that there is a justification for liberal hegemony (that is to say, the hegemony of liberal politics in the corporate person of the United States) in the conditions of contemporary world politics.[78]

Of course, Brilmayer's argument is not one that would necessarily be accepted by any of the liberal democratic peace theorists I have already discussed (indeed many would probably indignantly repudiate it). However, I want to suggest that there is a powerful link between them and that this link tells us something very important about the conception of liberalism that underlies the liberal democratic peace thesis and, indeed, cosmopolitan liberal conceptions of world order in general.

Let me begin by just outlining Brilmayer's argument in rather more detail. She starts by remarking, as we did earlier, that most of the mainstream literature to deal with questions of world order, hegemony, etc., is 'descriptive, analytical or historical'. Her project, on the other hand, is primarily normative. She goes on to say that her argument is that

> the legitimacy of international hegemony should be evaluated in much the same way that we would evaluate the legitimacy of other authoritative political structures, in particular domestic governments ... powerful states have

the same sorts of moral responsibilities to the states they dominate as to individuals in their power.[79]

Obviously in saying this, Brilmayer is challenging some fairly widespread assumptions about world politics. To name but two, Kenneth Waltz and Hedley Bull would both, as we have seen, reject this view and Brilmayer is indeed siding with those who reject the way in which the notion of anarchy has been used in IR theory.[80] Having established this she moves on to the main task of the book which is the justification of a 'liberal theory of international hegemony'. She starts by admitting that on the surface hegemony seems 'quintessentially autocratic' and therefore anti-liberal. 'If any principles might be taken as constitutive of the international normative order, they would be sovereign autonomy and sovereign equality. How could an international order that violates both of these principles ever be morally acceptable?'[81] However, she thinks that we should keep in mind that the same problem arises in domestic politics. 'Hierarchies abound, despite our domestic commitments to analogous principles of personal autonomy and equality ... [most] agree that domestic political hierarchies are in some circumstances justifiable. The central question, of course, is why and in what situation a justification exists'.[82]

Her answer is to start with an understanding of liberal politics firmly in the mainstream. 'Two common themes link the theories we will characterize as liberal', she writes, 'The first is the emphasis on democratic participation, with governance resting on some form of popular consent. The second is the protection of a particular set of substantive human rights from oppression even by majorities'.[83] She then asks what sort of factors would make hegemony consistent with these liberal principles and does so by means of a consideration of the Somalian intervention. She emphasizes certain features of the Somalian case which explain why it was less controversial than might have been supposed. I will just quickly run through them, in her own words.

> The first is that it seemed to be generally welcomed by the Somali people ... what matters, then, under this justification for American hegemony is the consent of the target state and its people ... what we will call contemporaneous consent. The intervention was also both multi-lateral and supported by the United Nations. ... These international norms and institutions are authoritative because they were established in advance by the entire world community. The US intervention in Somalia ... was justified because it followed procedures that were agreed to beforehand by the involved parties ... what we will call ex ante consent ... (thirdly) it can be argued that it is enormously beneficial to the world community that some strong state take charge. In Somalia, it can be claimed, what matters is not so much whether other states agreed to strong state leadership as the fact that strong state leadership was necessary for the public good. The benefits of international peace and stability require international governance for the same reasons that the benefits of domestic peace and stability require domestic gover-

nance ... whether or not American leadership was agreed to, it was a rational solution to the problem, a solution that rational states would have agreed to (which we will call) hypothetical consent. Finally ... the human suffering in Somalia was simply beyond the comprehension of most westerners; it challenged us as human beings to do something to help. I will deal with these straightforward arguments of human rights and basic subsistence needs under the category of substantive morality.[84]

The next four chapters of Brilmayer's book take up each of these claims in turn elaborating and defending a liberal case. Finally she comes to consider 'global liberalism and the new world order'. In this chapter she suggests that the four claims she has just outlined represent an ordered progression:

> From the first to the fourth, there is increasing attention to moral norms and decreasing attention to the positive preference of states. Yet precisely because these points are points on a spectrum, there is continuity. ... Second the four are overlapping in what they justify. There will be many actions which could be explained in terms of more than one of the rationales.[85]

However, there are problems with this argument, as Brilmayer readily admits. The first is the tendency of actual US policy to 'pick and choose' and/or to defend policies in more obviously 'realist' terms (the defence of oil or hard 'national' interests). The second and third are more obviously theoretical.

These consist in various versions of the 'communitarian' argument to the effect that 'states and their interests are as much a product of the international system as the international system is a product of their interests. If this is the case then the supposed consent of states may be illusory.'[86] A further elaboration of this is the acknowledged tension between 'liberalism' (i.e. cosmopolitanism liberalism) and 'statism' (i.e. Brilmayer's version of communitarian/constitutive/reflective critiques). In the main body of her argument, she attempts to resolve this problem by adopting what she calls a 'qualified statism', which is similar to, but subtly different from, other prominent forms of cosmopolitanism such as that of Beitz, Pogge and Doyle, which she calls 'derivative statism'. It is worth pausing for a moment and investigating the differences on this point, since I shall want to come back to them later.

According to Brilmayer, the arguments of liberal cosmopolitans like Beitz and (although she does not mention him) Pogge might be seen in terms of a 'derivative' statism in that

> they treat the deference due to states as only presumptive and not conclusive. The problem in reconciling liberalism with statism is that there are two competing sets of primary concepts, states and individuals. Statism elevates the state above the individual (for international purposes at any rate). Liberalism seems to do the opposite. But if we treat the state's power as at most presumptive ... the state would have only derivative entity status; it

would be entitled to moral standing only in so far as it acted on behalf of individuals.[87]

While this argument seems to mesh perfectly with the general tenor of Brilmayer's argument she also sees certain problems with it. Her earlier argument, she admits, depended rather on a 'qualified' statism, which while limiting the rights of states in important respects still tries to take national and ethnic loyalty (for example) more seriously than derivative statism seems to. In this respect she seems closer to aspects of pluralistic liberalism. Brilmayer is disarmingly frank that she sees this tension as a largely irresolvable one at present; 'liberalism', she says, 'has no ready answers' to this tension and the questions it raises. However, it is still the best hope for consistent and ethical foreign policy.

Peace, hegemony and liberal international theory

What, then, are the similarities between the liberal democratic peace thesis and Brilmayer's liberal democratic hegemon thesis, if any? And what do they tell us about liberal theories of world order? To begin to answer this let me just emphasize one thing about both arguments. They are both 'anti-systemic' in the sense of claiming that whatever might be true about 'the international system' the central determining feature of state behaviour in it is not 'the logic of the system' but, rather, the character of the political regime. Both arguments are agreed, in other words, that the existence of liberal regimes makes a difference; it creates the possibility of peace and provides a justification for hegemony. As we have seen also both the liberal democratic peace thesis and Brilmayer's argument see liberal regimes in terms of a fairly straightforward SLD understanding of democracy. In other words, they both emphasize the 'liberal' half of 'liberal democratic'.

However, we can also put the two arguments alongside one another and reveal some interesting dissonances. One of the most obvious aspects of the liberal democratic peace argument is the claim that relations between liberal states will be peaceful and on a basis of equality. While Brilmayer does not suggest that such relations will not be peaceful (and, indeed, the assumption in her book is consonant with the liberal democratic peace thesis in that liberal states, she agrees, would have little to fight about) she certainly does argue that they will not be equal. That, of course, is the whole point of asserting 'American hegemony'. A hegemon is, by definition, not equal but superior. Arguing for leadership by one liberal state over others is the *sine qua non* of Brilmayer's case.

If we put this together with some of our earlier observations relating to the stipulative character of the definitions involved in the liberal democratic peace argument a rather less benign picture of the liberal peace and the liberal hegemon emerges. For, of course, it is perfectly clear that European 'hegemons' in the nineteenth century (even liberal ones like Britain) were quite happy to use force to secure interests that were consonant with (say) economic liberalism.[88] It is true, of course, that they did not directly fight other liberal states (though the range of near misses indicates that this might have been more due to luck than to anything else, as I suggested earlier). Nonetheless, the claim that there is a justification for *liberal* hegemony, but not other kinds, is tantamount to suggesting that liberal states have the right to organize the world as they see fit. In other words, it is to say that liberal world order should be constructed in terms of liberal interests

The point here is to emphasize what ought to be, I would have thought, a fairly obvious point. Liberal states are, of course, states. They have interests as states and interests as liberal states, some of which overlap and some of which do not. However, it seems unlikely that the two are easily or happily separable. The interests of the United States as a state – that is to say, as a territorially defined, political bounded unit – in the Gulf War had to do with things like oil and geopolitical influence in the Middle East. The interests of the United States as a *liberal* state had to do with things like the preservation of the rule of law in international affairs, the opposition to tyranny in the person of Saddam Hussein, and the protection of the basic rights of the Kuwaiti people.

However, simply telling the story in that way makes it obvious that there were going to be points at which the interests of the United States as a state and the interests of the United States as a *liberal* state would conflict. For example, geopolitical interests and liberal interests clashed fairly directly over the deposing of the tyrant. The geopolitical interests of the United States, as defined by the political elite (or at least those sections of it that managed to win the bureaucratic battles in Washington), were said to lie in as stable a Middle East as possible after the war; thus support for the Kurds in Iraq or deposing Saddam as a brutal tyrant who was unquestionably violating the human rights of his own citizenry were ruled out as they would not serve these interests. Yet in terms of the 'global liberalism' advocated, in their different ways, by liberal cosmopolitans such as Beitz, Doyle and Brilmayer, the interests of the United States as a liberal state could, plausibly, be said to lie in the removal of Saddam and the granting of self-determination (after all a right enshrined in the UN charter) to the Kurds or the marsh Arabs. Of course, due weight would need to be given to the concerns of (say) the Syrians or the Iranians, as to the possibility of an independent Kurdistan (perhaps financial aid, buffer forces and so on might need to be considered) or to the international legal problems that a drive to Baghdad to depose Saddam might have created. Nonetheless this would be a consideration within the context of accepting the main point; that is, that the interests of the United States as a liberal state should take precedence over its interests as a state *per se*.

It is on this point that Brilmayer's frankness about the problems of liberalism versus statism should be born in mind. The 'derivative statism', which is what – Brilmayer is right – the 'moral cosmopolitanism' of a Beitz or a Pogge actually amounts to, is still, practically speaking, committed to states being the major actors in world politics for all of the reasons that Brilmayer cites. However, in so far as this remains the case, it seems likely (as has certainly been the case up until now) that state interests will outweigh *liberal* state interests when push comes to shove. However, if this is true, it has some fairly stark implications for the liberal democratic peace thesis. Since if it is the case that ultimately it is state interests that will dominate then it is conceivable that two liberal states *might* come to have reasons to fight each other. It might also give some circumstantial support to Mueller's argument that, while travelling on the same road, the rise of war aversion and the rise of liberal democracy are separate and separable phenomena.

What are the implications of all this for liberal theories of world order? On this view, it seems, liberal states do indeed have the right to order the world, since they possess regimes that are the most normatively justifiable and that promote the things which all desire, such as peace and prosperity. However, the problem is that these theories of world order are predicated upon the state, despite the emphasis placed on the rights of individuals, and that this leaves liberal states (and therefore liberal world order) with what we might call the problem of conflicting interests, reasons of states versus liberal reasons.

Liberals have tried, of course, various ways around this problem. One way has been outlined by perhaps the most interesting utilitarian to write on international ethics in recent years, Bob Goodin.[89] In Goodin's case, he suggests that we define state responsibilities as what he calls 'assigned general responsibilities', that is to say, responsibilities we all have, but assigned to that particular collectivity, state X. I shall return to this argument in my concluding section of this chapter. However, it is not, by and large, the root that most liberals have taken. If the state is a problem, in that state interests 'trump' liberal ones, they seem to say, then we will reconfigure both the state and liberalism in such a way that this will no longer be an option. The result, most commonly, is an increasing focus on the character and role of rights, considered as the centrepiece of liberal cosmopolitan thinking on world order as on other things, and secondarily the institutional framework which can allow such rights to exist. In other words, the suggestion has increasingly been made, *contra* the liberal peace thesis, that it is not the fact of liberal states that makes the crucial difference to world order, rather it is the existence and institutionalization of liberal principles and practices – usually characterized as rights – that matters most. This is perhaps the logical terminus of a cosmopolitan liberal argument. However, as I shall now seek to show, it is in fact an equally unstable solution.

Liberal (and neo-liberal) institutionalism

Among the most influential versions of liberal thinking in contemporary IR theory properly so called has been what is usually called 'neo-liberal' institutionalism or sometimes simply 'neo-liberalism'.[90] As a number of scholars have pointed out, this has usually been the most prominent form of liberalism in international affairs. As Joseph Grieco has said, for example, in his penetrating critique of such theories, prior to the present wave, liberal institutionalism appeared in three successive waves, the functionalist integration theory of the 1940s and 1950s, the neo-functionalist regional integration theory in the 1950s and 1960s and the interdependence theory in the 1970s.[91] One might add that the earlier so-called 'idealist' writers of the interwar period also emphasized international institutions and organizations, in direct contrast to what they saw as the ruinous (and quite unrealistic) 'realism' of the nineteenth-century balance of power system.[92]

However, the most influential contemporary version of liberal institutionalism sees itself in rather different terms. To understand the similarities and differences between this version of institutionalism and the previous sorts let me quote probably the most influential 'neo-liberal institutionalist', Robert Keohane, at some length.

'Liberalism is sometimes identified' he writes, 'as a belief in the superiority of markets to state regulation of an economy ... another conception of liberalism associates it with a belief in the value of individual freedom'.[93] However, neither of these, he thinks is especially relevant to his analysis of international relations. But, he goes on,

> liberalism also serves as a set of guiding principles for contemporary social science ... (as such) it stresses the role of human created institutions in affecting how aggregations of individuals make collective decisions. It emphasises the importance of changeable political processes rather than simply immutable structures and it rests on a belief in at least the possibility of cumulative progress in human affairs ... institutions change as a result of human action and the changes in expectation and processes that result can exert profound effects on state behaviour ... [thus] we need to understand which institutional patterns lead to more rather than less cooperative behaviour among states ... which conventions, regimes and organisations promote cooperation. Since Neo-liberal institutionalists share with realists the assumption that leaders of states calculate the costs and benefits of contemplated courses of action, putting the issue this way implies that we need to ask how institutions affect incentives facing states.[94]

Keohane suggests that this 'neo-liberal' position is different from other common forms of liberalism in international relations.[95] For example, what he calls 'republican liberalism' (chiefly represented today by the liberal peace thesis we examined in the previous section) together with what he calls 'commercial liberalism' usually overemphasize the 'harmony of interests argument' typical of a good deal of liberal thinking and downplay the necessary role of international institutions in affecting state behaviour.

Rather, Keohane suggests, state actions depend to a considerable degree on the flow of information and the opportunities to negotiate, the ability of governments to monitor others' compliance and to implement their own commitments and prevailing expectations about the solidity of international agreements. 'Institutions' he understands as 'persistent and connected sets of rules (formal and informal) that prescribe behavioural roles, constrain activity and shape expectations'.[96] Thus, Keohane suggests that international institutions understood thus can take one of three forms. The first is formal governmental or cross-national non-governmental organizations. The second he describes as international regimes and he uses Oran Young's term 'negotiated orders' to describe them. Examples would be the Bretton Woods system, the Law of the Sea regime and the US–Soviet Arms Control regime that existed during the Cold War. The third he calls 'conventions', which he regards as informal institutions with implicit rules and understandings.

He believes that in many respects these all overlap, for example conventions are usually both temporally and logically prior to regimes or formal organizations. He believes further that institutionalization as he understands it can be measured along three dimensions: *commonality*, that is the degree to which expectations about appropriate behaviour and understandings about how to interpret action are shared by participants in the system; *specificity*, that is the degree to which these expectations are clearly specified in terms of rules, and *autonomy*, that is the extent to which the institutions can alter their own rules rather than relying on others to change them.

Let us now look at how this view of institutions operates in terms of providing a 'liberal order' in world politics. Keohane's *After Hegemony*,[97] justly celebrated as a central text for neo-liberal institutionalism, offers one of the most carefully argued versions of this claim. In brief, Keohane's argument is as follows. Taking his starting point from the fact of interdependence, certainly among so-called 'advanced' capitalist states – a fact which he thinks his earlier work has established[98] – he suggests that interdependence creates discord and argues that if discord is to be limited and conflict avoided governments' policies need to be adjusted to one another. This, of course means that co-operation is necessary. In terms of the world economy, Keohane's explicit focus in the book, this can be achieved in a number of ways. The best known, he suggests, is through the activities of a hegemonic power (e.g. Britain in the nineteenth century or the United States in the period 1945–71). In non-hegemonic situations or situations where the hegemon is losing either its will or capacity to be hegemonic – the position Keohane thinks that the United States is now (in 1984) in – then the conditions are favourable for the emergence of international regimes which facilitate co-operation. Institutions can help realize common interests in world politics and thus create at least a minimum of order. Inasmuch as such regimes have a particular 'liberal' colouring – as Keohane suggests that they do – then the order they create will be at least favourably disposed to certain key liberal principles and practices.

In the conclusion to his book, Keohane raises a question that I want to dwell on for a moment, since it is a convenient introduction to the question of the overall significance of this approach for international order. 'What is the moral value', he asks, 'of the patterns of cooperation discussed in the book?' He suggests that what he calls two competing doctrines could be used as the basis for an evaluation. These are what he calls the 'morality of states' view, where states and not persons are the subject of international morality, or a 'cosmopolitan view', where state boundaries have no deep moral significance. As we saw in the above section this problem is itself a major problem for liberal international relations theory, in general terms. For the moment let us see how Keohane discusses the topic. Keohane suggests that his neo-liberal institutions are broadly accept-able from a morality of states position, since state autonomy is protected by the fact that states secure interests through the co-operation facilitated by such insti-tutions. However, the question is much less clear on a cosmopolitan view. Cosmopolitan ethics would require a much more demanding set of criteria for evaluation. Keohane suggests that he is sympathetic to the cosmopolitan view and embarks on a discussion of consequentialist versus rights-based approaches within it, focusing on the implications for his argument of broadening the discus-sion from the capitalist West to developing countries and economies. He concludes that while it is true that the 'morality of states model' is probably inad-equate to the task of extending the conditional approval of international regimes once this focus is added, the fact is that some of the moral assumptions behind the regimes do not invalidate the regimes themselves. As he puts it:

> The principles underlying the rules and practices of the IMF, GATT or IEA reflect the interests and ideologies of the most powerful states in the interna-tional system The cooperation that the institutions themselves foster, however, probably works to mitigate some of the harsher inequities inherent in the principles ... on consequentialist grounds, therefore, contemporary international economic regimes may be superior to politically feasible alter-natives ... [though this] does not relieve citizens of the advanced industrialised countries of the obligation to seek to modify the principles on which these institutions are based ... (however) abstract plans for morally worthwhile international regimes which do not take into the reality of self interest, are like castles constructed in the air, or – if implemented in a fit of absentmindedness by governments – on sand.[99]

This view makes it clear that, for Keohane at least, at present it is international order – and not world order, as discussed in Chapter 2 above – that international institutions might enhance but that in the process the possibilities of a Bullian world order might themselves be enhanced. Cosmopolitan norms are, in other words, to be achieved through currently statist liberal forms through the mecha-nisms of international institutions. One would find in much of the contemporary literature of liberal international ethics much that would agree with this. Henry Shue, for example, in his influential book *Basic Rights*[100] takes a not dissimilar position, though his cosmopolitanism is rather more obvious than Keohane's. In this context we can see that, although not always explicitly, liberal institution-alism ends up with an approach to international order that is, as Aron would have predicted, both explanatory and normative and, at root, not perhaps that dissimilar to the cosmopolitan liberalism of a Beitz or a Pogge.

Critique

At this point, I think it is time we took stock of all of the various liberal institu-tionalisms we have now looked at and attempt some sort of general evaluation of their ability to offer a convincing way of dealing with the 'problem of order'. For reasons that will become clear I hope in the third section of the book, I am unconvinced by the currently most popular view, to wit that liberal states are inherently more able to create a stable and 'ordered' world simply by virtue of their being liberal states. However, the currently dominant versions of liberal institutionalism offer a rather more sophisticated reason for optimism, *ergo* that institutions can change the 'payoff structure' and facilitate co-operation. Of course, co-operation is neither necessarily liberal nor beneficial. However, co-operation between liberal states in an international system still largely dominated by 'embedded liberalism' in various ways is more likely than not to facilitate co-operation for liberal ends, or so the argument runs.

However, as we saw, the justification of contemporary regimes and institutions in the international system is plausible enough on morality of states grounds but much more problematic if we assume a cosmopolitan framework. Keohane's argument, and I imagine he would be followed in this by most, if not all, contemporary liberal institutionalists, is that one can adopt basically cosmopolitan norms and work for them through the existing structures of liberal states and international institutions. However, as I argued above, this seems to me to be – at the very least – highly questionable, at least inasmuch as it depended upon state action. However, if we cannot assume that states in the foreseeable future are likely to become 'local agents of the global common good' then the construction of a justifiable liberal world order will be dependent on a much more radical view of the possibilities and potentialities of international and transnational institutions than anything so far suggested by liberal institutionalism. In this respect, my conclusion here is not dissimilar to my conclusion to Chapter 2. The logic of this points towards a much more radically cosmopolitan account of world politics than the English school, constructivist or liberal accounts currently are able to envisage.

Conclusion

There is one final point here. In all the sound and fury generated by both dominant forms of liberal institutionalism in world politics, one basic fact has been overlooked. The central liberal insight, I agree with Shklar, is fear of arbitrary power. The usual locus of such power has been the state. However, it is quite possible for it to be other political forms as well: international institutions, companies, nations, other organized groups. All can – and often do – exercise arbitrary power. The danger for contemporary liberalism, or so it seems to me, is that in celebrating the achievements of liberal states – who, after all, would wish to live in a non-liberal state? – and in pointing to the very real fact that regimes, institutions and organizations can exert a powerful, and often a positive, effect on world politics, liberals tend to forget or downplay the equally clear fact that liberal states can also do terrible things and that international institutions and regimes can as easily be vehicles for oppression and exploitation as the reverse, indeed that, in the current context of world politics, they are *more likely* to do terrible things. This might be one of the unheralded meanings of 'globalization'. As another of liberalism's staunchest defenders of recent years has recently said, 'To put it pessimistically, states have not lost their capacity to do bad things (torture, "disappearances" and even genocide) but their capacity to do good things'.[101] A cosmopolitan approach to the problem of order, which, I have suggested, is the logical position of liberal thinking, will therefore lead us beyond liberalism, at least to the extent that we will need to broaden the range of our analysis to include the manner in which, the conditions under which and the reasons for liberal states – or liberal institutions – behaving in such a way or allowing – or even facilitating – such behaviour. We are, therefore, at last, brought to the family of responses which suggests that the 'problem of order' cannot be (justifiably) solved in the context of the contemporary structure of world politics: it can only be transcended.

Notes

1 For his development of this thesis, see Eric Hobsbawm, *Age of Extremes: The Short Twentieth Century* (London: Michael Joseph, 1995).
2 See Walzer, *Just and Unjust Wars*, 2nd edition (New York: Basic Books, 1992), p. xi.
3 For a withering critique of a good deal of international theory specifically on this point – and all the more withering for it being sympathetically expressed – see John Lewis Gaddis, 'International Relations Theory and the End of the Cold War', *International Security*, 1992–3, 17(Winter): 5–58.
4 See, for example, the excellent discussions in Terry Nardin and David Mapel (eds), *Traditions of International Ethics* (Cambridge: Cambridge University Press, 1992) – see especially Michael Joseph Smith's excellent chapter on liberalism and international reform, but also the chapters by Thomas Donaldson on Kant, Anthony Ellis on utilitarianism, David Mapel on contractarianism and John Vincent on rights. Other excellent discussions are offered by Torbjorn Knutsen in his *A History of International Relations Theory* (Manchester: Manchester University Press, 1992; 2nd edition, 1996), by Ian Clark in his *The Hierarchy of States* (Cambridge: Cambridge University Press, 1991) and by F. H. Hinsley's now dated but still excellent *Power and the Pursuit of Peace* (Cambridge: Cambridge University Press, 1963).
5 Francis Fukuyama, *The End of History and the Last Man* (London: Hamish Hamilton, 1992), p. 211. This is not the place to develop an extended treatment of Fukuyama. Suffice to say that his argument in the book is in many respects rhetorically conservative even as it celebrates liberal democracy. Fukuyama's 'liberalism', like the liberalism of others influenced by the late Leo Strauss – I think especially of Allan Bloom and Harvey Mansfield – is a pretty curious one, neither fish nor fowl, I would say, and for very clear – though little discussed – reasons. Fukuyama acknowledges his debt to Straussian political theory in the introduction of the book. Strauss is not mentioned, though Bloom is. Bloom's 'defence' of liberalism is developed most clearly – that is to say, most opaquely – in his *The Closing of the American Mind* (New York: Penguin, 1987). Mansfield's *The Spirit of Liberalism* (Cambridge, MA: Harvard University Press, 1978) displays his version as does his much more recent *Taming the Prince: The Ambivalence of Modern Executive Power* (New York: Free Press, 1989). An interesting discussion of the 'conservatism' of the Straussians – especially good on their foreign policy ideas – is Robert Devigne, *Recasting Conservatism: Oakeshott, Strauss and the Response to Postmodernism* (New Haven, CT: Yale University Press, 1994). A powerful, though sometimes over polemical, exposition and critique of Strauss can

be found in Shadia Drury, *The Political Ideas of Leo Strauss* (London: Macmillan, 1988). The links between Strauss and Kojeve and thence Fukuyama are explored in some detail in her *Alexandre Kojeve: The Roots of Postmodern Politics* (London: Macmillan, 1994). I have discussed Strauss in some detail in my *Political Theory, Modernity and Postmodernity: Beyond Enlightenment and Critique* (Oxford: Blackwell, 1995), though I would now be less sympathetic and much more critical even of Strauss himself (I was always critical of the Straussians!). See also my remarks in Ch. 1, n85.

6 Treatments of these themes are now legion, of course, but some good general ones would include John Gerard Ruggie (ed.), *Multi-lateralism Matters: The Theory and Praxis of an Institutional Form* (New York: Columbia University Press, 1993), Scott Lash and John Urry, *Economies of Signs and Space* (London: Sage, 1994), Eugene Skolnikoff, *The Elusive Transformation: Technology and International Politics* (Cambridge, MA: Harvard University Press, 1991). I have touched on some of the implications of them in my 'The Ethics of Trust in World Politics', *International Affairs*, 1997, 73(3): July.

7 Of course, it is fair to say that the 'rebirth' of liberal political theory has been far wider than simply Rawls and his epigones. There have been many variants of it. A sample list of 'Non-Rawlsian' titles, giving some idea of the range and variety of the 'liberal revival' in political theory, would include Charles W. Anderson, *Pragmatic Liberalism* (Princeton, NJ: Princeton University Press, 1992), George Kateb, *The Inner Ocean: Individualism and Democratic Culture* (Ithaca, NY: Cornell University Press, 1992), J. Donald Moon, *Constructing Community: Moral Pluralism and Tragic Conflicts* (Princeton, NJ: Princeton University Press, 1993), Thomas Spragens Jr, *The Irony of Liberal Individualism* (Durham, NC: Duke University Press, 1989). On the (more common) 'Rawlsian' front we would have to include, of course, Rawls' *magnum opus* itself together with his *Political Liberalism* (New York: Columbia University Press, 1993) and the essay, shortly to be a major book, 'On the Law of Peoples', in M. Shute and S. Hurley (eds), *On Human Rights* (Oxford: Oxford University Press, 1994). For work in a Rawlsian mode it is difficult to know where to begin but my own view of the most interesting successors to Rawls, who are very much their own men (they are all men), would include Brian Barry, especially his (so far) two-volume *Treatise on Social Justice, Vol. 1 Theories of Justice* (Hemel Hempstead: Harvester, 1989), *Vol. 2, Justice as Impartiality* (Oxford: Clarendon Press, 1994), and Will Kymlicka, *Liberalism, Community and Culture* (Oxford: Clarendon Press, 1989), and *Multi-cultural Citizenship* (Oxford: Clarendon Press, 1995). This is also a good time to mention two works of scholars who, at least to some extent, followed Rawls, but who are innocent of the tendency I noted above to ignore the international. Charles Beitz' *Political Theory and International Relations* (Princeton, NJ: Princeton University Press, 1979, second edn, 1999) is a very strongly argued defence of a Rawlsian liberalism applied directly to international relations. Thomas Pogge's *Realizing Rawls* (New York: Columbia University Press, 1992) is an equally powerful argument in a similar vein (though it is more wide ranging that Beitz' book, dealing with other aspects than the international). As I say, this list is merely a sample and I shall return to many of these authors, as my argument proceeds.

8 See Samuel Huntington, *The Third Wave: Democratization in the Late Twentieth Century* (Norman, OK: University of Oklahoma Press, 1991).

9 I would like to acknowledge here the stimulus my thinking on liberal politics has received from the writings and conversations of a number of political international theorists. Most particularly, Onora O'Neill, John Charvet, Brian Barry, Will Kymlicka and Richard Bellamy have all helped me to develop my ideas on liberalism on which the next few sections of this chapter are based. For books that give various accounts of liberal politics which differ in some ways from the account presented here but which agree with the fundamentals, see Richard Bellamy, *Liberalism and Modern Society* (Cambridge: Polity Press, 1992), Brian Barry, *Justice as Impartiality*

(Oxford: Clarendon Press, 1995), Will Kymlicka, *Multi-cultural Citizenship*, John Charvet, *The Idea of an Ethical Society* (Ithaca, NY: Cornell University Press, 1996).

10 The presentation of this aspect of liberalism has unfolded almost across the whole of her work over some thirty years. However, recent presentations of it, on which I have largely drawn, include her *Ordinary Vices* (Cambridge, MA: Harvard University Press, 1984) and 'The Liberalism of Fear', in Nancy Rosenblum (ed.), *Liberalism and the Moral Life* (Cambridge, MA: Harvard University Press, 1989). Good discussions of her life and work can be found in Bernard Yack's excellent edited collection *Liberalism without Illusions: Essays on Liberal Theory and the Political Vision of Judith Shklar* (Chicago: University of Chicago Press, 1996) .

11 Shklar, 'The Liberalism of Fear', p. 21.

12 Todorov's way of emphasizing this aspect of liberalism in best displayed in his *Nous et les autres: La Reflection française sur la diversité humaine* (Paris: Editions du Seuil, 1989). Almost equally good, however, are those essays collected together in *The Morals of History* (Minneapolis: University of Minnesota Press, 1992).

13 Shklar, 'The Liberalism of Fear', p. 26.

14 Shklar, 'The Liberalism of Fear', p. 28.

15 The still standard history of constitutionalism is C. H. McIlwain's now very old *Constitutionalism, Ancient and Modern* (Cambridge, MA: Harvard University Press, 1947). A new survey, very different in style and content but also valuable, is Jan Erik Lane, *Constitutions and Political Theory* (Manchester: Manchester University Press, 1996).

16 Samuel Brittan, *Capitalism with a Human Face* (Cheltenham: Edward Elgar, 1995), p. 1.

17 For example, among recent liberal political theorists, one of the most interesting in my view has been Will Kymlicka, who has developed a sophisticated and important case for liberals taking group rights seriously. However, his argument turns on a particular way of reading individual rights as, under some circumstances necessarily also group rights. See Kymlicka, *Liberalism, Community and Culture* (Oxford: Clarendon Press, 1989), and *Multi-cultural Citizenship*.

18 Bellamy, *Liberalism and Modern Society*, p. 2.

19 As is well known, Popper is one of the most influential philosophers of science of the twentieth century, with his *Logik der Forschung* among its most important texts. In political theory his *The Open Society and its Enemies* (London: Routledge & Kegan Paul, 1945, 2 vols) and his *The Poverty of Historicism* (London: Routledge & Kegan Paul, 1957) are considered by many among the most important works of liberal political thought.

20 Beitz, 'Cosmopolitan Liberalism and the States System', in C. Brown (ed.), *Political Restructuring in Europe: Ethical Perspectives* (London: Routledge, 1994).

21 The dominant forms of academic liberalism, in all disciplines, are virtually variants of this form. The *locus classicus*, in this as in so much else, is Rawls, *A Theory of Justice*.

22 The writings both of, and on, Berlin are now large and growing all the time. A personal selection of books of Berlin's own to consult on these themes, almost all of them collections of essays, would include *Against the Current: Essays in the History of Ideas* (Oxford: Oxford University Press, 1978) and *The Crooked Timber of Humanity* (London: John Murray, 1990). A good discussion of Berlin on these and related topics is Claude Galipeau, *Isaiah Berlin's Liberalism* (Oxford: Clarendon Press, 1994).

23 The transition, as I read it, from *A Theory of Justice* to *Political Liberalism*.

24 In Michael Shute and Susan Hurley (eds), *Human Rights* (London: Harper Collins, 1994).

25 See, for example, his essay 'Cosmopolitanism and Sovereignty', in Chris Brown (ed.), *Political Restructuring in Europe: Ethical Perspectives* (London: Routledge, 1994).

26 As a (relatively brief) sample of the range and variety of his work, see *Introduction à la philosophie de l'histoire: Essai sur les limites de l'objective historique* (Paris: Gallimard, 1938),

Paix et guerre entre les nations (Paris: Calman–Levy, 1961; translated as *Peace and War: A Theory of International Relations*, trans. Richard Howard and Annette Baker Fox (New York: Doubleday, 1966)), *Le Grand Debat* (Paris: Calman–Levy, 1963; translated as *The Great Debate: Theories of Nuclear Strategy*, trans. Ernst Pawl (New York: Doubleday 1965)), *Progress and Disillusion: The Dialectics of Modern Society* (New York: Praeger, 1970), *Penser la guerre, Clausewitz, Vol. 1 L'age europeen; Vol. 2, L'age planetaire* (Paris: Gallimard, 1976). General discussions of Aron are commoner than they used to be but, in International Relations at least, still rare. With the exception of those who are known to be admirers and friends of Aron, for example Stanley Hoffmann and Pierre Hassner, Aron is, as Bryan-Paul Frost has rightly said, still a 'neglected theorist in International Relations'. For Frost's own excellent attempt at rescuing Aron, see his 'Resurrecting a Neglected Theorist: The Philosophical Foundations of Raymond Aron's Theory of International Relations', *Review of International Studies*, 1997, 23(2): April.

27 I should add, in this context, though, that Aron's reputation in the United States – and to some extent in France as well – is being obscured, even distorted, by his appropriation by some wings of the Straussian party – it is far too elitist (and small) to be called a movement – in political theory, who are very different in overall approach and general assumptions to Aron. That Aron knew and admired Strauss is certainly true (he testifies to it in his autobiography); that he is admired – albeit rather archly – by some prominent Straussians, most notably Allan Bloom, is also true (see Bloom's appreciation of Aron after his death in 1983, reprinted in Bloom's *Giants and Dwarfs* (New York: Simon and Schuster, 1990)). Such mutual esteem should not, however, mask the very real differences that existed in their respective positions. Aron was, and remained, an unambiguous and unapologetic liberal. Strauss, Bloom and others are not liberals, however they might express sympathy for a certain view of liberalism in the modern world.

28 For good discussions of Aron's liberalism on which I draw here – though I also disagree with aspects of them – see John A. Hall, *Diagnoses of our Time* (London: Macmillan, 1981), Bloom, 'Raymond Aron: The Last of the Liberals', in *Giants and Dwarfs*.

29 Originally published as 'La definition de la liberté' in the *European Journal of Sociology*, 1964, V: 159–89, reprinted as 'The Liberal Definition of Freedom', in Miriam Bernheim Conant (ed.), *Politics and History: Selected Essays of Raymond Aron* (New York: Free Press, 1978).

30 Aron, 'The Liberal Definition of Freedom', p. 162.

31 Aron, 'The Liberal Definition of Freedom', p. 163.

32 Aron, 'The Liberal Definition of Freedom', p. 165.

33 A much more honest term, I think, than the rather tamer 'security studies' which appears to be flavour of the month these days.

34 In *Politics and History*, pp. 166–85.

35 Aron, 'What is a theory of international relations?', p. 171.

36 Aron, 'What is a theory of international relations?', p. 185.

37 Aron, *Peace and War*, pp. 573–7.

38 At a conference in 1965, as reported by Stanley Hoffmann, rapporteur of the conference. See Stanley Hoffmann (ed.), *Conditions of World Order* (New York: Simon and Schuster, 1970), pp. 1–2.

39 John A. Hall, *International Orders* (Cambridge: Polity, 1996).

40 Hall, *International Orders*, pp. 30–1.

41 Hall, *International Orders*, p. xiii.

42 Hall, *International Orders*, p. 32.

43 See Hall, *International Orders*, chapters 1 and 5; Aron, *War and Peace*, parts one and two.

44 See the *History of the Peloponnesian War*, Book 2, 35–46, usually referred to as 'Pericles' Funeral Oration'.

45 For an excellent account of this see Kurt Von Fritz' classic *The Theory of the Mixed Constitution in Antiquity* (New York: Columbia University Press, 1954). I discuss it in much more detail in 'Political Judgement and Public Ethics in Plato and Aristotle', Paper presented to the Colloquium on Theory and Practice, University of Durham, 14–16 July 1995.

46 For the transition period in Roman history the classic discussion is, of course, Mason Hammond, *The Augustan Principiate in Theory and Practice* (Cambridge, MA: Harvard University Press, 1933). A very good discussion can also be found in C. G. Starr, 'The Perfect Democracy of the Roman Empire', *American Historical Review*, 1952, Vol. LVIII. The Later Empire is magisterially surveyed in A. H. M. Jones' massive *The Later Roman Empire 284–602* (Oxford: Blackwell, 1964, 2 vols), see Vol. 1, esp. chapters XI and XII.

47 For the now standard account see R. W. and A. J. Carlyle, *A History of Mediaeval Political Theory in the West* (London: William Blackwood, 1936), Vol. VI, part I, chapters 2, 5, 6 and part 2, chapters 2 and 6. A superb modern discussion is in Quentin Skinner, *The Foundations of Modern Political Thought*, Vol. 1 (Cambridge: Cambridge University Press, 1978).

48 On the evolution and history of liberal thought, practice and politics there is a superfluity of good studies, though no standard history. Thomas A. Spragens, *The Irony of Liberal Reason* (Chicago: University of Chicago Press, 1981), is an excellent account of the travails of modern liberalism from the Enlightenment onwards. John Hall's *Liberalism: Politics, Ideology and the Market* (London: Paladin, 1987) is also very good and thorough with a commitment to practices and institutions as well as ideas. The most recent and the most interesting account of nineteenth- and twentieth-century liberalism, to my mind at least, is Richard Bellamy, *Liberalism and Modern Society* (Cambridge: Polity Press, 1992).

49 Or, depending how you count them, three. The first (or first two) being 'Kant, Liberal Legacies and Foreign Affairs', part 1, *Philosophy and Public Affairs*, 1983, 12(3): 205–35, and part 2, 1983, 12(4): 323–53. The second (or third) being 'Liberalism and World Politics', *American Political Science Review*, 1986, 80(4): 1151–69.

50 For other work see his *Empires* (Ithaca, NY: Cornell University Press, 1986).

51 Even a sample list of discussions of Doyle's arguments would be immense. Here I merely include the best known, most influential and those I shall be returning to in my argument here.

52 The articles and books on which I shall chiefly draw here for the debate between the advocates of the liberal democratic peace and their critics will be: Bruce Russett (with Carol Ember, Melvin Ember, William Antholis and Zeev Maoz), *Grasping the Democratic Peace: Principles for a Post-Cold War World* (Princeton, NJ: Princeton University Press, 1993), Ann Marie Burley, 'Law among Liberal States: Liberal Internationalism and the Act of State Doctrine', *Columbia Law Review*, 1992, 8(1): 1907–96, Steve Chan, 'Mirror, Mirror on the Wall … Are the Freer Countries more Pacific?', *Journal of Conflict Resolution*, 1984, 28(4): 617–48, Ernst Otto-Czempiel, 'Governance and Democratization', in James N. Rosenau and Ernst Otto Czempiel (eds), *Governance Without Government: Order and Change in World Politics* (Cambridge: Cambridge University Press, 1992), David Forsythe, 'Democracy, War and Covert Action', *Journal of Peace Research*, 1992, 29(4): 385–95, Francis Fukuyama, *The End of History and the Last Man* (London: Hamish Hamilton, 1992), John Mueller, *Quiet Cataclysm: Reflections on the Changes in World Politics* (New York: Harper Collins, 1995), David Lake, 'Powerful Pacifists: Democratic States and War', *American Political Science Review*, 1992, 86(1): 24–37, Peter Manicas, *War and Democracy* (Oxford: Blackwell, 1983), John Mearsheimer, 'Back to the Future: Instability in Europe after the Cold

War', *International Security*, 1990, 15(1): 5–56, Christopher Layne, 'Cant or Kant: The Myth of the Democratic Peace', David E. Spiro, 'The Insignificance of the Liberal Peace' and John M. Owen, 'How Liberalism Produces Democratic Peace', *International Security*, 1994, 19(2): 5–125, special section, 'Give Democratic Peace a Chance', George Kateb, *The Inner Ocean: Individualism and Democratic Culture* (Ithaca, NY: Cornell University Press, 1992), James Lee Ray, 'War between Democracies: Rare or Non-existent?', *International Interactions*, 1993, 18(3): 251–76, Melvin Small and J. David Singer, 'The War-proneness of Democratic Regimes', *Jerusalem Journal of International Relations*, 1976, 1(1): 50–69.

53 See his article 'Liberalism and World Politics Revisited', in Charles Kegley (ed.).

54 Fukuyama, in the *End of History and the Last Man*, for example, bases his chapter on this theme around Doyle's argument, and, indeed, around his table!

55 See 'Back to the Future: Instability in Europe after the Cold War'.

56 To use the well-known (and rather shopworn) expression of Kenneth Waltz.

57 A powerful argument arguing this point has, in any case, been made by Bruce Russett. See *Grasping the Democratic Peace*, chapter 2.

58 Russett, *Grasping the Democratic Peace*, p. 35.

59 A recent interesting version of the structural/institutional model that I shall not discuss in the detail it deserves is Jack Snyder's *Myths of Empire* (Ithaca, NY: Cornell University Press, 1992). Snyder's argument is that what he calls empire – 'the myth of security through over expansion' – is most likely to come about in what he calls 'heavily cartelized' political systems where a particular special interest has control. In liberal political systems – by definition, he suggests, relatively 'uncartelized' – the checks and balances prevent this from happening; hence they are much less aggressive.

60 Russett, *Grasping the Democratic Peace*, p. 14.

61 See his essay 'Democratic Theory and Self Transformation', *American Political Science Review*, 1992, 86(1). The emphasis in the quotation is mine.

62 Huntington, *The Third Wave: Democratisation in the Late Twentieth Century* (Norman, OK: University of Oklahoma Press, 1991).

63 Doyle emphasizes elements of a liberal economy as well, but in other respects he adopts a relatively uncomplicated proceduralist account.

64 Russett's understanding is avowedly informed by his Yale colleague Robert Dahl's work, as is most of the mainstream literature on this topic.

65 I am thinking here of two (very different) American political theorists in particular. Benjamin Barber (see especially his *Strong Democracy*) and George Kateb, in especially *The Inner Ocean*.

66 The thinkers I have in mind here would include writers like William Connolly, Ernesto Laclau, Chantal Mouffe, Bonnie Honig, and, amongst those political theorists who write on international topics, Rob Walker, Richard Ashley, James Der Derian and Michael Shapiro. See Connolly, *Identity/Difference: Democratic Negotiations of Political Paradox* (Ithaca, NY: Cornell University Press, 1991), Mouffe, *Rethinking the Political* (London: Verso, 1992), Honig, *Political Theory and the Displacement of Politics* (Ithaca, NY: Cornell University Press, 1993), Walker, *Inside/Outside: International Relations as Political Theory* (Cambridge: Cambridge University Press, 1992), and Der Derian and Shapiro (eds), *International/Intertextual Relations: Postmodern Readings of World Politics* (Toronto: Lexington Books, 1989).

67 Mueller, *Quiet Cataclysm*, p. 157.

68 He refers in fact to Smith's letter to a friend where he says

For God's sake do not drag me into another war. I am worn down and worn out with crusading and defending Europe and protecting mankind: I must think a little of myself ... no war, dear Lady Grey – no eloquence; But apathy, selfishness, common sense, arithmetic.

(Quoted in Mueller, *Quiet Cataclysm*, p. 163)

69 See Owen, 'How Liberalism Produces Democratic Peace'.

70 Outlined, of course, in his *Retreat from Doomsday: The Obsolescence of Major War* (New York: Basic Books, 1989).

71 See the discussion in Paul Wilkinson, *Terrorism and the Liberal State* (London: Macmillan, 1986), pp. 184–5.

72 This is argued in some detail in *Quiet Cataclysm*, though it draws on the much more substantial argument in his *Retreat from Doomsday*.

73 The former view would be – in different ways, of course – that of theorists like Barber but also of social theorists like Habermas. The latter view is my gloss on the work of Geoge Kateb.

74 For sample discussions that highlight this see, Andrew Linklater, 'Liberal Democracy, Constitutionalism and the New World Order', in R. Feaver and J. L. Richardson (eds), *The Post Cold War Order* (London: Allen and Unwin, 1993), David Held, 'Democracy: From City-States to a Cosmopolitan Order', in D. Held (ed.), *Prospects for Democracy* (Cambridge: Polity Press, 1993), William Connolly, *Identity/Difference: Democratic Negotiations of Political Paradox* (Ithaca, NY: Cornell University Press, 1991), and R. B. J. Walker, *Inside/Outside: International Relations as Political Theory* (Cambridge: Cambridge University Press, 1992).

75 For a good, if brief, account of the travails of war in liberal thought see Michael Howard, *War and the Liberal Conscience* (Oxford: Oxford University Press, 1977).

76 See, for example, the interesting and entertaining account in David Forsythe, *Human Rights and Peace* (Lincoln, NE: University of Nebraska Press, 1993), chapter 2 (an argument to which I shall return in the next chapter). See also for good discussions of the specific case of US-sponsored covert action, John Prados, *Presidents' Secret Wars: CIA and Pentagon Covert Operations since World War 2* (New York: William Morrow, 1986).

77 A good discussion of the use of economic instruments in traditional statecraft is David Baldwin, *Economic Statecraft* (New York: Columbia University Press, 1986).

78 Brilmayer, *American Hegemony: Political Morality in a One Superpower World* (New Haven, CT: Yale University Press, 1994). To some extent this picks up and elaborates arguments from her earlier and more general *Justifying International Acts* (Ithaca, NY: Cornell University Press, 1989).

79 Brilmayer, *American Hegemony*, pp. 5–6.

80 Her second chapter is an attempted rebuttal of it.

81 Brilmayer, *American Hegemony*, p. 61.

82 Brilmayer, *American Hegemony*, p. 61.

83 Brilmayer, *American Hegemony*, p. 61.

84 Brilmayer, *American Hegemony*, pp. 62–4.

85 Brilmayer, *American Hegemony*, p. 170.

86 Brilmayer, *American Hegemony*, p. 176.

87 Brilmayer, *American Hegemony*, p. 181. This argument is one which is echoed by many. See for example the cosmopolitan liberal arguments contained (along with some constitutive and communitarian critiques) in Brown (ed.), *Political Restructuring in Europe: Ethical Perspectives*. One particular version of this derivative statism that is especially interesting, that of Onora O'Neill. See her *Faces of Hunger* (London: Allen & Unwin, 1986).

88 See, for example, the discussions in William Langer, *The Diplomacy of Imperialism* (New York: Knopf, 1950), and Rosecrance, *The Rise of the Trading State* (New York: Basic Books, 1986).

89 For the best general treatment of his position see his *Utilitarianism as a Public Philosophy* (Cambridge: Cambridge University Press, 1995). See especially the three chapters on international ethics as, even more especially, in the current context, the essay 'What is so special about our fellow countrymen?'

90 The literature on this is now, predictably, vast. Prominent neo-liberals are headed, so to speak, by Robert Keohane, on whom more in a moment. However, other important advocates of this view would be many of the contributors to Kenneth Oye (ed.), *Co-operation under Anarchy* (Princeton, NJ: Princeton University Press, 1986), Vinod K. Aggarwal, *Liberal Protectionism: The International Politics of the Organized Textile Trade* (Berkeley, CA: University of California Press, 1985), Oran Young, *International Cooperation: Building Resources for Natural Resources and the Environment* (Ithaca, NY: Cornell University Press, 1989). Good discussions can be found in various essays in David Baldwin (ed.), *Neo-Realism versus Neo-Liberalism* (New York: Columbia University Press, 1993), and Charles W. Kegely (ed.), *Controversies in International Relations Theory: Realism and the Neo-Liberal Challenge* (New York: St Martins Press, 1995).

91 See Grieco, 'Anarchy and the Limits of Cooperation: A Realist Critique of the Newest Liberal Institutionalism', in Kegely (ed.), *Controversies in International Relations Theory*. The writers that Grieco has in mind are, respectively, for functionalism David Mitrany and Ernest Haas, for neo-functionalism, Haas again and Joseph Nye, and for interdependence theory Richard Cooper, Edward Morse and, especially, Nye (again) and Robert Keohane. One might add a range of writers on international organizations and institutions, albeit that they did not always fit easily into the functionalist and neo-functionalist camps. For example, Inis Claude in the United States and writers such as John Groom, Paul Taylor and, in a later generation, Mark Imber in Britain. See, *inter alia*, Mitrany, *A Working Peace System* (Chicago: Quadrangle Press, 1966); Haas, *Beyond the Nation State: Functionalism and International Organization* (Stanford, CA: Stanford University Press, 1964), and *The Uniting of Europe: Political Economic and Social Forces* (Stanford, CA: Stanford University Press, 1958), Richard Cooper, 'Economic Interdependence and Foreign Policies', *World Politics*, 1972, 24: January, Edward Morse, 'The Transformation of Foreign Policies: Modernization, Interdependence and Externalization', *World Politics*, 1970, 22: April, Robert Keohane and Joseph Nye, *Power and Interdependence: World Politics in Transition* (Boston: Little Brown, 1977; 2nd edition, 1989), Claude, *Swords into Plowshares* (New York: Random House, 1964), John Groom and Paul Taylor, *International Institutions at Work* (London: Pinter, 1988) and Mark Imber, *The USA, ILO, UNESCO and IAEA: Politicization and Withdrawal in the Specialized Agencies* (London; Macmillan, 1989). It is also worth pointing out, in the interests of continuity, that Keohane in *International Institutions and State Power* ends his second chapter with a eulogy of Ernst Haas, thus directly, I would suggest, claiming the mantle.

92 The most famous such treatment, and still one worth consulting, is Alfred Zimmern, *The League of Nations and the Rule of Law* (London, 1936). A good account in general of the debates of the interwar period in international relations is Peter Wilson and David Long (eds), *Thinkers of the Twenty Years Crisis* (Oxford: Clarendon Press, 1996).

93 Keohane, *International Institutions and State Power* (Boulder, CO: Westview Press, 1989), p.10.

94 Keohane, *International Institutions and State Power*, pp. 10–11.

95 See both his few remarks on this in *International Institutions and State Power* and also his much more detailed treatment in 'International Liberalism Reconsidered', in John Dunn (ed.), *The Economic Limits to Modern Politics* (Cambridge: Cambridge University Press, 1990).

96 This definition and the above and subsequent paragraph or two are adapted, sometimes directly, from *International Institutions and State Power*, pp. 2–7.

97 Princeton, NJ: Princeton University Press, 1984.

98 See, famously, *Power and Interdependence: World Politics in Transition* (Boston, Little Brown, 1977; 2nd edition, 1989).

99 Keohane, *After Hegemony*, pp. 256–7.

100 Shue, *Basic Rights: Subsistence, Affluence and US Foreign Policy* (Princeton, NJ: Princeton University Press, 1980; 2nd edition 1996).
101 Brian Barry, 'The Limits of Cultural Politics', *Review of International Studies*, 1998, 24(3): 307–20.

Part II
Ending order?

4 Emancipation

Almost coterminous with the birth of the modern states system have been the development of the many attempts to transcend it. At its conceptual inception in the late sixteenth and seventeenth centuries there were many who bitterly opposed it, seeing it as little better than a law of the jungle and a denial of everything they felt Christian Europe stood for. Perhaps the most eloquent, and still among the most interesting, of these figures, as I suggested in the Introduction, is Leibniz.[1] However, Leibniz' affection for the medieval conception of the *Respublica Christiana* was not the route that disaffection with the states system was increasingly to take in the eighteenth and nineteenth centuries.[2]

For those who felt that the 'order' created by the states system most strongly resembled the order of the grave, the procession of attempts, begun by the Abbé de St Pierre, to find a way of converting the system into one of 'perpetual peace', is perhaps the best known attempt to 'transcend' the states system. Commented on at the end of his long life by Leibniz, and throughout the eighteenth century by writers like Rousseau, perhaps the most famous version of this today is Kant's justly celebrated essay *On Perpetual Peace*, first published in 1795,[3] which sketched out a programme for the gradual transcendence of the states system in all but name and its replacement by a system of cosmopolitan law.

Kant is usually – and rightly – seen as a liberal. However, there is embedded in Kant's thinking a radicality which many liberals shy away from. It is perhaps most clearly displayed in his writings on international relations: it was, after all, Kant, who famously referred to his predecessors in the field – 'Grotians' and 'realists' alike – as 'sorry comforters'.[4] In his *Perpetual Peace* essay Kant spoke firmly in the accents of the European Enlightenment of which he was perhaps the greatest philosophical representative. It is worth remembering, in this context, his famous description of Enlightenment in one of his other essays, *An Answer to the Question 'What is Enlightenment?'*. Enlightenment, he writes, 'is the emergence of man from his *self incurred immaturity*'. In other words, for Kant, and arguably for the Enlightenment as a whole, the key to our 'emancipation' is to recognize that it is we who hold ourselves back.

In IR theory, Kant was famously referred to by Martin Wight as a 'revolutionist' and it is his hostility to the states system that makes him genuinely revolutionary, in that sense if not in others. He has, however, been joined in that hostility by a good many thinkers and traditions, especially in the twentieth century, even where they have shared almost nothing else with him. In the nineteenth century, it is the liberal Enlightenment that dominates and such hopes are largely forgotten, save for a few little-known – at the time – radicals like Karl Marx. In the twentieth century, however, such hopes of systemic transcendence, what we saw Richard Falk refer to as 'system-transforming' hopes, have become much greater, especially over the last few years when all sorts of possible agents have been fingered as the agent who will put the final nail in the coffin of the states system: technology, globalization, the world economy; the list goes on and on.

This 'revolutionism' that would seek to transcend the states system has two great advocates in the eighteenth and nineteenth centuries, Kant and Marx. As Andrew Linklater has called them they are 'the two great exponents of moral and political universalism within the tradition of philosophical history'.[5] For both of them the key was mankind's (we might now say humankind's) emergence from their 'self incurred' problems: in other words, its emancipation, though they did not entirely agree either on what was to do the emancipating nor on what humans were being emancipated from.

In the context of notions of international or world order, however, the tradition in which they stand is unambiguous. The 'order' of the current international system is no true order at all, for it has no place in it for justice and little for humans *qua* humankind rather than humans as members of their communities. The 'problem of order', understood as I have understood it here, then, can only therefore be 'solved' when it is effectively transcended. This tradition is thus rightly seen as a 'cosmopolitan' tradition – though it is not, of course, the only available cosmopolitanism.[6] An equally important point, to which I shall want to return later, is that it is also seen, again rightly, as a *universalist* tradition.

What I want to do in this chapter, then, is to examine the most prominent approaches to 'emancipation' and the 'transcending' of the states system – and thus of the problem of order – in contemporary IR theory. However, since a good deal of this literature is either derived from, or depends upon, assumptions and claims less familiar in International Relations than some of the others I have had occasion to discuss in this book, let me first say something about the range of 'critical' and 'emancipatory' projects in contemporary thought, by way of introduction.

The critical turn in twentieth-century thought

As I say, there are a number of approaches that seek to develop this line of reasoning, many of them unrelated to (academic) IR theory. In addition to the forms of critical theory that I shall be chiefly concerned with in the chapter (i.e. Frankfurt school critical theory and Gramscian theory, discussed below), for example, a good deal of liberation theology (and some continental 'political' theology, for example that of Jurgen Moltmann and Johann Baptist Metz), more general *dependencia* analysis (Gunder Frank, Amin) in political economy and world systems analysis in sociology (Wallerstein, Chase-Dunn), together with some still more heterodox work such as the critical pedagogy of Paulo Friere, the critical legal theory of, amongst others, Roberto Managebeira Unger, and the literary and political writings of Edward Said and a number of other 'post-colonial' literary theorists,[7] as well as a wide range of feminist work and also much post-structural thought, are all well-known manifestations, in different ways and to different degrees, of what we might call the 'project of critique'. To this might be added the recent turn in contemporary Christian theology which emphasizes the radical character of the Church's continuing challenge to secular polities, as the 'other city', most interestingly developed by the likes of John Milbank in Britain and Stanley Hauerwas in the United States.[8]

Needless to say there are enormous gulfs between many of these writers: it would be completely untrue to suggest that they agreed about most things at all. However, the very diversity of such thinkers helps to illustrate the general orientation of the critical turn. Despite their very real differences all of the above thinkers effectively share a perspective on what we might call the 'shape' of the modern world and modern life: they believe that it is profoundly alienating, unjust and exploitative. Of course they are not in agreement as to what aspects of it are chiefly to blame, how deeply rooted such tendencies are and whether we can do much about it; but they are all critical of the *current structure* of modernity.

It is obvious, therefore, that inasmuch as self-proclaimed liberal societies are, at least now, the dominant societies of modernity, a good deal of the project of critique is couched as a critique of liberalism. In this context, the project of critique has its origins, one might say, in the ambivalence one finds about a good deal of the liberal character of modern societies in many of the founding texts of modern social science, especially the thought and practice of Max Weber, who was, as we saw in an earlier chapter, both a liberal and, partly because of his suspicions about liberalism, a realist. Marxism, too – in most of its variants – has been a central aspect of the project of critique throughout the century, but in this context Marxism is in key ways *dependent* on liberalism, even parasitic on it. Many of those involved in the project of critique, as we shall see, are persuaded that the main problem with modernity is its currently incomplete state: liberalism is not so much wrong as, *qua* liberalism, *necessarily* incomplete.

It is perhaps on the anvil of this centrally ambivalent relationship between Marxism and liberalism that the most influential versions of the project of critique have been hammered out. As far as IR theory is concerned, two have been particularly important: the tradition of 'Frankfurt school' critical theory and ideas associated with the Italian Marxist Antonio Gramsci, and I will come on to these in a bit more detail in a moment. However, there is one final more general point I want to make.

Although I have spoken of the 'project of critique' as having a shared perspective, whatever differences also existed, it would perhaps be more accurate to say that the critical project, while sharing this perspective, has taken two paths. Many contemporary adherents to the project of critique have become increasingly sceptical of what are usually termed 'foundational' claims in accounts of knowledge, ethics and politics. That is to say, they are uncomfortable with the 'universalism' that was seen, rightly as I remarked above, as a hallmark of the project of critique as it developed in eighteenth- and nineteenth-century thought, when it was often seen as a partner and ally of liberal politics.

There are various reasons for this, many of them located in the ups and downs of contemporary philosophical and social scientific thought. Many, probably a majority, of contemporary philosophers are sceptical about traditional – so-called 'metaphysical' – realist accounts of truth/evidence/knowledge claims, etc.:[9] where, in other words, there is held to be some mechanism wholly outside human cognitive faculties which makes things true or false, right or wrong, etc. The result is that they have tended to split into those who believe in what the American philosopher Hilary Putnam has felicitously called 'realism with a human face',[10] or sometimes empirical realism – that is to say, where there is some standard, but a specifically human standard, by which truth claims, moral rightness or whatever can be measured – and a more or less radical 'anti-realism', which denies that there is anything of this sort that we can identify and that traditional distinctions between – for example – 'objectivism' and 'relativism' describe a fox that isn't there.

This debate is much more encompassing than the project of critique I am discussing here. There are plenty of participants in it (on both sides) who would have little if any truck with the other arguments associated with the various 'critical' theories discussed above. However, given that critical theory has divided roughly along these lines, and given that in this chapter I am discussing the 'project of critique' as it has become grafted onto contemporary IR theory, I should say what the implications of this debate are for that. The short answer is that a goodly number of the 'critical' or 'alternative' projects in contemporary social and political theory (including IR theory) have followed the 'antifoundational' path, what in a slightly different context I have called a 'radical' interpretivist path. In this context their response to the 'problem of order' as I sketched it in my opening chapter is clear. They think that it is a question that cannot, properly so called, be put at all. The attempt to 'create' an order must be an attempt to *impose* an order, that is all it can ever be. Thus the very act of posing the question becomes an act to be put into question.

In the context of international relations this tends to mean that the states system cannot, in the required sense, be 'transcended'. Rather its logics and hierarchies can and must be inverted, and/or reinterpreted and we must recognize the limits to our ability to corral truth in this, or any other, sphere. Since this argument effectively questions the problem of order as I formulated it in the Introduction, I shall put it to one side, and take it up in the next chapter.

However, another set of critical arguments follow the 'realism with a human face' option. They do think that there is some way of providing a vantage point for critique which can provide reasons for an emancipatory project in ethics and politics. They are, to use a phrase I used some years ago to describe this position, 'minimal' foundationalists.[11] The traditions most sympathetic to this line of argument and which have had the most influence on contemporary IR theory are the tradition of Frankfurt school critical theory, some versions of Marxist or *Marxisant* historical sociology,[12] the Gramscian tradition in political and social theory and some aspects of feminist theory. Thus it is to these developments I turn in this chapter. Let me introduce then by first, a brief discussion of the Frankfurt School and (much briefer still) of Gramscian and feminist theories.

The Frankfurt school and critical theory

I want to start with the Frankfurt school because I shall argue that it is this tradition which has perhaps most strongly influenced the emancipatory project in IR theory. Of course, the general story of the Frankfurt school is well enough known and has been sufficiently well told by others that I do not need to repeat it in detail here.[13]

What became known (after the Second World War) as the 'Frankfurt school' had its institutional and personal origins in the creation in 1921 of the Institute for Social Research, independently financed by a Jewish Marxist philanthropist called Felix Weil, but connected to the newly founded University of Frankfurt. Virtually all of the original members of the Frankfurt school were both Jewish and Marxist – at least in general orientation – and all were, in the Weimar context, *Vernunftrepublikaner,*[14] that is to say grudging, 'rationally led' supporters of Weimar, which they saw as a 'liberal' bourgeois republic. The tension between Marxism and liberalism which I mentioned above was therefore present from its foundation in the Frankfurt school.

Initially the institute was directed by a distinguished Marxist analyst of European labour, Carl Grunberg, who had been brought in from the University of Vienna, and who quickly established the institute as a major centre for research on the problems and prospects of the European working class. Under Grunberg, the institute grew rapidly but its methodology, empirical and social scientific, did not distinguish it from a number of other similar institutes that had sprung up in Germany and elsewhere, after the First World War. However, a few years after its foundation, Grunberg was forced to retire through ill health and he was succeeded by a brilliant young philosopher who had been a member of the institute for a very short time: Max Horkheimer.

It was Horkheimer, of course, who first referred to the theory he and his colleagues were developing as 'critical theory' and, as is well known, he did so to distinguish it from what he termed 'traditional theory'. This was theory seen as separate from that which is theorized about, as in 'traditional' pictures of the natural sciences and as the dominant traditions of social science, including those which dominated the institute under Grunberg, predominantly saw themselves. Critical theory, by contrast, saw itself as irretrievably situated and thus directly related to social and political life. Thus critical theory, but not traditional theory, can investigate the function of theory itself – who and what it serves and why and how – and this is put in service of the task of theory as conceived by the

Frankfurt school – as Horkheimer and his colleagues became known on their return to Frankfurt after the war – to investigate the historical and social evolution of society, tracing contradictions which might open up in it and offer the possibility of emancipation.

A wide range of different thinkers were influential on the evolution of critical theory. Karl Korsch, Georg Lukacs, Max Horkheimer, Theodor Adorno, Walter Benjamin, Eric Fromm, Leo Lowenthal and Herbert Marcuse, all were important and obviously given this range, critical theory from the beginning was necessarily interdisciplinary; it covered fields as diverse as history, political science, social theory, aesthetics, political economy, psychology, economic history and what was to become (partly as a direct influence of Frankfurt school theory) 'cultural studies'.

The three central influences on the early work of the institute under Horkheimer's direction, however, were unquestionably Marx, Freud and, rather less obviously but perhaps more powerfully still, Hegel. The institute's work retained the essentially Marxist orientation it had had under Grunberg but it became much more radical. Horkheimer and the group he had gathered around him – most especially from the 1930s onwards, the brilliant polymath Theodor Adorno – used Freudian psychology and, increasingly, many other techniques to supplement the broadly materialist and economic analysis of society and its formation familiar from traditional Marxist work. This mix became still more eclectic when, as a result of the Nazi takeover, the institute was forced to relocate to the United States, initially in New York (loosely attached to Columbia University) and then in California.

Partly as a result of the shift to the United States, however, the orientation of the school began to shift. The early, largely pre-war, work had been broadly optimistic, seeing the possibility for successful political action to help bring about the emancipation they all felt was required. Much critical theory indeed remained optimistic even after the war. The work of Herbert Marcuse, a central figure in the 1930s and one who opted to remain in the United States after the war, remained wedded to the idea of effective political action into the 1960s; hence his adoption by the students in the United States during that period as a leading exemplar of radical politics.[15] Similar points could be made of a number of other former Frankfurters, like Erich Fromm.[16]

However, the central duo of the Frankfurt school, Adorno and Horkheimer, displayed a very different trajectory. Their writing during the war, and Adorno's at least thereafter, was much more pessimistic. Indeed, it is difficult to resist the sense that from at least their joint authorship of *Dialectic of Enlightenment* during the 1940s the intellectual relationship between the two altered to the extent that whereas prior to the war Horkheimer had been the 'senior partner' as it were, after the war Adorno had been elevated to that position. The key text was the aforementioned *Dialectic of Enlightenment* and in it they presented a deeply pessimistic view of the Enlightenment as a whole and of the possibilities for transformation, in the contemporary context. For Adorno and Horkheimer, the illusion was that liberalism was the heir to the Enlightenment and fascism a barbarous reaction to it. Rather *both* were central to the evolution of Enlightenment ideas (especially the rise of science, technology and the instrumental conceptions of reason that such developments emphasized) and in fact they depended upon one another in dialectically powerful ways.

Unquestionably, the experience of the rise of Nazism in Germany and the revelations about the Holocaust played a powerful part in shaping this analysis, but other reasons lay deeper still. Adorno, in particular, came to believe that the exploitative and oppressive aspects of modern society were now so embedded – and so protean – that they were continuing to gobble up even those aspects of life that had previously remained potentially independent – such as Adorno's beloved 'culture'. Hence, of course, his mordant and bitter delineation of the emerging 'culture industry' – the commodification of creativity. His writings were, he came to believe, a 'message in a bottle' for some future generation that might, if they were lucky, live in a totally transfigured time. He remained the great Hegelian, still alive to the possibilities of dialectical contradictions to the end, but his overview was always pessimistic.

Gramsci and hegemony

At the same time that the Institute for Social Research was developing critical theory in Frankfurt, the Italian Marxist Antonio Gramsci was evolving a different but equally heterodox version of Marxism. Gramsci, who was leader of the Communist Party of Italy at the time of his arrest in the 1920s, offered a series of reflections of power, politics, and the possibility of critique, mainly in his so-called 'prison notebooks' written between 1929 and 1935. In these reflections he developed many ideas that have become increasingly influential on the left over the years, especially ideas about hegemonic forces in societies and how to counter them.

Feminist critique and critical theory

A third important part of the 'minimal foundational' project of critique has been the growth, throughout the twentieth century but especially since the 1960s, of feminist thinking. Even more than other parts of the project of critique, however, feminist theory is a highly variegated body of thought and rather than attempt to impose a false unity on such a wide range of material, in what follows I will simply discuss those aspects of feminist thought that have been most influential on the emancipatory project in IR theory.

Emancipation and critical theory in international relations

'Critical theory' in international relations, as I suggested above, is often used in an unhelpfully general way. To name but five, international relations theory influenced by post-structuralism, virtually all forms of feminist international theory, Gramscian-influenced theory, especially in international political economy, some 'interpretive' constructivisms such as that of Kratochwil,[17] and more traditional, if still hardly orthodox, Marxisms such as that outlined by Fred Halliday and Justin Rosenberg[18] are all often referred to as 'critical theory'.[19] The theology of the contemporary debate does not concern me here, except to repeat that in this chapter I shall be concerned only to discuss those 'critical theories of international relations' which make 'emancipation' central to their analysis and operation: those which are, in other words, 'minimally foundational', as I described them above. This effectively rules out most post-structural international theory and much feminist theory, to which I will return in the next chapter, and a good deal of 'constructivist' theory, which I have already in any event discussed.

The central set of arguments I will be concerned with here, then, are derived from or related to, 'Frankfurt school' critical theory, 'Gramscian' theory,[20] and include the 'historical materialism' of Halliday and Rosenberg, some feminist theory,[21] and emancipatory IR theory in the work of scholars like Andrew Linklater and Robert Cox. It is these bodies of literature that make up what I would call the 'emancipatory project' in contemporary IR theory. Of course, as I have already emphasized, one should not expect no disagreement between these approaches. Each is, to some extent or another, critical of the others and they are hardly, in any event, monolithic. However, enough links them to treat them together, even if with the caveat that one should acknowledge and respect the differences each displays from each.

There is, in this context, one general point I should make. Almost all emancipatory theory is, at least in general outline, optimistic about the *possibility* of meaningful systemic change, even if sometimes cynical – or at any rate resigned – about the current likelihood of it. Perhaps the most exhaustive defence of 'optimistic' views in general has been given by the most significant contemporary representative of the Frankfurt school[22] – significantly also, its most Kantian[23] – Jurgen Habermas. Habermas's influence on contemporary critical theory in all of its variants is almost impossible to overstate. Most especially in the current context, he has been far and away the most influential critical theorist as far as critical theory in International Relations is concerned. With rather more qualifications and hesitations such optimism is shared by one of the *éminences grises* of Gramscian critical international theory, Robert Cox, as well as by some of his friends and followers in the 'Gramscian camp', such as Stephen Gill. It is also the view of some feminist scholars of international relations, for example Ann Tickner,[24] and is shared with various emendations of content or temper by many working in what is now called 'critical security studies', for example, and especially, Ken Booth.[25] And, though this is less relevant here, it is a common assumption of virtually all the related 'critical theories' I referred to above, if one excepts the theological critique of a Milbank or a Hauerwas which in this context at least perhaps has much more in common with the anti-foundationalists I shall discuss in the final chapter. It is worth adding, I think, that in wider social and political theory one of the most powerful elements in this equation comes from those branches of feminist scholarship whose most distinguished representatives have wedded a broadly Habermassian critical theory to feminist concerns precisely over the issue of emancipation[26] and a good deal of this has echoes in the debate in International Relations.

Mark Hoffman, in what is still one of the best general essays on the trajectory of critical theory in international studies,[27] has called this general optimistic impulse 'Utopian' and, notwithstanding the extremely bad press this term has had in twentieth-century International Relations, I suggest that he is right to do so. It is 'Utopian' in the sense that all of the best 'emancipatory' theory is Utopian, and as the early Frankfurt school was, following the sense of Utopia made famous in a related work, Ernst Bloch's massive *The Principle of Hope*.[28]

I want to suggest, in fact, that the *emancipatory* project of critical theory in International Relations – as opposed, for example, to its value as a salutary discourse – *depends* on this answer being true, – in other words, that critical theory depends for its success in terms of world order on the possibility of reconciling emancipation and order by the former transcending the latter. Indeed, I want to suggest that, notwithstanding all their differences, *all* of those committed to an 'emancipatory' project in contemporary world politics will require something like this to be true and thus, however much they might differ from Frankfurt school critical theory in emphasis and orientation, they will perforce share something like this as an aim. They must.[29]

However, I also want to suggest that there are problems inherent in this view; that the project of emancipation carries, so to speak, a worm in its core that constantly threatens to pollute the whole project. It is this that was the source of Adorno and Horkheimer's pessimism in *Dialectic of Enlightenment* and it is this, I suggest, that critical theory in International Relations must confront if it is to make good on its emancipatory project and yet which it has not really sought to address at all. More of this, however, in a moment.

The 'achievements of critical theory'?

Before we can make any attempt at assessing critical theory in International Relations, however, we should see how it has set out its stall. I shall do so first of all through the work of the person who I would see as the foremost critical theorist of international relations, Andrew Linklater. Linklater is, without doubt, the most penetrating critical international theorist writing in the tradition of the Frankfurt school. His work so far consists of three major books[30] and a smattering of important articles[31] with more on the way. He will obviously develop and refine his particular version of critical theory in the years ahead. Indeed, there is some reason to suppose that Linklater is now in some ways more radical than the philosopher most influential upon him, i.e. Habermas.[32] Inasmuch as the future of critical theory lies with critical *international* theory, a view subscribed to by a number of 'non-international' critical theorists as well as – as you might expect – by a number of critical *international* theorists, it seems certain also that Linklater's influence will grow.[33]

Linklater has provided a useful and powerful overview of what he considers to have been the 'achievements' of critical theory in a recent article.[34] He thinks, in brief, that critical theory has four main achievements. *First*, it has taken issue with positivism by arguing that knowledge always reflects pre-existing social purposes and interests. This, of course, was Horkheimer's original insight as to what 'critical' as opposed to 'traditional' theory could do and it is echoed in Cox's celebrated division of IR theory into 'critical' and 'problem-solving' variants that I shall discuss in a moment. In the context of IR theory this has led to powerful criticisms of 'rationalist' theory and what Linklater calls a 'gradual recovery of a project of enlightenment and emancipation reworked to escape the familiar pitfalls of idealism'. *Second*, critical theory stands opposed to claims that the existing structures of the social world are immutable and 'examines the prospects for greater freedom immanent within existing social relations'. *Third*, critical theory learns from and overcomes the weaknesses inherent in Marxism, emphasizing forms of social learning, drawing very heavily on Habermas's reconstruction of historical materialism and opening up new possibilities for constructing an 'historical sociology with an emancipatory purpose' (which in the context of IR theory Linklater advertises as his next major project).[35] *Fourth*,

> critical theory judges social arrangements by their capacity to embrace open dialogue with all others and envisages new forms of political community which break with unjustified exclusion … critical theory … envisages the use of unconstrained discourse to determine the moral significance of national boundaries and to examine the possibility of post-sovereign forms of political life.[36]

Linklater is aware that there are many mansions in the house of critique. He has insisted, however – especially in his most recent book – that all of the various forms of 'post-positivist' theory in International Relations can at least agree that 'reaching an understanding [which may not culminate in a moral consensus] captures the most important respect in which critical theory, post-modernism, feminism and also philosophical hermeneutics are involved in a common project' in International Relations.[37] He goes on to suggest that it is this process, very much tied in his view to a Habermassian discourse ethics, that is the manner in which the states system can be transcended and human beings emancipated, since it is through this possibility that we can begin to articulate what it might mean to live in 'post-sovereign' communities, and thus transcend the 'sovereign' communities and all that goes with them, that defines the states system in its current form.

There are two points I want to draw attention to in this essay before moving on. The first is the extent to which, as Linklater presents it, critical theory has a 'project' – the 'emancipatory project' – which comprises a fourfold set of developments each of which build upon each other and reinforce each other, thus opening the way to still further 'achievements' in which critical theory will 'maintain its faith in the Enlightenment project and defend universalism in its ideal of open dialogue not only between fellow citizens but, more radically, between all members of the human species'.[38] The second is the extent to which this view of critical theory subsumes a good deal of the substantive agenda of international society theory and constructivism and the liberalism discussed in the previous chapter, without necessarily accepting the methodologies of any of the above. In other words, for Linklater at least,[39] critical IR theory develops much of the agenda of more traditional theories, but does it so as to complete what Habermas famously referred to as the 'unfinished project of the Enlightenment'.

As recent work in critical international theory demonstrates, the crux of this is whether or not the discourse ethics that Linklater eloquently sketches in the final chapter of his new book provides for genuinely emancipatory theory. As Richard Devetak has recently noted, 'Emancipation', for critical international theory,

> can be understood as the establishment of a community which allows, and protects the development of universal autonomy ... the question (thus) arises as to how ... to reconstruct world politics so as to extend to the entire species a rational, just and democratic organization of politics.[40]

The answer that the leading critical international theorists give is drawn very largely from Habermas's attempt to develop a 'discourse ethics' that recognizes the necessity of universalist principles whilst not doing violence to the fact of diversity.

Discourse ethics, of course, depends on Habermas's general theory of communicative action[41] which emphasizes the centrality of consent to intelligible communication. As Devetak puts it,

> communicating subjects [need] to rationalize or account for their beliefs and actions in terms which are intelligible to others and which they can then accept or contest. Similarly, social norms and institutions must also be submitted to scrutiny and argumentation if they are to maintain legitimacy. At such moments when a principle, social norm or institution loses legitimacy or when consensus breaks down, discourse ethics enters the fray as a means of consensually deciding upon new principles or institutional arrangements ... newly arrived at political principles, norms or institutional arrangements can only be said to be valid if they can meet with the approval of all those who would be affected by them.[42]

He goes on to point out three things about discourse ethics: it is universalist, it is democratic and it is a form of moral 'practical reasoning' which is 'not simply guided by utilitarian calculations or expediency, nor is it guided by an imposed concept of the good life. Rather, it is guided by justice'.[43]

The implications of this for world politics have been developed in differing ways by different critical theorists. However, in general terms, as Devetak says, three broad implications stand out, and it is worth discussing each of these in turn.

The first is concerned with the evolution of more generally democratic forms of global governance and is predicated on an explicit critique of the state as simply inadequate, both practically and ethically, for contemporary decision making. As David Held, the critical theorist who has perhaps done most to develop this line of argument notes, 'whose consent is necessary and whose participation is justified in decisions concerning, for instance, AIDS, or acid rain, or the use of non-renewable resources? What is the relevant constituency, national, regional or international?'[44]

Second, and perhaps potentially most obviously fruitfully for one of the central tasks of traditional IR theory, discourse ethics offers a way of thinking about and regulating conflict. The critical theorist who has developed this line of argument most thoroughly and interestingly is Mark Hoffman[45] though it also figures prominently in some feminist thinking on these questions, see for example the exemplary work of Ann Tickner.[46] Again, discourse ethics offers a way of being inclusive without denying difference.

Third, Devetak suggests that discourse ethics 'offers a means of criticizing and justifying the principles by which the species organizes itself politically, that is it reflects on the principles of inclusion and exclusion'.[47] Since in principle no one should be excluded from anything that affects them, actually or potentially, this becomes a very clear cosmopolitan universalism which suggests that the 'problem of order' can only be overcome through the progressive evolution of what Linklater calls the 'social bond of all with all'.[48] Thus, this analysis, of course, is committed to an institutional as well as to a moral cosmopolitanism, to use terms introduced in the previous chapter. Indeed, Linklater, towards the end of *Beyond Realism and Marxism*, has made explicit that in his view the future of critical theory *depends* on its ability to develop analyses and institutions which actually help to restructure world politics along the lines suggested by this analysis and repeats this view in the opening to his most recent book where he insists that 'critical theory is to be judged not only by its contribution to ethics and sociology but by the extent to which it sheds light on existing political possibilities'.[49]

This is a theme I want to return to in a moment. However, before I move on to this let me just look at a couple of alternative routes the emancipatory project in IR has taken.

Historical materialism

As I suggested above, there is a considerable body of related work also derived from Marxian and related themes that has offered powerful analyses of contemporary international relations. Two thinkers who have been especially interesting in this regard are Fred Halliday and Justin Rosenberg and, with apologies to some others whose work might have also been included here, it is on their work I shall concentrate.

Halliday's *Rethinking International Relations* and Rosenberg's *The Empire of Civil Society*, the two texts I shall focus on here, are interestingly different in tone, style and range (in what follows references in brackets are to these two books).

Halliday's book is a collection of essays, mostly previously published (though revised, updated and rewritten), a double response, he says, 'to developments in political and social theory and the academic study of international relations, and to changes in the international system itself over the past years, most particularly the collapse of the Soviet bloc'. The essays cover a wide variety of topics, running from the straightforwardly meta-theoretical (chapter 2 on theories in contention, chapter 3 on historical materialism and international relations) to issue based (chapters 4–7 on, respectively, state and society, international society, revolutions and women and the international arena) and finally to three chapters on the end of the Cold War and its significance. However, as his title implies, Halliday has a double agenda: he is engaged both in rethinking 'international relations', the events in the real world in the aftermath of the Cold War, and in rethinking 'International Relations', the academic discipline that seeks to explain those events. His third chapter ('A necessary encounter: historical materialism and international relations') makes plain the manner (or perhaps that should be the matter!) of the rethinking.

Rosenberg's book, at least on the surface, is primarily engaged in the second of the tasks outlined by Halliday. As its subtitle announces, Rosenberg's book is an extended critique of 'realism'. The book is divided into three sections, the first of which outlines what Rosenberg takes to be the most important arguments upon which realism depends, and indicates their weaknesses, focusing specifically on what he calls the 'ahistorical and presociological' (p. 6) nature of realist thought. Preparing the ground for the argument of the rest of the book, Rosenberg outlines 'a broad historical materialist framework for analysis and then challenges the realist axiom that the geo-political core of the discipline's subject matter is ontologically distinct from the wider structures of social reproduction' (p. 6). The second section discusses a series of historical examples of ways in which 'social structures have been implicated in geopolitical systems'. Chapter 3 discusses the claims of state autonomy, by means of a comparative analysis of the modern states system with those of Renaissance Italy and Classical Greece, the argument being that their surface similarities cannot be understood without seeing the ways in which a particular form of the state is specific to a particular kind of society. Thus, the usual (realist) claim that there are transhistorical continuities between these three systems (as well as some others) is directly challenged. Chapter 4 discusses some pre-modern equivalents to the contemporary world market to point up, as it were, the differences.

The third part of Rosenberg's book develops an ambitious and intellectually rich version of Marx's social theory of capitalist society as an alternative (i.e. non-realist) way of understanding the modern international system. Two categories made much of in the first section, sovereignty and anarchy, are redefined in Marxian terms, and an agenda for future work laid out which points to a radically different understanding of the emergence and development of international relations (the events in the world) from that most usual in 'International Relations' (the self-proclaimed discipline).

At one level, these books are both attempts to 'explain' contemporary world politics; to lay bare, as it were, the lineaments of the contemporary international 'order'. However, both Halliday and Rosenberg are distinguished not just by a scholarly commitment, but by what we might call a practical commitment; to a sense of its urgency, indeed its centrality, in shaping (or, perhaps more likely at the moment, marring) human lives. In this context they both also share a commitment to human emancipation.

Halliday ends his book with a section entitled 'The challenge of the normative', in which he argues that normative questions are central to the new research programme for which he has been elaborating the building blocks in the book as a whole. He accepts that ethical principles, such as they are, are historically created and maintained, but refuses to accept that this requires us to accept 'relativism'. Indeed, he suggests:

> On matters of primary normative and political concern there is a measure of international consensus around a set of values that, on grounds quite independent of their origin, can be based on reason and which bear, for reasons that social scientists can happily argue over, on economic prosperity and peace, both domestic and international. It is a pity, indeed it is very dangerous, that just at the moment when a new international situation emerges, there should be a faltering of political nerve in the countries with the greatest political influence on what does, and does not, constitute a desirable political system.
>
> (p. 241)

Rosenberg is less given to such pronouncements. However, a small but powerful normative genie lurks in Rosenberg's argument, just waiting for the right rub of the lamp to bring it forth. The stirrings of the genie are felt from time to time: 'it is in this determined rediscovery of our own collective human agency in the anonymous social forces and processes around us', we find Rosenberg writing in his conclusion, 'that social theory finds both its surest methodological and its deepest political premise' (p. 173). However, the genie does not appear fully in *The Empire of Civil Society*, remaining, like the workings of capitalism in Rosenberg's argument, a powerful but shadowy form, operating largely beneath the surface.

It materializes with a vengeance, however, in a recent article of Rosenberg's. Here, he proclaims that he is in search of that alternative approach to International Relations which combines 'historical understanding, substantive explanation, totalizing theory and a moral vocation of reason'. This powerful theory is to be found, we are told, by reflecting upon the 'classic social analysis' outlined by C. Wright Mills in his *The Sociological Imagination*. In this book, says Rosenberg, Mills outlines freedom and reason as the evaluative guiding thread of 'classic social analysis' which involves 'tirelessly rendering visible and public the actual structures of power within a society in order to enlarge the possible realm of democratic self government' (p. 93). The theoretical agenda that results from Rosenberg's assumption of Mills' mantle (his version of the agenda sketched by

Halliday at the end of *Rethinking International Relations*) is fourfold. It is concerned, first, with 'the real international system of modern world history, that set of geo-political forms and relations which emerged out of the debris of European feudalism and expanded geographically to incorporate the rest of humanity' (p. 102). Second, it is thus concerned with history 'but not for antiquarian reasons'. Citing Mills again, he argues for a concern with history because 'the climax of the social scientist's concern with history is the idea he comes to hold of the epoch in which he lives' (p. 102, quoting Mills p. 65). Third, the international imagination is 'committed to understanding the social world in general – and our international system in particular – in terms of a complex but recognizable totality of real historical relations between individuals' (p. 104), as well as the history of 'the combined and uneven development of a large number of different kinds of society' (p. 105). Finally (the genie now manifesting itself in all its glory), the 'international imagination' 'does not eschew ethical judgment' but

> nor does it suppose that an intellectual method exists which can itself resolve moral dilemmas. Its principal contribution is the illumination of the objective, structural responsibility of individuals and groups for particular outcomes – whatever formal bonds of obligation are held to obtain. And its purpose is to educate moral choice by drawing out the real human relations involved – not to replace it with philosophical guarantees or technical formulae.
>
> (p. 105)

The implication of this is that

> what systematic moral reasoning could do is explain why [ethical dimensions of power relations] recur in (a particular) form, and what is at stake in them, what is their social content. What it arguably cannot do is to provide an intellectual resolution of those dilemmas – for the simple reason that those dilemmas are not at root intellectual: rather they reflect real tensions and contradictions in the characteristic social relations of the society in question.
>
> (p. 106)

Rosenberg's essay has been (rightly) seen as a powerful programmatic statement of the general approach I have ascribed to both him and Halliday, and it has been praised and criticized (in almost equal measure) by a number of writers. However, it is also worth pointing out that it is precisely in this 'normative area' that the argument he and Halliday put forward has, I suggest, most problems. More of this, too, in a moment.

'Gramscian' IR theory

A similar problem is visible, I suggest, in the other most prominent 'historical materialism' in contemporary international studies, that sometimes called

'Gramscian' critical theory.[50] As I remarked above, this version of critical theory originated with one of critical theory's most original voices, Robert Cox. A wide range of scholars, with a variety of interests and backgrounds, have contributed to it. Among the more prominent and interesting, I think, would be Steven Gill, Craig Murphy,[51] Kees van der Pijl[52] and Barry Gills. The most systematic exposition of what this implies has recently been given, in fact, by Gill.[53] He has suggested that the 'Gramscian' research programme would involve (at least) four aspects:[54]

1   ongoing attempts to reconsider epistemological and ontological aspects of world order, in the context of past, present and future;
2   continuous efforts in methodological, theoretical and conceptual innovation;
3   concrete historical studies of the emerging world order in terms of its economic, political and socio-cultural dimensions with a view to its emerging contradictions and the limits and possibilities these imply for different collectivities, a task which would involve work along three dimensions, analysis of the structures and agents of globalization; analysis of social formations such as state and civil society, the market and the family; analysis of the persistence of, and changes in, patterns of interest and identity;
4   directly addressing and developing related ethical and practical approaches to global problems.

As he concludes, this

> post hegemonic research agenda can be viewed as generating a perspective which needs to be understood as a part of the historical process, that is its form of engagement involves human knowledge, consciousness and action in the making of history and shaping our collective futures.[55]

It is noteworthy, of course, how similar this is to some of the themes in Halliday and Rosenberg treated above. Again the 'normative' dimension – the dimension which presumably tells us what is emancipatory and how we judge it – is, so to speak, the tailpiece of the programme. And again, we are rooted in notions of 'concrete historical studies' of the emerging world order. However, as we have seen, the sense of order involved is necessarily normative and it is the sense of the dialectic that is central.

Negative dialectic?

Enough has been said, I hope, to give a flavour of the various ways in which emancipatory theories of International Relations seek to offer their view of the manner in which the 'problem of order' might be conceptualized and even – perhaps – transcended. I want to start by commenting on Halliday's notion of an ethical 'consensus' in contemporary world politics. Halliday is, of course, scarcely alone in placing a good deal of weight on such consensus. He is, moreover, quite right that there are often considerable degrees of consensus about certain ethical principles in world politics, usually to do with concerns about peace, justice and prosperity. One very important part of a genuinely ethically sensitive account of world politics is to accept that and trace the relations between these claims and others in the light of it.

However, that very assumption requires that we are also able to evaluate the particular manifestations of any consensus. Nobody supposes (or do they?) that the mere fact of consensus generates any kind of obligation. The way in which Halliday and Rosenberg actually express their claims about 'norms or moral reasoning' is actually the result of adopting a certain 'ethical' understanding, in that they quite explicitly state that in their view there is no path away from the material realities that govern social practice in any given place and time. For the claims they wish to make, that admission is deeply damaging. It is one thing to say that 'moral reasoning' cannot and should not be completely divorced from the practicalities with which it has to deal, but quite another to say that the only way of understanding or situating the ethical is to consider the specifics of the here and now. I would happily agree with the former statement but would strongly resist the latter. Indeed, I would go further and suggest that in order for the former statement to be true, then the latter one would have to be false. If it is not, then Halliday and Rosenberg are left with a form of the relativism of which they are so strongly critical in others. Richard Rorty once wrote that one is always harshest on what one most dreads resembling. This perhaps accounts for the rather uncharacteristic shrillness in Halliday's critique of 'post-modernism'. Without the ability to go beyond the specifics of time and place, I suggest, ethical judgement and therefore, of course, what counts as 'emancipation' is impossible.

Halliday and Rosenberg have one major problem, therefore. On the one hand they want to avoid the charge of relativism and be committed to a universalistic ethic that would emancipate. Since they would claim that there is nothing transcendental on which they might choose to base that ethic, their ethic must be resolutely material and empirical. However, denying themselves the relentless 'negativity' and dialectical approach of the older Frankfurt school and disassociating themselves from the (from their perspective) suspiciously idealistic discourse ethics of a Habermas means relying effectively on some sort of ethical 'consensus' to which they might appeal as a 'fact'. On the other hand, such an appeal must of necessity recognize the contingent, situated, local, character of such ethical consensus, and then the question arises how it is possible to evaluate one 'factually' based ethical consensus against another and thus say one represents 'emancipation' and the other 'oppression'.

This points to an even broader question: even on its own terms, can critical theory be 'emancipatory' in the required sense? I want to suggest that critical theory has a profound ambiguity about the question of emancipation, an ambiguity which weakens, possibly fatally, the sense of 'emancipation' as the possible route out of the problem of order and that critical theory is engaged, in a sense, in a negative dialectic with itself on this question. The ambiguity can be most clearly seen in the work of Adorno and so it is to him I shall turn first, before assessing the implications of this reading for critical international theory.

It would obviously be impossible to offer even a sketch of a thinker as complex and nuanced (and as committed to the claim, as he often insisted, that 'true philosophy resists paraphrase')[56] as Adorno in the space I have available to me here. All I want to do here is illustrate why I think that Adorno's thought is problematic for the 'emancipatory project' on which, I have suggested, the versions of critical theory (both general and international) that I discussed above depend.[57]

To do this, I first want to develop Jay Bernstein's recent reformulation of critical theory along Adornoesque, rather than Habermassian lines. He argues first that

> critical theory is not a theory of society or a wholly homogenous school of thinkers or a method. Critical Theory, rather, is a tradition of social thought that, at least in part, takes its cue from its opposition to the wrongs and ills of modern societies on the one hand, and the forms of theorizing that simply go along with or seek to legitimate those societies on the other hand.[58]

The three basic criteria of this tradition are a non-instrumental conception of reason and cognition, and non-functionalist conception of culture and the harmonization of both of these.[59] However, the central root of critical theory, for Bernstein, is the recognition – originally laid out by Adorno – that the dilemmas of modernity have a common root, directly or indirectly, in the abstractive achievements of instrumental reason which produces two things. First, it produces 'domination' in the sense of what he calls the domination of 'exchange value over use value' seen as the result of the 'universal development of the exchange system', part of a continuous rationalization process within modern societies which leads to the 'domination' of institutions over people. Second, it produces 'nihilism' in that this 'rationalization process' possesses 'three logically discriminable features; proceduralism (formalism or methodologism as applied to social situations), substitutability and end-indifference', which lead to a continuous devaluation of the highest values. Effectively, these questions become the 'problem of justice' and the 'problem of reason'. As we saw in the Introduction, taken together, these represent in important respects the Nietzschean and Weberian departure point for the contemporary 'problem of order'. Each of these issues has, however, tended to be analysed apart from one another. As Bernstein puts it:

> Traditional Marxism tends to focus on the question of injustice ... making its trajectory at one with the most advanced moments of liberal political theory. Conversely, the tradition of existentialism and phenomenology ... directs itself to the problem of nihilism ... Adorno's original insight ... was

the identification of the common root ... and hence the demand for a theory that would address each dilemma without losing sight of the other.[60]

In terms of the basic criteria for a critical theory that Bernstein lays out, it is clear that the first requirement – a non-instrumental conception of reason – addresses the first problem, and the second – a non-functionalist conception of culture – addresses the second. However, as Bernstein puts it, 'the harmonization requirement constrains the satisfaction of the first criterion such that it becomes answerable to the demands of the second'.[61]

This discussion provides Bernstein with a way of viewing the obvious differences between Habermas and Adorno. 'Fundamentally,' he says,

> they differ with respect to the weight and focus they offer to the justice and meaning questions: Habermas believes that Adorno slights the question of justice in his engagement with the nihilism question, hence giving undue significance to the role of art in his theory and, by implication, espousing a position which could only be satisfied through a Utopian re-enchantment of the social and natural worlds. From an Adornoesque perspective, Habermas' focus on the justice problem entails surrender over the question of nihilism, falsely assuming that total disenchantment would not be extentionally equivalent to total reification.[62]

Bernstein's argument is centred on the claim that in his complex and profoundly important reworking of the central assumptions of critical theory, Habermas holds to the basic project (what he calls the 'very idea' of a critical theory) but that the theory that results is skewed because in evolving the centrepiece of this theory, the theory of communicative action, he develops it primarily in the context of the problem of justice and it is this which then leads to an account of the problem of nihilism. In other words, the problem of nihilism is constrained by the problem of justice, rather than, as Bernstein and Adorno would suggest, having the problem of justice constrained by the problem of nihilism. The result of this is that the dialectic on which critical theory depends becomes inverted, negative in a profoundly un-Adornoesque way.

If this reading is a plausible one and, as I say, in my view it is, then there is an equally profound implication for the 'emancipatory project' that is held to be at the centre of critical international theory. As we saw above, one of the features of contemporary critical theory – and especially of critical international theory – is the sense that critical theory should not only be able to critique modern societies, it should also answer the 'where's the beef?' question. It should also be able to offer action-guiding principles or have institutional/political recommendations of an institutionally cosmopolitan kind.

However, on the Adornoesque reading offered by Bernstein, such a view is untenable. 'In locating a form of reasoning that is not instrumental and which, remember, includes a cognition of ends, and a materialist conception of culture which is compatible with such a practical reason, we *exhaust* the demand that theory be practical',[63] he says. Moreover, first, 'whether or not, at any given time, the contradictions, suppressions and forms of domination in a society entail macro-potentialities for collective action is itself a historically contingent matter', and second, the demand that theory must have a 'praxial dimension' itself runs the risk of collapsing critical theory back into traditional theory by making it dependent on instrumental conceptions of rationality.[64]

Emancipation, critique and ambiguity

It is this danger, especially the last one, I want to suggest, that critical international theory is currently courting and, at least to some extent must court, if it is to perform the task it has set itself. In the first place, it is critical theory as an *emancipatory* project that requires, as Linklater suggests, 'light cast on present possibilities' and thus runs the risk alluded to above. It is therefore the notion of 'emancipation' in this context that creates the problem – rather than the project of critical theory *per se*. It is noteworthy, however, that 'emancipation' was not one of Adorno's major concerns. It is precisely this, of course, that has irritated so many emancipatory critical theorists.[65] However, if critical theory *cannot* be emancipatory in the required sense then it remains silent on the 'problem of order' as far as world politics is concerned, since it can add nothing to reflection on *it as critical theory*. Everything would remain, as it were, contingent on history and context. Whatever critical theory might be able to say about the problems of justice and nihilism held together, it would be silent on the question of praxis.

This is especially so, I suggest, for critical international theory. Think, for example, of Linklater's four 'achievements of critical theory' in international relations. The first two are facets of critical theory that I think both Habermas and Adorno would accept as a legitimate part of the three requirements of critical theory discussed by Bernstein. However, the last two are fashioned, as Linklater emphasizes, around the 'reconstruction' of historical materialism developed by Habermas and as such would be vulnerable, I think, to the charges levelled by Bernstein and others at that project. The point here is to suggest that the 'emancipatory project' in this context runs the risk of tipping critical theory back into traditional theory and that, as a result, it could not offer a separable solution to the problem of order, after the manner I have suggested that its advocates have hoped. *Only* if Habermas's reconstruction – and that developed by some of his more recent followers – can escape the Adornoesque critique would emancipation in the sense deployed above be a possible solution to the 'problem of order'.

Conclusion: strategic 'emancipation', 'tactical ethics' and world order

So, what is the trajectory of 'emancipatory' attempts to transcend the states system and thus the 'problem of order', as we approach the twenty-first century?

In many respects, the accounts of world politics discussed in this chapter seem to me to represent the most humane and generally hopeful accounts available. They also have, at least in principle, a way of seeking to 'solve' the problem of order that actually engages with it and seeks to understand its evolution historically and normatively and thus contribute to that dialectical sense of order that Aron, rightly I have argued, suggested was central.

However, 'Adorno's problem', if I may call it that, is real and, I want to suggest, has not yet been adequately dealt with by any of the 'critical theories' discussed above. In this conclusion I want to offer one reading as to why that might be so and suggest some implications of this reading for the 'emancipatory project' in IR theory.

Let me begin this reading by making an observation, the full implications of which will only surface in the Epilogue. In the *Republic*, in perhaps the most famous of his many images, Plato portrays society (any and all societies) as a cave. Some insist that the cave is all there is, but others claim that there is light outside the cave and that, perhaps, it is only because of this light that we see in the cave at all. In our current context, let us suggest that most 'International Relations' scholarship, realist, liberal, constructivist and societal, either assumes that the 'cave', that is to say, international society, the international system or what you will, is all there is (that is relevant), or is agnostic (and uninterested) concerning the possibility that there might be anything 'outside' the cave, however outside is understood. Therein in many respects lies its attraction (a clear focus, an agreed set of problems) but also the site of its greatest weaknesses. In Platonic terminology, it is left trying to see in the cave by virtue only of the pale light that exists there, and what it sees, of course, is shadows. That does not mean that some very interesting accounts of the shadows cannot be given, nor does it mean that the shadows are unimportant, for we all remain in the cave and the shadows are, of course, real for us.

Emancipatory theory in International Relations stands outside this 'mainstream' of contemporary 'International Relations' scholarship, however. Theorists of this persuasion seek their anchorage in that proud and much broader tradition that encompasses Kant and Hegel, Marx and Weber, Durkheim and Freud. They know there is light outside the cave – the light of real historical processes and they seek to let it in, so that the cave can be seen whole, in a full light. Doing that, they believe, would transform the cave, for it would be observable by all who care to see it for what it truly is. This is what Rosenberg means, I think, when he quotes with evident approval (indeed, relish) Mills' statement that the vocation of social science involves 'tirelessly rendering visible and public the actual structures of power within a society in order to enlarge the possible realm of democratic self-government'.

It is in this context, however, that Rosenberg comes closest to joining hands with those critical theorists who follow the Gramscian agenda laid out by Gill, or those critical theorists who, following Habermas's lead, have argued that world politics, no less than the individual societies which make it up, requires a comprehensive account of the public sphere and its logic. For all of them, the task of letting in the light would mean transcending the cave as it currently stands.

The reason in each case is the same; the historical materialists and the critical theorists and those feminists who work in a similar vein see themselves as defending the 'project of modernity', the further development of the emancipatory project that lies at the heart of the tradition of Enlightenment social science. In a certain sense their response to the Keohane challenge is much more potentially damaging than any other, for they – unlike the post-structuralists I will discuss in a moment and in many respects unlike most constructivists as well – lay claim to the mantle of 'social science' explicitly in its Enlightenment – or anyway Enlightenment-derived – guise.

Indeed, their challenge is precisely that it is the *corruption* of the Enlightenment project by the growing dominance of instrumental rationality that has made IR theory the tool of the powerful, rather than the weapon of, critique it should, and could, be. Ethically, this tradition is, of course, the tradition of universalism *par excellence*.

However, 'Adorno's problem' casts a dark shadow on this claim. For Adorno, the danger is that Marxism in its traditional mode and, as Bernstein suggests, critical theory in its Habermassian mode run the risk of 'becoming' traditional theory, of becoming domesticated or co-opted by instrumental rationality. Surely, however, this cannot be so. For all of the approaches I have looked at here are deeply aware of the problems of instrumental rationality, indeed in large part build their critique on their distrust of it.

This is, I think, true, but it misses the full force of Adorno's suspicion. To bring that out, I want to refer to a distinction taken from the French thinker Michel de Certeau.[66] De Certeau distinguishes between strategy and tactics. For de Certeau, strategy is

> the calculus of force relationships which becomes possible when a subject of will and power (a proprietor, an enterprise, a city, a scientific investigation) can be isolated from an environment. ... A Strategy assumes a place that can be circumscribed as proper and thus serve as the basis for generating relations with an exterior distinct from it (competitors, adversaries ... targets or objects of research. Political, economic and scientific rationality has been constructed on this model.[67]

In other words, and although there are differences, to which I shall come back in a moment, he understands this term analogously to the way in which Adorno deploys the sense of 'instrumental rationality'.

Tactics, on the other hand, is a 'calculus' which cannot count on a 'proper' (a spatial or an institutional) localization;

> the place of the tactic belongs to the other ... the 'proper' is a victory of space over time. On the contrary, because it does not have a place, a tactic

depends on time ... it must constantly manipulate events in order to turn them into opportunities.[68]

It is obvious to see that 'rationalist' IR theory is, in de Certeau's sense, a strategy. The case of traditional realism, some forms of liberalism and the English school would be less clear, however, and there would probably be plausible readings of them all as both a strategy or tactics in de Certeau's sense. However, what about those theories and accounts usually referred to by the derivation 'post-positivist'?

It seems to me that most contemporary constructivist theory would be 'strategic' in de Certeau's sense, the chief exceptions being the interpretive constructivist accounts of, for example, Kratochwil. However, the real question is over critical theory. The danger, I think, is that virtually all versions of the 'emancipatory project' are in danger of becoming at the very least 'strategic' – if not fully a 'strategy'. In other words, just as realism – on my reading – contains within it a 'tactics' that is at war with its general 'strategic' form, so critical theory contains an inherent strategy that is, I suggest, threatening to overwhelm its 'tactical' deployment. To explain, let me go back to Plato.

In Plato's story – and contrary to the emancipatory project as I have presented it here – Socrates taught that the cave cannot be fundamentally transformed. This is not to say that there is no change possible, rather it is a claim about the kind of understanding the 'light outside the cave' can provide. Socrates is a guide; he does not seek to bring light to the cave, but to help those who wish to 'leave' the cave (and are able to do so) to experience the light themselves and, as a result, understand themselves and the cave better. In so doing, we can balance understanding of the 'realities of the cave' – the shadows – with our knowledge of what the sun illuminates in us. Socrates suggests that when the philosopher returns to the cave, it is the philosopher who is transformed, not the cave.

The sort of 'knowledge' we have, if we take Socrates' route seriously, I suggest, is 'tactical' knowledge as outlined by de Certeau. As Adorno suggests, the cave remains what it has always been, it is us – as analysts, as actors, as humans – who are changed, but of course, we cannot be properly changed in the absence of change in the cave. The dilemma that I think Adorno could not escape (and that for all their power modern Adorno advocates like Rose and Bernstein cannot escape either) is that in trying to 'change the cave' one *inevitably and inescapably* becomes embroiled in the clutches of instrumental reason. This is why Adorno was reduced, finally, to suggesting that his work was 'messages in a bottle' for an age which had – somehow – escaped from the clutches of instrumental reason. He effectively abandoned any search for a way of getting to such a world because he realized that, on his own analysis, he could only get there by using the methods that would forever block his passage.

In other words, the problem is simply that in acting in the world as it is, as we must do to bring about change (even for the better), we have to partake of the forms of instrumental rationality, in which case we tip back into 'traditional' theory and any 'emancipation' that results would have to be seen in that way. To develop a 'research agenda' for this must therefore be moving towards a 'strategic' conception of what is required to develop or 'open up' the system, rather than simply a tactical response to what the system imposes on us. Tactics, as de Certeau says, is always reactive; the emancipatory project in its dominant modes in contemporary IR theory is not, it is – and must be – proactive.

If this is plausible, then the 'emancipatory project' in IR theory faces a central and complex task. To make good on its emancipatory agenda, it will have to show both that the 'Adorno problem' can be resolved and that it can add something to other ways of dealing with the task of social change that distinguish it from the more radical forms of liberalism. Otherwise its attempt to transcend the problem of order – to 'end order' – will be seen to be, at best, a descant over the main themes of liberalism, and at worst, a repeated wailing at the intractability of fate!

Notes

1   The most detailed and helpful discussion of Leibniz' political thought – including international thought – is Patrick Riley's magisterial *Leibniz' Universal Jurisprudence: Justice as the Charity of the Wise* (Cambridge, MA: Harvard University Press, 1996). He has also edited the best collection of Leibniz' political writings in English, *Leibniz' Political Writings*, revised and expanded (Cambridge: Cambridge University Press, 1992), which has most of Leibniz' major writings on international politics included. Alternatively the relevant sections of Terry Nardin, Chris Brown and N. J. Rengger, *Texts in International Relations* (Cambridge: Cambridge University Press, forthcoming), provide a summary and selections from Leibniz' writings.
2   Though, significantly, it is perhaps increasingly relevant today.
3   See the text in Hans Reiss (ed.), *Kant's Political Writings* (Cambridge: Cambridge University Press, 1970).
4   Those specifically mentioned included Grotius, Pufendorf and Vattel.
5   Andrew Linklater, *Men and Citizens in the Theory of International Relations* (London: Macmillan, 1982; 2nd edition, 1990), p. 205.
6   For a rather different cosmopolitanism see N. J. Rengger, 'Cosmopolitan Political Theory and International Ethics in the Twenty First Century', in D. Warner and J.-M. Cociaud (eds) *New Issues in International Ethics* (Tokyo: United Nations University, forthcoming).
7   An interesting overview which offers a good overview of the interpenetrations and interconnections of many of these with critical theory is Stephen Leonard, *Critical Theory and Political Practice* (Ithaca, NY: Cornell University Press, 1994). For Unger, who is not discussed here, see the three volumes of his *Politics* (Cambridge: Cambridge University Press, 1987). For political theology, probably the most able representative is Jurgen Moltmann; see especially his *Theology of Hope* (London; SCM, 1967), which draws on the work of Ernst Bloch, also very influential on the Frankfurt school, of course. For Metz, his *Political Theology* is paradigmatic. For *dependencia* arguments, a classic statement is Andre Gunder Frank, *Capitalism and Underdevelopment in Latin America* (New York, 1967). Wallerstein's world systems analysis has been expounded exhaustively (and exhaustingly) in the (so far) three volumes of *The Modern World System* (New York: Academic Press, 1974, 1980 and 1989) and in such collections as *The Capitalist World Economy* (Cambridge: Cambridge University Press, 1979). Slightly different versions, though indebted to Wallerstein, can be found in Christopher Chase-Dunn, *Global Formation* (Oxford: Blackwell, 1989), and Giovanni

Arrighi, *The Long Twentieth Century* (London: Verso, 1994). For Halliday's version of Marxism, his best presentation is his *Rethinking International Relations* (London: Macmillan, 1994) and Rosenberg's in his *The Empire of Civil Society: A Critique of the Realist Theory of International Relations* (London: Verso, 1994), which won the Deutscher Prize that year. Marxist accounts of international relations are also well discussed by Andrew Linklater, 'Marxism', in Scott Burchill *et al.*, *Theories of International Relations* (London: Macmillan, 1996), by Chris Brown, 'Marxism and International Relations', in Terry Nardin and David Mapel (eds), *Traditions of International Ethics* (Cambridge: Cambridge University Press, 1992), and, rather more confusingly but certainly thoroughly, by V. Kublakova and A. Cruikshank, in both *Marxism-Leninism and the Theory of International Relations* (London: Macmillan, 1980) and *Marxism and International Relations* (Oxford: Oxford University Press, 1985). The work of Paulo Friere is discussed by Leonard but also see Friere, *Pedagogy of the Oppressed* (New York: Continuum, 1983). For Said, see, especially, *Culture and Imperialism* (London: Chatto and Windus, 1994).

8   For Milbank the best text to consult is his massive *Theology and Social Theory: Beyond Secular Reason* (Oxford: Blackwell, 1990). Hauerwas's writings are so numerous it is difficult to pick out a representative text. However, let me suggest *The Church as Polis* (South Bend, IN: University of Notre Dame Press, 1995). I should emphasize that for writers like Milbank and Hauerwas, secular society can *never* be redeemed (for most of those listed above there are ways of redemption, however difficult). There is a simple choice between the secular city and the 'other city'. Thus their version of the project of critique is much closer to post-structuralism than to most versions of critical theory, as discussed below. However, they are certainly part of the 'critical project', if that term is used as broadly as I am using it at the moment.

9   This is not the place, and we certainly do not have the time, to attempt even a brief overview of the ins and outs of the realist versus anti-realist debates in philosophy (this 'realism' does not, of course, have much to do with 'political realism' in International Relations).

10   See his book of the same name, *Realism with a Human Face*.

11   See N. J. Rengger and Mark Hoffman, 'Modernity, Post-Modernism and International Relations', in Joe Doherty, E. Graham and Mo Malek (eds), *Post-modernism and the Social Sciences* (Basingstoke: Macmillan, 1992).

12   I would like to emphasize some very particular thanks here to a number of people whose writings, conversations and support have been particularly useful in helping me to come, rather belatedly, to realize the power and acuteness of the Marxian tradition in political thought. Pride of place must go to my long-suffering former colleague at Bristol, Terrell Carver, whose many writings, joint teaching with me, and many hours of conversations at various hostelries around Bristol, to say nothing of the bar of New College Oxford most Januaries since the mid 1980s, did more than anything else to persuade me that my long-standing doubts about Marx and the tradition which he inspired were, in part at least, misplaced. Once the dam had been breached many others helped educate me further. At Bristol, Mark Wickham-Jones' and Chris Bertram's knowledge of every minor twist in the seemingly endless saga of Marxist party splits world-wide, as well as their rigorous defence of democratic versions of social democracy, enlivened many a lunch in the helpfully Stalinist interior of Bristol's staff cafeteria. At the Oxford Political Thought Conference, for many years held at New College Oxford every January, Ian Forbes would often make a welcome insinuation into Terrell's attempts to remedy my lack of education and reading his *Marx and the New Individual* (London: Macmillan, 1989) was a revelation. At the LSE, on leave in 1992, Justin Rosenberg and Fred Halliday educated me still further. Finally, Andrew Linklater's writings and conversations, over many years now, are a master class in how to blend sympathetic interpretations of Marx with a thorough and insightful interpretation of Kant and Hegel to develop an original and powerful position in normative

international theory. Alas, I am still a resolute anti-materialist, but this is hardly their fault!

13 Standard histories of critical theory would include Martin Jay's excellent *The Dialectical Imagination* (Boston: Little Brown, 1973), Rolf Wiggershaus' exhaustive (and exhausting) *The Frankfurt School* (Cambridge: Polity Press, 1994) and David Held's *An Introduction to Critical Theory: Horkheimer to Habermas* (Cambridge: Polity Press, 1980).

14 For the origin of this term see Peter Gay's still outstanding cultural history of Weimar, *Weimar Culture: The Insider as Outsider* (Harmondsworth: Penguin, 1974).

15 On Marcuse, see, especially, his *Negations* (Harmondsworth: Penguin, 1972). Good discussions of Marcuse are contained in Stephen Eric Bronner, *Of Critical Theory and its Theorists* (Oxford: Blackwell, 1994) (see especially chapters 10 and 11), and John Bokina and Timothy J. Lukes (eds), *Marcuse Revisited* (Kansas City: University of Kansas Press, 1995).

16 On Fromm, an excellent discussion, sensitive to his originality while not uncritical, is Bronner, *Of Critical Theory and its Theorists*, chapter 10.

17 I have obviously already discussed Kratochwil in Chapter 2 and so will not repeat the discussion here.

18 See Fred Halliday, *Rethinking International Relations* (London: Macmillan, 1994), and Justin Rosenberg, *The Empire of Civil Society: A Critique of the Realist Theory of International Relations* (London: Verso, 1994). For an extended discussion of these two books, see N. J. Rengger, 'Clio's Cave? Historical Materialism and the Claims of Substantive Social Theory in World Politics', *Review of International Studies*, 1996, 22: 213–31, on which I draw here.

19 And sometimes an even wider use is intended. Many contemporary IR theorists, for example, refer to other kinds of constructivists as critical theorists as well. This is clearly the view that lies behind the recent critiques of 'critical theory' of, for example, John Mearsheimer and Stephen Walt. See, for example, Walt's otherwise excellent *Revolution and War* (Ithaca, NY: Cornell University Press, 1996) and Mearsheimer's 'The False Promise of International Institutions' in *International Security*.

20 Especially the work of Robert Cox and Stephen Gill. See, especially, Cox's *Approaches to World Order* (Cambridge: Cambridge University Press, 1996) and Gill's *American Hegemony and the Trilateral Commission* (Cambridge: Cambridge University Press, 1989) and Gill (ed.), *Gramsci, Historical Materialism and International Relations* (Cambridge: Cambridge University Press, 1993).

21 Especially the work of Ann Tickner. See, especially, Tickner, *Gender in International Relations* (New York: Columbia University Press, 1993).

22 It is probably true to say, and not irrelevant in the present context, that we are now witnessing the effective emergence of a 'third generation of critical theorists' in both Europe and North America whose concerns are still wider and certainly include increasingly questions which are traditionally central questions for International Relations (such as development, globalization, democratization, etc.). This 'third generation' of theorists would include, by my reckoning, Axel Honneth, who has inherited Habermas' chair at Frankfurt, Seyla Benhabib at Harvard, Nancy Fraser at the New School, Ken Baynes at SUNY, James Bohman at St Louis University, David Held at the OU and, possibly, such scholars as Maurizio Passerein d'Entreves at Manchester. Many of these have written on International Relations (Fraser and Baynes have chapters in the volume on *Critical Theory and International Relations* (Boulder, CO: Lynne Rienner, 1998) and Held has been a powerful advocate of 'cosmopolitan democracy', one of the real growth areas in contemporary International Relations). Taken together with the work of scholars like Linklater, who is more or less of an age with these figures, these developments presage a real growth in critical international theory over the next few years.

23 Good general introductions to Habermas that are accessible and accurate do not exactly abound. Two personal favourites would be William Outhwaite, *Habermas*

(Cambridge: Polity Press, 1994) and David Held, *An Introduction to Critical Theory*, part two.

24 See especially her *Gender in International Relations* (New York: Columbia University Press, 1993).

25 Again a degree of caution is in order here. Booth and some of his allies, for example Peter Vale, certainly fit pretty clearly into the 'emancipatory' category. However, a number of other critical security studies scholars are rather more difficult, being drawn to post-structural themes and thinkers as well. See for example Mike Williams and Keith Krause's edited collection *Critical Security Studies* (Minneapolis: University of Minnesota Press, 1996), which contains both. For Booth, probably the best articles to look at are 'Security and Emancipation', *Review of International Studies*, 1989, 19(5): 49, and 'Security in Anarchy: Utopian Realism in Theory and Practice', *International Affairs*, 1991, 67(3): 527–45, and 'Human Wrongs and International Relations', *International Affairs*, 1995, 71(1): 103–26.

26 I am thinking especially of scholars like Seyla Benhabib and Nancy Fraser, both of whom have made very powerful contributions to both feminist thought and critical theory. For a sample see Benhabib, *Situating the Self* (Cambridge: Polity Press, 1992), and Fraser, *Justice Interruptus*.

27 Mark Hoffman, 'Critical Theory and the Inter-Paradigm Debate', *Millennium: Journal of International Studies*, 1987, 17(3): Summer. I should add that one of the 'contributions' of mine to IR theory that I referred to in the Preface of this book was originally cast as a response to this essay (see N. J. Rengger, 'Going Critical? A Response to Hoffman', *Millennium*, 1988, 18(1): Spring, and Hoffman's reply in the same issue). Since there has been some comment on this exchange (see, for example, Yosef Lapid, 'Quo Vaid International Relations? Further Reflections on the next Stage of International Relations Theory', *Millennium*, 1989, 19(1): Spring; Jim George's *Discourses of Global Politics: A Critical (Re)introduction to International Relations* (Boulder, CO: Lynne Rienner, 1994), pp. 185–8, and Steve Smith, 'Self Images of a Discipline', in Ken Booth and Steve Smith (eds), *International Relations Theory Today* (Cambridge: Polity Press, 1994)) and since, despite the fact that Hoffman and I later published a joint essay amending our respective positions ('Modernity, Postmodernism and International Relations', in Joe Doherty *et al.* (eds), *Postmodernism and the Social Sciences* (London: Macmillan, 1992)), some of this comment has been rather inaccurate as to our respective positions, it seems appropriate to correct any misperceptions that there might have been. Hoffman is usually seen (correctly) as an advocate of critical theory, I often (and incorrectly) as an opponent of it from a broadly post-structural position. At the risk of sounding like a witness to the House UnAmerican Activities Committee, I am not now, nor have I ever been … a post-structuralist. As I will say in the Epilogue, there is a good deal in post-structural international theory with which I agree – as I do indeed with critical theory – but there is also much that I dissent from. My intention in my original response to Hoffman was merely to point out that 'critical theory' in international studies was *already* a mixture of the emancipatory and the post-structural and that, as a result, Hoffman's version of critical theory (i.e. Frankfurt- and Gramscian-inspired emancipatory critical theory) was unlikely to be the 'next stage of International Relations theory'. I would, of course, now put this rather differently, and indeed, that is what I am doing, in this chapter and in the Epilogue.

28 Bloch's masterpiece, as well as earlier works such as *Spirit of Utopia*, were influential on the early Frankfurt school partly through his friendship with two of the school's most powerful intellects, Adorno and Benjamin. Significantly also, his work was hugely influential on 'political theology', especially on Moltmann, whose first major work, *Theology of Hope*, owes, explicitly, an enormous amount to Bloch. A good general study of Bloch is Vincent Geoghan, *Ernst Bloch* (London: Routledge, 1995).

29 It is worth pointing out here, since it will not really be appropriate to come back to it later, that a number of the early critical theorists became increasingly 'mystical', even 'theological', in their old age (this is even true of Adorno, though he also remained a resolute atheist, a mixture very reminiscent of Bloch) and I suggest that the reason is simply that one of the strongest 'ways' of being Utopian in the required sense is a theological way, even if there is the minor inconvenience of (probably) having to believe in God. Contemporary critical theorists, for example Habermas and Linklater, do not do this, of course – at least not yet.

30 *Men and Citizens in the Theory of International Relations* (London: Macmillan, 1982; 2nd edition, 1990); *Beyond Realism and Marxism: Towards a Critical Theory of International Relations* (London: Macmillan, 1989); *The Transformation of Political Community* (Cambridge: Polity Press, 1998).

31 'What is a good international citizen?', in Paul Keal (ed.), *Ethics and Foreign Policy* (Canberra: Australian National University Press, 1992); 'The Question of the Next Stage in International Relations Theory: A Critical Theoretic Point of View', *Millennium: Journal of International Studies*, 1992, 21(1); 'Community, Citizenship and Global Politics', *Oxford International Review*, 1993, 5(1); 'Community', in Alex Danchev (ed.), *Fin de Siècle: The Meaning of the Twentieth Century* (London: Tauris, 1995); 'Neo-Realism in Theory and Practice', in Ken Booth and Steve Smith (eds), *International Relations Theory Today* (Cambridge: Polity Press, 1994); 'The Achievements of Critical Theory', in Steve Smith, Ken Booth and Marysia Zalewski (eds), *International Theory: Positivism and Beyond* (Cambridge: Cambridge University Press, 1996). Most of these have been incorporated in some form or another into his most recent book.

32 Linklater has remained strongly committed to a broadly (left) Hegelian understanding of emancipation and of politics and society. Habermas, as I have already remarked, has become increasingly Kantian in recent years. A good discussion of Habermas' 'Kantian turn' – denied by Habermas himself, it seems fair to add – is Onora O'Neill, 'Kommunikative Rationalitat und praktische Vernunft', *Deutsche Zeitschrift für Philosophie*, 1992.

33 It is interesting in this context that Linklater is virtually ignored in mainstream attacks on 'critical theory', especially from the United States. There are any number of reasons for this. For one thing, he has tended to publish with British (or Australian) publishers and in British (and Australian) journals and this is a sure way to reduce your visibility for a US audience. However, I suggest that another reason might be that it is difficult for 'mainstream' scholars to attack Linklater without engaging in genuine debate with his Habermassian-derived project. It is much safer and far easier – given their own assumptions – to restrict their criticisms to constructivists that they can co-opt (or try to) or post-structuralists or feminists that they can patronize (or try to). As Linklater's own brilliant demolition job on neo-realism shows, critical theory is extremely difficult to do either with, partly because it seeks to radicalize the very project mainstream scholars like Keohane (for example) see themselves as committed to.

34 Linklater, 'The Achievements of Critical Theory'.

35 See his introduction to *The Transformation of Political Community*.

36 All quotations from Linklater, 'The Achievements of Critical Theory', pp. 279–80.

37 Linklater, 'The Achievements of Critical Theory', p. 293.

38 Linklater, 'The Achievements of Critical Theory', p. 296.

39 Linklater himself is especially interested in the 'societal' body of theory I discussed in Chapter 2. Another ongoing project he announced in the introduction to *The Transformation of Political Community* is a book on the English school and the Grotian tradition, co-authored with his Keele colleague Hidemi Suganami, which will consider 'the relationship between the Grotian analysis of different forms of international society and the notion of a universal communication community' (p. 10).

40 Devetak, 'Critical Theory', in Scott Burchill *et al.*, *Theories of International Relations* (London: Macmillan, 1996), p. 169.
41 See Habermas, *The Theory of Communicative Action. Vol. 1. Reason and the Rationalization of Society. Vol. 2. The Critique of Functionalist Reason* (Cambridge: Polity Press, 1991). A superb general discussion can be found in William Outhwaite, *Habermas* (Cambridge: Polity Press, 1994), chapters 5–7. More specific discussions from a rather more critical (and Adorno-leaning) critical theorist can be found in Jay Bernstein, *Recovering Ethical Life: Jurgen Habermas and the Future of Critical Theory* (London: Routledge, 1995). See especially chapters 2 and 4.
42 Devetak, 'Critical Theory', p. 171.
43 Devetak, 'Critical Theory', p. 171.
44 This quotation is quoted by Devetak on p. 171. It is taken from Held's chapter in Held (ed.), *Prospects for Democracy: North, South, East, West* (Cambridge: Polity Press, 1992). Held's major statement of his position can be found in his *Democracy and the Global Order* (Cambridge: Polity Press, 1995).
45 In addition to his general theoretical work, Hoffman has worked for many years in conflict and peace research, both academically and, as it were, practically, by running conflict resolution workshops. He has been close to, and actively involved in, the conflict resolution work of John Burton and his associates like Michael Banks (Hoffman's dissertation supervisor at LSE), John Groom and Chris Mitchell. However, his work in this area has been increasingly shaped by his continuing engagement with critical international theory, and especially with Habermas and Linklater. In particular his work on third-party mediation both benefits from and contributes to his versions of critical international theory. See especially his essay 'Third Party Mediation and Conflict Resolution in the Post Cold War World', in John Baylis and N. J. Rengger (eds), *Dilemmas of World Politics: International Issues in a Changing World* (Oxford: Clarendon Press, 1992). More recently, he has offered a superb medi-tation on the relevance of this perspective for conflict resolution in his paper to the Critical Theory and International Relations Conference at Aberystwyth, 1996. This appears as a chapter in Roger Tooze and Richard Wyn Jones (eds), *Critical Theory and International Relations* (Boulder, CO: Lynne Rienner, forthcoming).
46 See her 'Revisioning Security', in Booth and Smith (eds), *International Relations Theory Today* (Cambridge: Polity Press, 1994).
47 Devetak, 'Critical Theory', p. 172.
48 Linklater, 'Community, Citizenship and Global Politics', *Oxford International Review*, 1993, 5(1): 119.
49 Linklater, *The Transformation of Political Community*, p. 5.
50 Or, equally, sometimes called the 'Italian school' of International Relations, in keeping, I assume, with the 'English' school.
51 See, for example, *International Organization and Industrial Change* (Cambridge: Polity Press, 1994). See also his chapter in Tooze and Wyn Jones (eds), *Critical Theory and International Relations*, and his 'Understanding IR: Understanding Gramsci', *Review of International Studies*, 1988, 24 (July): 417–25.
52 See *The Making of an Atlantic Ruling Class* (London: Verso, 1984).
53 See the introduction to Gill (ed.), *Gramsci: Historical Materialism and International Relations*.
54 These are taken from Gill (ed.), *Gramsci: Historical Materialism and International Relations*, pp. 16–17.
55 Gill (ed.), *Gramsci: Historical Materialism and International Relations*, p. 17.
56 This saying is quoted at the outset of Martin Jay's excellent *Adorno* (Cambridge, MA: Harvard University Press, 1984), p. 11.
57 Treatments of Adorno relevant to this task, and which I am happy to acknowledge that I have benefited greatly from reading, include Jay Bernstein's *Recovering Ethical Life* which I shall use here for general convenience – Gillian Rose's *The Melancholy Science:*

An Introduction to the Thought of Theodor W. Adorno (London: Macmillan, 1978) and *The Broken Middle* (Oxford: Blackwell, 1992), and Axel Honneth's *Kritik der Macht: Reflexionsstufen einer kritischen Gesellschaftstheorie* (Frankfurt: Suhrkamp Verlag, 1985) and *Kampf um Ammerkennung* (Frankfurt: Suhrkamp, 1992). I am particularly indebted to Rose and Bernstein, whose readings I am broadly in agreement with. Bernstein's forthcoming book on Adorno will, I have no doubt, be a major contribution.

58 Bernstein, *Recovering Ethical Life*, p. 11.
59 Bernstein, *Recovering Ethical Life*, p. 28.
60 Bernstein, *Recovering Ethical Life*, p. 28. Bernstein is drawing in this analysis on Adorno's extremely important essay 'Society' included in Stephen Bonner and Douglas Kellner (eds), *Critical Theory and Society* (London: Routledge, 1989).
61 Bernstein, *Recovering Ethical Life*, p. 28.
62 Bernstein, *Recovering Ethical Life*, p. 29.
63 Bernstein, *Recovering Ethical Life*, p. 19.
64 Bernstein, *Recovering Ethical Life*, p. 19.
65 See, for example, Stephen Bronner's criticisms of Adorno in his *Of Critical Theory and its Theorists*, pp. 199–200.
66 In his *The Practice of Everyday Life* (Berkeley, CA: University of California Press, 1988).
67 De Certeau, *The Practice of Everyday Life*, p. xix.
68 De Certeau, *The Practice of Everyday Life*, p. xix.

5   Limits

It is obvious – indeed, I have sought to emphasize it – that the above attempt to deal with the problem of 'order' by transcending it is hardly problem free. Is it the case, then, that 'Adorno's problem' is, as he feared, insoluble? Are we indeed destined to remain forever locked in an increasingly constricting and depersonalizing 'iron cage', as some contemporary pessimists would suggest? Are we witnessing, in any event, the end of 'order', not in the sense that we are transcending it, but in the sense that perhaps it of necessity transcends us?

Among the most interesting developments over the last few years has been the emergence of a variety of voices who would answer this question in the affirmative, though, as we shall see, for widely differing reasons. This chapter will thus explore what I take to be the two most influential of these approaches. I want to suggest that both of them emphasize the limits on our capacity to promote or recognize 'order' and suggest, as a result, that we should be much more hesitant than traditional approaches (within IR theory, that is) have usually been to suppose that the 'problem of order' is solvable or manageable. In that sense, they too, like the critical theorists discussed in the previous chapter, suggest that in its usual form, at least, we should end the search for 'order'.

However, though they share much, I want to suggest they differ a good deal as well. In this chapter, therefore, I shall first outline each of them, before going on to discuss both in the context of order and limits.

Deconstruction, post-structuralism and political criticism in IR theory

It would not, I think, be too much to say that for many – if I may borrow a well-known phrase – a spectre is haunting mainstream IR theory: the spectre of 'post-modernism'. In book after book, article after article, the full weight of the rationalist mainstream is brought to bear on the allegedly 'destructive', 'relativistic', 'nihilistic'[1] even – on one occasion and albeit in a semi-jocular fashion – 'evil'[2] proclivities of post-modernism and/or – for they are often seen as one – post-structuralism, for International Relations. Even in Britain, normally a relative backwater in the academic jousting stakes in International Relations, vitriolic attacks aimed largely or wholly at post-structuralism have occasionally whipped up a storm over the otherwise placid waters of British IR journals in the last few years.[3]

It is surely appropriate to begin by remarking that to anybody who is even moderately well read in (so-called) post-structural IR theory, let alone the vast swathe of relevant literature outside International Relations that might, in some sense, be seen as or called post-structural, this reaction is mystifying. 'Post-structuralism' is no more unified than any other broad intellectual trend; indeed it is a good deal less unified than many.[4] 'Post-structuralism' as a term is, in any case, simply a convenient – and sometimes not that convenient – shorthand for a wide variety of methods, assumptions and theoretical approaches which derive, in variously differentiated ways, from Nietzschean and post-Nietzschean turns in philosophy and social theory.

Among the more ironic results of this lumping together of often very disparate points of view is that the weapons chosen by the critics of post-structural IR theory often seem to consist largely of boomerangs. For example, post-structuralist A is accused of – say – 'relativism' (by far the commonest charge) whereas in fact A has made it plain that he or she is *not* a 'relativist'; rather A is someone who denies that the distinction between objectivism and relativism can be made meaningful in the manner in which a good deal of contemporary thought supposes. This view can, of course, be contested (I would, indeed, contest it myself).[5] However, it is a perfectly defensible view, versions of which go back (at least) to the Cynics, and can hardly be said, therefore, to be startlingly radical or very new. It is a depressing commentary on the general level of awareness of intellectual history amongst some contemporary scholars of international politics that they seem to think that it is both.[6]

It is true, of course, that post-structuralists occasionally talk a kind of short-hand that only the initiated can fully respond to. However, 'rationalist' social scientists are hardly exactly innocent of that particular failing of the modern academy. Anyone who cares to look at the latest article by (say) Bruce Bueno de Mesquita – I cite him simply because his work, it seems to me, is a particularly good example of the type – will clearly see what I mean.

Are there, however, any other reasons besides ignorance or wilful misreading, for the unholy row about 'post-structuralism' in International Relations? I think the answer to this is yes. Partly there is the knock-on effect from more general academic rows believed to have relevance to post-structuralism (Paul de Man and Heidegger as Nazi fellow travellers or worse,[7] Alan Sokal's 'hoax' in *Social Research* and the associated brouhaha, etc.). However, there is another point lurking beneath the surface of the hostility more relevant to our present concerns, and it is in fact one much more concerned with substance than method, for all that most of the charges laid at the door of post-structuralism in International Relations wear methodological dress.

Whatever their differences, most, if not all, of those usually termed 'post-structuralists/post-modernists' in IR theory challenge, often in very radical ways, the self-understanding of those discourses which have created International Relations as a 'separate' focus of study by accepting the dualism that grew from what I earlier called the 'practices' of sovereignty: inside/outside; domestic politics/international relations. As we have seen, they are hardly alone in this. Other forms of theory, especially versions of critical theory, would also challenge it. But they would do so from within a range of reference still broadly committed to a project 'rationalists' could recognize as being at least a distaff version of their own.

This is often referred to as the divide between those who believe in something called 'The Enlightenment Project' and those (the post-structuralists) who are supposed to reject it. On this view, critical theorists – for example – might criticize 'rationalists' because their sense of the requirements of the project is too attenuated, not radical enough – to paraphrase Habermas, still 'incomplete' – but it is still part of that project nevertheless. I have elsewhere criticized this view fairly strongly[8] and so will not go into it in any detail here. Let me merely say that I do not believe that there was – in the required sense – an 'Enlightenment Project' to be for or against and even if there was, traditional – classical – realists would be at least as suspicious of it as post-structuralists.

However, in a different sense this particular challenge does indeed cut to the bone of why post-structural work has been greeted with such hostility in International Relations. And in fact, I want to suggest that the source of the tension lies precisely in what I have been calling here the 'problem of order'. Let me explain.

Post-Nietzschean thought and International Relations

Before I can, however, it is worth emphasizing that post-structural IR theory is hardly monolithic. Variations of style, temper and topic abound. To give just a few examples, James Der Derian's elegant, witty and often mordant essays are indeed full of discussions of the major figures of French (and US) post-structural thought but his topics – diplomacy, terrorism, war, espionage – read like a cornucopia of very traditional IR concerns[9] – though not, as he remarks, concerns which have been the subject of much reflection by 'IR theorists'. David Campbell, too, balances a clear concern with obvious International Relations subject matter – war, foreign policy, security – with an increasingly powerful ethical orientation derived from, principally, Derrida and Levinas.[10] Rob Walker, however, though dealing with a range of subjects certainly central to international relations – sovereignty, structure, anarchy – has tended to prefer the writings of classical political theorists as foils. Machiavelli, Hobbes and Weber all recur in his thinking, and although his manner of approaching these texts shares certain themes with Der Derian or Campbell,[11] he often reads like – and sounds like – a fairly traditional political theorist and interpreter of texts.

Other prominent theorists associated with this approach – a representative sample of better known writers would usually include Richard Ashley, Michael Shapiro, William Connolly, Brad Klein, Mick Dillon, and some feminists, such as Spike Peterson, Christine Sylvester and Cynthia Weber – would add to the sense that post-structural IR theory is a broad church: they would often disagree with each other quite as much as any 'rationalist' would disagree with any of them, though to be sure not usually with the same bewildering vituperation.[12]

What, therefore, if anything do such disparate theorists share? To begin with, they share, to a greater or a lesser extent, a range of assumptions about the failures of conventional International Relations scholarship and share also a commitment to a (variety) of approaches derived from traditions of European thought that, until recently at least, have been alien to the Anglo-American social sciences. As has recently been suggested,[13] a good deal of post-structurally inclined scholarship in IR theory follows a (broadly) Foucauldian genealogical approach or adopts a number of now fairly familiar post-structural textual strategies or offers a combination of the same. Equally, a good deal of related International Relations scholarship increasingly adopts an ethical stance derived from the likes of Levinas and/or Derrida's later work.[14] As I suggested above, both of these strategies are recognizably indebted to Nietzsche.[15]

These approaches combine with other so-called 'post-positivist' approaches in bringing a powerful set of critical arguments to bear on the 'rationalist' dominance of the field – one reason, of course, why the dominant methodologies often lump them all together – but they have also developed powerful and original criticisms of, amongst others, constructivist and critical theory as well.

What is it, however, that such theorists actually *do*? As is indicated above, they certainly deal with real issues (sovereignty, war, intelligence, terrorism, etc.), and as I have already emphasized more than once, they do so in ways that are themselves distinct. They do not all speak with one voice, nor do they all say the same thing. However, I want to suggest that they do display, as Michael Oakeshott might have put it, a consistent disposition of mind; or let us say, they speak in a similar tone of voice.

This was nicely brought out a few years ago by a friendly disagreement between two leading post-structurally inclined scholars, Richard Ashley and William Connolly. Ashley argues that 'poststructuralism cannot claim to offer an alternative position or perspective [to any other] because there is no ground upon which it might be established'.[16] Connolly gently disagrees. For him, post-structuralists

> contend, in a way that overtly presents itself as a contestable supposition, that we live in a time when a variety of factors press thought into a rather confined and closed field of discourse ... the political task at a time of closure and danger is to try and open up that which is enclosed, to try to think thoughts that try to stretch and extend the normal patterns of insistence.[17]

To what he calls the 'modernist' question, 'do you yourself not presuppose "truth" in repudiating it?', he replies that post-structuralists think in a code of paradox and thus this question, which depends for its force on the view that only the code of 'truth' or 'falsity' can work, loses its power. However, recognizing paradox, complexity and uncertainty does not mean, he thinks, that *no* position can be taken, only that this 'position' must be taken in full knowledge of its own provisional character.

In his more recent work, Connolly puts the same point rather differently. Modernity, he thinks, is 'a systemic time without a corresponding political place',[18] and suggests that we develop

> an ethical sensibility, anchored in an ontological problematic, rendered through genealogies of the possible, cultivated through tactics applied by the self to itself, embodied as care for an enlarged diversity of life in which plural communities coexist in more creative ways than those simply sustained by a communitarian idea of harmony of a liberal idea of toler-ance, politicized through a series of engagements with established dualities of good/evil, normal/abnormal, guilt/innocence, rationality/irrationality, autonomy/dependence, security/insecurity.[19]

It is, I suggest, largely this 'sensibility' that we can observe in post-structural IR theory. Though some still veer to Ashley's view, most – perhaps even Ashley now – would subscribe to some version of Connolly's. Note, however, what this implies for any conception of 'order'. Rather than seeking to 'solve' the problem of order, this approach 'problematizes' *the problem itself*. 'The problem of order' should not be seen as a *question* of what produces order/disorder, rather it suggests that the 'problem of order/disorder' be seen in the light of this sensi-bility and continually probed and interrogated as the other dualities that Connolly listed should be.

And this, indeed, is what a good deal of post-structurally inclined work in 'International Relations' – as elsewhere – has done. In this sense it declines *any* of the four ways of 'coping with' or 'resolving' the problem of order that I have discussed in earlier parts of this book. Rather it looks at how they involve each other, interpenetrate and interrogate each other. They ask what is silenced, marginalized or repressed in them. There is no 'solution' to the 'problem of order', rather there is an ongoing interrogation of the manner in which 'solu-tions' (or resolutions) are tried. There is, indeed, an 'end' of order, in the sense traditionally meant for, as Connolly puts it in his most recent book, 'Nothing is fundamental ... therefore almost everything counts for something ... one element of a generous ethic is the recognition that neither it nor its competitors is grounded on something that is fixed, automatic, solid, commanded or neces-sary'.[20] In his most recent book David Campbell has put an essentially similar point in a particularly felicitous way. It is worth quoting him at length:

> The logic of inquiry that informs the argument of this book (and by exten-sion much so-called poststructural writing) is encapsulated by the idea of political criticism constituting an *ethos*. ... Undertaking a critique involves an intervention or series of interventions in established modes of thought and action. Such interventions are thus positioned in a particular relationship to those practices they wish to critique. They involve an effort to disturb those

practices that are settled, untie what appears to be sewn up, and render as produced that which claims to be naturally emergent. The positioning of the interventions means that there is an ethico-political imperative inherent to them, not a predetermined or established politics, but a desire to explore and perhaps foster the possibilities being foreclosed or suppressed ... it is in this context that the notion of ethos – which Foucault identifies as a manner of being or practice implicated in the philosophical life of Enlightenment criticism – is pivotal for the idea of political criticism ... critique is a lived experience.[21]

For Campbell, this implies that the one thing one should not try to do is create a 'theory' of international relations (still less a theory of ethics for international relations). Political criticism as an ethos, he suggests, has the function (he is para-phrasing Susan Sontag) of showing *how* something is what it is rather than what it means or why it is what it is: thus we should 'direct our attention away from a preoccupation with a search for the cause or origin of something and focus instead on the political consequences and effects of particular representations and how they came to be'.[22]

I suggest most 'post-structural' thinkers in International Relations would agree, at least in broad terms, with these formulations. To show how they work in practice, however, let me just briefly review two especially acute practitioners of such political criticism: Rob Walker and James Der Derian.

Rob Walker's work, as I indicated above, is rooted in traditional political theory. However, from his earliest work onwards[23] Walker has consistently argued that the problem with 'International Relations theory' is that it is increas-ingly distant from the world of real world politics, that in other words, it does not explain or interpret what it supposedly studies. Whilst this has been a permanent feature of IR theory, predicated upon the distinction between inside and outside, it has become more and more obvious with the epistemological and ontological orientation of IR as a 'discipline' over the last thirty years or so. As he has put it in a recent essay:

> Theories of international relations can ... be read as a primary expression of the limits of modern politics ... they, especially, frame these limits spatially. Politics, real politics, they suggest, can occur only as long as we are prepared – or able – to live in boxes.[24]

Walker's work is a persistent attempt to disrupt the claim that we either can or should live in boxes and, obviously, that claim is a central part of the problem of order as conventionally understood. What Walker seeks to do, both in his most influential text[25] and in much of his more recent work, is to explore, as he puts it, 'what it might now mean to speak of world politics rather than just inter-state or international relations'.[26] His manner of interpreting this task has been chiefly to focus on a series of dichotomies through which the conditions of modern politics have become actualized; most importantly inside/outside, identity/difference, and time/space, but also self/other, inclusion/exclusion, unity/diversity and universality/particularity.[27]

In doing this he is careful to suggest that he is mediating between – and implicitly outside – dichotomous choices of the sort posed by the contrast between attempts to solve the problem of order by 'managing' it – in other words, the responses discussed in Chapters 1–3 of this book – and attempts to solve it by 'transcending' it – that response we looked at in the last chapter.[28] Thus, for Walker, *any* claim that one might solve the 'problem of order' is an obvious capitulation to the languages of politics he is trying to break out of, though he is careful always to emphasize how difficult this will be. At the same time his constant concern with interrogating the discourse of state sovereignty, for him the master discourse of modernity, forces questions about identity, difference, culture, gender, space, time and place onto the agenda of an 'International Theory' that previously only seemed to have two categories, states and nations. 'Order', on this analysis, will be infinitely variable depending upon what the question is: no universal question, thus no universal answer, thus no 'problem of order' in the accepted or traditional sense.

Walker's work therefore makes perfectly clear the basic lineaments of this particular version of the claim that we have reached the 'end of order'. The languages of modern politics are the languages that make the claim to seek or to secure order plausible; thinking against/beyond such languages, which is what, Walker thinks, the conditions of late modern politics and especially its rearticulations of political space and time require, thus makes such a claim irretrievably problematic.

This last point, that it is the re-articulation of political space and time that, perhaps more than anything else, is changing the character of contemporary politics, is a particular hallmark of perhaps the most seductive and silver-tongued post-structural rhetor of all, in international studies at least, James Der Derian. Der Derian's most influential book to date, *Anti-Diplomacy*, is subtitled 'Spies, Terror, Speed and War', and in his introduction he points out that his focus is on three forces that 'stand out for their discursive power and shared problematic'.[29] These forces are (obviously) 'spies (intelligence and surveillance), terror (global terrorism and the national security culture) and speed (the acceleration of pace in war and diplomacy)'; their discursive power, he suggests, 'is chronopolitical and technostrategic ... they are "chronopolitical" in the sense that they elevate chronology over geography, pace over space in their political effects'.[30]

These effects and the way they combine and interpenetrate are the basic subject matter of Der Derian's book. Together, he suggests, they constitute an 'anti-diplomacy' which 'constitutes and mediates estrangement by new techniques of power and representations of danger'.[31] To focus on these relations and representations a post-structuralist approach is, he thinks, especially helpful since it 'proceeds by recognizing and investigating the interrelationship of power and representational practices that elevate one truth over another, that subject one identity to another, that make, in short, one discourse matter more than the next.[32]

Post-structural political criticism and the problem of order

Unlike those critical theorists we discussed in the previous chapter, then, there is no sense that 'emancipation' from the states system would lead, however gradually, to a change in this situation, since even assuming 'emancipation from the states system' were a plausible interpretation of the current development of world politics it would not alter the need for political criticism and would not really change the assumptions on which it is based (though to be sure aspects of the institutional furniture would be rearranged). For this reason, 'the problem of order' is largely refused as a 'problem' by the advocates of political criticism. This particular 'disposition of thought' suggests that we end the search for 'order' because in searching to secure it we are looking for a chimera. In this respect, the post-Nietzscheans indeed go beyond Nietzsche, who, as we saw in the Introduction, sought to create a 'new world order' out of the remnants of the old.

And here, perhaps, lies the chief source of tension between the rationalist mainstream and the political critics, for all that it is usually unacknowledged (at least by the mainstream). To make this clear let me cite a remark of Stephen Krasner's, discussed by Campbell. Krasner, in the course of a survey and overview of IPE, emphasizes the centrality of what he calls the 'Western rationalist tradition', understood as issuing in the methodological assumptions of mainstream 'rationalist' social science. While he accepts that such a tradition and such a social science offers no panacea,

> it does offer the best hope for academicians to make a positive contribution to the larger society because it can, in some instances, suggest a wise course for public policy and in others demonstrate that a policy is wrong. Postmodernism, in contrast, in its more extreme versions provides no such check. On the contrary it leads directly to nihilism which can produce an intense and burning flame but which hardly moves society towards peace and justice.[33]

As Campbell says, so much is skated over in this that it is difficult to know where to begin, but he himself accepts that the challenge of 'nihilism', 'relativism', etc., must be faced and his book is largely shaped by that acceptance. In this he is also implicitly answering that long (and growing) line of critics of post-structuralism/political criticism in International Relations who have made similar points, though usually with less chutzpah than Krasner! I will come back to this debate in a moment but for now it is simply worth pointing out what is often not acknowledged. *Both* Campbell and Krasner think that what they are doing is to intervene practically in political events. The character of the interventions is, of course, totally different. But it is not that one is seeking to give advice to princes and one is not. It is simply that the relevant constituency – who the prince is – is different; as is, of course, the assumptions underlying the possibility of intervention as such.

The key point here is that *if* Campbell is correct, then the problem of order cannot really be asked and so not answered either. Thus, the attempts to create a settled ground on which the 'Western rationalist tradition' can start to provide its 'positive contribution to the larger society' is simply not there. Unlike critical theory, which however critical it is of 'rationalism' is critical of it chiefly for not being *really* rationalist, that is to say of having too attenuated a notion of rationality, political criticism à la Campbell, Walker, Der Derian, etc., really does seek to knock the struts away from the complicated construction of modern social science. But doing so does not mean it is not interested in the 'facts', it merely suggests that all relevant facts are themselves complex constructions whose stories should be told before we seek to relate them and interpret them. Ontologically and epistemologically too, the political criticism discussed here is, indeed, the nemesis of rationalist social science – though it would be fairly hard on other accounts discussed here as well. Often for all the wrong reasons – the usual charges of relativism etc. – the mainstream senses this and that is why the confrontation between them is usually so harsh.

Elshtain: the limits of/to order

There is, then, the question of whether or not the political critics are correct. Before I turn to that, however, there is another related, though significantly rather different, formulation of a similar case. This is perhaps best represented by a writer who is usually regarded as the single most influential feminist voice in contemporary international political theory, Jean Bethke Elshtain. Yet Elshtain is extremely hard to describe simply in those terms. She has made a career of denying the usual disciplinary boundaries, starting off as a political theorist, but with a solid grounding in International Relations (taught amongst others by Kenneth Waltz, no less), and spreading herself broadly across the fields of the human sciences. Her feminism is real, important and influential but she also has made a strong critique of aspects of feminist thought and has been criticized in turn by many contemporary feminists.[34] She is amongst the most powerful critics of contemporary realisms in international relations, yet among her recent books is a study of that thinker she does not hesitate to say she 'loves', that selfsame Augustine who was so influential on realists like Niebuhr. She has also admitted, more than once, a sneaking admiration for those realists who refused what she calls (in *Women and War*) the 'rush to scientize',[35] even admitting herself to their company in a recent lecture[36] and a recent book.[37] She celebrates what she calls (it is the title of a recent collection of her essays) the 'real politics of everyday life'[38] and emphasizes, most obviously in her book on Augustine, a 'politics of limits' that is close to, yet at the same time worlds away from, the 'limits' of the realists or the English school, closer indeed to the ambiguities and dissonances of the post-structuralism/political criticism wherein many of her early allies and admirers were to be found.

It is both the ambiguity and the emphasis on limits that is most important for our current context. Elshtain is suspicious about the 'problem of order' because she suspects any attempt to 'solve' it will involve denying in some way or another

our humanness, expressed for her most importantly by our limitations and failings, our vulnerabilities and flaws. She expresses this powerfully in her reading of
Augustine:

> Augustine creates a complex moral map that offers space for loyalty and
> love and care, as well as for a chastened form of civic virtue ... wisdom
> comes from experiencing fully the ambivalence and ambiguity that is the
> human condition. That is what Augustine calls our business 'within this
> common mortal life' and any politics that disdains this business, this caring
> for the quotidian, is a dangerous or misguided or misplaced politics.[39]

Yet Elshtain's suspicion of the contemporary formulations of the problem of
order is not quite the same as, say, Walker's or Campbell's or Connolly's. She
does not refuse it quite the way they do. Her sense of its 'limits' is different
though related.

To fill this out a little, let us start with the point I closed with above. Like
Campbell, Elshtain would criticize Krasner for assuming the 'Western rationalist
tradition' can do what he thinks it can do. Elshtain suggests that the 'contemporary "scientization of realism"' (and, we might add, she would say the same
about the scientization of liberalism as well) invites 'fantasies of control over
events that we do not have'.[40] If we start from *assuming* a 'problem of order'
which we have to 'manage' or 'resolve' (by transcending?) then we will surely
lock ourselves into the logic that it generates. Following Hannah Arendt,
however, Elshtain suggests we focus instead on a logic that denies not the reality
of force or violence (that would be pointless) but one which allows us to address
it from a different vantage point. This logic is a logic of hope rooted in what
Arendt calls, in a memorable phrase from *The Human Condition*, 'the fact of
natality'.[41] For Elshtain the importance of this is simply that natality reminds us
of our common vulnerability and our 'beginning' (a beginning which, not incidentally, is dependent upon female rather more than male capacities), and that

> a full experience of the capacity rooted in birth helps us to keep before our
> mind's eye the living reality of singularities, differences and individualities
> rather than a human mass of objects of possible control or manipulation
> towards ends dictated by others ... [this view] shifts the ground on which we
> stand when we think about states and their relations. We become skeptical
> about the forms and claims of the sovereign state; we deflate fantasies of
> control inspired by the reigning technology ... we recognize the (phony)
> parity painted by a picture of equally sovereign states and are thereby alert
> to the many forms hegemony can take. Additionally, Arendt grants forgive-
> ness a central political role as the only way to break remorseless cycles of
> vengeance and the repetition they invite.[42]

In other words, we recognize the centrality of *limits* to what we can achieve and
to what we should expect. We recognize that 'order' is usually maintained by one

group at the expense of others and should not expect such a situation to be radically changed, but – equally – we should recognize that it is a permanently unstable affair. With hope, and the sense of shared vulnerability and uniqueness it engenders, we can work to bolster those elements of our 'orders' that can create what, in her most recent book, she calls

> power as primus inter pares – ... power deployed to promote a common good; to help to create more decent and generous societies ... (understanding ethics and politics) in a way that is, yes, realistic yet hopeful – hopeful that human beings are capable of responding to calls to brotherhood and sisterhood, even as we know all too well that they are too often seduced by hate mongers and fear peddlers.[43]

Note the similarities to the two sets of theorists she most resembles, the 'political critics' we have just discussed and the traditional realists discussed in Chapter 1. Her sense of the interrelationship between ethics and politics is very close to that of Niebuhr and especially to that of Morgenthau. It is perhaps no accident that one of the strongest influences on her, Arendt, was an extremely close personal friend of Morgenthau, whose general political and theoretical position was a lot closer to Arendt's than is generally recognized.[44] Equally, her sense of the ways in which identities and discourses are mutually shaping and reinforcing echoes that of the 'political critics' discussed above.

However, note, too, the differences. Morgenthau and the other traditional realists remained largely content with a conception of the way to deal with the 'problem of order' focused on balance. Balance is not dissimilar in some ways to an emphasis on limits. However, it is not the *same* as such an emphasis. Elshtain's emphasis on limits develops from her very different starting point: her focus on hope, on birth and vulnerability. No traditional realist would have thought or talked like that. However, she is more forthright than the political critics about the need to act in a world *made up of* identities, however constructed, and *through* discourses, however compromised and flawed. Perhaps it is the realist in her! She is also both interested in, and committed to, certain religious and even theological positions and assumptions – the aforementioned importance of forgiveness perhaps among the most important – which marks her out from the 'political critics' but symbolizes her sympathy (it perhaps does not get *much* stronger than that) with more 'traditional' (but certainly not positivist) readings of world politics such as that of Martin Wight or Herbert Butterfield, to say nothing of Rheinhold Niebuhr.

Elshtain, then, offers a powerful reading of world politics that shares much with the advocates of 'political criticism' discussed earlier. Like them she problematizes the problem of order and suggests we abandon grand attempts to resolve it and at least most of the past centuries' attempts to manage it do not meet with her approval either. Yet here, close to the terminus of our argument, we can hear powerful echoes of that realism with which much of our story began.

The limits of political criticism

At which point we should really move to the final discussion of these themes which I have reserved for the Epilogue. Before I do this, however, let me just make a general remark on this last general 'response' to the problem of order.

As we saw, perhaps the commonest charge aimed at post-structurally inclined IR theory is relativism. However, as we also saw, such a charge is largely baseless and can only be made through a combination of ignorance and malice. The 'political criticism' of a Campbell, a Der Derian or a Walker is, doubtless, 'relativistic' in the sense that they would claim that Truth (capital T) is not available. However, that hardly marks them out as enemies of the 'Western rationalist tradition' which boasts many varieties of relativism in its long and tangled history, up to and including Isaiah Berlin,[45] whom I imagine Professor Krasner would not wish to include among the enemies of Western rationalism.

What both these political critics – and Elshtain – do emphasize is the limits of our knowledge and of our practice and the sense that they are always complex and often hidden constructions of meaning. For these reasons, we should always be suspicious of the attempts to (literally and figuratively) 'discipline' knowledge or to suggest that (say) the 'problem of order' is a clear problem with a clear solution.

In this emphasis they are, I think, correct. However, there does remain a problem. When Campbell, for example, says that the interventions he practises have an ethico-political imperative to them we would be wise to take him at his word and not offer sarcastic jibes or muttered comments about nihilism. Nonetheless, it does seem pertinent to ask in what, precisely, the ethico-political imperative lies. It, too, presumably is a complex set of constructed meanings, and therefore open to similar acts of disruption. If we are to understand why this ethico-political imperative deserves more respect than the presumably dominant ones being critiqued we should surely be offered some reasons for a preference for ethico-political imperative A over ethico-political imperative B. The aim, remember, is to explore 'the possibilities being foreclosed or suppressed' but surely not *all* such possibilities. Some presumably are thought better (both ethically and practically) in any given context than others. But how are such judgements made and what processes of reasoning might be framed to justify them? Note that I am not saying that everything has to be argued from scratch. We do not normally need complex philosophical argumentation to justify the claim that as a general rule peace is to be preferred, on both practical and moral grounds, to war and anyone who does feel the need for a complex argument proving this probably has need of something rather more than philosophy.

But of course the point is that it is *the context* which will suggest whether such argumentation is necessary, but *if* it is, we need to know how it might be pursued. This is not something that the political critics, or for that matter Elshtain, seem to have very clear or well-formulated views on and it is, I think, the most powerful general weakness in their position. In its absence, one is left with the uncomfortable feeling that for all their skill in tracing hidden meanings, untying false unities and unsettling established discourses, the 'ethico-political imperative' requires a lot more fleshing out for the full potential of these approaches to begin to be realized.

Notes

1 This claim is made by many. Among the more moderate attacks (at least in print) is Stephen Krasner's in his 'The Accomplishments of International Political Economy', in Steve Smith, Ken Booth and Marysia Zalewski (eds), *International Theory: Positivism and Beyond* (Cambridge: Cambridge University Press, 1996). Krasner saves his blast against what he refers to as 'post-modernism' chiefly for his conclusion. 'What defines social science', he argues,

> is a methodology based on argument and evidence ... the conventional episte-mology that has informed the study of international political economy stands in sharp contrast with those variants of postmodernism that reject the Western rationalistic tradition. For these postmodernists there are many analytic cate-gories each of which contains its own truth ... postmodernism provides no methodology for adjudicating among competing claims ... it leads directly to nihilism.
>
> (pp. 124–5)

There is much else in the attack but this is the core. I cannot forbear to comment on a couple of points. Social science is indeed based on argument and evidence. The problem is, I know of virtually no post-structuralist who would deny such an obvious point. *All* enquiry is based on argument and evidence to some degree. The point is what counts as argument and what as evidence and, crucially, how are they related? Moreover, the 'Western rationalistic tradition' that Krasner invokes, or at least large parts of it, is, of course, also rejected by the 'rationalism' of which he is such a distin-guished representative. After all a goodly part of this tradition would have regarded it as tantamount to nihilism to abandon the notion that rationality can and must reason always for and to the good life. The notion that 'reason' was a category that could exert no influence on ends, being merely about means – the point of claiming that preferences are exogenous, of course – would have been rejected by virtually all the dominant figures of the Western rationalistic tradition until Hume and by most after Hume until Mill. 'Nihilism' is a weapon that can cut more than one way. However, I absolve Professor Krasner from blame in this matter and shoulder it myself. There are no direct references to any post-structuralists – in or out of International Relations – in his article. There is, however, a reference to an article of mine ('No Time Like the Present? Postmodernism and Political Theory', *Political Studies*, 1992, 40: 561–70). Clearly, I failed to convey adequately in this article the varieties and permutations that characterize post-structural thought, though the article was chiefly written with this task in mind. *Mea culpa.*

2 This is cheating really. This charge, made (I think) at least semi-jocularly, was used by Professor Krasner in an exchange with Rick Ashley at the 75th Anniversary Conference of the Department of International Politics at the University of Wales Aberystwyth, at which I was privileged to be a participant. The *International Theory: Positivism and Beyond* book quoted above is the published version of the conference papers.

3 I am thinking principally of two articles here. Roy Jones' characteristically mischievous attack on Rob Walker, which ended up with him suggesting Walker take hemlock, and William Wallace's heartfelt, if ill-tempered and, to my mind at least, rather ill-conceived, attack on all things critical and post-structural delivered initially

as an after-dinner speech at the annual British International Studies Association (BISA) conference a few years ago and then written up, once passion had cooled a little, for the *Review of International Studies*. The articles concerned together with responses are: Roy Jones, 'The Responsibility to Educate', and R. B. J. Walker, 'On Pedagogical Responsibility: A Response to Roy Jones', in *Review of International Studies*, 1994, 20(3): 299–312, 313–22; William Wallace, 'Truth and Power, Monks and Technocrats: Theory and Practice in International Relations', *Review of International Studies*, 1996, 22(3): 301–22; Ken Booth, 'A Reply to Wallace', *Review of International Studies*, 1997, 23(3): 371–7; Steve Smith, 'Power and Truth: A Reply to William Wallace', *Review of International Studies*, 1997, 23(4): 507–16.

4   This is part of the argument of my *Political Theory, Modernity and Postmodernity: Beyond Enlightenment and Critique* (Oxford: Blackwell, 1995).

5   See *Political Theory, Modernity and Postmodernity*, chapters 3 and 4, for my initial way of disputing it.

6   Examples of this are legion. I have time only for a couple of examples here. I cite initially Krasner's article in note 2 above. The claim that 'postmodernism provides no methodology for adjudicating among competing claims' is simply false. Various post-structuralists would provide a variety of ways of ranking competing claims and justify those ways under different headings. They would, it is true, usually be hesitant to use terms like 'methodology', but that is hardly the point. Any, even brief, acquaintance with the writings of, say, Bill Connolly shows what a canard this view is, and some of those post-structuralists in International Relations close to Connolly, for example James Der Derian, show a similar sensitivity. Equally Zygmunt Bauman's *Postmodern Ethics* (Oxford: Blackwell, 1995) shows just how powerful some post-structural assumptions can be for ethical reasoning.

7   Discussions of these *affairs* are legion. I simply refer the reader to my more general discussion in *Political Theory, Modernity and Postmodernity*, chapter 2.

8   In *Political Theory, Modernity and Postmodernity*, chapter 2.

9   Der Derian's general writings on 'International relations' – in the academy – are supplemented also, as one might expect, by essays in journals popular in the post-structural and information age areas – such as *Wired* magazine and by TV documentaries and commentaries. His major writings would include *On Diplomacy* (Oxford: Blackwell, 1987), *Anti-Diplomacy: Spies, Speed, Terror and War* (Oxford: Blackwell, 1992) and the forthcoming *Virtual War*. It is also worth pointing out the pioneering collection he edited with Michael Shapiro, *International/Intertextual Relations: Postmodern Readings of World Politics* (Toronto: Lexington Books, 1989), the first collection of clearly post-structural essays on International Relations and also worth pointing out the close influence on him – and of him on them – of two very prominent US political theorists with more than half a foot also in IR theory, namely William Connolly and Jean Elshtain. Connolly is one of the more important post-structurally inclined political theorists in the United States and Elshtain, though hardly post-structural, is one of the most influential political theorists now writing there. Moreover, she has had an important role in looking at the role of gender in international politics as well as linking gender, ethics and world politics in a number of books and articles, as I shall discuss in a moment. Both have testified to Der Derian's influence on them, an influence stemming from their period as colleagues at the University of Massachusetts at Amherst, where Der Derian (at the time of writing) remains. A final point worth noting is that Der Derian's balancing of (relatively) traditional subject matter with (often very) radical theoretical approaches shows traces of his sympathy for the 'international society' approach discussed in Chapter 2. His doctorate – later *On Diplomacy* – was supervised by Bull and his sympathy for the 'English school' type of theorizing is quite marked.

10 This particular orientation was less observable in his first book *Writing Security: US Foreign Policy and the Politics of Identity* (Manchester: University of Manchester Press, 1993) than in his second, or in his book on Bosnia.

11 The central text for Walker's (œuvre is *Inside/Outside: International Relations as Political Theory* (Cambridge: Cambridge University Press, 1993). However, Walker's trajectory is out of other forms of critique in world politics. He has been for many years, and remains, a close associate of Richard Falk, Saul Mendlowitz and others in the World Order Models Project (WOMP), whose house journal, *Alternatives*, has become, under his (joint) editorship, probably the flagship journal for critical international theory in general but certainly for post-structural international theory. He also works on various aspects of political theory and the politics of social movements.

12 See, for examples of their work, Ashley, 'The Achievements of Post-structuralism', in S. Smith, K. Booth and M. Zalewski (eds) *International Theory: Positivism and Beyond* (Cambridge: Cambridge University Press, 1996); Shapiro, *Violent Cartographies: Mapping Cultures of War* (Minneapolis: University of Minnesota Press, 1996); Dillon, *Politics of Security* (London: Routledge, 1996); Peterson, *Gendered States: Feminist (Re)Visions of International Relations Theory* (Boulder, CO: Lynne Rienner, 1992); Sylvester, *Feminist Theory in International Relations* (Cambridge: Cambridge University Press, 1994); Weber, *Simulating Sovereignty* (Cambridge: Cambridge University Press, 1994).

13 By Richard Devetak, in Burchill *et al.*, *Theories of International Relations*, pp. 180–93.

14 It is, I think, significant that few post-structurally inclined International Relations scholars have taken Heidegger as a main point of departure, though a number are concerned with typically Heideggerean themes at the margins and most are deeply indebted to Heideggerean strategies as filtered through some of his recent French disciples (of whom Derrida and Levinas are two conspicuous examples). The most obvious exception is Mick Dillon whose *Politics of Security* (London: Routledge, 1996) is a powerful example of how Heideggerean themes *can* be used in the 'International' context. A different example, not a self-conscious 'International' theorist but a polit-ical theorist who is very much concerned with some 'international questions', is Fred Dallmayr, particularly in his two most recent books, *The Other Heidegger* (Ithaca, NY: Cornell University Press, 1994) and *Beyond Orientalism: Essays on Cross Cultural Encounter* (New York: SUNY, 1996).

15 The theorist who has done most to explore the specific political orientation of what we might call the 'left' post-Nietzscheans is William Connolly. See especially his essay, 'Beyond Good and Evil: The Ethical Sensibility of Michel Foucault', *Political Theory*, 1993, August: 365–89, and his book (in the Borderlines series edited by Campbell and Shapiro) *The Ethos of Pluralization* (Minneapolis: University of Minnesota Press, 1995).

16 See Ashley, 'Living on Borderlines: Man, Poststructuralism and War', in James Der Derian and Michael Shapiro (eds), *International/Intertextual Relations*, p. 278.

17 Connolly, 'Identity and Difference in Global Politics', in Der Derian and Shapiro (eds), *International/Intertextual Relations*, p. 338.

18 Connolly, *Identity/Difference: Democratic Negotiations of Political Paradox* (Ithaca, NY: Cornell University Press, 1991), p. 215. For a fuller discussion of Connolly's argu-ments see my *Political Theory, Modernity and Postmodernity*, chapters 2 and 3.

19 Connolly, *The Augustinian Imperative* (New York: Sage, 1993), pp. 151–2.

20 Connolly, *The Ethos of Pluralization*, p. 40.

21 Campbell, *National Deconstruction: Violence, Identity and Justice in Bosnia* (Minneapolis: University of Minnesota Press, 1998), p. 4.

22 Campbell, *National Deconstruction*, p. 5.

23 'Political Theory and the Transformation of World Politics', World Order Studies Program, Occasional paper No. 8 (Princeton University, Center for International Studies, 1980).

24 'International Relations and the Concept of the Political', in Ken Booth and Steve Smith (eds), *International Relations Theory Today* (Cambridge: Polity Press, 1994), p. 307.

25 *Inside/Outside: International Relations as Political Theory.*

26 *Inside/Outside*, p. 20.

27 In a recent and perceptive essay on Walker, Lene Hansen suggests that the three key either/ors are inside/outside, self/other and universality/particularity. My own view would be that time/space plays more of a role than self/other – this latter is central, by contrast to the work of David Campbell. See Lene Hansen, 'R.B.J.Walker: deconstructing IR', in Iver B. Neumann and Ole Wæver (eds), *The Future of International Relations: Masters in the Making* (London: Routledge, 1997).

28 Though he is also clear that he is, obviously, more sympathetically disposed towards the latter than the former.

29 James Der Derian, *Anti-Diplomacy*, p. 3.

30 Der Derian, *Anti-Diplomacy*, p. 3.

31 Der Derian, *Anti-Diplomacy*, p. 3.

32 Der Derian, *Anti-Diplomacy*, p. 7.

33 Krasner, 'The Achievements of IPE', in Smith, Booth and Zalewski (eds), *International Theory: Positivism and Beyond*, p. 124. Discussed in Campbell, *National Deconstruction*, p. 7.

34 Her book *Women and War* (Brighton: Harvester, 1987) has been an enormously influential treatment of issues of war and peace from a feminist perspective. At the same time, in her recent *Democracy on Trial* (Toronto: University of Toronto Press, 1993), she is very critical of many aspects of contemporary feminist thought and practice.

35 Jean Bethke Elshtain, *Augustine and the Limits of Politics* (Notre Dame, IN: University of Notre Dame Press, 1995). The quotation is from *Women and War*, p. 89.

36 Elshtain, 'Women and War: Ten years on', *Review of International Studies*, 1998, 24(4): 447–60. See especially p. 449, where she remarks 'I consider myself a realist but I am not a scientized realist of the sort that now dominates in the academy, at least in the United States'.

37 Jean Bethke Elshtain, *New Wine and Old Bottles: Ethical Discourse and International Politics* (Notre Dame, IN: University of Notre Dame Press, 1998), see p. 4.

38 Jean Bethke Elshtain, *Real Politics in Everyday Life.*

39 Elshtain, *Augustine and the Limits of Politics*, p. 91.

40 See Jean Bethke Elshtain, *Meditations on Modern Political Thought: Masculine/Feminine Themes From Luther to Arendt* (Pittsburgh, PA: Pennsylvania University Press, 1992 [1986]), p. 107.

41 See Arendt, *The Human Condition* (Chicago: University of Chicago Press, 1958).

42 Elshtain, *Meditations on Modern Political Thought*, p. 111.

43 Elshtain, *New Wine and Old Bottles*, p. 5.

44 An indication of the closeness of their relationship is that when her second husband died, Morgenthau proposed to her. An even stronger indication is that her gentle refusal left their friendship largely untouched. A good discussion of their relationship can be found in Elizabeth Young-Breuhl's excellent biography of Arendt, *For Love of the World* (New Haven, CT: Yale University Press, 1978). The work of a PhD student of mine, Mitchell Rologas, has also begun to uncover strong echoes of their mutual influence.

45 For Berlin's own sense of his 'relativism' see the recent biography by Michael Ignatieff, *Isaiah Berlin: A Life* (London: Weidenfeld and Nicolson, 1998).

Epilogue
Ordering ends?

> I have not troubled myself about the great wars ... I am not altogether on anybody's side, because nobody is altogether on my side.
>
> Fangorn, in J. R. R. Tolkien, *The Lord of the Rings*

A book like this cannot really be concluded. All of the responses, theories and interpretations discussed herein are living options strongly argued for (and against) in the academy and outside and all will continue to play their parts in the attempt to understand 'how it all hangs together', as John Ruggie (quoting Edward Teller) has it.[1] However, just as Michael Dummett once remarked that authors owe their readers a preface,[2] I think they owe them some sort of conclusion as well. Thus, I offer this epilogue to the book as a whole as a substitute for the 'conclusion' I do not think can be written.

It has three parts. In the first, I want to offer a brief sketch of where I think 'we are now', in IR theory. Then, second, I want to consider briefly one particular trajectory embryonic in contemporary international studies, but growing rapidly – as indeed it is, more or less, in most social sciences – and suggest what at least some of the implications of this might be. Third and lastly, I want to outline, in the briefest possible manner, how the 'problem of order' might be reconceptualized in the light of a rather different 'disposition of thought' to those discussed herein and frame some of the implications of this reconceptualization.

From IR theory to international political theory

So where are we now? To begin, as I did in the Introduction, with the obvious: IR theory is now *irretrievably* plural. Of course, some scholars have suggested that serious plurality has characterized international studies at least since the early 1980s. Kal Holsti, after all, famously wrote about the 'dividing discipline' at that time.[3] However, the plurality I have discussed here cuts more deeply still, consisting, as we have seen, of both methodological (indeed deeply 'philosophical') as well as 'substantive' or 'normative' differences. Moreover, 'International Relations' as an academic study is now far too broad and diverse, spread way beyond its original heartlands of Britain and the United States (however much the latter is still dominant), for this to cease; indeed, as more cultures and more viewpoints become part and parcel of the debate in international studies, it is likely to increase greatly.

This is one of the reasons why I think that attempts, both intellectual and institutional, to stifle debate or at least to direct it and channel it into 'appropriate' methodological or normative forms are pointless. Those who seek to implement such practices will simply come to resemble an increasingly ineffective and ridiculous Canute, seeking to hold back the waters of methodological and normative diversity as they lap around their necks! Surely it would be better to seek to engage rival or alternative accounts (as, to be fair, some have certainly started to do) as at least genuine 'others', worthy of respect and critical attention.

In a rather different context, as I have already remarked, the philosopher James Sterba has discussed the advantages he sees in replacing what he characterizes as a 'warmaking way of doing philosophy' – where arguments are 'attacked' and sunk (like a ship) or shot down (like a plane) – with what he calls a *peacemaking* way, where real attempts to produce agreement, change minds or, anyway, seriously consider alternative or rival views are placed at the centre of debate.[4] I suggest this applies not just to philosophy but to the academic project as a whole.

If this plurality is, as I have suggested, now a permanent feature of International Studies in the academy – reflecting, of course, the increasingly hybrid (though also interconnected) multicultural, multilateral character of the world it studies – then surely we should relax some of the hard and fast assumptions that have come to play so large a role in the contemporary academy. But in this case, then, what counts as international studies must surely increase dramatically and the methodological and theoretical eclecticism will of course increase with it.

As far as theoretical reflection upon this diversity is concerned it is worthwhile pointing out that to reflect upon politics in this context will inevitably mean drawing upon the tradition of thought in the West usually termed political theory (and on analogous traditions elsewhere) as well as on much that at least traditionally political theorists do not reflect upon. In this context, then, we will be witnessing the transition from an 'International Relations Theory' where the traditional concerns of political theory are largely excluded to an 'International *Political* Theory' where such concerns are commonplace *but* where the more traditional concerns of 'IR theory' are not excluded but are part and parcel of the range of enquiries as well as where a growing range of new issues will be important.

In the context of the accounts of international relations that I have discussed in this book this has some fairly obvious implications. Let me start by referring back to that debate between 'rationalism' and 'reflectivism' we visited briefly in the Introduction. Manifestly, Keohane hit on an important aspect to contemporary debates in 'IR theory', and as we have seen, many contemporary writers and theorists have at least half an eye on that debate. However, the main 'debate' in the US-based literature has been, of course, within 'rationalism'. Yet the differences between the 'rationalists' are growing smaller all the time. What

Ole Wæver has referred to as the 'neo–neo' debate – the debate between neo-realism and neo-liberalism – has rapidly shrunk to the status of a parish pump debate. As Ruggie has put it,

> neo-realism and neoliberal institutionalism have been able to converge to the extent that they have because they now share very similar analytical foundations ... [the debate's] tenor is barely a faint echo of the titanic intellectual and moral struggles between realism and liberalism down the centuries.[5]

Without denying the differences that still exist between neo-realists and neo-liberals it seems to me that this growing rapprochement is not only a fact, but also likely to become more and more important. This is simply because the general assumptions that underlie the 'rationalist' mode of argument seem to me at least to be weighted heavily in favour of neo-liberalism, not least the effective adoption within neo-realism of a methodological individualism that is predicated on a model of *homo œconomicus* which is in its turn highly sympathetic to (indeed on some readings dependent upon) certain readings of liberalism.

The likely result of this is a 'rationalist' mainstream (in self-conscious 'IR theory') which is progressively more and more 'neo-liberal' in general orientation, though doubtless still with some neo-realist hold-outs. Even neo-realists, however as we saw in Chapter 1 – are increasingly moderating or subsuming old-style Waltzian neo-realism and replacing it – or supplementing it, if replacing sounds too heterodox – with a much more nuanced and complex 'neo-realism' that looks increasingly like, well, neo-liberalism! The implications of this are simple. The only alternative path which would retain a *distinctive* realist world view would be a return of realism to its roots as an essentially normative theory or at least one that is much closer to aspects of constructivist thought than either neo-realism or neo-liberalism could be. In other words, the future of realism seems to lie precisely in the evolution of an 'international political theory' that is both normative and explanatory and that can therefore allow newer and more nuanced versions of traditional realist ideas (necessity versus ethics, the balance of power, etc.) to flourish.

On the 'reflectivist' side of the debate, as we have seen, the hurried promotion of 'constructivism' as the 'acceptable face' of critical theory conceals far more than it illuminates. Constructivist accounts themselves are, in any case, hardly all of a piece. My own view is that one of the most interesting sites of major debate over the next few years will be *within* the constructivist camp as those who want to make over 'constructivist' themes to tie into more mainstream debates are challenged by those constructivists who see their agenda as one which links ever more closely with the growing and broadening agenda of critical theories in international studies.

Yet these latter accounts themselves are likely to be the site of some major debates. For all that Linklater has tried heroically to keep the initial partners in the critical project together, I suspect that the wheels are going to come off the chariot with a vengeance in the next few years. Debates over the extent to which it is possible to realize the sorts of projects that Linklater and Held – for example – have developed (post-Westphalian citizenship, cosmopolitan democracy) are already showing the considerable differences between the views of a Walker and those of a Linklater. While their critiques of mainstream IR theory are not dissimilar, Linklater's broadly Habermassian account of society and politics seems to me, substantively speaking, to have more in common with certain radical liberal projects than with those of Walker or Der Derian, for all the mutual respect there is between them and for all that Linklater certainly wants to keep all the critical players on the same team. At the same time, both critical theory and post-structurally informed theory in international studies have already been the target of critical sallies by some feminist theorists for allegedly ignoring or downplaying the significance of gender.

However, whilst these differences are real and important enough, there are also other powerful forces working to increase these pluralities. One of the most powerful of these has surfaced several times in the previous chapters, namely the dichotomy between the universal and particular. This is likely to become more and more central, though not really as a question of universal or particular (though to be sure many express it like that) but how one *combines* universality and particularity and which, so to speak, is in the driving seat.

This is brought out most clearly in the 'critical' literatures – or we might say those literatures happiest with the notion of 'international political theory' – which is one reason, in addition to their own intrinsic merits, for their exponential growth and growing influence. It is those associated with these bodies of thought that have done most work thinking through this dichotomy, though they link hands here with realists like Morgenthau and chastened liberals like Aron, Hoffmann and Shklar. The character of the debate within and between them is consequently especially powerfully shaped by this dichotomy. And it is not accidental, of course, that it is in the process of working through this dichotomy that some of the most pressing concerns about 'order' are raised. Moreover, in this problem especially, the methodological and substantive debates I reflected on in the Introduction become fused in interestingly ironic ways. Those *discoursi* which seek to stay within the frame of 'modern' politics – with an inside and an outside – as realism does, and indeed as at least rationalistically minded versions of liberalism seem to do as well – will inevitably come down on the side of particularism in substance, though they very often are wedded to (differing) versions of universalism in method. Those versions which challenge modern conceptions of politics, as to varying degrees most of the critical literatures do, tend to be universalistic in substance, but rather more pluralist in methodological terms, though post-structuralism is obviously something of an exception here. Indeed, in an irony that some on both sides will appreciate, on the problem of order at least, the post-structuralists end up in some ways closest to those realists who were always sensitive to the complexity, fluidity and fragility of the 'balance' on which, for them, order had to rest.[6]

As we saw in Chapter 4, this is why critical theory 'proper', as it were, is the most consistent – though that does not necessarily mean the most correct – approach; for it displays a thoroughgoing universalism 'all the way down' (normatively, substantively and methodologically), one which, moreover, is giving enormous thought to the question of how such universality can be combined with the obvious diversity of human life. The success of critical theory in general, as I suggested, will therefore depend upon it being able to balance this successfully and, of course, in a world of globalization this will require that it is a theory of 'international relations' – indeed of world politics – whatever else it also is.

This issue is, however, by no means unique to 'International Relations'. It is worth remembering the increasing disciplinary interpenetration among the social sciences as a whole – with the partial and always problematic exception of economics – and to remember also how central the question of universal and particular is for the social sciences generally. It is now not uncommon to find books on IR theory that contain essays by literary critics, anthropologists, geographers and philosophers, but the newness of this can be overdone: though these disciplines may be new, the fact of interpenetration is not; it was always the case that IR theory had close relations with history, law and even theology. *Diplomatic Investigations*, let us remember – published deep in the mists of antiquity, 1966 – contained essays by historians, theologians and diplomats as well as scholars of international relations and, as Dunne's history of the English school makes clear, the British Committee was always such a hybrid affair.[7] However, the newer interpenetration is having the obviously beneficial effect that methodological debates within IR theory are part and parcel of more general debates elsewhere, though obviously they will have their own particular ramifications and distinctions. This is likely to grow, it seems to me, and it will surely be all to the good that it does. As it does, though the subject matter of 'International Relations' will remain distinct as a field of learning – and whether it is still called 'International Relations' or by some other name (world politics?) – the general questions relevant to its orientation will be part of the wider questions in the human sciences. Which is surely as it should be. And, as an added bonus (from my point of view at least) it is in the context of these debates in all their plurality that 'international political theory' will find itself most at home as one of the most significant ways that political theorists can ply their trade in late modernity.[8]

International political theory and naturalistic social science

There is, however, one particular development which could easily revolutionize this growing plurality by offering very specific solutions *both* to the question of universal and particular *and* the problem of order. This is the growing recognition among many social scientists that they ignore the literature and arguments of what are now generally referred to as the 'life sciences' at their peril,[9] and the consequent growth of what we might call an ever more obviously 'naturalistic' social science.

If well established, a naturalistic social science would, of course, represent an extremely attractive way of dealing with the problem of order, for it could explain what order is, at least in general terms and for beings biologically and psychologically structured as human beings are. It would also, I suggest, incline towards a 'managerial' rather than an emancipatory framework, though it is only fair to add, that – as in the work of Amartya Sen, Martha Nussbaum and their colleagues[10] – at least some versions of a naturalistic approach could also be used very powerfully to ground criticisms of the political status quo.

The basic arguments in support of such a view are quite simple. To begin with, advocates of this view would claim that it is quite absurd to seek knowledge about human beings and their social structures without using the rapidly advancing knowledge about human *biological* processes and properties achieved by evolutionary biology, cognitive psychology and neurology and a number of other major areas of the contemporary 'life sciences'. The doyen of sociobiologists, Edward O. Wilson, has recently advanced an especially clear statement of this view, which he terms (following William Whewell) 'consilience'[11] and he also gives the clearest intimation of what this will mean in practice. He suggests that:

> If the world really works in a way so as to encourage the consilience of knowledge, I believe the enterprises of culture will eventually fall out into science, by which I mean the natural sciences, and the humanities, particularly the creative arts. These two domains will be the great branches of learning in the twenty first century. The social sciences will continue to split within each of its disciplines, a process already rancorously begun, with one part folding into or becoming continuous with biology, the other fusing with the humanities. Its disciplines will continue to exist but in a radically altered form. In the process the humanities, ranging from philosophy and history, to moral reasoning, comparative religion and interpretation of the arts, will draw closer to the sciences and partly fuse with them.[12]

I shall return to this prediction in a moment, but for now what evidence is there for this view in contemporary IR theory? While it has not been much in evidence till now, there are signs that it is growing in strength. Perhaps the most obvious manifestation of this trend relevant to date can be found in the work of Robert Axelrod, whose original motivation for the book that established his reputation, *The Evolution of Co-operation*,[13] was, he tells us, 'to help to promote co-operation between the two sides of a bipolar world';[14] that is, it was intended in large part as a contribution to mainstream – and 'rationalist' – IR theory.

Both in that book and in his subsequent work, he has emphasized the extent to which new areas of science in general and the life sciences in particular, especially those which draw on evolutionary biology and complexity theory, can contribute to what Keohane termed 'rationalist' social science. The essays in his most recent book carry such a project much further and challenge one of the central assumptions of the 'game theoretic' methods that dominate his – and many others' – work, to wit the notion that actors' preferences are, to use the jargon, 'exogenous', that is to say, given outside the parameters of the 'game' (whatever it might be). It is not insignificant, I think, that one of those who have signalled that such a move opens up very considerable opportunities for 'social science' is the aforementioned Professor Keohane.[15]

But the point, of course, is what you mean by 'social science'. 'Rationalists' are not alone in moving towards methods and models drawn from complexity theory and the life sciences. Hayward Alker is another figure in contemporary international studies whose work is increasingly influenced by such concerns,[16] and yet he is almost always cited by rationalists as a leading 'reflectivist'. In truth, Alker, perhaps more than any other scholar working in international relations today, *combines* rationalism and reflectivism. A recent collection of his essays[17] contains pieces that would not be out of place alongside those of leading rationalist scholars[18] together with pieces that could happily grace an anthology of post-structural writing[19] and several which are neither! Alker is quite clear himself that such a combination is precisely what he is trying to achieve. His work, he suggests, is

> a fresh attempt at ... synthesis, uniting the inclusive subject matter, the concern with discovering and shaping meaning, and the value orientations of the humanities with the methodological discipline, the formal rigour and the explanatory concerns one normally associates with the natural sciences.[20]

If we are looking for an apostle of 'consilience' in contemporary IR theory, then Hayward Alker is surely it!

The point of the above discussion is to emphasize that *on both sides* of the alleged rationalist/reflectivist divide there is a growing sense of the importance of what we might call 'naturalistic' methods and styles of argument.[21] In part, simply because of the aforementioned explanatory power of evolutionary biology and of the life sciences that stem from it and also because it develops a trend quite visible and influential already in mainstream social science, which has already given rise to game theory, rational and public choice and many other similar movements.

As evolutionary models become more influential – and as they themselves change – there will be profound implications for IR theory, as for the social sciences more widely. To begin with, the 'rationalist' models so beloved of the mainstream will have to change. Once preferences are no longer seen as exogenous for game theory – to give just one example – there would be much more chance of linking aspects of this to at least some versions of constructivism or even to critical theory, as some scholars have already suggested.[22] In other words, as life science models become more commonplace in political and social science, and also therefore in International Relations, then the divisions between 'rationalist' and 'reflectivist' – or let us say between those that seek inspiration in broadly economistic naturalistic models and those that seek inspiration in broadly sociological naturalistic models – will become progressively harder to draw. There will still be differences, of course, but these differences will be much less clear than those that currently exist between 'neo-utilitarian' and 'reflectivist' accounts: much more to do with matters of interpretation and much less to do with 'methodology'. A good example of the manner in which a concern with evolutionary systemic models can lead even the most acute 'traditional' International Relations scholar is Robert Jervis' recent *System Effects: Complexity in Political and Social Life.*[23]

Of course, it is far from true that this view will *necessarily* triumph; it certainly has plenty of opponents, who would seek to pull international studies (and indeed social science more generally) away from the increasing links with the natural – or at any rate the life – sciences. This trend we might call 'a-naturalist' – for few of its advocates would wish I think to call themselves *anti*-naturalists – and it consists chiefly of those who are suspicious of the natural sciences in this sort of (human/social) context, whatever their achievements might be in other settings. This tendency too, of course, has a long history in the social sciences.

However, the growing sense that the life sciences necessarily have something important to say about human motivations and behaviour[24] – and thus also about the traditional concerns of all social sciences – will force the a-naturalists into a series of difficult choices. Either they will have to confront the assumptions about human social life and behaviour that dominate evolutionary biology – and thus social science informed by it – head on, or, as they largely do now, they will simply have to continue to try and ignore it. Yet, for all of the reasons just given, the latter choice will become increasingly difficult. However, if they do seek to confront naturalistic methods head on then they will have two further choices. Either they will have to decide to deny the life sciences outright or, second, they will have to deny either its coherence and/or its relevance.

Most a-naturalists will, I suspect, opt for the latter and attack on the ground of relevance. It has been their time-honoured strategy of defence and has for the most part worked. However, its effectiveness in the past was at least in part generated by the model of science that self-conscious 'social scientists' tended to adopt (i.e. a model of science based upon physics). With the changes in scientific method and style and with the growing importance of biology and life sciences, it is harder and harder to deny these arguments *some* role at least in the explanation and understanding of human affairs, though of course it will remain defensible to say that they are not the whole story and there will be room for considerable debate as to just what the implications of this development are.

For this very reason, however, some a-naturalists are likely to take a different tack and attack the *coherence* of naturalistic arguments, at least in the context of human affairs and not just their relevance. Many post-structuralists, I think, effectively take this line. Not because they deny that 'science' can offer us insights that we should use. Rather – and most ingeniously – they will carry the offensive to the enemy. It is not the 'social sciences' that will collapse into the humanities and natural sciences, rather it is the natural sciences which will increasingly come to resemble the humanities and (properly configured) the social sciences. It is the *natural* sciences which will be most affected by the changes in perspective, not other areas of enquiry: 'we' do not have to become 'them', because, increasingly, 'they' will become us!

As I say, this is an ingenious stratagem and it may well contain more than a kernel of truth (even the illustrious Professor Wilson's 'consilience' model could be roped in, suitably rearranged). The problem with it is that it fails to address the most important questions that the growing 'naturalization' – if I may so put it – of the social sciences raises. However, it is not alone in this. These questions are pretty much completely ducked by most social scientific disciplines at present, since the possible consequences of thinking them through might prove to be especially painful.

I should emphasize, by the way, that these questions have nothing – or at any rate not very much – to do with such traditional old chestnuts as the possibility of prediction in social science or determinism versus free will in human action. Rather, they cut to the quick of the very diversity and 'professional status' of the social sciences as such. Simply put, if the naturalization of the social sciences is to continue then the whole way in which the social sciences are conceived of, and social scientists trained, will have to change. How many professors in the social sciences today have any real knowledge of the recent developments in evolutionary biology? How many even have a sound grasp of the essence of the theory of evolution? How many could tell you who are the leading figures in cognitive psychology today? The point is not to say that none do (I can think of several who certainly do) but to emphasize how marginal such questions currently are in the training of social scientists in general and political scientists and International Relations scholars in particular.

All of the above is simply to emphasize that I do not think it very likely that International Relations can be any more insulated from this particular trend than it has been from other similar intellectual trends, like the attraction of rational choice theory or post-structuralism. Moreover, given technological advance in areas such as genetics and biotechnology, the implications of our growing knowledge of human biological processes and all that goes with them for human (and including international) affairs more generally will be increasingly impossible to ignore. This does not, I think, dictate any particular direction in International Political Theory as the new millennium unfolds but it does suggest a range of issues that it will inevitably have to deal with.

From international political theory to cosmopolitan political theory? The 'order of ends'

Notwithstanding the power and appeal of this naturalistic approach, however, I think it likely that the current 'theory wars' in International Relations, as elsewhere in the human sciences, are here to stay. I think, moreover, it would actually be a bad thing if they were not. Real dialogue requires strongly held and powerfully expressed points of view – as well, of course, as a *commitment* to dialogue as such. There is no shortage of the former in contemporary international studies and the presence of the latter is certainly growing, though to be sure in fits and starts. At the same time as welcoming the plurality of 'international political theory' – and this is not, I would claim, the contradiction it might appear – I also think that many aspects of current debates in international studies are essentially distractions from what I take to be one of its central tasks.

Like Tolkien's Fangorn, therefore, if I have not bothered myself too much about the great (theory) wars, in the sense of feeling that, in this book at least, I have to take one view over another, it is because I am not, in fact, on anybody's *side* for the simple reason that none of the theories I have examined here are exactly on *my* side – though naturally, some are closer than others.[25] Having suggested, therefore, that 'mainstream' IR theory is substantively and methodologically too limited, but that most of the available alternatives, though preferable, are still hardly without problems, it is only fair to end this book by outlining this 'central task' to which I have just averred and to suggest how and why its way of seeing the 'problem of order' might be preferable to the others we have examined, and what, as a result, it might imply for 'international political theory' more generally.

Essentially, this central task is simply a reconfiguration of a very old question in political theory – arguably indeed the oldest, since it is Socrates' question – 'how should we live?'[26] Politics, all politics, must, I believe, start with this question. Even if we see our task as 'explaining' politics rather than, in any sense, recommending one choice over another, we only rule it out of bounds by simple fiat. Specifically, in the circumstances of our own time, I understand the question to mean three related things. First, it asks us to identify what we might call the 'manner' of our living. Our understandings of where we[27] are and how we arrived there, and an assessment of our successes and failures, our hopes and fears, the values we profess to love or to loathe and the extent to which we succeed in instantiating the one and repudiating the other. Second, it asks how we should thread a path *through* the matrix of associations, obligations and identities and what they bring, and specifically how we might *judge* such associations, obligations and identities and their implications and what follows from such judgement. Finally, and in the light of our answers to these questions, it asks what we should seek to build – what associations, what institutions, what identities – to live our lives better, to minimize our failures and our fears, and increase our chances of, as Socrates would have put it, living *well*.[28]

These tasks are tasks of '*international* political theory', both because it must inevitably take in questions the salience of which cannot be limited to one particular form of political community and because it must face the sorts of questions which are at the centre of much contemporary international relations (for all that they have often been ignored by International Relations): identity, the claims of political obligation within states, the character of the claims states traditionally make externally, the interpenetration and interrelations of states and nations, the character of the ethical obligation to community as such (any community) and so on.

In many ways, of course, it would simply be easier to call all of this by what is, so to speak, its proper name: political theory. Yet in doing this we run the risk of forgetting that 'political theory', just like International Relations, has a history in the academy and outside, and that this history is impregnated with certain assumptions, many of which bear the same hallmarks as those which suggested that the 'problem of order' was no longer a problem 'inside' the state and that thus its only real resonance is 'outside' the state.[29] To call the sort of concerns I am talking about here 'international' political theory is in part largely a rhetorical – and for that reason, as any Aristotelian will tell you, therefore a political – strategy which should hopefully serve to remind us that it is not just International Relations that needs rethinking, but political theory as well, and that we cannot take any of the assumptions on which contemporary politics rests simply for granted – neither state nor states system, not liberalism or realism. Rather all must be put into question when we ask 'how should we live?'

This also indicates clearly why the task is one of international *'political'* theory. It is the character of 'the political' that is at issue,[30] how it has evolved, and how it *might* evolve and what such trajectories as can be identified might imply. There is a tendency, I think – especially in some of the so-called 'neo-medieval' literature and in the huge (and growing) literature on globalization – to mask the fact that 'the political' has always been contested and contestable, a point where we would find the likes of Morgenthau agreeing with an Elshtain or a Walker. The point is how we *frame* the political and what such frames include and exclude, allow and disavow.

Which emphasizes, of course, why, finally, it is also a task for international political *theory*. As many have emphasized in very different ways, we need theory when we do *not* know 'how it all hangs together', not when we do. There are, of course, many ways of theorizing, but it seems to me that one of the central assumptions we should make is that the type of 'theory' we need the most is in fact one which is rooted in practice. As Stephen Toulmin and Albert Jonson have put it in a related context, 'the kernel of moral wisdom [and, we might add, serious political theory] consists not in a hard-line commitment to principles which we accept without qualification, but in understanding the human needs *and relations* that are nurtured by a life of reflective moral action' (emphasis added).[31] The key notion here is the sense that human life – and certainly human ethico-political life – is a matter of organizing our relations with other entities – other humans, other sentient beings, our environment itself – in appropriate contexts. Being able to do this requires the exercise of judgement and practical reason in the sense that Aristotle meant them, even if we do not necessarily want to follow Aristotle completely in how he understood that task. It is such a view that the ancients averred when they suggested that all the wise were friends, in 'that great city "walled and governed by reason" to which their first loyalty is given'[32] and to which the Renaissance and Enlightenment referred when they suggested that wherever liberty was, there was their country.

Global 'order' and cosmopolitan 'ends'

This view, of course, is usually seen as a cosmopolitan one. However, understood properly, I think, it is not a *universalist* one. Now, I have already suggested that universalism and particularism are powerful, if often subterranean, themes in contemporary international political theory. In normative theory especially, as we briefly saw earlier, they have most often been cashed out in terms of what are usually called 'cosmopolitan' and 'communitarian' frameworks,[33] which

> relate ... directly to the most central question of any normative interna-
> tional relations theory, namely the moral value to be credited to
> particularistic political collectivities [the communitarian/particularist view]
> as against humanity as a whole or the claims of individual human beings
> [the cosmopolitan view].[34]

In this context, it has often been pointed out that cosmopolitanism can come in two versions, called by Charles Beitz 'moral' and 'institutional' cosmopolitanism. He understands 'cosmopolitanism' as 'both inclusive and non perspectival', that is it 'encompasses all local points of view' and 'it seeks to see each part of the whole in its true relative size'.[35] Given this understanding, *moral cosmopolitans* are those who suggest that each individual is equally a subject of moral concern and that, in the justification of choices, one must take the prospects of everyone equally into account. *Institutional cosmopolitans*, on the other hand, suggest that in order to do this, the world's political structure would have to be reshaped so that states and other political units are brought under some other kind of authority. Beitz clearly suggests that this is most likely to be an incipient world government but as we saw in Chapter 4, for example, Linklater's arguments about the normative significance of 'cosmopolitan law' as a mechanism of emancipation would also qualify as an 'institutional cosmopolitanism'.

Obviously, when the distinction is put this way then 'cosmopolitans' are rightly seen as 'universalists', and their 'communitarian' opponents as 'particularists'. However, there is a problem to which a number of writers (amongst them most persuasively Brown himself) have recently pointed, and to which I also alluded earlier. Simply put, few cosmopolitans would wish to deny the value *in toto* of the sorts of associations and communities championed by communitarians. They simply want to suggest that the admitted value of particular communities – be they states, nations, linguistic or religious groups or whatever – should not 'trump' other more fundamental values, for example human rights.

Equally, few communitarians would be entirely comfortable with a thorough-going communally based relativism. Rather they tend to opt for some version of what one of their most illustrious writers has called the 'thick and thin' solution,[36] wherein some, very abstract and 'thin' notions – freedom, democracy, self-government, – are treated as effectively 'universal' but where the real work is done in 'thick', local, particularistic contexts – freedom *in the case of* Bosnia, the United States, Vietnam, etc.

As with many other alleged dichotomies discussed in this book, in other words, the universal/particular (or cosmopolitan/communitarian) one seems less substantial the closer one looks at it. Surely, the devil, as always, is in the details, the details being the specific sorts of questions being asked, in specific sorts of contexts. And yet in specific contexts how – on what criteria – do we balance the claims of (say) our fellow citizens' right to security against the civil rights claims of an alien who might perhaps be a guilty subversive or might, equally possibly, be an innocent dupe, or simply completely innocent? Surely particularism and universalism pull in different directions, however much each tries to pay tribute to the other; they end up resembling one another it is true, but the resemblance is that of the mirror not that of the copy.

There is a way of splitting the difference, however, and we can best see it if we return to the problem of order. The modern sense of the problem of order, remember, begins with Nietzsche and with Weber, seeking somehow to render whole the sense that the human world had been sundered from its 'natural' wholeness. This is what Nietzsche referred to as 'decadence', Weber as 'the iron cage' or 'disenchantment'. In International Relations, it is in so many ways that Weberian sensibility that sets the scene for the manifold ways in which order is theorized – and practised and *as* a practice – as scholars as distinct as Morgenthau and Walker would agree. In all the sound and fury that has enveloped international theory in the twentieth century, it is very easy to forget that the realism of a Morgenthau or a Wolfers, the critical theory of a Linklater and the post-structuralism of a Walker or a Der Derian, while of course differing about a good deal, have not forgotten where 'International Relations theory' – and a good deal else in the twentieth century – came in – with the intellectual reaction to Nietzsche and Weber and with the political (and, of course, intellectual) reaction to the social forms Nietzsche and Weber reflected upon.

Even more than realism, perhaps, critical theory and post-structuralism are the children of Nietzsche and Weber, however much they might have rebelled at parental authority. Along with a lot of other twentieth-century thought, they are deeply suspicious rebels against the rise of an instrumental 'science' that seems unstoppable and unanswerable. It is this, for example, that gives rise chiefly to Adorno's despair at the modern world. If instrumental rationality is the villain, and yet the two greatest and most protean forces of the modern world, capitalism and science, are precisely the areas where instrumental rationality is most at home, it would be difficult not to despair.

Yet, the one refusal post-structuralism does not make is to deny the initial assumption that Nietzsche and Weber (and then Heidegger, Adorno and on into our own times) make: to wit, that the developments they trace – which are I think often extremely acute – *must* mean what they take them to mean. That they often *have* meant them is certainly true; that they *must* seems to me simply an article of faith. In other words, one is free, I think, to put together science, history and society in different ways, without assuming – as the twentieth century in general has seemed to do – that the way they are together now is the only way. Moreover, and more significantly still, the manner in which we relate to such developments will depend on how we view them in the light of our sense of what it is, precisely, that is the 'natural' wholeness of human beings. If our sense of 'naturalness' is different from that of Nietzsche or Weber we may not feel quite so 'disenchanted' with the world as they seemed to, even if we also feel that, in many respects, it is a hellish place and mostly, in most places, always has been. If we seek to make a better place of it, it does not seem to me that starting where most contemporary thought starts is very helpful. In the words of the old joke, 'If I were you and wanted to get there, I wouldn't start from here'.

Thus, I want to distinguish the sense of 'cosmopolitan' from both 'universalist' and particularist. George Steiner has recently expressed something of the sense I have in mind when he remarks:

> To be a guest among other men is a possibility. All of us ... are guests of the planet ... we did not make our world, we were thrown into it. We are born without knowing why. We haven't planned it. We are trustees of a dwindling space for survival. We had better learn very quickly that we are guests or there will not be much left to live in.[37]

And he goes on to suggest that the implication of this is both simple and stark:

> There is no synagogue, no *ecclesia*, no *polis*, no nation, no ethnic community *which is not worth leaving*. ... A nation is a place always worth leaving, because it will behave in ways that we may or must come to find unacceptable. A synagogue will one day excommunicate Spinoza. It must [emphasis in original].[38]

To be a cosmopolitan in *this* sense is, most emphatically, not to be a universalist, because one can accept the centrality of particularism to our lives – the *fact* of particularism, that is – and still refuse its *intrinsic* moral worth. It recognizes only the fact that, whatever communities we live in and however central they are for our lives – indeed *because* they are likely to be so central – the responsibility for judgement is always ours alone. It can never be sloughed off to anyone, friend or family, local or ethnic community, state or international society.

Such a view, of course, would require a much more elaborate working out to be convincing and this is neither the time nor the place. It is worth adding, however, that on this view, 'order' becomes simply the continuous process of *ordering (and reordering) ends*. It is neither moral nor institutional cosmopolitanism, as Beitz describes them, though it may – depending on the context – resemble either or both. It is, equally, not dissimilar to Bill Connolly's claim that in our current circumstances we have to develop a loyalty to our time, as such, without any corresponding loyalty to a specific political place.[39]

Such a cosmopolitanism would agree with a good deal of what I have traced here as the critique of instrumental reason, but would refuse to accept what these critiques think follows from such criticisms. It would substitute, in Stephen Toulmin's words, the *reasonable* for the rational[40] (or for despair about the rational). In its specific applications, it would be context driven, casuistical and committed to no specific institution or agent in advance of the circumstances or issue. Thus, by definition, it would be 'critical' of most established discourses in International Relations which privilege one (or more) above others. Finally, it would suggest that the 'problem of order' is a permanent feature of politics, whether global or otherwise, though of course it can and does take historically and geographically distinct forms. It would hold also that it cannot be 'transcended' as those who advocate emancipation suppose, but that we have to do more than simply 'manage' it (as, in their various ways, the advocates of balance, society and institutions, at least in this century, have tended to suppose). However, what it also suggests is that the 'problem of order' is perhaps better seen not as one overarching question – how best to secure 'world order' – but rather as a *series* of multiple and overlapping questions, which map onto the various different issues as they arise in world politics, *together with* a more general question about what ends the variously complex institutions and agents involved in these issues and questions should serve and how they should serve them. The 'problem of order' on this view, then, is how to 'order our ends' in these contexts – not how to end the problem of order.

It is clear enough that on the view that I have outlined here the 'problem of order' for the twenty-first century should look very different from the way it has been addressed in the twentieth. In the first place it requires a melding of 'political' and 'international' theory and the rewriting of the resulting fusion in ways which are sensitive to 'reasonable' rather than 'rational' ends and thus to particular (*and* cosmopolitan) circumstances but not universal (and thus timebound) 'truths'. In the second, it will require what Toulmin has rightly called a complex 'ecology of institutions that has, as yet, scarcely come into existence'.[41]

This 'ecology of institutions' is perhaps amongst the most important tasks that explicit 'International Relations' as an area of study can perform, though of course it is hardly likely to be absent from the concerns of Political Science or Sociology either. The world of the twenty-first century is likely to be a world of much greater multilateralism and of radical degrees of interdependence – political, economic, environmental and other – whatever one thinks of the wilder shores of the globalization/neo-medieval literatures. How international institutions might work effectively in this context or how not; how they relate to states and state structures and to global and national civil societies; what would give them legitimacy and what remove or erode it – such questions are likely to be central to the study of International Relations in the twenty-first century.

Yet without a profound focus on normative concerns such questions are likely to be impossible even properly to address, still less answer. The greatest failing of most mainstream 'rationalist' IR theory is its refusal (indeed incapacity) adequately to address normative questions; the greatest advantage of much traditional literature (realist, liberal and English school) and most post-positivist literature is that they foreground such questions. However, none of these literatures has yet sought to develop quite the focus on 'ordering ends' that I have suggested is appropriate here. There are, of course, specific reasons for this. In the case of traditional realism, and to some extent also the English school, this is largely because the centrality of the state in their analysis and also – especially in the case of the English school – the sense that it is *the society of* states that should be the central focus. In the case of some (non-rationalist) liberal writing, where perhaps one might expect a focus on an 'ecology of institutions', the failure has been largely due to a similar emphasis only in reverse, as it were. The 'liberalism of fear' for all that it is sceptical about or critical of the arbitrary exercise of power criticizes it largely in the context of a focus on *state* power which, as Shklar and Hoffmann have quite correctly pointed out, was indeed the usual concern of the liberals they seek to emulate.

In the case of post-positivist theories, there is obviously a different general orientation. Neither critical theory nor the various forms of political criticism I discussed in Chapter 5 are committed to the state as the principal legitimate political agent, though of course they recognize its centrality in contemporary international politics. However, in the case of critical theory its historicism and universalism – the central building blocks in other words of its attempt to transcend the problem of order – create an ironic problem for it in that while its historicism makes it sensitive to context historically speaking, its universalism creates a rigidity in the normative sphere which leads it towards an unhelpful abstraction from the context of ethical (and political) judgement. The problem of order thus remains simply as a problem to be 'transcended' and once it is, it will dissolve.

For the 'political critics' of Chapter 5, the reverse is the case. They are, certainly, sensitive to the contexts and dissonances of contemporary ethical and political life and it is fair enough to say that they seek to disrupt established accounts of how things come to be. But *all* accounts? Come what may? And then how might they determine what action to follow if all accounts are to be equally problematized? Political criticism, let us recall, is an *ethos* – a manner of being – but why should such an ethos be prioritized? What makes it valuable? Note that I am not suggesting that no answers could be given to these questions, but in answering them it seems to me that some reasons for preferring action x over action y would need to be given. In which case it is true that not all accounts are equally problematized.

In contrast, the approach outlined above will offer reasons, specific to context a or b, as to what actions are preferable, what institutions appropriate, where legitimacy lies in any given context. Moreover, this approach has an additional advantage. Over time, it could build up a picture of the evolving moral, political and institutional universe and could thus develop, or so I want to suggest, a sensitivity to the sorts of responses appropriate to discrete situations. It could also pick up actual or potential dangers and weakenings of the fabric as a whole. Such a picture would, of course, be constantly revised and revisable. It would not seek to create a Utopia, it would indeed be rooted in our world as we live it, but at the same time it would speak to the most powerful ethical and political impulses we have developed as a species.

In this sense the view I have briefly sketched here would share a good deal with the position I ascribed to Elshtain in Chapter 5, with this difference. Elshtain's 'realism', powerful as it is (indeed powerful though *realism* is, if understood without the scientizing squint that has so disfigured it), is committed to a conception of power that is still shaped by the politics of state sovereignty. For all that she is a critic of sovereignty, at least unfettered sovereignty, Elshtain herself retains this emphasis. From my perspective, however, such an emphasis is still too committed to a particular institution *in advance of the context of judgement.*

It is this context of judgement that makes the point about 'ordering ends' central. The ends we set for ourselves and our institutions should be dependent on the contexts we are in and appropriate for them. Rather than there being *a* 'problem of order' the differing and disparate contexts of contemporary world politics would set many discrete problems of 'ordering' which would thus replace the 'problem of order' as an orientation for both reflective observer and practical actor in world politics. Such a world would require a highly developed, historically sensitive, conceptually sophisticated set of scholarly tools, many of which we have, some of which we have doubtless yet to develop adequately. It should also – I would argue – be able to encompass much of the emerging 'naturalistic' social science that I discussed above, without becoming wholly naturalistic in the process.

Such a trajectory surely offers much for students of world politics. It would (and will) require, in the first place, a much more developed account of political judgement than we currently have and perhaps, more all embracingly, it will require a proper understanding of the parameters of 'cosmopolitanism' into which such a conception could be embedded. Obviously, therefore, it will require a theoretical engagement far broader than that currently dominant in self-conscious 'International Relations Theory' would allow, as well as building in a political theory that is itself a lot broader than much work in that field has sometimes been. Even so, as I hope this study has shown, the theoretical diversity of contemporary IR theory is in fact very rich; there is much that can be built on. And that is good; for if my suggestion in this epilogue is at all plausible, managing or even perhaps trying to solve our multiple questions of order, our problems not of 'order' but of *ordering*, will provide international political theory with a very full in-tray in the coming century. We will need all the help we can get!

Notes

1 See John Gerard Ruggie, *Constructing the World Polity: Essays on International Institutionalization* (London: Routledge, 1998).
2 A remark he makes in his Frege book and which is quoted, also with approval, by Grady Scott Davis in his remarkable *Warcraft and the Fragility of Virtue* (Moscow, ID: University of Idaho Press, 1992).
3 K. J. Holsti, *The Dividing Discipline: Hegemony and Diversity in International Theory* (London: Allen and Unwin, 1985).
4 See James Sterba, *Justice for the Here and Now* (Cambridge: Cambridge University Press, 1998).
5 Ruggie, *Constructing the World Polity*, p. 10.

6   Though the sympathy with which some post-structuralists treat major realists, or figures influential on realism, displays the similarities better than any narrow 'agreement' would. See, for example, Der Derian's sympathy for aspects of realist thinking in his chapter in Francis A. Beer and Robert Hariman (eds), *Post-Realism: The Rhetorical Turn in International Relations* (Minneapolis: University of Minnesota Press, 1995), Walker's considerable sympathy for and understanding of Machiavelli, Hobbes and Weber in *Inside/Outside* and Connolly's extremely sympathetic, though opposed, reading of Augustine in *The Augustinian Imperative*.

7   See the discussion in Chapter 2.

8   Although it is expressed differently, this is one of the arguments at the end of my *Political Theory, Modernity and Postmodernity: Beyond Enlightenment and Critique* (Oxford: Blackwell, 1995); see especially chapter four.

9   There are, of course, a large and growing variety of ways of recognizing this. Perhaps the most interesting general approach, aside from that of Axelrod which I will discuss in a moment, is that of Roger Masters. See especially his *The Nature of Politics* (New Haven, CT: Yale University Press, 1990). See also the journal *Politics and the Life Sciences*.

10   See A. Sen and M. Nussbaum (eds), *The Quality of Life* (Oxford: Clarendon Press, 1994).

11   See Edward O. Wilson, *Consilience: The Unity of Knowledge* (New York: Knopf, 1998).

12   Wilson, *Consilience*, p. 12.

13   Axelrod, *The Evolution of Cooperation*, (New York: Basic Books, 1984).

14   In the introduction to his most recent book, *The Complexity of Cooperation: Agent Based Models of Competition and Collaboration* (Princeton, NJ: Princeton University Press, 1997), p. xi.

15   In an admiring tribute on the back cover of *The Complexity of Cooperation*.

16   With better credentials than most. Interestingly, and like Axelrod, Alker's first degree is in mathematics, his PhD in political science. Also, and again like Axelrod, he has been a fellow at the Sante Fe Institute, the Mecca for those interested in complexity theory.

17   Hayward Alker, *Rediscoveries and Reformulations: Humanistic Methodologies for International Studies* (Cambridge: Cambridge University Press, 1996).

18   See Alker, *Rediscoveries and Reformulations*, chapters 8, 9 and 10.

19   See Alker, *Rediscoveries and Reformulations*, chapters 1, 3, 4, 12.

20   Alker, *Rediscoveries and Reformulations*, p. 2.

21   If one wants another example, think of Roger Spegele's realism discussed in Chapter 1.

22   For how a skilful and artful constructivist might use aspects of game theory see the wonderfully ingenious discussion in Kratochwil's *Rules, Norms, Decisions: On the Conditions of Practical and Legal Reasoning in International Relations and Domestic Affairs* (Cambridge: Cambridge University Press, 1989), pp. 74–94. For a more general and pragmatic argument about how one might link critical theoretic and public-choice-type arguments see John Dryzeck, 'How far is it from Virginia and Rochester to Frankfurt? Public choice as critical theory', *British Journal of Political Science*, 1992, 22: 397–417.

23   Princeton, NJ: Princeton University Press, 1997.

24   For obvious examples of this see Matt Ridley, *The Origins of Virtue: Human Instincts and the Evolution of Co-operation* (New York: Viking, 1997).

25   It is obvious that I have a good deal of sympathy for aspects of critical and post-structural theory, though I do not identify with either. Equally they would share, with me, many criticisms of both the matter and the manner of much contemporary IR theory, without wanting to share my views about the appropriate way to proceed.

26   For his framing of it, of course, see, most especially, *Republic*, bk 1.

27   And I emphasize that by 'we' I imply *any* human subject.

28 For those who have read my *Political Theory, Modernity and Postmodernity*, this is now the way I would reconfigure the rather conventional framing of the 'tasks of political theory' that I borrowed from John Dunn and discussed in Chapter 1.

29 For one of the most thoughtful meditations on this, as I have already remarked, see R. B. J. Walker, *Inside/Outside: International Relations as Political Theory* (Cambridge: Cambridge University Press, 1992).

30 Amongst those thinkers discussed above perhaps Jean Elshtain and Rob Walker have developed this point most articulately, though their positions are still evolving and in Walker's case at least, published statements of it remain rather elusive. See, for example, Jean Bethke Elshtain, *Women and War* (Brighton: Harvester, 1987); see also her retrospective essay, 'Women and War: Ten years on', *Review of International Studies*, 1998, 24(4): 447–60. See also R. B. J. Walker, 'International Relations and the Concept of the Political', in Ken Booth and Steve Smith (eds), *International Relations Theory Today* (Cambridge: Polity Press, 1994).

31 Albert Jonson and Stephen Toulmin, *The Abuse of Casuistry: A History of Moral Reasoning* (Berkeley, CA: University of California Press, 1988), p. 342.

32 Stephen R. L. Clark, *Civil Peace and Sacred Order* (Oxford: Clarendon Press, 1989), p. 154.

33 The distinction is developed most fully in Chris Brown's *International Relations Theory: New Normative Approaches* (London: Harvester, 1992), though he is drawing on a wide range of other work. A similar argument, though put rather differently, can be found in Janna Thompson's, *Justice and World Order* (London: Routledge, 1992).

34 Brown, *International Relations Theory*, p. 12.

35 Though he has deployed it elsewhere, this version of his distinction is taken from Beitz' essay, 'Cosmopolitan Liberalism and the States System', in C. Brown (ed.), *Political Restructuring in Europe: Ethical Perspectives* (London: Routledge, 1994), p. 124.

36 The writer I have in mind, of course, is Michael Walzer. See especially his book *Thick and Thin: Moral Argument at Home and Abroad* (Notre Dame, IN: University of Notre Dame Press, 1994).

37 George Steiner, *No Passion Spent: Essays, 1978–1996* (London: Faber, 1996), p. 237.

38 Steiner, *No Passion Spent*, p. 237.

39 And this is also, I think, where it would share something of the sensibility displayed in many of the essays in Cheah and Robbins (ed.), *Cosmopolitics*, cited above. However, it would also be committed to a sense of the requirements of practical reason that such a sensibility would refuse, in that it would be committed to a form of ethics that post-structural thought tends to problematize.

40 See Toulmin, *Cosmopolis* (Chicago: University of Chicago Press, 1992), for a discussion of this. It also plays a prominent role, of course, in his co-authored book *The Abuse of Casuistry*.

41 See the last sentence of *Cosmopolis*.

Select bibliography

What follows is a list of those works referred to in the text that I have found most helpful, most stimulating or most generally relevant to the argument of the book as a whole. More specific references are also found in the notes to individual chapters. Translations, except where noted, are my own.

Acheson, Dean, *Morning and Noon* (Boston: Houghton Mifflin, 1965).

Acheson, Dean, *Present at the Creation* (New York: Norton, 1969).

Adorno, T. and M. Horkheimer, *Dialectic of Enlightenment* (New York: Continuum, 1989 [1947]).

Aggarwal, Vinod K., *Liberal Protectionism: The International Politics of the Organized Textile Trade* (Berkeley, CA: University of California Press, 1985).

Alker, Hayward, *Rediscoveries and Reformulations: Humanistic Methodologies for International Studies* (Cambridge: Cambridge University Press, 1996), pp. 19–20.

Allott, Philip, *Eunomia: New Order for a New World* (Oxford: Oxford University Press, 1990).

Anderson, Charles W., *Pragmatic Liberalism* (Princeton, NJ: Princeton University Press, 1992).

Ansell-Pearson, Keith, *Nietzsche contra Rousseau* (Cambridge: Cambridge University Press, 1991).

Arendt, Hannah, *The Human Condition* (Chicago: University of Chicago Press, 1958).

Aron, Raymond, *Introduction à la philosophie de l'histoire: Essai sur les limites de l'objective historique* (Paris: Gallimard, 1938).

Aron, Raymond, *Le Grand Debat* (Paris: Calman–Levy, 1963); translated as *The Great Debate: Theories of Nuclear Strategy*, trans. Ernst Pawl (New York: Doubleday, 1965).

Aron, Raymond, *Paix et guerre entre les nations* (Paris: Calman–Levy, 1961); translated as *Peace and War: A Theory of International Relations*, trans. Richard Howard and Annette Baker Fox (New York: Doubleday, 1966).

Aron, Raymond, *Progress and Disillusion: The Dialectics of Modern Society* (New York: Praeger, 1970).

Aron, Raymond, *Penser la guerre, Clausewitz, Vol. 1 L'age europeen. Vol. 2, L'age planetaire* (Paris: Gallimard, 1976).

Aron, Raymond, 'La definition de la liberté', *European Journal of Sociology*, 1964, V: 159–89, reprinted as 'The Liberal Definition of Freedom', in Miriam Bernheim Conant (ed.), *Politics and History: Selected Essays of Raymond Aron* (New York: Free Press, 1978).

Aron, Raymond, *Memoirs: Fifty Years of Political Reflection* (New York: Holmes and Meier, 1990).

Arrighi, Giovanni, *The Long Twentieth Century* (London: Verso, 1994).

Ashley, Richard, 'Living on Borderlines: Man, Poststructuralism and War', in James Der Derian and Michael Shapiro (eds), *International/Intertextual Relations: Postmodern Readings of World Politics* (Lexington, KY: Lexington Books, 1989).

Ashley, Richard, 'The Achievements of Post-Structuralism', in Steve Smith, Ken Booth and Marysia Zalewski (eds), *International Theory: Positivism and Beyond* (Cambridge: Cambridge University Press, 1996).

Axelrod, Robert, *The Evolution of Cooperation* (New York: Basic Books, 1984).

Axelrod, Robert, *The Complexity of Cooperation: Agent Based Models of Competition and Collaboration* (Princeton, NJ: Princeton University Press, 1997).

Baldwin, David, *Economic Statecraft* (New York: Columbia University Press, 1986).

Baldwin, David (ed.), *Neo-Realism versus Neo-Liberalism* (New York: Columbia University Press, 1993).

Baraclough, Geoffrey, *History in a Changing World* (Oxford: Basil Blackwell, 1955).

Barker, E., *Social and Political Thought in Byzantium from Justinian I, to the last Palaeologus* (Oxford: Clarendon Press, 1956).

Barry, Brian, *Theories of Justice* (Hemel Hempstead: Harvester, 1989).

Barry, Brian, 'Social Criticism and Political Philosophy', in *Liberty and Justice: Essays in Political Theory 2* (Oxford: Clarendon Press, 1991).

Barry, Brian, *Justice as Impartiality* (Oxford: Clarendon Press, 1994).

Barry, Brian, 'The Limits of Cultural Politics', *Review of International Studies*, 1998, 24(3): 307–20.

Bartelson, Jens, *A Genealogy of Sovereignty* (Cambridge: Cambridge University Press, 1995).

Bauman, Zygmunt, *Postmodern Ethics* (Oxford: Blackwell, 1995).

Beer, Francis and Robert Hariman (eds), *Post-Realism: The Rhetorical Turn in International Relations* (Minneapolis: University of Minnesota Press, 1996).

Beetham, David, *Max Weber and the Theory of Modern Politics* (London: Allen and Unwin, 1974).

Beitz, Charles, *Political Theory and International Relations* (Princeton, NJ: Princeton University Press, 1979).

Beitz, Charles, 'Cosmopolitan Liberalism and the States System', in C. Brown (ed.), *Political Restructuring in Europe: Ethical Perspectives* (London: Routledge, 1994).

Bellamy, Richard, *Liberalism and Modern Society* (Cambridge: Polity Press, 1992).

Benhabib, Seyla, *Situating the Self* (Cambridge: Polity Press, 1992).

Beranger, J., *Principatus. Etudes de notion et d'histoire politiques dans l'antique greco-romaine* (Droz: Galle, 1973).

Berlin, Isaiah, *Against the Current: Essays in the History of Ideas* (Oxford: Oxford University Press, 1978).

Berlin, Isaiah, *The Crooked Timber of Humanity* (London: John Murray, 1990).

Bernstein, Jay, *Recovering Ethical Life: Jurgen Habermas and the Future of Critical Theory* (London: Routledge, 1995).

Biersteker, Thomas and Cynthia Weber (eds), *State Sovereignty as Social Construct* (Cambridge: Cambridge University Press, 1995).

Bishop, Jerry E. and Michael Waldholz, *Genome: The Story of the Most Astonishing Scientific Adventure of our Time – the Attempts to Map all the Genes in the Human Body* (New York: Simon and Schuster, 1990).

Black, Antony, *Political Thought in Europe 1250–1450* (Cambridge: Cambridge University Press, 1992).

Bloom, Allan, *The Closing of the American Mind* (New York: Penguin, 1987).

Bloom, Allan, *Giants and Dwarfs* (New York: Simon and Schuster, 1990).

Blumenberg, Hans, *The Legitimacy of the Modern Age* (Cambridge, MA: MIT Press, 1983).

Bokina, John and Timothy J. Lukes (eds), *Marcuse Revisited* (Kansas City: University of Kansas Press, 1995).

Booth, Ken, 'Security and Emancipation', *Review of International Studies*, 1989.

Booth, Ken, 'Security in Anarchy: Utopian Realism in Theory and Practice', *International Affairs*, 1991, 67(3): 527–45.

Booth, Ken, 'Human Wrongs and International Relations', *International Affairs*, 1995, 71(1): 103–26.

Brezinski, Zbigniew, *The Grand Chessboard: American Primacy and its Geostrategic Imperatives* (New York: Basic Books, 1997).

Brierly, James, *The Law of Nations* 2nd edition (Oxford: Oxford University Press, 1936).

Brilmayer, Lea, *Justifying International Acts* (Ithaca, NY: Cornell University Press, 1989).

Brilmayer, Lea, *American Hegemony: Political Morality in a One Superpower World* (New Haven, CT: Yale University Press, 1994).

Brittan, Samuel, *Capitalism with a Human Face* (Cheltenham: Edward Elgar, 1995).

Bronner, Stephen Eric, *Of Critical Theory and its Theorists* (Oxford: Blackwell, 1994).

Brown, Chris, *International Relations Theory: New Normative Approaches* (London: Harvester, 1992).

Brown, Chris, Terry Nardin and N. J. Rengger, *Histories of International Political Thought* (Cambridge: Cambridge University Press, forthcoming).

Brown, Peter, *Augustine of Hippo* (London: Faber, 1967).

Bull, Hedley, *The Control of the Arms Race* (London: Weidenfeld and Nicolson, for the International Institute for Strategic Studies, 1961).

Bull, Hedley, 'The Theory of International Politics, 1919–69', in B. Porter (ed.), *The Aberystwyth Papers* (Oxford: Clarendon Press, 1972).

Bull, Hedley, *The Anarchical Society* (London: Macmillan, 1977).

Bull, Hedley, *Justice in International Relations: The Hagey Lectures* (Waterloo, Ontario: University of Waterloo, October 1984).

Bull, Hedley, Adam Roberts and Ben Kingsbury (eds), *Hugo Grotius and International Relations* (Oxford: Clarendon Press, 1990).

Bull, Hedley and Adam Watson (eds), *The Expansion of International Society* (Oxford: Clarendon Press, 1986).

Burchill, Scott *et al.*, *Theories of International Relations* (London: Macmillan, 1996).

Burley, Anne Marie, 'Law among Liberal States: Liberal Internationalism and the Act of State Doctrine', *Columbia Law Review*, 1992, 8(1): 1907–96.

Burns, J. H. (ed.), *The Cambridge History of Medieval Political Thought* (Cambridge: Cambridge University Press, 1988).

Butterfield, Herbert and Martin Wight, *Diplomatic Investigations* (London: George Allen and Unwin, 1966).

Buzan, Barry, *People, States and Fear* (Brighton: Harvester; 2nd edition, 1991).

Buzan, Barry, 'The Levels of Analysis Problem Reconsidered', in Ken Booth and Steve Smith (eds), *International Relations Theory Today* (Cambridge: Polity Press, 1994).

Buzan, Barry and Richard Little, 'The Idea of International System: Theory Meets History', *International Political Science Review*, 1994, 15(3): 231–55.

Buzan, Barry and Richard Little, *The International System: Theory Meets History* (Oxford: Clarendon Press, forthcoming).

Buzan, Barry and Gerald Segal, *Anticipating the Future: Twenty Millennia of Human Progress* (New York: Simon and Schuster, 1998).

Buzan, Barry and Ole Wæver, 'Slippery? Contradictory? Sociologically Untenable? The Copenhagen school replies', *Review of International Studies*, 1997, 23: 241–50.

Buzan, Barry, Charles Jones and Richard Little, *The Logic of Anarchy* (New York: Columbia University Press, 1993).

Buzan, Barry, Ole Wæver and Jaap de Wilde, *Security: A New Framework for Analysis* (Boulder, CO: Lynne Rienner, 1997).

Campbell, David, *Writing Security: US Foreign Policy and the Politics of Identity* (Manchester: University of Manchester Press, 1993).

Campbell, David, *National Deconstruction: Violence, Identity and Justice in Bosnia* (Minneapolis: University of Minnesota Press, 1998).

Carlyle, A. J., *A History of Medieval Political Theory in the West* (London: William Blackwood, 1903–36).

Carr, E. H., *The Twenty Years Crisis* (London: Macmillan, 1939).

Carty, Antony, *The Decay of International Law* (Manchester: Manchester University Press, 1986).

Chadwick, Henry, *The Sentences of Sixtus: A Contribution to Early Christian Ethics* (London: Texts and Studies, 1959).

Chan, Steve, 'Mirror, Mirror on the Wall … Are the Freer Countries more Pacific?', *Journal of Conflict Resolution*, 1984, 28(4): 617–48.

Chase-Dunn, Christopher, *Global Formation* (Oxford: Blackwell, 1989).

Clark, Ian, *The Hierarchy of States* (Cambridge: Cambridge University Press, 1989).

Clark, Stephen R. L., *Civil Peace and Sacred Order* (Oxford: Clarendon Press, 1989).

Claude, Inis, *Swords into Plowshares* (New York: Random House, 1964).

Connolly, William E., *Political Theory and Modernity* (Oxford: Blackwell, 1988).

Connolly, William E., *Identity/Difference: Democratic Negotiations of Political Paradox* (Ithaca, NY: Cornell University Press, 1991).

Connolly, William E., 'Beyond Good and Evil: The Ethical Sensibility of Michel Foucault', *Political Theory*, 1993, August: 365–89.

Connolly, William E., *The Augustinian Imperative: A Reflection on the Politics of Morality* (London: Sage, 1993).

Connolly, William E., *The Ethos of Pluralization* (Minneapolis: University of Minnesota Press, 1995).

Cooper, David, *World Philosophies* (Oxford: Blackwell, 1996).

Cooper, Robert, 'Economic Interdependence and Foreign Policies', *World Politics*, 1972, 24 (January).

Cox, Robert, *Approaches to World Order* (Cambridge: Cambridge University Press, 1996).

Czempiel, Ernst-Otto, 'Governance and Democratization', in James N. Rosenau and Ernst Otto Czempiel (eds), *Governance without Government: Order and Change in World Politics* (Cambridge: Cambridge University Press, 1992).

Dallmayr, Fred, 'Eric Voeglin's Search for Order', in *Margins of Political Discourse* (Notre Dame, IN: University of Notre Dame Press, 1984).

Dallmayr, Fred, *The Other Heidegger* (Ithaca, NY: Cornell University Press, 1994).

Dallmayr, Fred, *Beyond Orientalism: Essays on Cross Cultural Encounter* (New York: SUNY, 1996).

Davis, Grady Scott, *Warcraft and the Fragility of Virtue* (ID: University of Idaho Press, 1992).

Deane, H. A., *The Political and Social Ideas of St Augustine* (New York: Columbia University Press, 1963).

De Certeau, Michel, *The Practice of Everyday Life* (Berkeley, CA: University of California Press, 1988).

de la Blanche, Vidal, *Principles of Human Geography* (London: Constable, 1936).

Der Derian, James, *On Diplomacy* (Oxford: Blackwell, 1987).

Der Derian, James, *Anti-Diplomacy: Spies, Speed, Terror and War* (Oxford: Blackwell, 1992).

Der Derian, James, *International Theory: Critical Investigations* (London: Macmillan, 1995).

Der Derian, James and Michael Shapiro (eds), *International/Intertextual Relations: Postmodern Readings of World Politics* (Lexington: Lexington Books, 1989).

Deudney, Daniel, 'Geopolitics and Change', in Michael Doyle and G. John Ikenberry (eds), *New Thinking in International Relations Theory* (Boulder, CO: Westview Press, 1997).

Devetak, Richard, 'Critical Theory', in Scott Burchill *et al.*, *Theories of International Relations* (London: Macmillan, 1996).

Devigne, Robert, *Recasting Conservatism: Oakeshott, Strauss and the Response to Postmodernism* (New Haven, CT: Yale University Press, 1994).

Dillon, Michael, *Politics of Security* (London: Routledge, 1996).

Dolger, F., *Byzanz und die europaische Staatenwelt. Ausgewahlte Vortrage und Aufsätze* (Buch-Kunstverlag Ettal, 1956).

Donelan, Michael (ed.), *The Reason of States* (London: Allen and Unwin, 1978).

Doyle, Michael W., 'Kant, Liberal Legacies and Foreign Affairs', part 1 in *Philosophy and Public Affairs*, 1983, 12(3): 205–35; part 2 in 1983, 12(4): 323–53.

Doyle, Michael W., 'Liberalism and World Politics', *American Political Science Review*, 1986, 80(4): 1151–69.

Doyle, Michael W., 'Liberalism and World Politics Revisited', in Charles Kegley (ed.), *Controversies in International Relations: Realism and the Neo-Liberal Challenge* (New York: St Martins Press, 1996).

Drury, Shadia, *The Political Ideas of Leo Strauss* (London: Macmillan, 1988).

Drury, Shadia, *Alexandre Kojeve: The Roots of Postmodern Politics* (London: Macmillan, 1995).

Dryzeck, John, 'How far is it from Virginia and Rochester to Frankfurt? Public choice as critical theory', *British Journal of Political Science*, 1992, 22: 397–417.

Dunne, Timothy J., 'International Society: Theoretical Promises Fulfilled?', *Co-operation and Conflict*, 1995, 30(2): 125–54.

Dunne, Timothy J., 'The Social Construction of International Society', *European Journal of International Relations*, 1995, 1(3): 368–72.

Elshtain, Jean Bethke, *Meditations on Modern Political Thought: Masculine/Feminine Themes from Luther to Arendt* (Pittsburgh, PA: Pennsylvania University Press, 1992 [1986]).

Elshtain, Jean Bethke, *Women and War* (Brighton: Harvester, 1987).

Elshtain, Jean Bethke, *Democracy on Trial* (Toronto: University of Toronto Press, 1993).

Elshtain, Jean Bethke, *Augustine and the Limits of Politics* (Notre Dame, IN: University of Notre Dame Press, 1995).

Elshtain, Jean Bethke, *Real Politics: At the Centre of Everyday Life* (Baltimore, MD: Johns Hopkins University Press 1997).

Elshtain, Jean Bethke, 'Women and War: Ten years on', *Review of International Studies*, 1998, 24(4): 447–60.

Elshtain, Jean Bethke, *New Wine and Old Bottles: Ethical Discourse and International Politics* (Notre Dame, IN: University of Notre Dame Press, 1998).

Falk, Richard, *The End of World Order* (New York: Holmes and Maier, 1983).

Forsyth, Murray, 'The Classical Theory of International Relations', *Political Studies*, 1978, 13(1): 32–57.

Forsyth, Murray, *Unions of States: The Theory and Practice of Confederation* (New York: Holmes and Maier, 1981).

Forsyth, Murray, H. M. A. Keens-Soper and Peter Savigear (eds), *The Theory of International Relations* (London: Allen and Unwin, 1970).

Forsythe, David, 'Democracy, War and Covert Action', *Journal of Peace Research*, 1992, 29(4): 385–95.

Forsythe, David, *Human Rights and Peace* (Lincoln, NE: University of Nebraska Press, 1993).

Frank, Andre Gunder, *Capitalism and Underdevelopment in Latin America* (New York, 1967).

Frankel, Benjamin, *Realism: Restatements and Renewal* (Ilford: Frank Cass, 1996).

Frankel, Benjamin, *Roots of Realism* (Ilford: Frank Cass, 1996).

Friere, Paulo, *Pedagogy of the Oppressed* (New York: Continuum, 1983).

Frost, Bryan-Paul, 'Resurrecting a Neglected Theorist: The Philosophical Foundations of Raymond Aron's Theory of International Relations', *Review of International Studies*, 1997, 23(2).

Fukuyama, Francis, *The End of History and the Last Man* (London: Hamish Hamilton, 1992).

Galipeau, Claude, *Isaiah Berlin's Liberalism* (Oxford: Clarendon Press, 1994).

Gay, Peter, *Weimar Culture: The Insider as Outsider* (Harmondsworth: Penguin, 1974).

Geoghan, Vincent, *Ernst Bloch* (London: Routledge, 1995).

George, Jim, *Discourses of Global Politics: A Critical (Re)introduction to International Relations* (Boulder, CO: Lynne Rienner, 1994).

Gill, Stephen, *American Hegemony and the Trilateral Commission* (Cambridge: Cambridge University Press, 1989).

Gill, Stephen (ed.), *Gramsci, Historical Materialism and International Relations* (Cambridge: Cambridge University Press, 1993).

Goldstein, Joshua, *Long Waves: Prosperity and War in the Modern Age* (New Haven, CT: Yale University Press, 1988).

Gong, Gerritt, *The Standard of Civilization in International Society* (Oxford: Clarendon Press, 1984).

Goodin, Robert E., *Utilitarianism as a Public Philosophy* (Cambridge: Cambridge University Press, 1995).

Gray, Colin, *The Geopolitics of Superpower* (Lexington, KY: University of Kentucky Press, 1988).

Gray, Colin, *War, Peace and Victory: Strategy and Statecraft for the Next Century* (Oxford, 1991).

Grieco, Joseph, 'Anarchy and the Limits of Cooperation: A realist critique of the newest liberal institutionalism', *International Organization*, 1988, Vol. 42.

Grieco, Joseph, *Cooperation among Nations* (Ithaca, NY: Cornell University Press, 1990).

Groom, A. J. R. and Paul Taylor, *International Institutions at Work* (London: Pinter, 1988).

Haas, Ernst, *Beyond the Nation State: Functionalism and International Organization* (Stanford, CA: Stanford University Press, 1964).

Habermas, Jurgen, *The Theory of Communicative Action. Vol. 1 Reason and the Rationalization of Society. Vol. 2 The Critique of Functionalist Reason* (Cambridge: Polity Press, 1991).

Hall, John A., *Diagnoses of Our Time* (London: Macmillan, 1981).

Hall, John A., *Liberalism: Politics, Ideology and the Market* (London: Paladin, 1987).

Hall, John A., *International Orders* (Cambridge: Polity Press, 1996).

Halliday, Fred, *Rethinking International Relations* (London: Macmillan, 1994).

Halliday, Fred and Justin Rosenberg, 'An Interview with Ken Waltz', *Review of International Studies*, 1998, 24(3): 371–86.

Hammond, Moses, *The Augustan Principiate in Theory and Practice* (Cambridge, MA: Harvard University Press, 1933).

Hampsher-Monk, Ian, *A History of Modern Political Thought: Hobbes to Marx* (Oxford: Blackwell, 1994).

Hansen, Lene, 'R.B.J. Walker: Deconstructing IR', in Iver B. Neumann and Ole Wæver (eds), *The Future of International Relations: Masters in the Making* (London: Routledge, 1997).

Hass, Ernst, *The Uniting of Europe: Political Economic and Social Forces* (Stanford, CA: Stanford University Press, 1958).

Heim, Michael, *The Metaphysics of Virtual Reality* (Oxford: Oxford University Press, 1993).

Held, David, *An Introduction to Critical Theory: Horkheimer to Habermas* (Cambridge; Polity Press, 1980).

Held, David (ed.), *Prospects for Democracy: North, South, East, West* (Cambridge: Polity Press, 1992).

Held, David, *Democracy and the Global Order* (Cambridge: Polity Press, 1995).

Herman, Arthur, *The Idea of Decline in Western History* (New York: Free Press, 1997).

Hinsley, F. H., *Power and the Pursuit of Peace* (Cambridge: Cambridge University Press, 1963).

Hobsbawm, Eric, *Age of Extremes: The Short Twentieth Century* (London: Heinemann, 1994).

Hoffman, Mark, 'Critical Theory and the Inter-Paradigm Debate', *Millennium: Journal of International Studies*, 1987, 17(3): Summer.

Hoffman, Mark, 'Third Party Mediation and Conflict Resolution in the Post Cold War World', in John Baylis and N. J. Rengger (eds), *Dilemmas of World Politics: International Issues in a Changing World* (Oxford: Clarendon Press, 1992).

Hoffmann, Stanley (ed.), *Conditions of World Order* (New York: Simon and Schuster, 1970), pp. 1–2.

Hoffmann, Stanley, *Janus and Minerva: Essays in the Theory and Practice of International Politics* (Boulder, CO: Westview Press, 1987), pp. 85–6.

Hoffmann, Stanley, 'International Society', in J. D. B. Miller and R. J. Vincent (eds), *Order and Violence: Hedley Bull and International Relations* (Oxford: Clarendon Press, 1990).

Hollis, Martin and Steve Smith, *Explaining and Understanding International Relations* (Oxford: Clarendon Press, 1990).

Holsti, Kal, *The Dividing Discipline: Hegemony and Diversity in International Theory* (London: Allen and Unwin, 1985).

Honig, Bonnie, *Political Theory and the Displacement of Politics* (Ithaca, NY: Cornell University Press, 1993).

Horton, John and Sue Mendus (eds), *After MacIntyre* (Cambridge: Polity Press, 1992).

Howard, Michael, *War and the Liberal Conscience* (Oxford: Oxford University Press, 1977).

Hume, David, *Essays* (London: Routledge, 1907).

Hume, David, *Treatise of Human Nature*, ed. L. A. Selby Bigge, rev. P. H. Nidditch (Oxford: Clarendon Press, 1978).

Huntington, Samuel P., *The Third Wave: Democratization in the Late Twentieth Century* (Norman, OK: University of Oklahoma Press, 1991).

Ignatieff, Michael, *Isaiah Berlin: A Life* (London: Weidenfeld and Nicolson, 1998).

Imber, Mark, *The USA, ILO, UNESCO and IAEA: Politicization and Withdrawal in the Special-ized Agencies* (London: Macmillan, 1989).

Jackson, Robert, *Quasi-States: Sovereignty, International Relations and the Third World* (Cambridge: Cambridge University Press, 1990).

Jackson, Robert, 'The Political Theory of International Society', in Ken Booth and Steve Smith (eds), *International Relations Theory Today* (Cambridge: Polity Press, 1994).

Jackson, Robert, 'Is there a classical international theory?', in Steve Smith, Ken Booth and Marysia Zalewski (eds), *International Theory: Positivism and Beyond* (Cambridge: Cambridge University Press, 1996).

Jay, Martin, *The Dialectical Imagination* (Boston: Little Brown, 1973).

Jervis, Robert, *System Effects: Complexity in Political and Social Life* (Princeton, NJ: Princeton University Press, 1997).

Joel, Rosenthal, *Righteous Realists: Responsible Power and American Culture in the Nuclear Age* (Baton Rouge, LA: Louisiana State University Press, 1991).

Johnson, James Turner, *Ideology, Reason and the Limitation of War* (Princeton, NJ: Princeton University Press, 1975).

Johnson, James Turner, *Just War Tradition and the Restraint of War* (Princeton, NJ: Princeton University Press, 1981).

Jones, A. H. M., *The Later Roman Empire 284–602*, 2 vols (Oxford: Blackwell, 1964).

Jones, Roy E., 'The English School of International Relations: A Case for Closure', *Review of International Studies*, 1981, 7(1): 1–12.

Jonson, Albert and Stephen Toulmin, *The Abuse of Casuistry: A History of Moral Reasoning* (Berkeley, CA: University of California Press, 1988).

Kant, E., (Carlyle Lectures in Oxford, 1992, forthcoming).

Kaplan, Robert, *The Ends of the Earth: A Journey at the Dawn of the Twenty First Century* (New York: Random House, 1996).

Kateb, George, *The Inner Ocean: Individualism and Democratic Culture* (Ithaca, NY: Cornell University Press, 1992).

Katzenstein, Peter (ed.), *The Culture of National Security* (New York: Columbia University Press, 1997).

Kegely, Charles W. (ed.), *Controversies in International Relations Theory: Realism and the Neo-Liberal Challenge* (New York: St Martins Press, 1995).

Kenyon, John, *The History Men* (London: Weidenfeld and Nicolson, 1983).

Keohane, Robert, *After Hegemony* (Princeton, NJ: Princeton University Press, 1984).

Keohane, Robert, *International Institutions and State Power* (Boulder, CO: Westview Press, 1989).

Keohane, Robert, 'International Liberalism Reconsidered', in John Dunn (ed.), *The Economic Limits to Modern Politics* (Cambridge: Cambridge University Press, 1990).

Keohane, Robert and Helen Milner, *Internationalization and Domestic Politics* (Cambridge: Cambridge University Press, 1995).

Keohane, Robert and Joseph Nye, *Power and Interdependence: World Politics in Transition* (Boston: Little Brown, 1977; 2nd edition, 1989).

Kissinger, Henry, *Diplomacy* (New York: Simon and Schuster, 1994).

Knutsen, Torbjorn, *A History of International Relations Theory* (Manchester: Manchester University Press, 1992; 2nd edition, 1996).

Krasner, Stephen, *Defending the National Interest* (Princeton, NJ: Princeton University Press, 1978).

Krasner, Stephen, *Structural Conflict: The Third World Against Global Liberalism* (Berkeley, CA: University of California Press, 1985).

Krasner, Stephen, 'The Accomplishments of International Political Economy', in Steve Smith, Ken Booth and Marysia Zalewski (eds), *International Theory: Positivism and Beyond* (Cambridge: Cambridge University Press, 1996).

Kratochwil, Friedrich, *International Order and Foreign Policy: A Theoretical Sketch of Post War International Politics* (Boulder, CO: Westview Press, 1978).

Kratochwil, Friedrich, 'Of Systems Boundaries and Territoriality: An Inquiry into the Formation of the States System', *World Politics*, 1986, Vol. 39.

Kratochwil, Friedrich, *Rules, Norms and Decisions: On the Conditions of Legal Reasoning in International Relations and Domestic Affairs* (Cambridge: Cambridge University Press, 1989).

Kublakova, Vendulka and A. Cruikshank, *Marxism-Leninism and the Theory of International Relations* (London: Macmillan, 1980).

Kublakova, Vendulka and A. Cruikshank, *Marxism and International Relations* (Oxford: Oxford University Press, 1985).

Kymlicka, Will, *Liberalism, Community and Culture* (Oxford: Clarendon Press, 1989).

Kymlicka, Will, *Multi-cultural Citizenship* (Oxford: Clarendon Press, 1995).

Lake, David, 'Powerful Pacifists: Democratic States and War', *American Political Science Review*, 1992, 86(1): 24–37.

Lane, Jan Erik, *Constitutions and Political Theory* (Manchester: Manchester University Press, 1996).

Langer, William, *The Diplomacy of Imperialism* (New York: Knopf, 1950).

Lapid, Yosef, 'Quo Vaid International Relations? Further Reflections on the next Stage of International Relations Theory', *Millennium*, 1989, 19(1): Spring.

Lash, Scott and John Urry, *Economies of Signs and Space* (London: Sage, 1994).

Layne, Christopher, 'Cant or Kant: The Myth of the Democratic Peace', *International Security*, 1992, 19(2): 5–125, special section, 'Give Democratic Peace a Chance'.

Leonard, Stephen, *Critical Theory and Political Practice* (Ithaca, NY: Cornell University Press, 1994).

Levy, David, *Political Order: Philosophical Anthropology, Modernity and the Challenge of Ideology* (Baton Rouge, LA: Louisiana State University Press, 1987).

Lewontin, R. C., *The Doctrine of DNA: Biology as Ideology* (Harmondsworth: Penguin, 1993).

Linklater, Andrew, *Beyond Realism and Marxism: Towards a Critical Theory of International Relations* (London: Macmillan, 1989).

Linklater, Andrew, *Men and Citizens in the Theory of International Relations* (London: Macmillan, 1982; 2nd edition, 1990).

Linklater, Andrew, 'What is a good international citizen?', in Paul Keal (ed.), *Ethics and Foreign Policy* (Canberra: Australian National University Press, 1992).

Linklater, Andrew, 'The Question of the Next Stage in International Relations Theory: A critical theoretic point of view', *Millennium: Journal of International Studies*, 1992, 21(1).

Linklater, Andrew, 'Community, Citizenship and Global Politics', *Oxford International Review*, 1993, 5(1).

Linklater, Andrew, 'Liberal Democracy, Constitutionalism and the New World Order', in R. Feaver and J. L. Richardson (eds), *The Post Cold War Order* (London: Allen and Unwin, 1993).

Linklater, Andrew, 'Neo-Realism in Theory and Practice', in Ken Booth and Steve Smith (eds), *International Relations Theory Today* (Cambridge: Polity Press, 1994).

Linklater, Andrew, 'Community', in Alex Danchev (ed.), *Fin de Siècle: The Meaning of the Twentieth Century* (London: Tauris, 1995).

Linklater, Andrew, 'Sovereignty and Citizenship in the Post-Westphalian State', *European Journal of International Relations*, 1996, 2(2).

Linklater, Andrew, 'The Achievements of Critical Theory', in Steve Smith, Ken Booth and Marysia Zalewski (eds), *International Theory: Positivism and Beyond* (Cambridge: Cambridge University Press, 1996).

Linklater, Andrew, *The Transformation of Political Community* (Cambridge: Polity Press, 1998).

Lintott, Andrew, *Violence, Civil Strife and Revolution in the Classical City* (London: Croom Helm, 1982).

Lipschutz, Ronnie, 'Towards a Global Civil Society', *Millennium: Journal of International Studies*, 1992, 21(3): Summer.

Little, Richard, *Intervention: External Involvement in Civil Wars* (London: Martin Robertson, 1976).

Little, Richard and M. Smith (eds), *Perspectives on World Politics* (London: Croom Helm, 1976; 2nd edition, Routledge, 1990).

Lowith, Karl, 'Nature, History and Existentialism', *Social Research*, 1952, 19(1).

Lowith, Karl, *Weltgeschichte und Heilsgeschehen* (Stuttgart: Kohlshammer, 1955).

Lowith, Karl, *Marx and Weber* (London: Routledge, 1992).

Luard, Evan, *Types of International Society* (New York: Free Press, 1976).

Luban, David, 'The Romance of the Nation State', in Charles Beitz *et al.*, *International Ethics* (Princeton, NJ: Princeton University Press, 1981).

Mackinder, Halford, 'The Geographical Pivot of History', *Royal Geographical Society Journal*, 1904.

Mackinder, Halford, *Democratic Ideals and Reality* (New York: Henry Holt, 1919).

Mahan, Alfred Thayer, *The Influence of Sea Power upon History, 1660–1783* (Boston: Little Brown, 1890).

Manicas, Peter, *War and Democracy* (Oxford: Blackwell, 1983).

Mansfield, Harvey, *The Spirit of Liberalism* (Cambridge, MA: Harvard University Press, 1978).

Mansfield, Harvey, *Taming the Prince: The Ambivalence of Modern Executive Power* (New York: Free Press, 1989).

Mapel, David and Terry Nardin (eds), *International Society: Diverse Ethical Perspectives* (Princeton, NJ: Princeton University Press, 1998).

Marcuse, Herbert, *Negations* (Harmondsworth: Penguin, 1972).

Markus, R. A., *Saeculum: History and Society in the Theology of St Augustine* (Cambridge: Cambridge University Press, 1970).

Masters, Roger, *The Nature of Politics* (New Haven, CT: Yale University Press, 1990).

Mayall, James (ed.), *The Community of States* (London: Allen and Unwin, 1982).

Mayall, James, *Nationalism and International Society* (Cambridge: Cambridge University Press, 1990).

McCormick, John P., *Carl Schmitt's Critique of Liberalism: Against Politics as Technology* (Cambridge: Cambridge University Press, 1997).

McIlwain, C. H., *Constitutionalism, Ancient and Modern* (Cambridge, MA: Harvard University Press, 1947).

McKinley, R. D. and R. Little, *Global Problems and World Order* (London: Frances Pinter, 1986).

Reiss, Hans (ed.), *Kant's Political Writings* (Cambridge: Cambridge University Press, 1970).

Rengger, N. J., 'Going Critical? A Response to Hoffman', *Millennium*, 1988, 18(1): Spring.

Rengger, N. J., 'Serpents and Doves in Classical International Theory', *Millennium: Journal of International Studies*, 1988, 17(2): 215–25.

Rengger, N. J., 'Incommensurability, International Theory and the Fragmentation of Western Political Culture', in John Gibbins (ed.), *Contemporary Political Culture* (London: Sage, 1989).

Rengger, N. J., 'Discovering Traditions? Grotius, International Society and International Relations', *Oxford International Review*, 1991, 3(1): Winter.

Rengger, N. J., 'Arms Control, International Society and the End of the Cold War', *Arms Control*, 1992, April.

Rengger, N. J., 'Culture, Society and Order in World Politics', in John Baylis and N. J. Rengger (eds), *Dilemmas of World Politics* (Oxford: Clarendon Press, 1992).

Rengger, N. J., 'No Time Like the Present? Postmodernism and Political Theory', *Political Studies*, 1992, 40: 561–70.

Rengger, N. J., 'The Ethics of Trust in World Politics', *International Affairs*, 1997, 73(3): July.

Rengger, N. J. and Mark Hoffman, 'Modernity, Postmodernism and International Relations', in Joe Doherty, E. Graham and Mo Malek (eds), *Postmodernism and the Social Sciences* (Basingstoke: Macmillan, 1992).

Ridley, Matt, *The Origins of Virtue: Human Instincts and the Evolution of Co-operation* (New York: Viking, 1997).

Riley, Patrick, *Leibniz' Political Writings* (Cambridge: Cambridge University Press, 1992).

Riley, Patrick, *Leibniz' Universal Jurisprudence: Justice as the Charity of the Wise* (Cambridge, MA: Harvard University Press, 1996).

Rose, Gillian, *The Melancholy Science: An Introduction to the Thought of Theodor W. Adorno* (London: Macmillan, 1978).

Rose, Gillian, *The Broken Middle* (Oxford: Blackwell, 1992).

Rosecrance, Richard, *The Rise of the Trading State* (New York: Basic Books, 1986).

Rosenau, James N. and Ernst-Otto Czempiel (eds), *Governance without Government: Order and Change in World Politics* (Cambridge: Cambridge University Press, 1992).

Rosenberg, Justin, *The Empire of Civil Society: A Critique of the Realist Theory of International Relations* (London: Verso, 1994).

Ruggie, John Gerard (ed.), *Multi-lateralism Matters: The Theory and Praxis of an Institutional Form* (New York: Columbia University Press, 1993).

Ruggie, John Gerard, *Constructing the World Polity: Essays on International Institutionalization* (London: Routledge, 1998).

Russett, Bruce (with Carol Ember, Melvin Ember, William Antholis and Zeev Maoz), *Grasping the Democratic Peace: Principles for a Post-Cold War World* (Princeton, NJ: Princeton University Press, 1993).

Said, Edward, *Culture and Imperialism* (London: Chatto and Windus, 1994).

Sagan, Scott and Kenneth Waltz, *The Spread of Nuclear Weapons: A Debate* (New York Norton, 1997).

Sandel, Michael, *Liberalism and the Limits of Justice* (Cambridge: Cambridge University Press, 1982).

Sandoz, Ellis (ed.), *Eric Voeglin's Significance for the Modern Mind* (Baton Rouge, LA: Louisiana State University Press, 1991).

Santayana, George, *Dominations and Powers: Reflections on Liberty, Society and Government* ([1950] New Jersey: Transaction Books, 1995).

Scaff, Lawrence, *Fleeing the Iron Cage* (Berkeley, CA: University of California Press).

Scott, D. (trans.), *Friedrich Meinecke Machiavelism: The Doctrine of Raison D'état and its Place in History* (London: Westview Press, 1984).

Searle, John, *Minds, Brains and Science* (Oxford: Oxford University Press, 1990).

Searle, John, *The Construction of Social Reality* (New York: Free Press, 1995).

Seeley, John, *The Expansion of England* (Chicago: University of Chicago Press, 1971 [1888]).

Sen, Amartya and M. Nussbaum (eds), *The Quality of Life* (Oxford: Clarendon Press, 1994).

Serba, James, *Justice for Here and Now* (Cambridge: Cambridge University Press, 1998).

Shapiro, Michael, *Violent Cartographies: Mapping Cultures of War* (Minneapolis: University of Minnesota Press, 1996).

Shklar, Judith, *Ordinary Vices* (Cambridge, MA: Harvard University Press, 1984).

Shklar, Judith, 'The Liberalism of Fear', in Nancy Rosenblum (ed.), *Liberalism and the Moral Life* (Cambridge, MA: Harvard University Press, 1989).

Shue, Henry, *Basic Rights: Subsistence, Affluence and US Foreign Policy* (Princeton, NJ: Princeton University Press, 1980; 2nd edition, 1996).

Simon, Herbert, 'Human Nature in Politics: The Dialogue of Psychology with Political Science', *American Political Science Review*, 1985, 79: 293–304.

Sinclair, T. A., *A History of Greek Political Thought* (London: Routledge & Kegan Paul, 1967).

Singer, J. David, 'International Conflict: Three Levels of Analysis', *World Politics*, 1960, 12(3): 453–61.

Singer, J. David, 'The Levels of Analysis Problem in International Relations', in K. Knorr and S. Verba (eds), *The International System: Theoretical Essays* (Princeton, NJ: Princeton University Press, 1961).

Skinner, Quentin, *The Foundations of Modern Political Thought*, 2 vols (Cambridge: Cambridge University Press, 1978).

Skinner, Quentin, *Reason and Rhetoric in the Philosophy of Hobbes* (Cambridge: Cambridge University Press, 1996).

Skolnikoff, Eugene, *The Elusive Transformation: Technology and International Politics* (Cambridge, MA: Harvard University Press, 1991).

Small, Melvin and J. David Singer, 'The War-Proneness of Democratic Regimes', *Jerusalem Journal of International Relations*, 1976, 1(1): 50–69.

Smith, Michael Joseph, *Realist Thought from Weber to Kissinger* (Baton Rouge, LA: Louisiana State University Press, 1986).

Smith, Steve, 'Self Images of a Discipline', in Ken Booth and Steve Smith (eds), *International Relations Theory Today* (Cambridge: Polity Press, 1994).

Snyder, Jack, *Myths of Empire* (Ithaca, NY: Cornell University Press, 1992).

Sorabji, Richard, *Time Creation and the Continuum* (London: Duckworth, 1983).

Spegele, Roger, *Political Realism in International Theory* (Cambridge: Cambridge University Press, 1996).

Spiro, David E., 'The Insignificance of the Liberal Peace', *International Security*, 1994, 19(2): 5–125, special section, 'Give Democratic Peace a Chance'.

Spragens, Thomas, Jr, *The Irony of Liberal Individualism* (Durham, NC: Duke University Press, 1989).

Spykman, Nikolas, *America's Strategy in World Politics* (New York: Harcourt Brace, 1942).

Starr, C. G., 'The Perfect Democracy of the Roman Empire', *American Historical Review*, 1952, Vol. LVIII.

Steiner, George, *No Passion Spent: Essays, 1978–1996* (London: Faber, 1996).

Strong, Tracy, *Nietzsche and the Politics of Transfiguration* (Berkeley, CA: University of California Press, 1975; 2nd edition, 1988).

Struasz-Hupe, L., *Geopolitics* (New York: Putnams, 1942).

Sylvester, Christine, *Feminist Theory in International Relations* (Cambridge: Cambridge University Press, 1994).

Thompson, Janna, *Justice and World Order* (London: Routledge, 1992).

Tickner, Ann, *Gender in International Relations* (New York: Columbia University Press, 1993).

Tickner, Ann, 'Revisioning Security', in Ken Booth and Steve Smith (eds), *International Relations Theory Today* (Cambridge: Polity Press, 1994).

Todorov, Tzvetan, *Nous et les autres: La reflection française sur la diversité humaine* (Paris: Editions du Seuil, 1989).

Todorov, Tzvetan, *The Morals of History* (Minneapolis: University of Minnesota Press, 1992).

Toulmin, Stephen, *Cosmopolis* (Chicago: University of Chicago Press, 1992).

Toynbee, Arnold, *A Study of History* (Oxford: Oxford University Press, 1954).

Toynbee, Arnold, *Constantine Porphryogenitus and his World* (Oxford: Oxford University Press, 1973).

Tuck, Richard, *Natural Rights Theories* (Cambridge: Cambridge University Press, 1979).

Tuck, Richard, *Sorry Comforters: Political Theory and International Order from Grotius to Unger, Roberto Managebeira, Politics*, 3 vols (Cambridge: Cambridge University Press, 1987).

Tully, James (ed.), *Meaning and Context: Quentin Skinner and his Critics* (Cambridge: Polity Press, 1988).

Vincent, R. J., *Non-Intervention and the International Order* (Princeton, NJ: Princeton University Press, 1978).

Vincent, R. J., *Human Rights and International Relations* (Cambridge: Cambridge University Press, 1986).

Voeglin, Eric, *The New Science of Politics* (Chicago: University of Chicago Press, 1951).

Voeglin, Eric, *Order and History* (all volumes published by Louisiana State University Press, 1956–1987).

Voeglin, Eric, 'World Empire and the Unity of Mankind', *International Affairs*, 1962.

Voeglin, Eric, *Anamnesis: Zur Theorie der Geschichte und Politik* (Munich: Piper Verlag, 1966).

Von Fritz, Kurt, *The Theory of the Mixed Constitution in Antiquity* (New York: Columbia University Press, 1954).

Wæver, Ole and Iver Neumann (eds), *The Future of International Relations: Masters in the Making* (London: Routledge, 1996).

Wæver, O., B. Buzan, M. Kelstrup and P. Lemaitre with D. Carlton, *Identity, Migration and the New Security Agenda in Europe* (London: Pinter, 1993).

Walker, R. B. J., 'Political Theory and the Transformation of World Politics', World Order Studies Program, Occasional paper No. 8 (Princeton University, Center for International Studies, 1980).

Walker, R. B. J., *Inside/Outside: International Relations as Political Theory* (Cambridge: Cambridge University Press, 1992).

Walker, R. B. J., 'International Relations and the Concept of the Political', in Ken Booth and Steve Smith (eds), *International Relations Theory Today* (Cambridge: Polity Press, 1994).

Wallerstein, Immanuel, *The Modern World System*, 3 vols (New York: Academic Press, 1974, 1980 and 1989).

Wallerstein, Immanuel, *The Capitalist World Economy* (Cambridge: Cambridge University Press, 1979).

Walt, Stephen, *Revolution and War* (Ithaca, NY: Cornell University Press, 1996).

Waltz, Kenneth, 'The Stability of a Bi-polar World', *Daedalus*, 1964, 93: 881–909.

Waltz, Kenneth, *Man, the State and War* (New York: Columbia University Press, 1979).

Waltz, Kenneth, *Theory of International Politics* (Reading, MA: Addison-Wesley, 1979).

Waltz, Kenneth, ' The Spread of Nuclear Weapons: More may be Better', *Adelphi*, 1981, No. 171.

Walzer, Michael, *Spheres of Justice* (Cambridge: Cambridge University Press, 1983).

Walzer, Michael, *Interpretation and Social Criticism* (Cambridge, MA: Harvard University Press, 1987).

Walzer, Michael, *Just and Unjust Wars*, 2nd edition (New York: Basic Books, 1992).

Walzer, Michael, *Thick and Thin: Moral Argument at Home and Abroad* (Notre Dame, IN: University of Notre Dame Press, 1994).

Warren, Mark, *Nietzsche and Political Thought* (Cambridge, MA: MIT Press, 1988).

Warren, Mark, 'Democratic Theory and Self Transformation', *American Political Science Review*, 1992, 86(1).

Watson, Adam, *The Evolution of International Society* (London: Routledge, 1992).

Weber, Cynthia, *Simulating Sovereignty* (Cambridge: Cambridge University Press, 1994).

Weber, Max, *Gesammelte Politische Schriften* (Munich, 1921).

Weber, Max, *Weber's Political Writings* (Cambridge: Cambridge University Press, 1992).

Wendt, Alexander, 'The Agent-Structure Problem in International Relations Theory', *International Organization*, 1987, 41(3): 335–70.

Wendt, Alexander, 'Anarchy is What States Make of it: The Social Construction of Power Politics', *International Organization*, 1992, 46(2): 391–425.

Wendt, Alexander, 'Collective Identity Formation and the International State', *American Political Science Review*, 1994, 88(2): 84–96.

Wendt, Alexander, 'Constructing International Politics', *International Security*, 1995, 19: 71–81.

Wendt, Alexander, 'Identities and Structural Change in International Politics', in Yosef Lapid and Friedrich Kratochwil (eds), *The Return of Culture and Identity to IR Theory* (Boulder, CO: Lynne Rienner, 1996).

Wendt, Alexander, *Social Theory of International Politics* (Cambridge: Cambridge University Press, 1999).

Wheeler, Nicholas J., 'Guardian Angel or Global Gangster? A Review of the Ethical Claims of International Society', *Political Studies*, 1996, 44(2): 123–35.

Wheeler, Nicholas J., 'Pluralist or Solidarist Conceptions of International Society: Bull and Vincent on Humanitarian Intervention', *Millennium: Journal of International Studies*, 1992, 21(3): 463–87.

Wheeler, Nicholas J. and Timothy Dunne, 'Hedley Bull's Pluralism of the Intellect and Solidarism of the Will', *International Affairs*, 1996, 72(1): 91–107.

Wiggershaus, Rolf, *The Frankfurt School* (Cambridge: Polity Press, 1994).

Wight, Martin, 'Western Values in International Relations', in Herbert Butterfield and Martin Wight (eds), *Diplomatic Investigations* (London: Allen and Unwin, 1966).

Wight, Martin, *Systems of States* (Leicester: Leicester University Press, 1977).

Wight, Martin, *International Theory: The Three Traditions*, ed. Brian Porter and Gabrielle Wight (Leicester: Leicester University Press, 1992).

Wight, Martin, *Power Politics* (London: Macmillan, 1992).

Wilkinson, Paul, *Terrorism and the Liberal State* (London: Macmillan, 1986).

Williams, Mike and Keith Krause, *Critical Security Studies* (Minneapolis: University of Minnesota Press, 1996).

Wilson, Edward O., *Consilience: The Unity of Knowledge* (New York: Knopf, 1998).

Wilson, Peter and David Long (eds), *Thinkers of the Twenty Years Crisis* (Oxford: Clarendon Press, 1996).

Winkleman, F. (ed.), *In Praise of Constantine: A Historical Study and New Translation of Eusebius' Tricennial Orations* (Berkeley, CA: University of California Press, 1975).

Wolfers, Arnold, *Discord and Collaboration: Essays on International Politics* (Baltimore, MD: Johns Hopkins University Press, 1962).

Wright, Quincy, *The Study of International Relations* (New York: Appleton Century Crofts, 1955).

Wyn Jones, Richard and Roger Tooze (eds), *Critical Theory and International Relations* (Boulder, CO: Lynne Rienner, forthcoming).

Yack, Bernard (ed.), *Liberalism without Illusions: Essays on Liberal Theory and the Political Vision of Judith Shklar* (Chicago: University of Chicago Press, 1996).

Young, Oran, *International Cooperation: Building Resources for Natural Resources and the Environment* (Ithaca, NY: Cornell University Press, 1989).

Young-Breuhl, Elizabeth, *For Love of the World* (New Haven, CT: Yale University Press, 1988).

Zimmern, Alfred, *The League of Nations and the Rule of Law* (London, 1936).

Index

Subject matter in the endnotes has not been included in the index except where a substantial issue has been raised. In such cases the location is indicated by the page number followed by the note number: for example 28n23 refers to endnote number 23 on page 28.